The Nation-State
and Global Order

SECOND EDITION

THE NATION-STATE AND GLOBAL ORDER

A Historical Introduction to Contemporary Politics

Walter C. Opello, Jr.
Stephen J. Rosow

LYNNE
RIENNER
PUBLISHERS

BOULDER
LONDON

Published in the United States of America by
Lynne Rienner Publishers, Inc.
1800 30th Street, Boulder, Colorado 80301
www.rienner.com

and in the United Kingdom by
Lynne Rienner Publishers, Inc.
3 Henrietta Street, Covent Garden, London WC2E 8LU

Library of Congress Cataloging-in-Publication Data
Opello, Walter C.
    The nation-state and global order : a historical introduction to
contemporary politics / Walter C. Opello, Jr., Stephen J. Rosow—2d.ed.
    Includes bibliographical references and index.
    ISBN 978-1-58826-289-9 (pbk. : alk. paper)
    1. State, The. 2. State, The—Origin. 3. Comparative government.
I. Rosow, Stephen J. II. Title.
JC11.063 2004
321'009—dc21

                                                2004-001840
                                                CIP

British Cataloguing in Publication Data
A Cataloguing in Publication record for this book
is available from the British Library.

Printed and bound in the United States of America

⊗   The paper used in this publication meets the requirements
     of the American National Standard for Permanence of
     Paper for Printed Library Materials Z39.48-1992.

    15   14   13   12   11   10   9   8   7

For my daughter, Katherine
—W. C. O., Jr.

To the memory of Bernard Rosow
—S. J. R.

Contents

Maps

Preface

We are pleased that *The Nation-State and Global Order* has been adopted widely enough to warrant a second edition. This suggests to us that there is a significant number of scholars who are dissatisfied with the mainstream texts and seek an alternative approach to understanding politics, the state, and global order. We can only hope that the historical approach we take, one with "an attitude" according to one reviewer of the first edition, will continue to resonate with those concerned with understanding and teaching about the current political order.

The second edition has afforded us the opportunity to refine central arguments of the first edition. Within the historical account we have clarified the mutual constituting of the state and the states system. Together these make up ensembles of forces—political, technical, economic, and cultural—that establish forms of political order at specific times and places, creating the need for historical understanding. We have more tightly structured the historical account around the idea of epochs of global order, which was left more implicit and thus more loosely formulated in the first edition.

The concluding argument, that the neoliberal state is not a new form of the state, but a reconstituting of the managerial state in the context of the newest forces of globalization, has also been strengthened. Although we recognize that the trend toward managerialism is not inevitable, we contend that it does define a new terrain of political struggle within states and the global order.

This new edition also corrects a number of errors of historical fact, and we are grateful to those who pointed these out to us. Recent scholarship published since the appearance of the first edition has been consulted and cited when appropriate, and the case studies have been updated.

We owe a sincere debt to Christina Wilder for cheerfully preparing the manuscript for this book, even when we changed our minds and gave her additional adjustments to sections she had already finished.

A thousand years scarce serve to form a state;
An hour may lay it in the dust: and when
Can Man its shattered splendour renovate,
Recall its virtues back, and vanquish Time and Fate?
　　　　　—Lord Byron, from "Childe Harold's Pilgrimage"

We shall . . . dwell on scenes of the past with the sole object
of throwing light on matters of the present . . .
No society is possible in which power and compulsion are
absent, nor a world in which force has no function.
　　　　　—Karl Polanyi, from *The Great Transformation*

Introduction:
A Historical Approach to
the State and Global Order

During the 1970s, Prime Minister Margaret Thatcher blamed Britain's economic malaise and decline as a world power on the welfare-state programs put in place by the Labour Party after World War II. She and her Tory Party began to dismantle the welfare state by selling off nationalized industries, reducing social programs, and implementing monetarist economic policies. In the 1980s, Ronald Reagan, president of the United States, was elected on a similar neoliberal agenda. To the Thatcherite critique of the welfare state, Reagan and his Republican Party added to their list of causes of the United States' economic malaise the hedonism of the 1960s, the rise of the new left, the anti–Vietnam War movement, the radicalization of the civil rights movement, and, later, the rise of feminism.

In 1989, the Soviet Union withdrew from Eastern Europe and, in 1991, collapsed, thus ending the bipolar system that had divided the world into two spheres of influence, one American and one Soviet, since the end of World War II. As Russian power faded and the United States emerged during the 1990s as the world's only superpower, the neoliberal agenda articulated by Thatcher and Reagan began to spread to the major states in Europe, including Russia and the states of Eastern Europe, and beyond to states in Asia, Latin America, and even Africa. Since then, the United States has become a hegemonic "hyperpower" and neoliberalism has become the dominant ideology within the global order.

These events prompted much speculation about their deeper meaning.[1] The first President Bush wrote that the collapse of the Soviet Union and the emergence of the United States as the world's only superpower represented something more profound than just the ending of hostilities between two superpowers. For him, it marked the end of an old world order and the beginning of a new one.[2] Francis Fukuyama, then the deputy director of the Department of State's policy-planning staff, also saw in these events a deep significance. He published an article in which he argued that they proved that liberal democratic states, such as the United States, represented a kind of terminus toward which all states were evolving and at which all states would eventually arrive. Fukuyama also claimed that the gradually forming global consensus around neoliberalism meant that history, manifested in ideological conflict, was coming to an end.[3] Samuel Huntington, then a professor of government at Harvard University, saw these events as the beginning of a new phase of global history in which the fundamental conflicts will not be between nation-states, but rather between civilizations. For Huntington, the clash of civilizations will dominate global politics in the future.[4]

Does the collapse of the Soviet Union, the ending of the bipolar global order of the Cold War, the subsequent emergence of the United States as the global hegemon, and the spread of neoliberalism to all regions of the world represent a fundamental shift to a new global order devoid of conflict over ideology and rife with conflict along the fault lines between and among civilizations? Does the liberal democratic state represent the end of history? The only way that the significance of these events can be judged satisfactorily is by placing them into a broad and deep historical context. An analysis of how the current global order came to be will provide the frame of reference necessary to judge the claims of scholars who, like Huntington, see them as a fundamental watershed from an era dominated by conflicts within Western civilization to an era dominated by clashes between Western and non-Western civilizations and among non-Western civilizations or, like Fukuyama, see them as the ending of a long historical process of change through succeeding epochs because the final form of human governance has been finally achieved.

The Nation-State

Although Fukuyama's analysis recognizes the importance of the nation-state in these events, Huntington does not. Despite a brief passage in which he says that states will remain "the most powerful actors in world affairs," Huntington dismisses them as secondary to "civilization." In this regard Huntington is wrong. Civilizations do not exercise politico-military power, nation-states do.[5] Although they are being challenged by the forces of globalization, about which we will say more later, nation-states, having eclipsed all other types of politico-military rule that have existed on the planet, are, and will continue to be for the foreseeable future, the basic building blocks of the global order. Today, every square mile of land surface of planet Earth, except Antarctica, falls within the exclusive domain of one nation-state or another. In fact, the nation-state as a form of politico-military rule has become so ubiquitous that its existence is taken for granted, rarely noticed even by scholars of international relations.[6]

What is the nation-state? This is a difficult question to answer briefly because the words "nation-state" conjure multiple meanings and associations. Defining the nation-state is complicated by the fact that in contemporary English usage the words "nation" and "state" are used interchangeably. This problem is compounded among U.S. speakers of English because the received truth of U.S. political discourse is that the United States does not constitute a "state." This is because the Founding Fathers never used the word when speaking or writing about the new politico-military entity that they were creating in Philadelphia during the summer of 1787. Instead, they called it a "republic" or a "union." When they used the word "state," they were referring to one of the constituent parts of the new entity or to Britain. Thus, today, the word "state" to Americans means one of the several constituent parts of the union, such as New York State or the state of California. Americans tend to use the words "nation" or "country" to refer to what we mean by the word "state."[7]

Nonetheless, the following characteristics can be recognized as the common currency of nation-states in the current global order. The nation-state is a type of politico-military rule that, first, has a distinct geographically defined territory over which it exercises jurisdiction; second, has sovereignty over its territory, which means that its jurisdiction is theoretically exclusive of outside interference by other nation-states or entities; third, it has a government made up of public offices and roles that control and administer the territory and population subject to the state's jurisdiction; fourth, it has fixed boundaries marked on the ground by entry and exit points and, in some cases, by fences patrolled by border guards and armies; fifth, its government claims a monopoly on the legitimate use of physical coercion over its population; sixth, its population manifests, to a greater or lesser degree, a sense of national identity; and, seventh, it can rely, to a greater or lesser degree, on the obedience and loyalty of its inhabitants.[8]

Political Science and the State

Throughout the nineteenth and into the early twentieth century the state received much scholarly attention. It was something that needed to be explained by political scientists who, at that time, were professors of law, history, and philosophy. Their understanding of the state was based on its formal-legal structures, that is, on constitutions, governmental structures, and lawmaking, especially among the European democracies.[9] After World War II, especially among U.S. academics, scholarly attention shifted away from the formal-legal structures of the state to the "informal" politics within "society," because formal-legal studies were thought to be too legalistic and too narrowly focused on state structures. The new focus, which can be called pluralism, sought out the ways in which the diversity of social interests, organized into political parties and pressure groups, produced public

The Nation-States of the World

Afghanistan
Albania
Algeria
Andorra
Angola
Antigua and Barbuda
Argentina
Armenia
Australia
Austria
Azerbaijan
Bahamas
Bahrain
Bangladesh
Barbados
Belarus
Belgium
Belize
Benin
Bhutan
Bolivia
Bosnia and Herzegovina
Botswana
Brazil
Brunei Darussalam
Bulgaria
Burkina Faso
Burundi
Cambodia
Cameroon
Canada
Cape Verde
Central African Republic
Chad
Chile
China
Colombia
Comoros
Congo
Costa Rica
Côte d'Ivoire
Croatia
Cuba
Cyprus
Czech Republic
Democratic People's Republic of
   Korea
Democratic Republic of the Congo
Denmark

Djibouti
Dominica
Dominican Republic
Ecuador
Egypt
El Salvador
Equatorial Guinea
Eritrea
Estonia
Ethiopia
Fiji
Finland
France
Gabon
Gambia
Georgia
Germany
Ghana
Greece
Grenada
Guatemala
Guinea
Guinea-Bissau
Guyana
Haiti
Honduras
Hungary
Iceland
India
Indonesia
Iran (Islamic Republic of)
Iraq
Ireland
Israel
Italy
Jamaica
Japan
Jordan
Kazakhstan
Kenya
Kiribati
Kuwait
Kyrgyzstan
Lao People's Democratic Republic
Latvia
Lebanon
Lesotho
Liberia
Libyan Arab Jamahiriya

Liechtenstein
Lithuania
Luxembourg
Macedonia (the former Yugoslav
    Republic of)
Madagascar
Malawi
Malaysia
Maldives
Mali
Malta
Marshall Islands
Mauritania
Mauritius
Mexico
Micronesia (Federated States of)
Monaco
Mongolia
Morocco
Mozambique
Myanmar
Namibia
Nauru
Nepal
Netherlands
New Zealand
Nicaragua
Niger
Nigeria
Norway
Oman
Pakistan
Palau
Panama
Papua New Guinea
Paraguay
Peru
Philippines
Poland
Portugal
Qatar
Republic of Korea
Republic of Moldova
Romania
Russian Federation
Rwanda
Saint Kitts and Nevis
Saint Lucia

Saint Vincent and the Grenadines
Samoa
San Marino
Sao Tome and Principe
Saudi Arabia
Senegal
Serbia and Montenegro
Seychelles
Sierra Leone
Singapore
Slovakia
Slovenia
Solomon Islands
Somalia
South Africa
Spain
Sri Lanka
Sudan
Suriname
Swaziland
Sweden
Switzerland
Syrian Arab Republic
Tajikistan
Thailand
Timor-Leste
Togo
Tonga
Trinidad and Tobago
Tunisia
Turkey
Turkmenistan
Tuvalu
Uganda
Ukraine
United Arab Emirates
United Kingdom of Great Britain
    and Northern Ireland
United Republic of Tanzania
United States of America
Uruguay
Uzbekistan
Vanuatu
Venezuela
Viet Nam
Yemen
Zambia
Zimbabwe

Source: UN member states, 2004

policy. Pluralists assumed that society was separate from and prior to the state. The state did what the groups in society wanted or pressured it to do. In short, politics was to be explained by what happened in society and the state was seen as being little more than one social group among the many that existed.

The new focus on society was connected to the extension of U.S. power after World War II. Political scientists in the United States sought to generalize the Western liberal democratic model of state and society, especially the U.S. version, to newly independent states. In this way, new states could be more easily incorporated into a world order in which U.S. interests and values would prevail, and communism would be unable to gain a foothold in the non-European world. In order to project the Western model of state and society, U.S. political scientists sought a "general" theory to explain how societies, no matter where they were, could function smoothly, if their economies, politics, and social structures were integrated and balanced. "Disequilibrium" among these balanced parts, it was feared, would create an instability that could be exploited by leftist groups in their bids for power and, thus, increase the influence of the Soviet Union.

Ironically, the disinterest of the discipline of political science in the state was, in part, a product of the state's success. In the advanced capitalist states, such as the United States, Japan, and the states of Western Europe, the state more or less successfully managed increasing economic prosperity and steady advances in the welfare of their subject populations. Public policies considered "socialistic" when initially proposed, such as Social Security, healthcare for the poor and aged, unemployment insurance, and the minimum wage, became staples of these states. The so-called welfare state did not need serious analytic attention from political scientists because it seemed to provide a common good that few questioned. This positive view was reinforced by the fact that Western European states and the Japanese state had successfully transformed war-ravaged economies into prosperous, dynamic, capitalist powerhouses.

By the early 1970s, however, all was not well and the pluralist approach came under intellectual scrutiny and political challenge. Among mainstream political scientists, a new subfield of the discipline called "policy analysis" arose out of new bureaucratic-politics models of government and a new interest in decisionmaking. Policy analysis had two concerns in the United States. One was to explain how the United States became embroiled in the Vietnam War in spite of widespread domestic dissent and expert advice that the war could not be won. The hope was that models of bureaucratic politics would shed light on how foreign policy decisions could be better made to prevent future Vietnams.

The second concern was the search for answers to the vexing question of how state programs could be more efficiently managed in the face of challenges by those who deemed them wasteful. While not reviving an interest in the state per se, and while accepting the prevailing pluralist model of the state, the policy-analysis approach did refocus on the activities of government bureaucracies. Eschewing an explicit concept of the state, policy analysis drew on theories of organizational behavior and decisionmaking that, in turn, were drawn from mathematics (game theory), social psychology, and cybernetic engineering. As with pluralism, the implicit normative emphasis of policy analysis was on promoting order, routine, and efficiency against the messy indeterminacy and contingency of politics. Hence, this backdoor reintroduction of the state envisioned it without politics.

The first political and social scientists to renew an interest in the state per se were crisis theorists, many drawing on various Marxist traditions.[10] These theorists sought to explain why the welfare state seemed no longer able to sustain the prosperity and security of the postwar era. Many of these theories were inspired by Marx and traced the failures of the state to its inability to extract sufficient resources or to maintain its legitimacy in the context of a capitalist economy. Some argued, on the one hand, that the state could not take in enough money to pay for all its programs, along with Cold War military budgets (which were seen as necessary to ensure foreign outlets for capital and sources of raw materials); and some, on the other hand, argued that the legitimacy of the state, which rested on its promotion of equality, could not overcome the class inequality produced by capitalism.[11]

Increasingly, in reaction to pluralism, policy analysis, and crisis theory, certain political scientists began to focus explicitly and look more favorably upon the state. These scholars examined how the state had functioned historically both as an organization of domination and as a promoter of reforms that might make good on the promises of the welfare state.[12] This effort to "bring the state back in" was critical of the way the state had been subordinated to society by the pluralists and neo-Marxist crisis theorists.[13] Instead, these scholars began to look at how state institutions made decisions, under what influences, and with what effects. These statist theories viewed the state as an agent in itself, as an autonomous entity in the sense of being institutionally separate from society, which could take independent action, even against society's wishes. Statist theories have led to fruitful studies of particular states by integrating historical sociology and political science. However, while statists have been attuned to the historical nature of particular states, they have assumed an ahistorical and reified concept of the state; states are historical, but the state as a form of politico-military rule is not.[14]

For the most part, these theorists have largely ignored international politics, although some crisis theorists did locate the state in the world capitalist economy.[15] Also, pluralism had international parallels in theories of international integration, which sought to identify those behavioral principles of social integration among states and international organizations capable of producing international peace.[16] The statist theories that did introduce the international dimension into a theory of the state were not very successful because of their ahistorical concept of the state. Eventually, these theories accepted the point of view of realist international relations that all states were conceptually the same; each sought to maintain sovereign territoriality against others in a systematic balance of power. Just as the state was seen domestically as autonomous because it was institutionally separate from the economy and society, the same was assumed to follow for the "states-system." That is, states somehow existed autonomously from their societies, on the one hand, and from the global system of states, on the other.[17]

In the 1980s and 1990s constructivist theories developed that have contributed to a more thoroughly historical account of the state.[18] These theories have explored how aspects of the state that pluralist and statist theories largely take for granted and do not explain historically are themselves historical constructs, especially the two primary aspects of the modern state: territoriality and sovereignty. Constructivist theories have also shown how war and violence constitute the state, and cannot be analyzed simply as resources or tools used by states, as well as how the distinction between the domestic "inside" of the state (a presumed sphere of order and law) and the international "outside" (a sphere of presumed anarchy and war) are not given ontological categories but are historically constituted of and by states.

A Historical-Constructivist Approach

The approach to the state taken in this book is inspired by these constructivist theories. It examines the formation of the modern sovereign, territorial state and the current states-system historically. It constitutes an archaeology of the transformations in the state and the states-system that led to the contemporary way of imagining and understanding political life and to the imposition across the globe of the territorial state as the only acceptable form of politico-military rule.

What are the advantages of a historical-constructivist approach? First, it shows that the assumption of most scholars of international relations that the nation-state, or something like it, has always existed and consequently is a universal manifestation of human nature, is wrong. A historical-constructivist approach shows that the state and the current states-system have not always existed and, therefore, are not products of human nature. It shows that the nation-state and the states-system have histories that can be discerned. From these histories, it can be seen that there was a time on the planet when there were no nation-states and no states-system as presently constituted. Historical-constructivism shows that there was a time when there was a plethora of politico-military forms of rule that rivaled the state and were, eventually, surpassed by it.

One such historical rival and alternative was the city-state, which was a small, independent, self-governing, urban conurbation, surrounded by agricultural land, that engaged in trade and war with neighboring city-states. The city-state was unable to expand itself to incorporate additional territory in order to enhance its politico-military power because to do so would make it too large to be self-governing. The best historical examples of this form of politico-military rule are the city-states of ancient Greece (Athens, Sparta, etc.); the free cities of the Hanseatic League of North German cities (Bremen, Hamburg, Danzig, etc.) during the Middle Ages; and the republican cities (Venice, Genoa, Pisa, etc.) of what is today northern Italy during the Renaissance.[19] A contemporary city-state is Singapore, which occupies only 641 square kilometers, but is dealt with by the current global system as if it were a nation-state.

Another historical rival and alternative form of politico-military rule was the empire.[20] The classical traditional empire, such as those of the Romans, Chinese, Incas, Syrians, Persians, Zulus, etc., was a form of politico-military rule that had only indirect and limited control over an extensive territory and heterogeneous population. Traditional empires were ruled by an elite that shared a language and culture among itself but ruled conquered subject peoples who were linguistically and culturally distinct from one another and from the ruling elite. The elite ruled indirectly through local rulers from the various ethnic and linguistic groups enclosed within the empire.

A traditional empire was, theoretically, expandable to encompass the entire globe because such empires did not have fixed borders. Imperial borders were merely frontiers that marked the empire's temporary outer limits where its army happen to have stopped and could be moved outward at will. In other words, the boundaries of a traditional empire did not demarcate an area of exclusive territorial jurisdiction based on a shared national identity, but defined a flexible zone of military and economic contact between the empire and the peoples outside of it.

Moreover, traditional imperial governments did not have a monopoly of physical coercion within the empire's jurisdiction and ordinary people did not have regular contact with imperial officials. Contact was occasional, usually only at tax-collection time, and often mediated by local elites from the various conquered peoples. Essentially, empires did not have, nor did they seek to engender systematically, a uniform shared imperial identity among subject peoples. Recent traditional empires include the Ottoman Empire, Austro-Hungarian Empire, and the Russian (later Soviet) Empire. Like Singapore, these empires were dealt with by the global system as if they were nation-states. Their disappearance, about which we will say more in later chapters, can be seen as a consequence of the increasing legitimization of the nation-state as the only acceptable form of politico-military rule on the planet.

A third historical rival to the nation-state is the tribe. A tribe is a non-territorial social group composed of numerous extended families grouped into clans, which are believed to be related to one another by being the descendants of a common mythical ancestor. Social solidarity is based on ties of blood and kinship, not territorialized national identity. Governance of the tribe is in the hands of a hereditary chief from one of the families or clans, usually assisted by a council of elders or warriors. The vast majority of human beings who have ever lived on the planet have lived in tribes. Tribes exist today, especially in Africa, but have been surpassed and overlain by the nation-state. Occasionally a tribe is given a state of its own (e.g., Botswana, Swaziland); more typically, however, a state contains many tribes (e.g., the Yorubas, Ibos, and Hausa-Fulani, to mention the largest in Nigeria), or a tribe straddles the borders between one or more states (e.g., the Kurds in Iraq, Syria, Turkey, and Iran).

A historical-constructivist approach shows that war has been central to the formation of the nation-state. Military activity and the formation of the nation-state have been inextricably linked. Selection by competition, especially in war fighting, gave rise to the modern nation-state, although this should not be taken to mean that the process was determined by some transcendent logic.[21] The organizational and technological innovations in warfare during the fifteenth and sixteenth centuries gave a war-making advantage to the form of politico-military rule that had access to large volumes of men (for soldiers) and capital (money to pay, equip, and arm them) from their own subject populations. Competitive advantage also came to those politico-military forms of rule that were able to construct a coherent collective identity (i.e., a sense of nationhood) that overrode regional, class, and tribal loyalties, which in turn allowed entire societies to be mobilized for war.

Historical-constructivism shows that the form of politico-military rule that was the most efficient at mobilizing the men, money, and matériel for war was hierarchically organized within a sizable, but not *too* sizable, territory.[22] In such forms of politico-military rule, rulers were able to take advantage of their territorial authority to construct uniform, centrally administered, territorially wide systems of law, taxation, weights and measures, coinage, tariffs, etc., which regularized and homogenized social and economic life and made the efficient extraction of the human and nonhuman resources necessary for making war possible. As we will show below, from the fifteenth century onward, the hierarchical authority over a sizable demarcated territory exercised by kings gave European monarchies a strong competitive advantage over rival forms of politico-military rule such as city-states and empires, which were eventually eliminated from the system as independent actors.

A historical-constructivist approach shows that the evolutionary success of such hierarchically organized and territorial demarcated forms of rule was not due to internal factors alone. Rather, success was also owed to the simultaneous construction of a system of similarly organized forms of politico-military rule from which emanated pressures and demands that units within the system conform to the forms of politico-military rule that dominated the system. Forms that violated the emerging dominant organizational logic came to be seen as illegitimate by the system and were forced to adapt to it or were eliminated from it. Thus, the formation of the nation-state and the formation of the current global states-system were mutually constitutive, interactive processes. In effect, once the states-system gradually transformed itself into a network of like states, it imposed structural limits on the types of states that were permitted and able to exist in the system. The construction of a particular ordered system of states involved interventions justified by reference to the norms that regulate state governing practices. When state practices did not fit the agreed-upon understanding within the system of governing practices of what these practices ought to be, powerful states sought to reinforce acceptable forms of rule by regulating the sovereignty of the nonconforming state. In other words, a state's relations with other states has had a historically mutually reinforcing effect on the whole structure of the states-system. The form of the state has tended to reproduce itself, internally and externally, by interventions from the most powerful states in the system, and within the confines of systemic rules and norms.[23]

Moreover, a historical-constructivist approach shows that the characteristics of the modern state mentioned above came about very slowly, over a long period of time. Therefore, what constitutes a state differs over time. Different forms of the state have appeared and disappeared. The history of the state and the current global order of nation-states is a history of variation, change, and transformation from one dominant reality to another marked by a profound change in the basic units that compose global society and the way that they relate to one another. Change from one dominant reality to another defines different epochs or eras in the history of global society.[24]

Four "great" or primary transformations from one epoch to another can be discerned. The first of these great transformations was the movement from the heteronomy of coexisting and competing politico-military forms of rule (city-states, order-states, monarchies, principalities, duchies, coun-tries, fiefs, bishoprics, theocracies, and empires) that existed in medieval Europe to the homonymous system of territorially segmented sovereign states hierarchically organized with clearly defined geographical bound-aries and within which there exists a monopolization of politico-military power and coercion on the part of the central government.[25] This first great transformation, marked by the Peace of Westphalia that ended the Thirty Years Wars (1618–1648), was the culmination of a thousand years of politi-co-military consolidation after the collapse of the Western Roman Empire that gave rise to territorialized politico-military rule in Europe.

The second great transformation was the imposition of the state and the European states-system on other areas of the globe. Outside of Europe, European states encountered traditional empires (Inca, Chinese, Ottoman, Persian, etc.) and a wide assortment of tribal peoples. These entities of politico-military rule were not recognized by Europeans as states in the European sense, nor were they accorded the privileges of sovereign state-hood. There was no homogeneous interstate society at this time. Gradually, European states partitioned the globe into spheres of influence for trade and, finally, established colonies throughout. The colonies that the British, French, Dutch, Portuguese, Belgians, Americans, and Germans held in the Americas, Asia, the Middle East, and Africa were, in effect, entities through which the European states-system was extended to the entire globe.

The third great transformation was the movement from a mixed global system of sovereign states in Europe and European colonial empires out-side of Europe to the current global order in which sovereign, territorial statehood is the only legitimate and acceptable form of politico-military rule on the planet. This transformation began in Europe when the idea that sovereign authority flowed from God and was invested in a king (the "divine right") was replaced with the idea that sovereign authority flowed from the people and was invested in leaders chosen by them. The rise of popular sovereignty during the late eighteenth century began to transform the European states-system, in which hereditary monarchy was the only legitimate form of the state, to the present global order in which the state based on some type of popular sovereignty, usually some type of liberal-ism, is the only legitimate form.[26]

The third great transformation led to the fourth, which began at the end of the eighteenth and beginning of the nineteenth century, with the rise of nationalism.[27] Appearing first in Europe's colonial possessions in the Americas as liberal nationalism, this fourth great transformation continued piecemeal until after World War II, when the idea of the self-determination of peoples—which held that colonized peoples were entitled to rule them-selves, that is, to have their own sovereign state—became a principle of the global system of states. The legitimation of the principle of self-determination led to a large number of colonies in Africa and Asia becoming independent sovereign states, however weak their governments, scant their control over their territory, and inchoate their people. Once independent, these former colonies became full members of the globalized European states-system with all the rights and privileges that sovereign statehood entailed. This fourth transformation is still going on as "nations" in various regions of the world demand their own sovereign states and receive them.

Finally, a historical-constructivist approach shows that these great transformations are slow and never "clean" or "neat." A certain number of previously existing units of politico-military rule have survived, or have been allowed to survive, into subsequent epochs despite the fact that they were less efficient makers of war and should have disappeared from the states-system, and despite the fact that they have a form of governance that is at variance with the form that is accepted as legitimate in that epoch. Take the Vatican City, the globe's smallest (109 acres) fully sovereign state, for example. It is the remnant of the once powerful and legitimate papal states (themselves a remnant of the Roman Empire) that stretched across the Italian Peninsula's midsection and were part of the Holy Roman Empire during the Middle Ages. The Vatican City survived the above-mentioned great transformations not because it was able to compete militarily with its rivals nor because it was able to adjust its form of governance (absolute monarchy) to that which is legitimate within the current European states-system. Rather, it was allowed to continue to exist by the powerful units within the system, especially the Italian state within which it is entirely enclosed.

The Plan of the Book

The following chapters constitute an archaeology of the nation-state and the current global states-system. The focus of these chapters is on the transformations in institutions, ideologies, and governing practices that produced the nation-state and the current states-system. They contain a rich load of historical data and a number of case studies that show the importance of contingent historical conditions in the formation of particular states. They emphasize the role of war in the formation of the state as a form of politico-military rule.

The book is divided into four parts. Part 1 describes the first great transformation from the heteronomy of coexisting and competing forms of politico-military rule that existed in medieval Europe after the fall of the Roman Empire to the homonymous system of territorially segmented states of the early modern period. Part 2 discusses the specific forms that the territorially segmented sovereign states have taken within the spatiotemporal framework of Europe and simultaneous construction of a states-system within that geographical space. Part 3 discusses the second and third great transformations: the extension of the territorially segmented sovereign state to areas of the globe outside of Europe and the movement from a global system of sovereign territorial states inside Europe and colonial empires outside of Europe to the current global order in which sovereign territorially segmented states are the only legitimate and acceptable form of human politico-military rule on the planet. Part 4 focuses on the challenges to the territorially segmented sovereign states as the dominant form of politico-military organization presented by globalization and technological change. In this last part of the book we will seek to answer the questions raised at the beginning of this chapter: Is the world experiencing its last great transformation to a new global order in which the territorially segmented sovereign state will no longer be the dominant form of politico-military rule and will be replaced by a form organized at the level of civilizations, at which time history as we know it will have ended? Or, are we witnessing the consolidation within the states-system of a particular form of the state to the detriment of others?

Notes

1. Ian Clark, "Another 'Double Movement': The Great Transformation After the Cold War?" in Michael Cox, Tim Dunne, and Ken Booth (eds.), *Empires, Systems and States: Great Transformations in International Politics* (Cambridge: Cambridge University Press, 2001): 237–255; and Richard Falk, *Law in an Emerging Global Village: A Post-Westphalian Perspective* (Ardsley, NY: Transnational Publishers, 1998), chapter 1.

2. George Bush and Brent Scowcroft, *A World Transformed* (New York: Knopf, 1998).

3. Francis Fukuyama, "The End of History?" *The National Interest* (summer 1989): 3–18.

4. Samuel P. Huntington, "The Clash of Civilizations?" *Foreign Affairs* (summer 1993): 22–49.

5. Fouad Ajami, "The Summoning," *Foreign Affairs* (September-October 1993): 2–9.

6. Alexander B. Murphy, "The Sovereign State System as Political-Territorial Ideal: Historical and Contemporary Considerations," in Thomas J. Biersteker and Cynthia Weber (eds.), *State Sovereignty as Social Construct* (Cambridge: Cambridge University Press, 1996): 81–120.

7. Christopher W. Morris, *An Essay on the Modern State* (Cambridge: Cambridge University Press, 1989), 19–21.

8. Andrew Vincent, *Theories of the State* (Oxford: Basil Blackwell, 1987), 19–21.

9. Robert MacIver, *The Modern State* (London: Oxford University Press, 1926); W. C. MacLeod, *The Origins of the State* (Indianapolis, IN: Bobbs-Merrill, 1924); Franz Oppenheimer, *The State* (Indianapolis, IN: Bobbs-Merrill, 1914); and

G. E. Smith and W. J. Perry, *The Origins and History of Politics* (New York: Wiley, 1931).

10. A useful review of Marxist theories of the state as they revived in the 1960s, largely in France and Britain, and then entered U.S. political science is Clyde W. Barrow, *Critical Theories of the State* (Madison: University of Wisconsin Press, 1993). More sophisticated is Bob Jessop, *The Capitalist State* (New York and London: New York University Press, 1982).

11. See especially James O'Connor, *The Fiscal Crisis of the State* (New York: St. Martin's Press, 1973); Jürgen Habermas, *Legitimation Crisis,* trans. Thomas McCarthy (Boston: Beacon Press, 1973); Claus Offe, "The Theory of the Capitalist State and the Problem of Policy Formation," in L. Lindberg et al. (eds.), *Stress and Contradiction in Modern Capitalism* (Lexington, MA: D. H. Heath, 1975).

12. See especially Charles Tilly (ed.), *The Formation of National States in Western Europe* (Princeton, NJ: Princeton University Press, 1975).

13. Theda Skocpol, "Bringing the State Back In: Strategies of Analysis in Current Research," in Peter B. Evans, Dietrich Rueschemeyer, and Theda Skocpol (eds.), *Bringing the State Back In* (Cambridge: Cambridge University Press, 1985).

14. For a more detailed critique of this type, see Timothy Mitchell, "The Limits of the State: Beyond Statist Approaches," *American Political Science Review* 85:1 (1991): 77–96.

15. Most notable are Marxist theories of capitalist imperialism and dependency, as well as Immanuel Wallerstein's "world systems theory." See his *The Modern World System: Capitalist Agriculture and the Origins of the European World Economy in the Sixteenth Century* (New York: Academic Press, 1974).

16. See, for example, Ernest B. Haas, *The Uniting of Europe: Political, Social, and Economic Forces, 1950–1957* (Stanford, CA: Stanford University Press, 1958).

17. The most famous rendering of this was Kenneth Waltz, *Man, the State, and War* (New York: Columbia University Press, 1954). For a critique of realist international-relations theory, which connects its disdain for theories of the state to its ahistorical positivism, see Richard K. Ashley, "The Poverty of Neorealism," *International Organization* 38:2 (spring 1984): 225–286.

18. Two forms of critical international theory prevail, a neo-Gramscian approach following Robert Cox, and a postmodernist approach following the work of Richard Ashley, R.B.J. Walker, Michael Shapiro, and James Der Derian, although these categories hardly account for the diversity of recent approaches to international relations and political economy. For a useful review, see Scott Burchill, Andrew Linkleter, et al., *Theories of International Relations* (New York: St. Martin's Press, 1996).

19. Charles Tilly and Wim P. Blockmans (eds.) *Cities and the Rise of States in Europe A.D. 1000 to 1800* (Boulder, CO: Westview Press, 1994).

20. Rey Koslowski, "Human Migration and the Conceptualization of Pre-Modern Politics," *International Studies Review* 46 (2002): 375–399.

21. Hendrik Spruyt, *The Sovereign State and Its Competitors: An Analysis of Systems Change* (Princeton, NJ: Princeton University Press, 1994).

22. Robert Gilpin, *War and Change in World Politics* (Cambridge: Cambridge University Press, 1981).

23. Cynthia Weber, *Simulating Sovereignty: Intervention, the State, and Symbolic Exchange* (Cambridge: Cambridge University Press, 1995).

24. The classic work is Karl Polanyi, *The Great Transformation: The Political and Economic Origins of Our Time* (Boston: Beacon Press, 1957). See also Philip Bobbitt, *The Shield of Achilles: War, Peace, and the Course of History* (New York:

Anchor Books, 2002); Barry Buzan and Richard Little, *International Systems in World History: Remaking the Study of International Relations* (Oxford: Oxford University Press, 2000); Philip G. Cerny, *The Changing Architecture of Politics: Structure, Agency, and the Future of the State* (Newbury Park, CA: Sage Publications, 1990); Rodney Bruce Hall, *National Collective Identity: Social Constructs and International Systems* (New York: Columbia University Press, 1999); Andreas Osiander, *The States System of Europe, 1640–1990: Peacemaking and the Condition of International Society* (Oxford: Clarendon Press, 1994); Daniel Philpott, *Revolutions in Sovereignty: How Ideas Shaped Modern International Relations* (Princeton, NJ: Princeton University Press, 2001); John Gerard Ruggie, *Constructing the World Polity: Essays on International Institutionalization* (London/New York: Routledge, 1998).

25. John Gerard Ruggie, "Territoriality at Millennium's End," in John Gerard Ruggie, *Constructing the World Polity: Essays on International Institutionalization* (London/New York: Routledge, 1998): 172–197.

26. Weber, *Simulating Sovereignty*.

27. Hall, *National Collective Identity*.

PART I

THE EMERGENCE OF THE TERRITORIAL STATE

In Part 1, we discuss the first great transformation that brought into being the territorial state and the European Westphalian states-system. We examine the legacies of the Roman Empire, feudalism, and medieval monarchies in the formation of the territorial state. We focus on the emergence of institutions—such as standing armies, centralized administrations, and economies framed by territory-wide legal structures— as well as the transformations of political language and knowledge that made the modern territorial state possible. In addition, we establish an interpretive framework in which the specific histories of contemporary states, within and beyond Europe, can be understood.

Part I

THE EMERGENCE OF THE PREDATORY STATE

I

The Ancient Roman State: Imperial Rule

We begin with a discussion of the ancient Roman imperial state to show how the disappearance of the western portion of the empire created the conditions out of which emerged the territorial state. We will see that the Western Roman Empire was followed by a number of Germanic kingdoms that eventually were transformed by the necessities of war into territorial states.

The political history of Roman rule can be divided into two broad periods: the first is the period of the Republic, which stretches from the founding of the city of Rome in 508 B.C. to the rule and assassination of Julius Caesar on the Ides of March in 44 B.C. The second is the period of the Empire, which extends from the rule of the Emperor Caesar Augustus (ruled 27 B.C.–14 A.D.) until the sacking of Rome by Alaric, a Visigothic chieftain, in 410 A.D.[1]

The Roman Republic

During the republican period, the Roman state was governed by the Senate, which represented the patricians, or persons of high birth, wealth, and cultivation who could trace their ancestry to one of the original clan heads appointed to govern the city of Rome by its mythical founder, Romulus. The patricians held most formal positions within the state administration, and articulated the ideology that justified or legitimated the institutions and structure of the Roman state. In short, the Senate represented the ruling aristocratic class of Rome.

During the early Republic, class warfare between the patricians and the plebeians, or the ordinary people, was common. In order to still this internal strife, the Senate allowed wealthier plebeians to gain access to the consul, the highest office of magistrates in the Republic, as early as 356 B.C. It also created the tribunate, which was composed of tribal representatives and functioned as a parallel executive office to the consul. The tribunate was designed to give the poor a voice in governing Rome, but was ineffective because, as one scholar puts it, "the tribunes, normally men of considerable fortunes, . . . [were] for long periods docile instruments of the Senate itself."[2]

In effect, the political institutions of the Roman Republic were "a complex mechanism that provided both an outlet for, and a restraint upon, the dynamics of class conflict, group rivalries, and personal ambitions."[3] In addition to the institutional flexibility of the Republic, a flexibility always kept from bending too far by the Senate, the Roman state managed political conflict and allegiance through the oratory of its politicians and their skill at playing the "seamier side of politics . . . patronage, bribery, vote-buying, tampering with electoral bodies, and the sale of public contracts."[4] So long as politics remained centered in the city of Rome itself, this political practice managed to maintain order and secure for Rome significant wealth and power. It generated a powerful military machine composed of all male citizens of Rome. By 275 B.C., the Roman army had conquered the Italian peninsula, defeated the Carthaginians in a century-long campaign known as the Punic Wars (264–202 B.C.), which gave the Republic control of the Western Mediterranean, and conquered Greece and Macedonia between 201 and 146 B.C.

The Roman Political Imaginary

Given the persistence of a political structure dominated by the patrician aristocracy, it is important to understand the ideas and cultural practices through which the state was imagined and represented under the Republic. These ideas and representational practices portrayed certain ideals and values as normal for all Romans, and presented them as universally valid, as if inscribed in the natural ways of the world.

The Roman sense of political space was intensive, consisting of a dense mythology and history that marked Rome as a special and privileged place that possessed a spiritual gravity over all other places without the Republic. This gave its institutions and governing practices an assurance of their ethical rightness and superiority over vanquished enemies. It also constituted the Roman way: its traditions and especially its time-worn status and class distinctions were seen as being rooted in the cosmological order. Even after absorbing a universalism drawn from Greek Stoic philosophy, which we will discuss shortly, Roman ideology assured Rome of its distinctive superiority and privilege as an ethical and political order.

The political ideas of Rome focused on two attributes of the patrician class: *virtus* and "nobility of birth and ancestry."[5] *Virtus*, or "manliness," as demonstrated by the great deeds and accomplishments of patricians, especially in the Roman army, provided the ruling class with a politically effective identity. To be a member of the Senate required one to be the descendant of a family that had contributed greatly to the city in the past. The civic virtue of the ruling class carried both honor and responsibility to look after the affairs of the city, inclining that class to define the essence of politics in terms that transcended private "interests," such as responsibility and honor. Even as the patrician lineages of senators came to be diluted by social reforms and the introduction of plebeians into the Senate in the later Republic, civic virtue remained part of the identity of the senator.

It is useful to talk about the conception of power embedded in the political ideas of Rome. To have power meant to act for the common good. Power prescribed a hierarchical decisionmaking structure, legitimating those "in power" to make and enforce decisions through a mixture of coercion, consensus, and organized violence. This republican idea of power and politics replaced the less hierarchical practices of earlier tribal, clan, and kinship systems in which politics involved ritualized reciprocity, such as gift giving, as well as noncoercive allocations of collective roles, privileges, honors, responsibilities, and resources.[6]

In Rome, political authorities were to be obeyed because they exercised certain offices, which were conceived of as having been created for the public good, not for the person who exercised the office. The idea that the public good was to be associated with political office rather than the particular officeholder would make possible the reference to Rome as an original source of the bureaucratic and legal authority of the modern state, and help to establish a historical lineage constituting the modern territorial state as the culmination of Western civilization.

In the Roman political ideology, masculinity was privileged. The deference given to ancestry associated power and authority with patriarchy, that is, the supremacy of the father of the family and the legal subordination of wife and children. Women were to be silent and invisible in the public world of Rome, considered by Roman law as under the *patria potestas,* or power of the father, which "committed women to male guardianship as perpetual minors."[7] In law, the power of the father was absolute, although in practice women exercised some political power. Only fathers had rights before the law, could own property, and make contracts. The father had the power of life and death over the members of his family. Moreover, the ideology of Roman civic virtue, indeed of "armed civic virtue," relegated women to the private world of the household dominated by their fathers or husbands, and constructed their public role as "civic cheerleaders, urging men to behave like men, praising the heroes and condemning the cowardly."[8] Women who were not under the power of their husbands and whose fathers had died, were independent, although they were supposed to have a male guardian because women were considered to be the "feeble sex" and in need of male protection and guidance. The subordination of women in the political imagination as well as in the legal practices of Roman citizenship, which represented it, was an essential part of the Roman state.

The durability of the Roman Empire was bolstered by Roman law, which, when it was finally codified by the Byzantine Emperor Justinian (ruled 527–565 A.D.), largely followed the patterns set centuries before in the Twelve Tables (451–450 B.C.).[9] Because the revival of Roman law will be central to the formation of the modern territorial states of Europe, it is important to discuss briefly some of its details.

Civil law was the most important element of Roman law. It dealt primarily with "the regulation of informal relationships of contract and exchange between private citizens."[10] Public law, which set forth the rights and duties of the citizen toward the state, and criminal law, which was the law regarding crimes and punishments, were based on the principle of different statuses (slave-freeman, husband-wife, men-women, rich-poor). The latter was especially concerned with keeping slaves, women, and the lower classes in check, and was often arbitrary and harsh.[11] One's status defined one's rights and duties.

Roman civil law was not concerned with regulating the relationships between individuals but with the transference and protection of private property. With respect to indebtedness, for example, it protected the creditor far more than the debtor.[12] Roman civil law did not give legal and political protection to the entire population, or even to all citizens, because it was based on the idea of "absolute private property," which separated property from political and moral restrictions.[13] As the preeminent principle of civil law, the institution of property itself never required justification.[14]

Parallel to Roman civil law was another system of law based on the practical principles used by the governors of towns and justices when they tried specific cases in the law tribunals. This law was more sensitive to regional differences and the needs and customs of the people living in specific areas. Eventually, this customary law became known as the *ius gentium* or "law of the nations."[15] It governed those economic and political relations that could not be adjudicated by the more traditional and inflexible civil law. With the introduction of the Greek philosophy of Stoicism into Rome, especially in the second century B.C., the *ius gentium* gained the idea of the normative law of nature, which embodied universal moral laws that could be perceived through reason. Stoics, such as Cicero, emphasized order, and taught people to live their lives in conformity to the natural order of the cosmos, which governed all physical and moral being. As practiced by Romans, Stoicism meant peacefully accepting one's duties and responsibilities even if such acceptance involved great personal pain and sacrifice.

Roman Expansion and Imperial Policy

The political structure and ideology of the Roman Republic were most appropriate to a city-state, a geographical and cultural space in which political life focused on the city of Rome itself. However, the expansion of the Roman republican state into an imperial state was driven in good part because, to increase wealth, its economy needed additional land. The state's revenues were drawn largely from agriculture, and its more ambitious public works were funded from tribute paid by conquered peoples. Also, important social reforms, such as the grain subsidies and distribution of provincial lands to the poor during the tribunates of Tiberius and Caius Gracchus (ruled 133–121 B.C.), were paid for largely by wealth drawn from Roman colonies in Asia Minor.[16] Moreover, the Roman economy was dependent on a continuous supply of slaves, whose primary source was conquered territory because slaves practiced various forms of birth control, which limited their numbers. In the words of one historian, the "result was a growing territory that needed even more troops to defend it, and a growing army that needed even more land to support it."[17]

Expansion from a republic into an empire was also propelled by the idea of *virtus,* which militarized Rome. War provided an important social and cultural arena where male Roman citizens distinguished themselves in the eyes of their fellow citizens. Hence, conquest was an integral part of Rome's view of itself. Almost every year, Rome's armies marched out, fought, and humbled an enemy. War was not the "continuation of politics" as it is today, but about a single-minded search for glory, noble self-sacrifice for the *patria* (fatherland), of adversity endured, and victory over increasingly formidable opponents.

The Roman Empire, which expanded greatly under Caesar Augustus (ruled 27–14 B.C.), reached its greatest territorial extent during the reign of Trajan (ruled 98–117 A.D.). Rome's army was stationed along the empire's *limes* (frontiers), which were demarcated with walls and fortifications. Rome's legions, which were made up of peasants recruited from the countryside, constituted the world's first standing army, that is, a permanent military force paid, fed, clothed, and armed by the state. Enlistments were long (twenty years), after which legionaries were given a lump-sum payment equal to thirteen years' service or a grant of land. The Roman army was the finest military organization of its time—highly trained, superbly disciplined, and extremely mobile. It was virtually invincible from the Punic Wars to the third century A.D. At the time of its greatest strength, the Roman army numbered about six hundred thousand men and consumed about 75 percent of the state's budget.[18]

Administratively, the Roman Empire was divided into Italy proper and the provinces. The city of Rome and the Italian peninsula, which had been

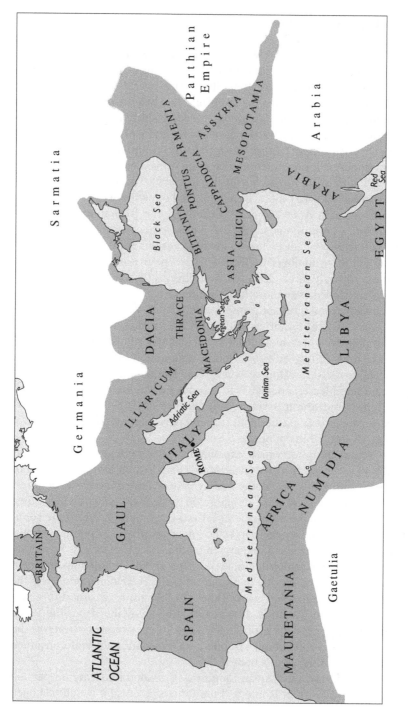

The Roman Empire, 117 A.D.

24

gradually Romanized, were governed by the Senate, the supreme council of the empire. The eastern and western provinces outside of the peninsula were governed by the emperor, the absolute ruler of the empire, and the supreme commander of the army, which provided the administrative staff. The purpose of Roman imperial administration was to collect the taxes that supported the army and paid for public works such as roads, temples, baths, and aqueducts. Administration and control were facilitated by the Roman road network (originally built to allow for the rapid movement of troops), which created a communications system within each province and connected each province to the capital city; hence the expression "all roads lead to Rome."

The practice of Roman imperial policy was not the same in all of its provinces, however. In Italy and the eastern provinces, especially Greece and Asia Minor as well as Egypt, Rome established its domination indirectly by spreading Roman ideology and manipulating local rulers. The Romans generally left these people to live according to their traditions and laws so long as they did not threaten Roman control and Pax Romana (Roman peace). When the Romans believed their hegemony was threatened, Roman provincial governors, called prefects, restored order by sending in the Roman army.

In the western provinces, military campaigns were constantly necessary to subjugate the largely seminomadic tribes of Celtic peoples, whom the Romans called "barbarians" (from the Sanskrit *varvara*, meaning a rough uneducated person), who inhabited these regions. Roman policy in the west required more direct forms of rule, which often amounted to brutal and violent repression of local populations and extensive exploitation by Roman businessmen, moneylenders, and tax collectors. Although the eastern provinces had provided Rome with much of its culture and wealth, the western provinces were a perpetual battleground, where generals of the Roman army gained power and prestige. Julius Caesar, the general in charge of military operations in the western province of Gaul, and other generals like him would play an important role in eroding the power of the Senate and, eventually, replacing the oligarchic Republic with an imperial state centered on the emperor.

Roman imperial expansion caused tremendous social upheaval that strained and eventually transformed the state. Expansion impoverished the small peasant farmers, who had been the backbone of the Roman economy and the chief source of recruits for the army, and enhanced the wealth and power of the patrician aristocracy. As peasant farmers were drafted into the army in ever greater numbers to increase its size so that the empire could be expanded and maintained, their farms were taken over by the patrician aristocracy. Such takeovers created *latifundia,* or large estates, and intensified the use of slave labor.[19]

The republican state was transformed into an empire dominated by emperors and military strongmen who ruled more and more autocratically. As one historian has put it, "The Republic had won Rome its Empire: it was rendered anachronistic by its own victories."[20] The Senate gradually declined in power. The position and role of the army changed. Its ranks were filled increasingly by dispossessed farmers and the poor, as well as by barbarians who agitated for land and, most important, Roman citizenship. When the traditional aristocracy refused and resisted their demands for land and citizenship, legionaries became increasingly loyal to their local military commanders, who promised such rewards. As the citizenry expanded to include the poor and non-Romans, the centralized political power and authority of Rome and the ideology that justified rule by the senatorial aristocracy were undermined and eventually collapsed.

Political Economy and Imperial Decline

The disappearance of the Roman Empire as a coherent politico-military entity was gradual, extending over several centuries. The disappearance of the empire was caused by four interrelated factors involving the inextricably interconnected state and economy.

First, the empire ceased to expand during the reign of Hadrian (ruled 117–138 A.D.). Lacking the regular influx of booty and tribute from newly conquered peoples, the empire could no longer pay for its vast army, large bureaucracy, and extensive public works. The only resources available to the state were drawn from the agricultural sector within the empire. Although Rome's economy was monetarized, it did not have a rich and extensive industrial and commercial base from which to draw revenues.[21]

As the expenses of the state increased, taxes had to be increased. In addition to money taxes, a tax-in-kind was levied on land and labor. A percentage of what was produced by farmers had to be turned over directly to state warehouses and granaries. Manual labor of a certain number of days per week had to be rendered on public roads, buildings, bridges, and aqueducts. Therefore, laws were passed that compelled farmers to fully cultivate their land and urban dwellers to stay in their occupations, for life. As taxation reached intolerable levels, tax evasion became widespread. Essentially, the Roman imperial state had become despotic as it sought to squeeze more and more money out of an economy incapable of expanding fast enough to meet growing financial needs.

Second, Rome's reliance on slave labor as the major source of economic productivity also contributed to imperial decline. Although the Roman economy was in certain respects quite innovative, having invented new agricultural techniques and machines, such as bread-kneading devices and the screw press to extract oil from olives, which increased productivity and wealth, throughout its history the economy remained predominantly unmechanized. This was because the aristocracy limited the use of labor-saving devices because it wanted to moderate unemployment and prevent idleness among slaves. With the concentration of land ownership in the *latifundia* system of the later republic and empire, a consequence of the movement of small peasant farmers off the land, reliance on slave labor expanded. This system of agricultural production depended on the state's continuing to expand militarily because military campaigns on the frontiers of the empire were the most significant source of new slave labor.[22]

Third, the empire's economic problems, especially the inflation of prices caused by falling productivity (a result of the dwindling supply of slave labor), were compounded by the expansion of public expenditures, especially on the building of cities. Rome was an urban culture because Romans imagined political order and the political good as being possible only within cities. The Romans invented concrete, which made possible the construction of large domed public buildings, such as the Pantheon and Colosseum, and aqueducts necessary to city life. Therefore, Romans constructed cities wherever they conquered. Each of these cities was a small replica of Rome itself, with a public square, colonnaded streets, basilicas, forums, triumphal arches, *thermae* (public baths), amphitheaters, and aqueducts. This urbanization, which accelerated as power shifted from Rome itself to the provinces, became increasingly difficult to pay for with the financial resources provided by a largely agrarian economy.[23]

Fourth, Rome's policy of recruiting barbarians into the army to maintain its strength eventually led to the de-Romanization of the army. Gradually, the ranks of the army were filled with legionaries whose commitment to Rome was slight. The influx of barbarians into the army was speeded up after the third century A.D. because the Roman state was facing a serious manpower shortage brought on by a declining birth rate and a high mortality rate among Roman peasant farmers, the chief source of soldiers. Both were the result of civil war, epidemic diseases such as the plague, and increasing economic hardship produced by confiscatory taxation.[24] One historian summed up the economic cause of the Roman collapse this way:

> Increased state expenditures on the army, bureaucracy, in welfare state commitments brought about a continual unbearable tax pressure. Tax pressure grew heavier and the tendency to evasion . . . on the part of high officials and large landowners, was increased . . . This vicious circle could lead to only one result, that which clearly shows itself in the course of the fifth century. The bankruptcy of the enormous [Roman] State at the same time as small privileged groups, while they evaded taxation, heap up riches and create around their villas economic and social microcosms, completely cut off the central authority. It was the end of the Roman world.[25]

In an attempt to stave off the end, the empire was divided, for administrative purposes, into eastern and western portions by the emperor Diocletian (ruled 284–305 A.D.). This division followed geo-social differences between the eastern and western portions marked by the Adriatic Sea. Diocletian ruled the eastern portion and appointed a co-emperor in the west. Diocletion gave the empire efficient administration by subdividing the two halves of the empire into four prefectures under the control of a praetorian prefect appointed by himself and his co-emperor. Each prefecture was subdivided into several dioceses. When Diocletian abdicated in 305 A.D., he was followed on the imperial throne by Constantine (ruled 306–337 A.D.), who established a new capital city on the Bosphorus called Nova Roma (New Rome), on the site of Byzantium, in 330 A.D. With the death of the emperor Theodosius in 395 A.D. the division into eastern and western empires became permanent and Byzantium, the capital of the Eastern Empire, was renamed Constantinople in honor of its founder.

Roman Religion and the Rise of Christianity

Something must be said about Roman religion because developments in this sphere eroded the ideology that justified an imperial state centered at Rome.

The official state religion of Rome was polytheism (i.e., the belief in many gods). Romans worshipped the gods of the Greco-Roman pantheon, such as Jupiter, Juno, Minerva, and Mars, as well as dead emperors who had been officially deified. These gods were tied to the life-world of the Romans and were seen as protectors of Rome itself.

In fact, Romans of the Republic thought of themselves as especially loved by their gods. Their success as a people was seen as a sign of divine favor and their piety to their gods entitled them to conquer other peoples. Rome invited the gods of their defeated enemies to join their pantheon. Hence, Rome was the center of many cults to their gods. As the disintegration of the empire and the harsh methods taken to counteract it created extreme economic hardship, Romans began to turn away from official polytheism. They turned either to foreign gods, such as Mithras, the militant god of the sun from the Persian Zoroastrian religion, especially popular with Roman legionaries, and Isis, the Egyptian goddess of motherhood, or to ancient natural and fertility gods from pre-Roman times. They also turned to a variety of mystery cults from the eastern provinces of the empire. Initially, the Roman state allowed people to follow these new religions, provided that they continued formally to recognize the gods of Rome and the cult of the deified emperors. The devotees of these new religions were largely, but not exclusively, from the lower and most economically distressed classes of Roman society, especially slaves and the very poor, who were desperately seeking relief from economic misery. Roman aristocrats continued to be loyal to the gods they believed had made Rome great.

One of these oriental religions was a Jewish sect that originated in the eastern province of Judea. At first the disciples of Jesus of Nazareth, an early nonconformist, itinerant teacher, and the sect's founder, proselytized among Jewish communities elsewhere in the eastern portion of the empire. After Jesus's crucifixion by the Romans, his disciples began to proselytize in the empire's western portion. Christianity (from the Greek *christos* or messiah, meaning "anointed one") was a revolutionary social movement that spread rapidly, especially among the lower social classes as well as aristocratic women, because its theology (1) was clear-cut (good versus evil), (2) was universalistic (all are equal in the sight of God), (3) satisfied emotional and psychological needs (belief in life after death), and (4) emphasized concern for the poor (charity). Christianity's rapid spread was facilitated by the Pax Romana and the existence of good Roman roads, which made movement about the empire relatively easy for its missionaries.[26]

At first the Roman state tolerated Christianity. However, because Christians refused to acknowledge the many gods of Rome and the cult of the deified emperors, they came to be seen as enemies of the Roman state. Its monotheism (i.e., the belief in the universality of one god) and its idea that all people everywhere were equal in the eyes of that one god threatened the way Rome had understood its relationship to the divine. The Christian emphasis on kindness, humility, charity, mercy, and love for one's neighbor proffered an alternative understanding of virtue, which undermined the Roman association of virtue with manliness and war. Christian virtue was manifested in individual acts of piety and charity rather than civic acts of courage and honor on the battlefield. Consequently, the most pious and energetic adherents to Christianity were women.[27] Moreover, monotheistic Christianity revised the Roman view that victory in battle was not a victory of one set of beliefs over others. Christianity saw victory/defeat as an all-or-nothing proposition (absolute good versus absolute evil), which seriously undermined the Roman social order.

In spite of persecution, the greatest of which came during the third century when many thousands were tortured and put to death, the number of Christians within the empire increased during the fourth century. Converts began to come from the upper classes of Roman society. The early Church, which was composed of small, independent congregations that elected their own deacons and bishops, was replaced by an ecclesiastical hierarchy modeled on the Roman system of provincial administration. On October 29, 312, the emperor Constantine, having defeated his rival in battle, entered Rome. Afterward, he let it be known that he owed his success to the god of

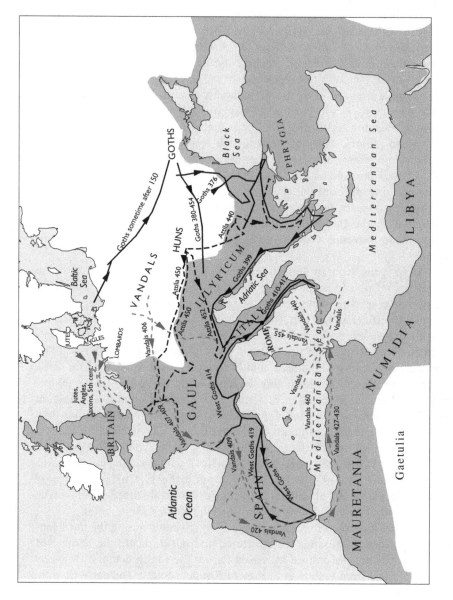

The Germanic Incursions, 300–400 A.D.

30

the Christians. In 313, he lifted the ban on Christianity and a few years later became a Christian himself and chose the Christian god to be the protector of the empire. When he died in 337, the Roman Empire was well on its way to being Christianized. The emperor Theodosius (ruled 379–395 A.D.) declared Christianity to be the official religion of the Roman Empire and outlawed polytheism. He prohibited blood sacrifices, closed temples, and sanctioned the use of physical force to enforce religious conformity. As the empire disintegrated as a coherent politico-military entity, the Christian Church replaced the institutions of Rome with its own law (canon law), ecclesiastical courts, and an administrative hierarchy of priests, bishops, and cardinals. The capital of the empire became the capital of the Catholic (meaning universal) Church. In the fifth century, the bishops of the diocese of Rome were able to achieve ascendancy over the Church's religio-administrative hierarchy by arguing that they had inherited their authority directly from St. Peter, the first bishop of Rome and the apostle to whom Christ reputedly gave the "keys of Heaven," and established the papacy. Christianity's message of kindness, humility, patience, mercy, purity, and chastity was fused with the governing practices of the Roman imperial state: hierarchy, order, *virtus*, patriarchy, and law. In effect, the Church had merged with the Roman Empire. In the words of one scholar, the Church "took over the vestments of pagan priests, use of incense and holy water in purification, burning of candles before the alter, worship of saints, the architecture of the basilica, Roman law as the basis for Canon law, the title Pontifex Maximus for the pope, the Latin language, and the vast framework of the government of the Empire."[28] At this point the Catholic Church had grafted itself onto the framework of Roman administration and became a form of organized rule that did not recognize territorial boundaries to its authority over its community of believers.

Germanic Infiltration

At the time the Roman Republic was expanding northwestward, Germanic tribes of Franks, Lombards, Frisians, Burgundians, Alemmani, Jutes, Angles, and Saxons were experiencing a population explosion that caused them to expand westward from the Baltic region and overrun the indigenous Celtic inhabitants of Europe. By 200 B.C. they had reached the Rhine River and by 100 B.C., the Danube. Other Germanic tribal peoples such as the Suevi, Visigoths, Ostrogoths, and Vandals expanded to the south and east.

The Rhine and the Danube became the frontier between the seminomadic Germanic peoples and the Roman Empire. Only in Scotland, Wales, Cornwall, the Isle of Man, Ireland, and Brittany did the Celts survive. In about 378 A.D. the Huns, a nomadic warrior people from central Asia, led by Attila, swept westward and pushed some of the Germanic peoples across the Rhine and Danube into Roman territory. The Romans allowed them to come into the empire and settled them on uninhabited land as self-governing allies of Rome and under obligation to furnish troops for the Roman army in exchange for land and money. The Germanic tribes accepted Christianity and Roman ways after being settled within the empire.

The Germanic tribes were stateless pastoral societies. Except for occasional temporary confederacy, forms of politico-military rule above village level were rare. A small number of families living on contiguous farmsteads were the basic unit of these societies. Their economies were based on primitive agriculture and animal husbandry, which required them to move perpetually, probably annually, to seek virgin land to cultivate and new pastures for their herds. Land was considered the property of everyone. Because tribes lacked formal institutions of government, decisions affecting the tribe, such as which clans and families would work which areas of land, were made by assemblies of leading warriors according to custom. Many of the clans that made up these tribes were matrilineal (i.e., they traced descent and inheritance through the female line), which gave women important social roles as clan leaders and involved them in decisionmaking. Finally, because the tribe was considered to be the family writ large, no distinction existed within the Germanic tribes between the public and the private.

In places along the Rhine and Danube Rivers where tribes had settled within the empire, there grew a hybrid society, a "social and cultural 'Middle Ground,'"[29] which blended Roman and Germanic institutions and practices. In many places, Germanic peoples abandoned communal ownership and accepted the Roman idea of private ownership. Leading Germanic warriors carved out *latifundia* for themselves, creating differences in social standing and status that had not existed before the encounter with Rome. Increasingly, women were subordinated to men as the Germanic tribes accepted Rome's patriarchal inheritance laws and Christianity's subordinating definition of the identity "woman" in relation to God and "man."[30]

For their part, the Romans gradually accepted the Germanic institution of the *comitatus* (from the Latin *comes,* or one who dines with the king), in which successful older warriors gathered around themselves elite groups of younger warriors who pledged unswerving loyalty and devotion to their leader in exchange for arms, horses, protection, and a share of the booty taken from defeated enemies. Bands of such retainers formed powerful politico-military units within the Roman army. As more and more Germanic peoples were brought into the Roman army, most generals during the last centuries of the empire were of Germanic origin. Gradually, loyalty to Rome was replaced by personal loyalty to a particular commander. Thus, the chain of command from the emperor downward was broken and the Roman imperial state was left without a reliable means of defense.[31]

Eventually, the slow infiltration of Germanic peoples became a full-scale invasion. From 407 to 429, the provinces of Italia, Galicia, and Hispania were invaded. In 410, Alaric, a Gothic chieftain who had fought with the Roman army, invaded the Italian peninsula and sacked Rome. Rome was sacked for a second time in 455 by Vandals who invaded from Africa after having infiltrated the Iberian peninsula. The frontier provinces were also overrun: Jutes, Angles, and Saxons invaded Britannia between 441 and 443; Galicia fell to the Franks, Burgundians, Alemmani, and Visigoths. Hispania was overrun by the Suevi, Vandals, and Visigoths. In 476, the last Western Roman emperor was deposed and replaced by the German chieftain Odoacer (433–493), who ruled the Italian peninsula as a king. The Roman Empire in the west had come to its end as a coherent politico-military entity. Visigoths attacked Constantinople in 378 but were defeated by the Byzantine emperor. After this victory, the Eastern Roman Empire was able to maintain itself until defeated by the Turks in 1453, after which it was subsumed within the Ottoman Empire.

Summary

Polytheistic Romans blamed the fall of the Western Roman Empire as a coherent politico-military entity on Christianity, and Christian Romans blamed the collapse on the polytheists, especially their continual "idolatrous" religious practices, which Christians believed angered the one God. The reality is that the Western Roman Empire did not "fall." Rather, it gradually melded with Germanic institutions and practices and continued to exist in hybrid form. Its religious aspect was carried on by the Catholic Church and its secular aspect by the Holy Roman Empire of Charlemagne. These two institutions formed the basis on which was built a hierarchically organized spiritual community of Christians that transcended the boundaries of the successor Germanic kingdoms called "Christendom," about which we will say more in the next chapter, that was seen to encompass Western Europe as a whole. The Roman Empire also lives on to the present day in all standing armies of the world; the Romance languages (e.g., French, Italian, Spanish, Portuguese, Catalan, and Romanian); the architecture of all cities of Western Europe, and in cities of the world colonized by Europeans; republican ideas about representative government; codified legal systems, especially on the continent of Europe; and scientific, medical, and technical languages that use thousands of words from Latin.

We now turn to the period of politico-military fragmentation that followed the period of Roman politico-military coherence and hierarchy from which the territorial state emerged.

Notes

1. Karl Lowenstein, *The Governance of Rome* (The Hague: Martinus Nijhoff, 1973), 3–5.

2. Perry Anderson, *Passages from Antiquity to Feudalism* (London: New Left Books, 1974), 55.

3. Sheldon S. Wolin, *Politics and Vision: Continuity and Innovation in Western Political Thought* (Boston: Little, Brown, 1960), 83.

4. Ibid., 85.

5. E. Badian, *Roman Imperialism in the Late Republic,* 2d ed. (Ithaca, NY: Cornell University Press, 1968), 8.

6. Alternative concepts of power and politics to sovereignty rooted in kinship and clan systems have been studied largely by anthropologists who usually focus on so-called non-Western societies. It is part of contemporary ideology not to recognize alternative concepts of power and politics as themselves part of the Western legacy and "heritage." For an account of clan and kinship concepts of politics as alternatives to sovereignty-based concepts of politics, see Pierre Clastres, *Society Against the State,* trans. Robert Hurley (New York: Zone Books, 1989).

7. Diana Coole, *Women in Political Theory: From Ancient Misogyny to Contemporary Feminism,* 2d ed. (Boulder, CO: Lynne Rienner Publishers, 1993), 36.

8. Jean Bethke Elshtain, *Women and War* (Chicago and London: University of Chicago Press, 1987), 121.

9. Hans Julius Wolff, *Roman Law: A Historical Introduction* (Norman: University of Oklahoma Press, 1951), 63.

10. Anderson, *Passages from Antiquity,* 65.

11. Ibid., 74.

12. Ernst Block, *Natural Law and Human Dignity,* trans. Dennis J. Schmidt (Cambridge, MA: MIT Press, 1986), 18.

13. Anderson, *Passages from Antiquity,* 66.

14. Block, *Natural Law,* 18.

15. Ibid., 19–20.

16. Badian, *Roman Imperialism,* 44 ff.

17. Norman Davies, *Europe: A History* (Oxford and New York: Oxford University Press, 1996), 159.

18. Graham Webster, *The Roman Imperial Army,* 3d ed. (Totowa, NJ: Barnes and Noble, 1985), 1–27.

19. Anderson, *Passages from Antiquity,* 60–62.

20. Ibid., 67.

21. Aurelio Bernardi, "The Economic Problems of the Roman Empire," in Carlo M. Cipolla (ed.), *The Economic Decline of Empires* (London: Methuen & Co., 1970): 16–83.

22. Ibid.

23. Ibid.

24. M. I. Finley, "Manpower and the Fall of Rome," in Carlo M. Cipolla (ed.), *The Economic Decline of Empires* (London: Methuen & Co., 1970): 84–91.

25. Bernardi, "The Economic Problems," 81–82.

26. Solomon Katz, *The Decline of Rome and the Rise of Medieval Europe* (Ithaca, NY: Cornell University Press, 1955), chapter 3.

27. William H. McNeill, *The Rise of the West: A History of the Human Condition* (Chicago: Chicago University Press, 1963), 338–339.

28. Will Durant, *Caesar and Christ: A History of Roman Civilization and of Christianity from Their Beginnings to A.D. 325* (New York: Simon & Schuster, 1944), 618–619.

29. Peter Brown, *The Rise of Western Christendom* (Oxford: Blackwell, 1996), 16.

30. See Anderson, *Passages from Antiquity*, 107–111; and Coole, *Women in Political Theory,* 35–40.

31. Joseph R. Strayer, *Feudalism* (Princeton, NJ: Van Nostrand Press, 1965), 156.

2

The Feudal "State": Indirect Rule

Against the disintegration of the Western Roman Empire, a gradual unification took place in Europe around Christianity. The Christianization of Europe was a struggle, a political act, that involved persuasion by missionaries, a great many of whom were Irish, and the use of military force. As they infiltrated the Roman Empire, Germanic peoples were converted to Christianity, the official religion of the empire, usually from the top down: a chieftain would be baptized and his people would follow. Conversion also took place by force. For example, in 785, Charlemagne ordered 4,500 pagan Saxons whom he had defeated to convert to Christianity or die. They chose to remain loyal to their pagan gods and all were killed.[1] Through such methods, then, "by the thirteenth century the cross was the universal symbol from the Black Sea to the Atlantic and from the Mediterranean to the Arctic Circle."[2]

The European-wide Christian community, which came to be called "Christendom," was the common basis of identity for European peoples after the fall of the Western Roman Empire. Despite its being the largest space with which European peoples identified, Christendom lacked the singular, unified politico-military hierarchy of rule that had existed within the Roman Empire. Neither the pope, the leader of the Catholic Church that claimed religious authority over Christendom, nor the Holy Roman Emperor, the Germanic heir to the Roman emperors who claimed secular authority over it, could control religious and political life within *res publica christiana*.

Christendom was deeply fragmented by rival secular Germanic kingdoms that had succeeded the Western Roman Empire. Although these kingdoms were initially quite centralized and covered extensive territory, they were gradually broken down into semiautonomous politico-military units (principalities, duchies, counties, fiefs) for administrative purposes. Germanic kings appointed family members, close companions, and retainers to administer them. Over time, this way of administering wide territories broke down the Roman conception of centralized, direct, public, politico-military rule and replaced it with the Germanic conception of politico-military rule being decentralized, indirect, and private such that it could be bought and sold, divided among heirs, mortgaged, and given in marriage. In other words, Germanic kings "considered their new kingdoms as their property, and the [Roman] distinction between public and private would have baffled them."[3]

Gradually, this situation of politico-military heteronomy began to reverse itself. From about the year 1200 A.D, rival semiautonomous units of politico-military rule began to consolidate around the idea of bounded, mutually exclusive territory and politico-military power began to centralize. Politico-military rule gradually became more direct and bureaucratic. The lineaments of territorially defined, mutually exclusive, sovereign states came into view.

To help understand this transformation from heteronomy to the homonymy of territorial states, we first discuss the reasons why politico-military rule was privatized in the Germanic kingdoms. We then take up the subject of feudal politico-military rule. We then turn to a discussion of the social organization of feudal "states." Finally, we turn to the subject of "feudal constitutionalism."

Germanic Kingdoms: Privatized Rule

What would become European kingdoms developed from Germanic tribal custom. As was mentioned in the previous chapter, the Germanic peoples were ruled by chieftains selected from certain clans. Chieftains were military, political, and religious figures who were expected to lead the tribe into battle, settle disputes among the tribe's members, and act as intercessors with the gods through the performance of religious rituals, such as making sacrifices for successful hunting and good crops, or victory in war. Successors were chosen from among a chieftain's direct male descendants. The choice was made by the still-living chieftain, but had to be confirmed through an act of acclamation by an assembly of the leading warriors of the tribe. Thus, loyalty among Germanic peoples was based on persons, which meant that followers were loyal only to a chieftain from a certain clan.[4]

Politico-military rule did not operate according to the same logic in Germanic tribes as it did in the Roman Empire. The chieftain was the leader *of* the tribe, not the ruler *over* the tribe's people. Chieftains did not have the power to command the obedience and actions of persons in the tribe. Rule was a matter of performing religious rituals, maintaining peace among the tribe's clans, and leading the tribe into battle. These activities accorded the chieftain honor and respect and, hence, authority, but did not give him "power over" fellow tribespeople.

The conversion of Germanic peoples to Christianity enormously enhanced the power and influence of the Catholic Church, which began to play an increasing role in secular rule. The Church was called upon to consecrate, and thereby authenticate, a new king. According to the Church, a king was appointed by God to maintain order, protect the weak, and defend the faith. Thus, Germanic kings in the area of the disappeared Western Roman Empire began to be seen as holding secular authority under the sacred authority of the Church—in contrast to the Eastern Roman Empire, where the emperor, seen as representing Christ on earth, held both secular and sacred authority. Consequently, in the west, kings wielded secular power, and the Church wielded sacred power, which it had, in its view, inherited through St. Peter from Christ.[5] Thus, in the west, a political imaginary emerged that defined politico-military rule as deriving from Church confirmation, which, as we will see later, resulted in the theory of the "divine right of kings."

The Germanic kingdoms had no formal "state," that is, no political organization, no specialized administrative departments, no civil service, and no standing army, as did the Roman Empire. Governance was handled by the king's household, which was not a problem when the kingdoms were small. As they grew larger, new governance structures had to be invented. When a kingdom reached a certain size, it was subdivided into counties, and a representative of the king, called a count, was selected to govern each one. Counts ruled their counties as the king ruled the kingdom: they had full military, judicial, and financial power, which they exercised with the aid of their household companions. Thus, the problem of governing the large Germanic kingdoms was solved by breaking them into subunits small enough to be ruled by a few individuals.[6]

This way of governing had a significant drawback: counts could become independent of the king and challenge his power in their counties. Kings attempted to stop such challenges in several ways. First, they tried to prevent counts from becoming too strong by directly supervising them, but such supervision was intermittent. Second, they sought to counterbalance the power of strong counts by establishing rival authorities in each county. Thus, at an early date the Church was taken under the protection of kings. Abbots of the monasteries and bishops of the dioceses were placed on the same level as counts, who were forbidden to enter Church property or territory. Third, kings would establish a few close and unswervingly loyal companions on estates scattered throughout various counties of the kingdom.[7]

Gradually, the large Germanic kingdoms, already fragmented into counties, became even more fragmented into a bewildering array of smaller kingdoms and independent principalities and duchies, each possessing its own military, financial, and judicial powers. Although this fragmentation resulted in part from the practice of delegating politico-military rule downward to counts, it was also in part the result of dynastic struggles provoked

The Final Partition of Charlemagne's Empire, 900 A.D.

by the dissatisfaction of the king's heirs with the subdivision of the kingdom at his death. The breakup of Charlemagne's Holy Roman Empire is the most famous example. Toward the end of his life, Charlemagne's son, Louis I, the Pious, who had received the Holy Roman Empire intact, having been made co-emperor before his father died, willed the empire to his oldest son, Lothar, and subkingdoms to his two younger sons, Charles, the Bald, and Louis, the German. When Louis I died in 840, a war broke out among Lothar and his brothers for possession of the throne of the empire. After a bloody internecine struggle, the combatants agreed, according to the Treaty of Verdun (843), to partition the empire into three new kingdoms: Charles received West Francia (France), Louis, the German, received East Francia (Germany), and Lothar received the Middle Kingdom (Lotharingia), which included the northern half of the Italian peninsula. Further partitions followed.

Fragmentation was also the result of a series of invasions: by the Saracens (a derogatory term derived from the Arabic *sharakyoun,* meaning easterner), a nomadic, Muslim people from North Africa, in 711; by the Vikings, a polytheistic land-hungry people from the north (Norse [North] men), whose descendants, the Normans, spread throughout Western Europe, including England (1066) and Sicily (1027); and by the Magyars, a nomadic horsed confederation from the steppes of central Asia, who eventually settled in the tenth century in what is now Hungary after being defeated by the Saxon king Otto I, the Great (936–973) at the Battle of Lechfeld (955). The brunt of these invasions was borne by local counts and their retainers, which encouraged their independence. Few kings were able to raise an army quickly enough to be effective against bands of swift-moving raiders. Therefore, local counts had to defend themselves. This led them to believe that the land they defended was their own personal property, not the king's. The people whom they defended also came to believe that the local count was their ruler, not the distant king. Great families began to take root in specific counties. In this way the principle of strong monarchy, which had been synonymous with the early Germanic kingdoms, was undermined, and politico-military rule became fragmented and indirect.[8]

Feudalism

The politico-military practices in the fragmented successor Germanic kingdoms have been known since the seventeenth century as "feudalism" because they appeared to be connected to the medieval institution of the fief; therefore, they were lumped together under the term feudalism, which comes from the medieval Latin *feodum,* itself from the old German *fee,* meaning cattle or property.[9] We look at feudalism to introduce some of the elements of this historical period that established political, economic, and social conditions from which the modern territorial state emerged.

Feudal society was thoroughly militarized. Violence everywhere impinged on many aspects of daily life. Legal disputes were often resolved by "trial by combat" or recourse to painful ordeals. Those convicted of felonies suffered death or mutilation. Brutality was common. The Church was contaminated by the violence and brutality of feudal society, and took an active role in warfare, especially against the Muslims. In the words of one historian, the "political units which had emerged from the slow and painful dissolution of the Western Roman Empire were dominated by aristocratic kindred which derived their wealth and power from the control of land and asserted their status by leadership in war."[10]

Feudal politico-military rule consisted of five interrelated activities and practices. First, vast castles were built with high, stone walls for defense, which embodied and projected the power and wealth of the warrior elite. Second, military campaigns were carried out against rival lords, which made reputations and established particular lords as leaders to be respected, obeyed, and feared. Third, religious leadership and patronage was provided, which furthered the reputations of certain lords as defenders of the Catholic Church and ensured its support. Fourth, dynastic alliances, primarily through strategic marriages, which expanded the wealth and politico-military power of rulers, were vigorously pursued. Fifth, the nobility provided justice throughout the realms they governed, be it kingdom, principality, duchy, or county.[11]

Such practices did not constitute a "state" in any formal sense, however. Feudal politico-military rule lacked key features of a state, such as permanent structures for decisionmaking, a standing army, or an extensive administration that operated according to codified law. Most important, though people were personally loyal to counts and kings, their identity as human beings was not bound up with a secular political order to which all belonged. To the extent people recognized an intersubjective social unity that linked them to people outside their immediate local surroundings, it was Christendom, that vast community of believers under the authority of the Catholic Church.

By the tenth century, feudalism had spread more or less to all former territories of the Roman Empire. Although more highly developed in some areas than others and exhibiting local variations, each feudal "state" was a pyramidal structure of individuals bound together by oaths of loyalty. The king was at the top of this pyramid and was the *suzerain*, or overlord, of the entire kingdom. Several dukes, who held huge tracts of land within the kingdom, were his direct vassals. Dukes, in turn, retained a number of direct vassals, and so on. At the bottom of this pyramid were the simple knights, who held sufficient land to maintain themselves and their families.

All land was someone's property and all landholders, except the king, were someone's vassals.[12] In some cases, kings were considered vassals of the pope, who, of course, was considered God's vassal on Earth.

The glue that held the feudal "state" together was "vassalage," which can be defined as "a system in which a free man binds himself personally to a lord, offering him loyalty and military service in return for protection and the use of property (usually land)."[13] It was entered into by doing homage, which was a ceremony in which the lesser man, kneeling before the greater man with hands joined as if in prayer, pledged himself and his loyalty to the greater man. In some areas, the pledge was "sealed with a kiss." Ties of vassalage lasted during the entire lives of both lord and vassal.[14] Vassalage was thus a complex politico-military system based on ties of personal dependence within which all men were the "men of other men," to whom they owed obedience and loyalty and from whom they expected unwavering assistance and beneficence. Thus, dukes, counts, marquis, and even bishops and abbots pledged themselves to their kings. Lesser knights pledged themselves to counts and marquis, and so on. As will be seen in the next chapter, the rise of the territorial state involved replacing an idea of politico-military power and authority rooted in the personal ties of loyalty and obedience to individuals with a conception of politics rooted in identity with and loyalty to the institutions of the sovereign territorial state.

Although some vassals resided in the households of their lords, more significant were those who were granted an estate called a fief, from which the vassal could derive sufficient income to feed, clothe, and arm himself and, if the fief was large enough, keep an armed retinue. Political power in the form of immunities—that is, the right to collect taxes and tolls, dispense justice, and coin money—were often delegated by the king to local lords. The granting of land from which the vassal could derive personal income became the most common way of rewarding service, because land was the primary source of wealth. From the king's point of view, granting fiefs to vassals was a way of shifting the cost of maintaining an army of heavy cavalry to the warriors themselves.[15]

Vassals provided the king with three forms of service. The first was military, which meant appearing fully armed when summoned by the king. The second was counsel, or advice on important decisions, a legacy of the German practice of involving all warriors in decisions affecting the tribe. The third was financial, which involved payments of money to the king to help him meet unusual expenses such as ransoming himself from his enemies, paying for the great feast given when his eldest son was knighted or when his eldest daughter was married.[16] As will be shown below, such aid evolved into modern systems of general taxation.

The feudal contract was binding on both lord and vassal for life, although it could be broken by mutual agreement or individual public renunciation. Nonetheless, at the beginning of the medieval period, the status of the lesser vassals was precarious. Their fiefs could be seized by the king for no reason at all or exchanged for others. Vassals had no assurance that their lands would be inherited by their heirs, because after a vassal's death, the fief legally reverted back to the king. In other words, the vassal had no hereditary right to the fief. As a consequence, vassals became obsessed with strengthening rights of inheritance in any way they could. The transference of a fief exclusively from father to son did eventually become hereditary under laws of primogeniture, although it was never automatic and had to be reaffirmed by the king. Kings gladly acquiesced to these efforts because they did not want fiefs to become too small by inheritance to provide protection. Laws of primogeniture replaced the earlier Germanic custom that favored equal inheritance among sons and daughters. Therefore, although there were occasionally exceptions, as a rule, women were unable to inherit fiefs. When a woman was permitted to inherit, it was always with the proviso that her husband perform vassalic duties in her stead. If the firstborn son was too young to meet the obligations of a vassal, an adult relative, usually a maternal uncle, was chosen to exercise vassalage until the minor came of age.

Fiefs were subdivided into manors, the basis of the feudal agricultural economy, which had been foreshadowed by the *latifundia* of the Roman Empire. The lord of each manor was a free man who owed feudal obligations to the lord of the fief. Thus, political and economic life were thoroughly intertwined within the feudal "state." The peasants who lived on the manor tilled plots of land owned by the lord, who gave them life tenure over these plots and military protection for as long as they paid an annual rent in produce, labor, and money.[17]

The Estates

Fuedal society was ordered into "estates" to which rights and privileges were attached. There were three estates based on the medieval assumption that humankind since the beginning of time had been divided into three parts: those who pray (*orators*), those who fight (*bellators*), and those who work (*laborors*).[18] The first estate was the clergy, which was composed of the official hierarchy of the Church (bishops, priests, archbishops, and cardinals) as well as the monks and abbots of its religious orders. The second estate was the nobility, which comprised a privileged politico-military ruling class. The third estate was composed of the merchants and artisans who lived in towns. In addition, there were various other groups—servants, beggars, prostitutes, and thieves—most of whom were poor and without legal status in the estates system.

Although not part of the formal estates system, women were often treated as a separate and distinct corporate group, a "fourth estate." In the feudal "state," women were dealt with under the sign "woman," which was not a description of a particular person but a social category.[19] In order to represent women as the social category "woman," medieval society primarily drew upon two Christian teachings. The first was the biblical narrative of the Creation, in which woman was seen as being created from Adam's rib and serving as his "helpmate." In this narrative, women were the ubiquitous reincarnation of Eve who lost the Garden of Eden for mankind, and, hence, were seen as the favored instruments of Satan for leading men, who could not resist women's tempting, to Hell. The second was the story of the virgin birth of Christ, in which woman, of whom Mary became a dominant representation, was seen as innocent and chaste.[20] The former teaching was openly misogynistic (i.e., hating and distrusting women), and the latter valorized "woman" as representing absolute purity, innocence, and goodness. When women failed to live up to the ideal of purity, they were subjected, and subjugated, as sin incarnate. Hence, these two seemingly opposite characterizations formed part of a singular representation of women that effectively subordinated them within medieval life.

In general, women were deemed incapable of exercising political power by reason of their physical constitution.[21] Women had no rights at all against ennobled males and were both legally and in custom subordinate to men in nearly all spheres. Once married, a woman could do little without the consent of her husband.[22] Describing the condition of women in marriage, one historian says: "In marriage, the husband predominated by force of law and with the guidance of homiletic [i.e., religious] literature. Many women feared their husbands, and some were even beaten by them. Law and custom permitted a man, whatever his class, to bring his superior physical strength to bear against the woman who was supposed to be his helpmate."[23]

Although they could not exercise political power and had no rights, women were in charge of the interior of the house, especially over the "women's rooms" and the women living in them.[24] Women shared the status of their husbands, which occasionally gave some women significant power and importance, especially because the life expectancy of their knighted husbands was quite low. For example, in some places in medieval Europe, such as France and Catalonia (although not in England), noble wives not only took responsibility for educating children but also protected their inheritances and otherwise safeguarded their futures. In several cases, noble wives took on the role of local governance and administration in the absence of their husbands,[25] the most famous being Eleanor, wife of Henry II of England, who ruled Aquitaine, his province in France, in his absence.

The First Estate: Those Who Pray

The clergy included the priests, bishops, archbishops, and cardinals of the regular Catholic Church hierarchy; the monks and abbots of its religious orders, such as the Cistercians, Benedictines, and Franciscans; and the knights, masters, and grand masters of its military orders, such as the Templars and the Hospitallers. Bishops, archbishops, abbots, masters, and grand masters were equal in status and power to the greatest dukes and counts of the secular nobility. Many dioceses and religious orders became extremely wealthy and controlled huge tracts of land. The military-religious orders were especially powerful because they were composed of armed monks. In fact, the order-states created by the Templars, Hospitallers, and Teutonic knights were powerful rivals and competitors to feudal kings. [26]

The great power and wealth of certain dioceses and religious orders created tension between the Church and feudal rulers. Feudal kings frequently sought to control the appointment of bishops and abbots and were always watching for any attempt by the Church to rob them of their rightful revenues and patrimony, that is, their property. The threat of excommunication was usually sufficient to persuade a recalcitrant king to bend to the Church's wishes. However, as feudal monarchs began to centralize their political power during the late medieval period, they were able to gain control over the appointment of important bishops and abbots within their realms. Eventually, the military-religious orders were suppressed and disbanded and their lands and properties were confiscated by the crown. The most famous of the disbandments was the brutal suppression of the Templars in France in 1310. The French king Philippe IV (ruled 1285–1314) arrested all Templar knights within his kingdom on charges of heresy, tried and tortured many, and executed about sixty who refused to recant, including the order's grand master, Jacques de Molay.

The clergy served an important politico-cultural function in medieval Europe. They comprised its intellectuals, and as such they interpreted the meaning of Scripture, elaborated Church doctrines, and carried on the traditions of classical philosophy and science inherited from Rome. Through its networks of monasteries and its cathedral schools, as well as its dominance of emerging universities, the clergy came to be respected for its learning as well as feared for its enforcement of canon law, under which, among other things, it could accuse people of heresy (i.e., adherence to a religious teaching contrary to Church dogma) and execute them, usually by burning at the stake. Few people outside the clergy and the nobility were literate, and within the nobility, men were more likely to be literate in Latin, the language of religion and government, and women in the vernacular, or the language of the common people. This gave the literate clergy enormous power because the Church communicated legal and moral ideas. As one historian put it, the Church was "the main, frail aqueduct across which the cultural reservoirs of the Classical World now passed to the new universe of feudal Europe, where literacy had become clerical."[27]

What unity there was beyond the local village or town came not through identification with a political association (e.g., a state), but through the system of religious signs institutionalized by the Catholic Church throughout Europe. This semiotic system was visual and aural. Therefore, the cathedrals and liturgy (i.e., rituals and ceremonies) of the Church served not only the religious function of reinforcing and strengthening faith, but the sociopolitical function of anchoring identity in Christendom, that universal community to which all Christians belonged.

Note that many areas within Europe were not thoroughly Christianized until well into the high Middle Ages, that is, the twelfth and thirteenth centuries. The clergy did not simply pronounce and propagate Catholic dogma on an already believing and, hence, accepting people. As was mentioned above, the establishment of Christianity was a struggle, a political act that often involved persuasion, the use of terror, and military force. Moreover, the Church's official liturgy was continually contested by local religious practices drawn from pagan religions. Pagan habits of mind remained strong. People of all ranks continued to pray to local deities, practice magic, and believe in miracles, all of which the Church combated. With respect to witchcraft, the Church targeted women especially, believing, according to one historian, that "legions of the Devil were led by evil women who anointed themselves with grease from the flesh of unbaptized children, who rode stark naked on flying broomsticks or on the backs of rams and goats, and who attended their nocturnal 'sabbaths' to work their spells and copulate with deamons."[28]

Thus, medieval political theory conceived of the world, God's creation, as a unity, a whole governed by Him for the good of His subjects. Humanity was potentially a single unity under God's rule. To define and interpret the meaning of community and collective life, the clergy relied on the idea of the *corpus mysticum,* the mystical body of Christ, which had roots in the early days of Christianity. Christ's body, the human element of which was believed to have died on the cross at Calvary, and the spiritual element, which is supposed to live forever at God's side, symbolized the unity of the spiritual and the secular, of faith and reason in human life. In St. Augustine's famous phrasing, human life is divided between the City of Man and the City of God. The City of Man referred to man's physical and secular needs, a world of necessities in which the potential for sin and evil was great, but in which men also needed to develop reason. The City of God referred to the spiritual in human life, the orienting of men and women toward eternal happiness in God. Reason, especially as expressed in classical philosophy, was the human means toward knowing God, hence the continuing importance of Roman and Greek legacies in feudal Christianity.

The universal idea of Christendom, then, both retarded the emergence of an understanding of a territorialized political community and made available a powerful alternative and competitive communal identity across the otherwise politically fragmented lives of medieval peoples.[29] Within this alternative imagined Christian community, the political was subordinated to the religious, as was reason to faith. Christianity rested on what one historian, trying to make sense of the motivations behind the Crusades, has called a "spiritual restlessness," the emotional, passionate, and all-consuming longing for God that was inscribed in the Christian idea of faith.[30] Rather than considering social conflicts as mediated and resolved by the institutions of secular rule, people in the Middle Ages relied on local religious practices informed by the Church's teachings. In order to use Christianity in constructing the modern territorial state, its principles and signs would have to be reinterpreted; and they were, as we will see.

The Second Estate: Those Who Fight

During the early centuries of the medieval period, no social or legal distinctions existed among vassals. By the twelfth century, all members of the feudal hierarchy, from the greatest lord to the pettiest knight, believed they belonged to the same social group, a belief based on their ownership of politico-military power. Thus a nobility (or aristocracy) was created whose social purpose was governing and fighting; it dominated European political and military affairs until the nineteenth century. Initially, the nobility was a military caste whose members often came from humble backgrounds. When they were not making war, vassal-knights passed their time practicing with arms, carousing, and intriguing in the lord's court. They engaged in tournaments, or mock combat, designed to maintain and improve their martial skills, in search of which some knights traveled far and wide across Europe. These knights-errant helped spread medieval culture and feudal institutions from northwestern Europe, where they had developed, to the Iberian Peninsula, southern Italy, Eastern Europe, the British Isles, and the Holy Land during the Crusades.[31]

The Crusades, which were holy wars instigated by popes and undertaken by the Christian kings from 1096 until 1270 to take the Holy Land from the Seljuk Turks, gave rise to the idea that the vassal-knight was a soldier of God, a defender of the Church, a protector of widows, orphans, and the poor, an avenger of evil, and a savior of "damsels in distress." This ideal of military virtue and skills was codified into a system of personal conduct called chivalry (from the French *chevel*, meaning horse), which prescribed that knights live according to strict rules called "courtesy." The gentleman (from the French *gentilhomme*, or man of good lineage), in addition to being a great warrior, was expected to have polished manners, a high moral sense, and knowledge and skill in the social arts of courtly life.[32] The cult of chivalry reestablished the Roman masculine ideal of virtue over the Christian feminine ideal, and encouraged the misogyny, pugnacity, and militarism of the feudal age.

The development of the notion that vassal-knights were socially superior to others because of their bravery and devotion to duty, honor, and good manners eventually gave rise to the idea that such status could be acquired only by birth, although lords could acquire more vassals, some even low-born. Thus, the right to be made a vassal-knight became hereditary. Gradually, the nobility became privileged, that is, subject to its own legally recognized rights and obligations. Certain occupations deemed incompatible with noble status, such as trade or commerce, were legally forbidden to the nobility. Nobles were also forbidden from working with their hands in agriculture or at manual occupations. Such activities were considered to be contrary to the honor and breeding of the nobility. The nobility itself came to be subdivided into various legally recognized ranks based on wealth and power, to which specific legal privileges and obligations were attached. The most powerful and prestigious were, of course, kings, followed by dukes, counts, viscounts, and knights.[33]

The development of recognized ranks and hereditary privilege gave rise to the art and science of heraldry, which arose from the need to identify armored knights, whose faces were hidden by their helmets during combat, and involved the painting of individual signs of recognition, such as a chevron, lion, or cross, on shields. Such signs came to be legally associated with a particular knight and were passed from father to son through the generations. Thus, the heraldic device became a legal symbol of family continuity and noble standing.

The Third Estate: Those Who Work

In some kingdoms, especially England, the third estate referred to all commoners, whereas in others it referred primarily or exclusively to town dwellers. In all kingdoms, the third estate was dominated by the bourgeoisie (from the Latin *bourg* meaning fortified town), who were for the most part merchants and artisans.

Towns came into existence when commercial activity in Europe revived after the disappearance of the Western Roman Empire. Initially, trade was of little importance for the Germanic kingdoms. Manors were self-sufficient and produced almost no surplus. Roman roads over which trade could flow had fallen into disrepair. By the eleventh century, however, commercial activity began to grow and urban life revived. Trade began between certain areas of Western Europe where a surplus of a locally produced good, such as woven woolen cloth in Flanders, was traded to another area that had a surplus of other locally produced goods, such as the honey, furs, and hunting hawks of Scandinavia. Surpluses of French wines were traded for the tin, lead, and silver of England, especially after the conquest by the Normans, who preferred wine to ale. The Crusades also were made possible by increased trade: the Crusader states in the Holy Land needed supplies, and pilgrims needed transportation. Thus the northern Italian towns of Genoa, Pisa, and Venice became important shipbuilding and trading centers.[34]

As commercial activity grew, a class of merchants who traveled from place to place developed. The fragmented structure of feudal politico-military rule created special problems for these merchants, especially the localized customary law that limited the validity and uniformity of contracts over time and across space. Laws governing commerce were "under the rule of a patchwork system of local customs, influenced in varying degrees by Roman law."[35] Moreover, "procedure in the secular feudal courts was uniformly slow, arbitrary, and unfair to the lower orders of society . . . characterized by reliance upon an oral tradition of custom maintained by the lord and his officers and judges."[36]

Eventually, these itinerant merchants looked for places where the local lord would allow them to settle and extend them the privileges necessary to carry out their commercial activities. This included stabilizing and extending the law that applied to commerce, often by combining elements of canon law and the law that traveling merchants had themselves devised to facilitate and normalize trading practices across multiple feudal legal jurisdictions, called "merchant law."[37]

Usually, merchants settled near ports, river crossings, castles, monasteries, or cathedrals. It was not long before major castles and monasteries had *bourgs* nearby, which had been granted a charter or franchise of privileges and rights in exchange for the payment of a sum of money or an annual income to the local lord.[38] Thus, those who lived in such settlements, many of which eventually grew into major cities, enjoyed a distinctive legal status that distinguished them from the nobility, clergy, and serfs. Town charters applied to the collective whole, not to individuals. Towns, because they were centers of commercial activity, became economically and militarily self-sufficient. Town dwellers surrounded themselves with defensive walls and raised their own militias, which was a way of placing the duty of military service on all fit male citizens of the city. People who lived in towns were free because they were immune from laws that regulated the feudal system beyond their walls. Serfs who escaped to a town and lived within its walls for a "year and a day," without being claimed or identified, became free persons and received the town's protection.

The merchants who settled the first towns organized themselves into a guild (from the Anglo-Saxon *geld,* meaning self-governing) for protection, mutual aid, and governance. As the towns grew and attracted artisans such as cobblers, weavers, dryers, fullers, butchers, bakers, tanners, wheelers, coopers, pullers, and smiths of various kinds, new guilds were formed in each trade or craft. Guilds regulated these occupations and their levels of activity by controlling the training and licensing of those who practiced them and by preventing competition. Each guild set forth detailed regulations concerning the method of manufacture, price, and quality of its goods. Before being admitted to a guild, one had to learn its trade or craft by becoming an apprentice to a master practitioner, the number of which in a particular area was controlled by the guilds. After a certain amount of time, the apprentice had to produce a masterpiece to be inspected by the officers of the guild to prove his ability to practice the trade or craft.[39]

At the bottom of the lord-vassal system were the serfs (from the Latin *servus* or slave), the lowest of whom were attached wholly to the land of the lord on whose manor they resided. Above these serfs were serfs who had land of their own. Serfs were not slaves because, unlike slaves, they had certain rights and privileges. The lord could not harm his serfs and was obligated to protect them from enemies. A serf had a right to his land and to his wife and family. As with the nobility, the male was considered the head of the serf's family, although women often performed considerable work. In addition, serfs enjoyed the right to rest on holidays (holy days), which could number as many as fifty a year in addition to Sundays. In exchange for these rights and protections, the serf gave the lord a portion of his produce or rent or labor for special tasks, as well as a tithe, that is, 10 percent, to the Church. He was also obliged to work several days each week on the lord's land as well as perform extra work for him during ploughing, sowing, and harvesting. The serf also had to pay to use the lord's mill, bake-oven, brewery, winepress, and stud animals.

Feudal Constitutionalism

Recall that rendering the king counsel was one of the major feudal obligations of every vassal. A king received advice from two sources: his court (from the Latin *curia,* meaning place of assembly), composed of his closest companions and household retinue, and a great council, usually convened on major holidays such as Christmas and Easter, composed of the upper members of the nobility and higher clergy of the realm as well as important members of the third estate. When the upper nobility and clergy became too numerous for the council to perform useful work, delegates were chosen from the three main estates (clergy, nobility, and bourgeoisie) of the realm to attend. These delegates did not represent individuals but were representatives from the estates from which they were chosen—that is, the group of people having the same legal status or position to which bundles of rights, privileges, and obligations were attached. Thus, representation in the feudal state meant the representation of corporate groups such as the nobility and clergy, and eventually included other corporate groups such as lawyers, professors, and physicians.[40]

Thus the feudal "state" was "constitutional" in that the great council of the three estates represented the realm to the king, voiced protest, restated rights, gave advice, and agreed to financial requests. We do not mean to say that the feudal "state" was democratic, but simply that the crown governed with the concurrence and under the surveillance of the estates. As the king needed the consent of the estates to obtain access to their financial resources, especially to raise taxes to fight wars, a struggle ensued between the crown, on the one hand, which needed the money, and the council of estates, on the other, which had it to give but expected justification.[41] This struggle intensified in the late feudal period when a military revolution increased the cost of war well beyond that which any individual monarch could afford from his private coffer. This struggle between the crown and the estates evolved in two main directions: in favor of the king to the exclusion of the estates, or in favor of the estates to exclusion of the king.[42] The consequence of which side won the struggle for the development of the form of the state will be discussed in Part 2.

Summary

The heteronomy of politico-military forms of rule that appeared in Europe after the disappearance of coherent Roman rule presses us to recognize that the modern territorial state is a historically contingent creation. The political space of the Roman Empire fragmented into multiple Germanic kingdoms, which themselves fragmented into a large number of rival and competing forms of politico-military rule, such as subkingdoms, principalities, dukedoms, counties, fiefs, bishoprics, and self-governing cities. Even feudal society was fragmented into three estates, each with its own rights and privileges. In the next chapter we turn to the long historical process by which the medieval condition of heteronomy was reversed and a new form of politico-military rule emerged, the territorial state.

Notes

1. Richard Fletcher, *The Barbarian Conversion: From Paganism to Christianity* (New York: Henry Holt, 1998), 215.

2. Denys Hay, *Europe: The Emergence of an Idea* (Edinburgh: Edinburgh University Press, 1957), 20.

3. Herbert H. Rowen, *The King's State: Proprietary Dynasticism in Early Modern France* (New Brunswick, NJ: Rutgers University Press, 1980), 7.

4. Reinhard Bendix, *Kings or People: Power and the Mandate to Rule* (Berkeley and Los Angeles: University of California Press, 1978), 21–35.

5. Ibid.

6. Joseph R. Strayer, *Feudalism* (Princeton, NJ: Van Nostrand, 1965), 29–30.

7. Ibid.

8. Ibid., 34.

9. Ibid., 11–12.

10. Marcus Bull, "Origins," in *The Oxford Illustrated History of the Crusades* (Oxford: Oxford University Press, 1997): 18.

11. R. W. Southern, *The Making of the Middle Ages* (New Haven, CT: Yale University Press, 1953), 86.

12. Ibid., 16–17.

13. Jeffrey Burton Russell, *Medieval Civilization* (New York: John Wiley & Sons, 1968), 193.

14. Ibid., 204.

15. Ibid., 204–205.

16. Ibid.

17. Ibid., 212–227.

18. Georges Duby, *The Three Orders: Feudal Society Imagined*, trans. Arthur Goldhammer (Chicago: University of Chicago Press, 1978).

19. Shulamith Shahar, *The Fourth Estate: A History of Women in the Middle Ages* (London and New York: Methuen, 1983), 14.

20. On the biblical sources, see Angela M. Lucas, *Women in the Middle Ages* (New York: St. Martin's Press, 1983), part 1, and R. Howard Bloch, *Medieval Misogyny and the Invention of Western Romantic Love* (Chicago and London: University of Chicago Press, 1991).

21. Georges Duby, "Women and Power," in Thomas N. Bisson (ed.), *Cultures of Power: Lordship, Status, and Process in Twelfth-Century Europe* (Philadelphia: University of Pennsylvania Press, 1995): 69–85.

22. "The law generally held that a married woman could not draw up a contract, take a loan, or take any person to court on civil matters without the consent of her husband, not only because the husband managed joint property, *but also because of her very status as a married woman.*" (Italics added.) Shahar, *The Fourth Estate,* 92.

23. Ibid., 138.

24. Duby, "Women and Power," 80–84.

25. Shahar, *The Fourth Estate,* 140–142, 145–152. This was the case in the towns as well. For example, in the thirteenth century one contemporary source reports that in "the guilds of Paris . . . out of a hundred occupations women engaged in eighty-six!" Ibid., 6.

26. For a complete discussion of the order-states, see Walter C. Opello Jr. "Early Competitors of the State: The Military-Religious Orders," paper presented at the 44th annual meeting of the International Studies Association, Portland, OR, February 25–March 1, 2003.

27. Perry Anderson, *Passages from Antiquity to Feudalism* (London: New Left Books, 1974), 131.

28. Norman Davies, *Europe: A History* (Oxford and New York: Oxford University Press, 1996), 437.

29. See especially Sheldon Wolin, *Politics and Vision: Continuity and Innovation in Western Political Thought* (Boston: Little, Brown, 1960), chapter 4.

30. For the idea of "spiritual restlessness," see Southern, *Making of the Middle Ages,* 50.

31. Robert Bartlett, *The Making of Europe: Conquest, Colonization and Culture Change, 950–1350* (Princeton, NJ: Princeton University Press, 1993); J.R.S. Phillips, *The Medieval Expansion of Europe* (Oxford and New York: Oxford University Press, 1988).

32. Andrea Hopkins, *Knights* (New York/London/Paris: Artabras, 1990), 99–123.

33. Sidney Painter, *The Rise of Feudal Monarchies* (Ithaca, NY: Cornell University Press, 1951), 29–30.

34. David Nicolas, *The Growth of the Medieval City* (New York: Longman, 1997).

35. Michael E. Tigar and Madeleine R. Levy, *Law and the Rise of Capitalism* (New York and London: Monthly Review Press, 1977), 26–27.

36. Ibid., 27.

37. Ibid.

38. Painter, *The Rise of Feudal Monarchies,* 72.

39. Ibid., 79–84.

40. Alexander Passerin D'Entrèves, *The Notion of the State* (Oxford: Clarendon Press, 1967), 90.

41. Painter, *The Rise of Feudal Monarchies,* 1–4.

42. Emile Lousse, "Absolutism," in Heinz Lubasz (ed.), *The Development of the Modern State* (New York: Macmillan, 1964), 46.

3

The Medieval State: Territorial Sovereignty Instituted

War gradually transformed the heteronomy of the medieval period into the homonomy of the current global order composed solely of territorial states.[1] Innovations in the technology of warfare resulted in a profound shift in the way that politico-military rule was organized and understood. By the end of the late Middle Ages, roughly from 1100 through the 1500s, a number of important elements of territorial states would be in place: large standing armies, hierarchies of government functionaries loyal to territorially based rulers, and a new language of politics that legitimated new territorial politico-military rule. In this chapter, we will see how these developments made human beings, the state's subjects, available to be used as objects by the state to enhance the power and prestige of the state, primarily through war.

Innovations in Military Technology

With the advent of the feudal "state," the large standing infantry-based army of imperial Rome was replaced with a multitude of small private armies composed primarily of retinues of mounted aristocratic warriors. From 1000 to about 1400, a band of heavily armored knights mounted on specially bred and trained warhorses (always 16 to 18-hand stallions) became the principal military organization of the medieval age and the massed cavalry charge its chief tactic.[2] Heavy cavalry was made possible by the arrival of large horses from Persia by way of Byzantium in the fifth century, the invention of the horseshoe, and the introduction of the stirrup into Europe from Asia.[3] A feudal army, known as a host, was a temporary coalescence of many private retinues called into military service by the prince or king. Knights were obliged to render this service in exchange for their fiefs. The non-noble groups of the feudal "state"—clergy, bourgeoisie, and serfs—had no military obligations and were, for the most part, excluded from military service. Knights were responsible for procuring their own military equipment, which included a chain-mail coat, helmet, sword,

Europe, 1200

shield, lance, and mace. Because of the expense of this equipment, especially the chain-mail coat, the number of men-at-arms in medieval armies was low. Knights were assisted by one or two squires, who were apprentice knights responsible for the packhorses and the maintenance of equipment.

Medieval warfare took several forms: wars of defense against invading Vikings, Muslims, and Magyars; wars of expansion such as the Norman Conquest of the southern Italian peninsula and the British Isles, the *reconquista* of the Iberian peninsula, and the Crusades; and wars of property manifested in local feuds over land and castles. As no entity could mobilize the resources for making war for long periods, wars tended to be short and warmaking episodic. As medieval Europe was a martial culture, high value was placed on the physical strength and fighting prowess of the individual knight, that is, his horsemanship, dexterity with weapons, and ferocity in combat.[4]

Between 1300 and 1600, three technological innovations were introduced onto the European battlefield that revolutionized medieval warfare.[5] The first was the longbow, the traditional weapon of the Welsh, which was capable of shooting ten arrows per minute at targets 300 yards away with great accuracy and penetrating power. The second was the pike, which, in the hands of well-drilled foot soldiers, could dislodge armored knights from their horses. During the century and a half after 1300, a number of battles—at Courtrai (1302), Crécy (1346), Poitiers (1356), Aljubarrota (1385), and Agincourt (1415), in which small contingents of longbowmen and pikemen were able to defeat larger contingents of heavily armored cavalry—demonstrated the effectiveness of these two weapons. To defend against longbows and pikes, armorers replaced the chain-mail coat with plate armor, which was worn by horses as well. Thus, heavy cavalry became even heavier, capable only of the direct charge. Infantry, or foot soldiers, when formed into phalanxes (i.e., closed into deep ranks and files), could easily break such charges and dislodge knights from their horses. On the ground, knights weighted down by their armor could be easily overwhelmed by infantrymen. As a consequence, armies increasingly became composed of infantry units armed with longbows and pikes.[6]

The third technological innovation that revolutionized medieval warfare was the introduction of gunpowder from China during the fourteenth century. The dominance of the heavily armored knight and the high, stone castle ended with the development of two weapons that used gunpowder: the arquebus and the cannon. The arquebus was a primitive, handheld firearm that fired a lead ball capable of penetrating the thickest plate armor. Gradually, longbows and pikes were replaced by arquebuses and, eventually, by muskets and, finally, rifles.

The second weapon that used gunpowder was the cannon. At first, cannons were small, poorly made, inaccurate, and unable to do more damage to medieval fortifications than the traditional, mechanical siege engines such as catapults, which fired stones by means of counterweighted levers. Gradually, metallurgical techniques were developed that permitted the manufacture of larger, more powerful, and more accurate cannons. It was learned that the best cannons were cast solid then bored out, which made a better fit between ball and tube and allowed barrel length to be increased. Cannon manufactured in this way became more reliable, lighter, and more accurate. Stone shot was replaced by round cannonballs of lead and iron. Improvements in the composition and manufacture of gunpowder called "corning" increased the muzzle velocity of projectiles fired from cannon, which multiplied penetrating power.

The development of effective artillery had a dramatic impact on the balance between offense and defense in medieval warfare. The offense gained the advantage because more-powerful cannons were able to penetrate the stone walls of medieval castles with ease. Castles that had held out for many months against traditional siege engines were reduced to piles of rubble within a matter of hours when they received direct fire from cannons. Consequently, the high-profile stone-walled castle was gradually abandoned and replaced by a low-profile fortification, first designed by Italian engineers and called the *trace italienne*, whose low, angled, earthen bastions could absorb the shock of concentrated artillery fire, even from the most powerful cannons.

As a result of the emergence of infantry, artillery, and *trace italienne* fortifications, armies increased in size and complexity. Table 3.1 shows the tremendous increase in military manpower for various emergent, European territorial states from the fifteenth to the eighteenth century.

As armies became bigger, they were divided into infantry, artillery, and

Table 3.1 Increase in Military Manpower, 1200–1800

Date	Spain	France	England	Prussia	Sweden	Holland	Russia
1200s		50,000	25,000				
1300s	37,500	60,000	32,000				
1400s	60,000	40,000	25,000				
1500s	200,000	80,000	30,000		15,000	20,000	
1600s	300,000	150,000	70,000	30,000	63,000	30,000	25,000
1700s	98,000	400,000	200,000	162,000	100,000	100,000	130,000
1800s		600,000	347,000	1,200,000		100,000	170,000

Sources: Karen A. Rasler and William R. Thompson, *War and State Making* (Boston: Unwin Hyman, 1980), 66; Brian M. Downing, *The Military Revolution and Political Change* (Princeton, NJ: Princeton University Press, 1992), 69; and Clifford J. Rogers (ed.), *The Military Revolution Debate: Readings on the Military Transformation of Early Modern Europe* (Boulder, CO: Westview Press, 1995), 44.

light-cavalry units. Training and discipline were introduced. Logistics (i.e., procurement, maintenance, and transportation of military matériel) systems developed. Privateers (i.e., armed private ships) were organized into navies and sailors were trained. To withstand the shock of rounds fired from ever more powerful and accurate artillery pieces, the *trace italienne* fort became larger and its earthen bastions thicker. Highly trained and disciplined infantry units, which were organized independently of their members and commanded by a hierarchy of officers, including noncommissioned officers, became the backbone of these massive armies. Troops began to wear distinctive, standardized clothes, called uniforms, and were issued standardized weapons. Individualistic displays of fighting prowess and heroism, which had been so important in medieval warfare, were discouraged. The warrior aristocratic caste and the feudal host were gradually replaced by a professional standing army.[7]

Initially, the ranks of most early infantry-based armies were filled by mercenaries, that is, individuals paid to fight who were recruited outside of the centralizing monarchy from peripheral regions of Europe that became specialized in providing them. Eventually, mercenaries began to be replaced by soldiers recruited exclusively from the monarch's own population because mercenary armies were notoriously unreliable: they frequently rebelled for higher pay, deserted the battlefield, changed sides, and even threatened the monarch's own throne by taking sides in internal power struggles.[8]

The regiment became the basic unit of military organization of domestically recruited armies. They became permanent institutions with a fixed headquarters in a provincial city, recruited their soldiers from the surrounding countryside, and were officered by the male members of the local aristocratic families.[9] Troops recruited and officered in this way fought better, were more reliable, and were less of a threat to the crown itself.

The summary effect of these technological innovations, then, was to change fundamentally the social and political reality of armed force and warfare. In the words of one scholar, "standing armed forces began to conform to bureaucratic regularity."[10] War became a complex of practices that required the regular disciplining of subjects and the organizing of logistics that could be used not only for defeating the enemy but also for the general production of social order. More and more, armies became objects, a unified (as in *uni*form) "body" of soldiers onto which the signs of the sovereign could be inscribed, through the design and color of uniforms and of various accoutrements such as insignia of rank, belt buckles, and buttons. Armies increasingly became more than just instruments of warmaking; they increasingly came to represent the sovereign for whom they fought—which tended to render mercenaries an anachronism—and to symbolize the sovereign's power, thereby helping create the right to govern. Thus the military revolution encouraged a new general view of the person and the body as an object to be molded and upon which could be inscribed signs of the state's power and legitimacy. Soldiers lost their individualism as uniforms marked the wearer as a servant, a person of restricted rights and liberties. Soldiers could no longer glory in their individual diversity of dress and prowess. Essentially, they became interchangeable cogs in a vast bureaucratic machine required to follow orders to the letter. In order to mold individuals into a united fighting force, Count Maurice of Nassau introduced drill and discipline that he had found in the manuals of the Roman legions.

Emergence of a State Apparatus

A sovereign who was able to recruit, train, equip, and maintain a large standing army as well as build low-profile fortifications could prevail over others. Hence, the advent of standing armies, regular navies, and *trace italienne* fortifications gradually transformed the indirect, fragmented, decentralized rule of feudalism into the direct, concentrated, centralized rule of the medieval state, an early form of the territorial state. In the words of one historian, "The modern state without the military revolution is unthinkable. The road from the arquebus to absolutism, or from the maritime mortar to mercantilism, was a direct one."[11]

Recall that feudal kings were not all-powerful rulers. They faced the three estates of the realm—nobility, clergy, and bourgeoisie—who had their own rights and privileges as corporate groups. Kings were *primus inter pares* (first among equals) with respect to the nobility and had special responsibilities to the realm: providing justice, coining money, designating bishops and abbots, granting town charters, and defending the realm. During the feudal period, wars were largely private affairs, paid for by revenues collected from the king's own demesne as well as by tolls charged for the use of his roads and bridges, fees for fairs, fines levied by his courts, customs placed on imports, and money from vassals.[12]

As armies and fortifications became larger and more expensive to maintain, kings increasingly found themselves in debt. Medieval kings were unable to tax or confiscate property, except that of Jews, because their power was circumscribed by the rights and privileges of the estates. In order to raise funds, kings borrowed money, debased the coinage of the realm, sold crown lands, and pawned the royal jewels.[13] Eventually, medieval monarchs began to levy taxes on the estates. At first, the concessions granted to the king to levy such taxes were valid only for the estate that had granted them and only for the purpose for which they had been requested. The idea of a general tax on all subjects came about slowly. Gradually, the financial institutions set up by kings to collect revenues from their private lands became public institutions that collected taxes conceded by the estates.[14]

Medieval monarchs were helped in their centralizing efforts by the support they received for such efforts by the bourgeoisie and the lower nobility. The burden of direct taxation fell most heavily on the bourgeoisie because movable property (i.e., commodities bought and sold) could be more easily taxed than fixed property such as land. Nevertheless, the bourgeoisie did not much resist because it benefited from the territory-wide legal systems that were also being developed by medieval kings at the time. Towns began to renounce their privileges and autonomy and integrated themselves into these emerging territory-wide legal frameworks, which came to link capitalism and state power in a single political formation.[15]

For its part, the lower nobility was also in favor of the centralizing efforts of medieval kings. Many lesser vassals were barely able to live as gentlemen because their lands were too small and unproductive. It was from their ranks that kings recruited tax collectors and judges. They were paid good salaries and given gifts of additional land. From the ranks of the lesser nobility, then, medieval monarchs began to build a corps of professional administrators; in this way monarchs could bypass the upper nobility.[16]

Emergence of Professional State Administration

Although certain practices of feudal governance remained within the medieval state, such as dispensing justice through personal rule, and dynastic politics based on family ties and feudal obligations, increasingly a new apparatus of politico-military power—a new set of institutions, offices, and techniques of exercising power—emerged; it was envisioned and created as separate and distinct from the persons of the rulers themselves.

As was mentioned in the previous chapter, all feudal lords, including kings, kept retinues of knights and household servants who helped them defend and run their castles and lands. The most important members of the king's household staff were the chancellor, who was in charge of the chancel (the altar area of the lord's chapel), and the steward, who was in charge of the great hall of the castle or manor house. The chancellor, in addition to saying Mass for the king, kept the king's seal, wrote his business letters (in Latin) to other kings or the pope, and directed the work of the king's scribes, clerks, and messengers. The steward, who was in charge of the household and the management of the king's demesne, required knowledge of accounting and document preparation. The steward was assisted by a number of bailiffs, who were put in charge of the sections of the king's demesne called bailiwicks.[17]

The king's properties were not contiguous, that is, they were scattered throughout the realm. Revenues from them were also shared with members of the nobility. Therefore, collecting what was due the king was difficult even when the exact amounts were known. The first permanent officials of the emergent state apparatus were the estate managers sent out by the king to collect revenue from crown lands and properties. In medieval England these estate managers were called reeves, and in France, provosts. After the Norman Conquest, England was divided into shires (counties), within each of which a reeve was appointed. These shire-reeves, or sheriffs, were responsible for collecting the king's revenue. As fines from local courts were part of the king's revenue, sheriffs and provosts were also responsible for ensuring the king's justice. Sheriffs and provosts frequently held court for petty offenses. Thus, the collection of the king's revenue and the provision of his justice were intertwined activities in the early medieval state.[18]

Gradually, feudal kings began to consider the administration of justice as more than a source of money. It was a way of asserting monarchical power and authority. Therefore, they began to increase the jurisdictions of courts. Serious criminal cases, such as murder, were reserved for the king's court; this allowed him to intervene in districts where he had no estates or local rights of justice. In civil cases, special procedures were developed that allowed litigants to bypass the local court and present their cases directly to a royal court. This allowed the lower nobility to protect themselves against their immediate lords. Because it was the duty of feudal kings to see that justice prevailed throughout the realm, appeals were allowed from lower courts to royal courts as a way of remedying injustice.[19]

Eventually, throughout medieval Europe the tasks of collecting revenue and providing justice were disentangled and two parallel sets of institutions and offices—legal and financial—began to evolve. While the same individual might be both judge and tax collector, when hearing a case he followed certain procedures and formalities that were different from those he followed when collecting revenue. As the law became more complicated, individuals who had been trained in the law, called judges and lawyers, began to appear and take charge of the provision of the king's justice. At the same time individuals trained in accounting began to take over the collection of the king's revenue.[20]

As legal and financial institutions and offices evolved separately, their work had to be coordinated. This was accomplished by the king's chancellor, who was always a high-ranking clergyman, either a bishop or a cardinal. The king's scribes and clerks, under the direction of the chancellor, developed and preserved regular administrative routines. They drafted orders and instructions, attempting to use unambiguous language. The chancery, or the office of the chancellor, became the nerve center of the medieval monarchy.[21]

A group of individuals thus appeared who spent their entire working lives as professional, full-time administrators. They were assisted by part-time agents who were willing to work for a portion of the year as estate managers, tax collectors, or judges. Although few existed at first, these individuals significantly increased in number during the thirteenth century. This growing band of administrators was recruited from the lesser nobility, who needed the money, and the bourgeoisie, who wanted the prestige and potential influence that came from being in the service of the king or prince.

The development of financial and judicial institutions staffed by a small but growing number of professional judges, tax collectors, law-trained clerks, and scribes meant that monarchs were able to control and administer wide territories without the help of the feudal aristocracy. Because the king's administrators were dependent upon the king for their livelihoods, they were loyal to him. Thus, the vassal-lord relationship ceased to be the glue that held the politico-military system together.

The development of territory-wide law courts and direct systems of revenue collection, as well as the growth of the general right to tax, led to the commercialization of economic life and the decline of the nobility as an effective political force. The nobility began to lose ground to the bourgeoisie and the king. It should be recognized that this was a gradual trend; it did not happen all at once. Medieval kings continued to support the nobility, although increasingly on the king's terms. The nobility was more and more subordinated to the king; those who were not recruited into the administrative apparatus were converted into the officer corps of the new infantry-based armies.

Thus, medieval kings gathered to themselves the instruments of politico-military rule that had been hitherto dispersed among the estates. They began to construct a centralized, territory-wide administrative apparatus that allowed them to supervise their realms directly down to the local level and to plan, organize, and direct large-scale military operations. Gradually, the castles of provincial lords were destroyed and the private armies of the nobility were disarmed. The production of battlefield weapons was monopolized in the king's arsenals. Larger and larger coherent territorial kingdoms emerged and politico-military rule became concentrated in the hands of the king and his court. Public officials eventually replaced individuals who held power as a private possession.[22]

As this apparatus of territorialized politico-military rule became more and more distinctive and visible, it gradually destroyed the multiple, unequal categories (estates and corporate groups) of the feudal "state" and increasingly constructed a realm peopled by a multitude of individuals who were all equally the subjects of the king. Eventually, neither allegiance to an estate nor membership in a corporate group stood between the individual and the king. The medieval monarchy itself became the individual's primary membership association.[23]

Emergence of the Modern Sovereign

As power and authority became more centralized and more abstract, in the sense of being lodged in the institutions and offices of monarchical power rather than in the person of the king, they were increasingly depersonalized. This involved, first, the development of impersonal systems of law and taxation and, second, the emergence of a new language of politics and rule.

With respect to the first, the emergence of the king's legal and financial institutions encouraged the evolution of uniform, impersonal systems of law. Two legal systems developed in medieval Europe. One was English common law (i.e., law common to all), which was an amalgamation of local customary law created by the king's judges, who were sent out to hear cases in local courts. The decisions they made in a multitude of local cases gradually became the law of the realm. Common law was based on cases, and as each case was different, judges were able to make constant changes in it until the nineteenth century, when the principle of *stare decisis* (i.e., to stand by the decision), or precedent, emerged and was consistently applied. Thus, English common law was judge-made law that became uniform across the realm when individual judges followed precedent.

The legal systems that emerged on the continent were heavily influenced by the rediscovery of Roman law. As was discussed in Chapter 1, the Romans developed a homogeneous body of codified law, which provided a framework that regulated political, economic, and social life throughout the empire. Medieval courts on the continent, influenced by canon law, looked to the Roman legal system as a model. Quite early, medieval monarchs on the continent began to write legal codes—which were published in the vernacular, not Latin—that regulated the management of the realm's forests, rivers, shipping, trade, fairs, and the like. Such codes fostered the development of official state languages such as French, Russian, English, Spanish, and Portuguese.

Thus, whether the judge-made law of England or the Roman-inspired code law of continental monarchies, uniform systems of public law came into existence that eventually replaced the various rights and privileges (literally, private law) claimed by each estate. Law came to be applied territorially, meaning that the same rules were applicable to all groups and in all regions within the realm. The law became an instrument for governing entire populations dispersed throughout the realm. At this point, the king's power to make law transcended his ability to do so based on discrete rights and privileges adhering to his person.[24]

The second element of the emerging depersonalized mode of governance was the development of a new language of political power and authority revolving around the idea of sovereignty. In feudal "states," the king was sovereign only in the sense of being "first among equals," and therefore his authority was limited by clearly recognized rights and privileges accruing to the estates. As centralization increased, medieval kings claimed a different kind of authority as the "head of state." Authority—that is, the legitimate right to exercise power—came to be lodged in the state itself, and in the person of the king only insofar as the king represented the imagined unity of the state. More important, as sovereign head of state, the king claimed to be not simply first among equals but a separate, overarching sovereign—that is, one whose power was free from control by all others. In doing so, the king exploited a legal fiction that had emerged, especially in England, according to which the king's body had a dual nature: it was simultaneously the physical body of the king and the symbolic, collective body that mediated between his realm and God.[25]

The purpose of politico-military rule changed during this period. In the classical Greek city-states and the Roman Republic, the purpose of rule was aimed at realizing a just and harmonious human community that embodied the best, most virtuous qualities of human beings, which was understood to be possible only in the "city," the highest and noblest form of human association. In feudal "states," the objective of rule was the soul. To the extent that the king (and his vassals) ruled, beyond protecting his private holdings, he understood himself to be acting for the moral and spiritual well-being of those he ruled, his subjects. In the late medieval period, from about the thirteenth century, there began to emerge a new idea about what ruling meant that contested these earlier conceptions. The objective of politico-military rule was neither to realize human virtue nor to serve religious redemption, but rather, to produce a perfectly formed state.[26] In this new language, the king became more and more the symbolic representation of the apparatus that managed public affairs, his symbolic body gaining precedence over his physical body. The state became identified less with the authoritative decisions of a private person who governed, and more as an ongoing apparatus of processes, offices, and institutions under the direction and supervision of the king. Its logic became less one of personal loyalty to rulers and overlords and more one of representation; that is, politico-military rule became hierarchical and mediated by a language and culture that represented to the people their own collective being. Once the state was understood in this way, and a language formed that made such an idea intelligible, the state could take itself as its own object of rule. That is, the art of ruling could become the act of managing the territorial space of the state so as to ensure its own power and security, and to secure the health and well-being of its subjects.

It is important to recognize that the development of the modern language of sovereignty was gradual, and, hence, we will look at its development further in the next chapter. The authority and the growing power claimed by centralizing monarchs were contested throughout this period, in some cases successfully, by the Catholic Church and the nobility. Moreover, kings did not yet clearly see themselves as representatives of the sovereign power of the state. Most kings, well into the early modern period, that is, into the seventeenth century, continued to frame their claims to authority and power in terms of their being the representatives of a universal Christendom in Europe. This allowed them to claim rightful authority in areas outside their territorial area and to extend their authority to inherited but noncontiguous areas.

Nonetheless, from the twelfth and thirteenth centuries on, a new mode of politico-military rule based on the sovereignty of the state rather than personal rule developed. The principle of state sovereignty first and foremost unified political rule within a specific territory. The stage was being set for the imagining of political space in a fundamentally novel way as a unified, contiguous territory. The king came to look on his subjects, the population of the territory he ruled, as an object, bounded by the limits of the physical space he ruled, as parts of the whole to be ordered and administered.

Secularism and the Emergence of Modernity

The formation of centralized politico-military power together with the idea of sovereignty affected the traditional Christian way of understanding the relationship between human actions and God; this, in turn, provoked a crisis in Christian beliefs. As the politico-military power of the medieval state grew and strengthened, the natural and human worlds began to appear more contingent; that is, more of what happened to human beings appeared to be the result of mere chance or the result of their own actions rather than being directly determined by God. The power of the emerging, centralized medieval state to order human affairs made the world increasingly subject to human will; this presented a challenge to the Christian idea that all human actions and laws fit neatly together as part of God's plan over which humans themselves have no control.

In the early fourteenth century, this crisis in Christian belief found expression in a philosophical movement called nominalism, which began to sever the link between reason and faith and emphasized God's inscrutability and fallen man's distance from him. Nominalists, such as William of Ockham (c. 1280–1349), defended the new power of the medieval monarchy by arguing that considering the world as a preexistent order prior to human action and determination was inconsistent with the Christian idea that God was omnipotent, an all-powerful being who created the world according to his own will. Ockham argued that the way the world is at any particular moment is finite and contingent. One contemporary political theorist describes the importance of nominalism this way: "Nominalism saves God's omnipotence by pushing him higher into the heavens, disconnecting him from the reason, experience, texts, and signs that make up the mundane world. It thereby sets the table for later secularization."[27]

This theological and spiritual crisis would continue to affect the rise of the state for several hundred years, and we will have occasion to return to it later. Here, we introduce three developments of the late medieval period that would be important to the development of the secularized, territorial state: (1) the idea of a civil society; (2) the revival of Roman republicanism, including the idea of "reason of state"; and (3) the idea that knowledge can and should improve human life.

Civil Society

As early as the writings of the Dominican friar Thomas Aquinas (1225–1274), the idea of a body of law that governed human social and moral life independently of direct religious supervision developed. Aquinas revived Aristotelian ideas concerning the ability of human reason to discover for itself the moral laws that governed human beings. To do this without denying God and defying the Church, he defined natural law as developing from the "participation in the eternal law by rational creatures."[28] In Aquinas's view, however, mankind still required direction from God. To express this need, he set natural law within a juridical hierarchy. At the pinnacle of this hierarchy was the eternal law by which God regulated the universe. Divine law—the law as expressed in the Bible—governed mankind's higher spiritual life. Natural law reflected humankind's nature as a rational being possessed of both a natural inclination to do good and the innate reason to discover moral laws. Below natural law was positive or human law, the body of law made by the state. For Aquinas, human institutions and actions, such as politics, were to be directed according to principles of natural law and were distinct from the canon law of the Church, which expressed divine law. Aquinas used the idea of natural law derived by reason to justify the growing autonomy of medieval kingship from the Church, and even went so far as to argue that the king was bound by natural law to do what was good for his subjects.[29] Natural law sought to preserve a link between the universal and the particular in the king who ruled for the common good, uniting the transcendent and the contingent that the crisis of Christianity seemed to sever.

The implications of the idea that politics is bound by a realm of universal rational rules that systematized the good of the "society" as a whole would develop over the next several centuries. It led to the concept of the "social" as a distinct realm of human actions and institutions. Natural law would become especially important in the seventeenth and eighteenth centuries, when it would be used to describe a system of social relations that were based in human nature itself, and only indirectly linked, if at all, to God's law.

Of particular importance to the construction of the idea of a society was the way in which women were related to natural law. This would lead to the subordination of women in the modern state by enabling them to be assigned to a private sphere cordoned off from the public world. Although natural law referred to both men and women, it did not do so in the same way or to the same degree. In both Aristotle's thought and in Christianity, the two sources of Aquinas's theory of natural law, women were secondary to men in a natural hierarchy. Aristotle believed that women were biologically inferior to men. Their natural function in the hierarchy of nature was to reproduce and care for children. Their natural place was the household and home. As was discussed in Chapter 2, Christianity considered women to be the "helpmates" of men, created by God to assist him in the Garden of Eden. Thus, Aquinas's theory freed the natural world from direct religious control, but continued to place women in a subordinate position within a presumed "natural" gender hierarchy.[30] The result was that the modern state and society became domains of male activities. Although individual women might occasionally participate in them, this was not the norm, and such women were most often viewed with suspicion and open disdain. The modern idea of society was constructed according to a presumed "natural" gender hierarchy and a sharp division of public and private spheres, the latter proper to women and the former proper to men.

Perhaps the most important consequence of natural law's conception of an independent social realm was that it freed commercial and economic activity from medieval constraints. The medieval Church taught that commerce was an immoral activity because it encouraged people's passions and desires and put material life above spiritual life. However, Aquinas's writings provided a justification for commercial activity and the accumulation of wealth and private property based on the idea of natural law. Aquinas argued that although God had given the world to human beings as a whole for the purpose of sustaining and reproducing life (the traditional Christian belief), this inheritance would be best taken care of, and peace would be more likely, if individuals owned property for themselves. Aquinas rea-

soned from his observations of his fellow human beings that they took better care of property they personally owned. Here is how Aquinas put it:

> Community of goods is said to be part of the natural law not because the
> natural law decrees that all things are to be possessed in common and
> nothing held privately, but because the distribution of property is not a
> matter of natural law but of human agreement which pertains to the posi-
> tive law, as we have said. Therefore private property is not against natural
> law but it has been added to natural law by the inventiveness of human
> reason.[31]

By justifying commerce and private ownership in this way, Aquinas
marginalized women within economic activity, because it was men who
legally owned property and therefore were the privileged caretakers of it.

Aquinas did not go so far as to describe an independent society, that is,
the self-regulating, individual action that would later underlie the free-
market economy. Nor is the theory of natural law in Aquinas's meaning a
part of the concept of civil society that emerges in the eighteenth century.
However, Aquinas's idea helped generate a linguistic space that made the
idea of civil society possible by leading people to think of their social
world as a creation of individual reason and their social interactions as governed by moral law, which they could know and justify to themselves.[32]

The Revival of Republicanism

Another effect of the general trend toward centralized politico-military
power in later medieval monarchies was the increasing construction of the
political realm as independent of religious authority. This trend was bound
up with the development of state sovereignty, which imbued the political
realm with a spirit of self-confidence. Just as the idea of natural law
allowed a freeing of the commercial spirit, the revival of Roman republican
ideas of a distinct political realm operating according to its own principles
freed the political will from the constraints of a divinely ordered world.

The new spirit of politics emerged most forcefully in the city-states of
Renaissance Italy. From the thirteenth through the sixteenth centuries, powerful Italian city-states such as Florence, Venice, Pisa, Milan, and Siena
struggled to establish their independence from both the Catholic Church,
which claimed the right to control them directly, and the Holy Roman
Emperor. Political theorists such as Marsiglio of Padua (c. 1275–1342) and
Dante Alighieri (1265–1321), among others, established the idea that the
pope had no jurisdiction at all over political matters.[33] They described the
pope as "a mere administrator of sacraments who could have no power and
make no laws in temporal fields."[34] Although this claim was made for the

specific purpose of establishing the supreme authority of the Holy Roman Emperor in Italy, the arguments about the autonomy of political matters would go on to have more general significance. The important legal thinker Bartolus de Saxoferrato (1314–1357) used the rediscovered Roman law to claim not only the autonomy of politics from religion, but the supremacy of particular secular rulers.[35]

Roman practices of self-governance had never been fully eradicated from the northern Italian cities during the Middle Ages; the peoples in them developed a fierce spirit of independence, which by the twelfth and thirteenth centuries led to the establishment of self-governing republics against prevailing monarchies. Thus, the political realm—the realm of struggle for independence and the conflicting strategies and passions of the factions that sought to rule these independent city-states—became a subject of interest in its own right. *Literati* (i.e., educated individuals) began to write pamphlets and books giving advice to rulers on how to maintain independence from outside forces as well as peace among different factions at home.[36]

The most significant proponent of this new spirit in politics was Niccolò Machiavelli (1469–1527), a Florentine bureaucrat and diplomat who served in the republican government of Florence until it was overthrown in 1494. Machiavelli reinterpreted the Roman republican ideas of citizenship and civic virtue as actions in the spirit of self-sacrifice for the good of the state. He most fully presented this concept in his commentary on Roman history, the *Discourses on the First Ten Books of Titus Livy* (1519). Machiavelli's political theory has been called "the first great experiment in a 'pure' political theory."[37]

Machiavelli described politics as an arena of human action governed not by religion and high moral purpose but by necessity and contingency (i.e., chance and unforeseen causes). He saw it through a new imagery drawn not from religion but from the Roman idea of *virtus* and from his long experience of the political realm itself. Politics, he declared, demanded that the ruler know the people and that the people know the ruler, and involved the power and manipulations inherent in such knowledge. Knowing politics from the lofty heights of the heavens was replaced with an earthly imagery:

> For in the same way that landscape painters station themselves in the valleys in order to draw mountains or high ground, and ascend an eminence in order to get a good view of the plains, so it is necessary to be a prince to know thoroughly the nature of the people, and one of the populace to know the nature of princes.[38]

Thus, for Machiavelli, the political spirit is within politics itself, within its struggles for power, honor, privilege, and security. For him, the laws that govern political action are those of strategy, prudence, and daring. To learn politics, one does not study theology or morals but the "deeds of great men" and their successes and failures in past political struggles.

For Machiavelli, the spirit of the political realm was distinctly human, able to recognize and, when possible, master the contingencies of Fortune (i.e., chance). In this struggle, great men could not afford either religion or its morals. They had to reduce the contingencies of Fortune through the prudent and instrumental use of violence for the "interest of the state," in order to maintain its glory, longevity, and greatness. One commentator on Machiavelli has called his focus on necessity and contingency an "economy of violence."[39]

This emphasis on mastery and its limits, prudence and valor in war, and violence reinforced the masculine character of the emerging state and continued the trend of estranging women from politics and public life. Fortune, Machiavelli said in a famous passage in *The Prince* (1513), "is a woman, and it is necessary, if you wish to master her, to conquer her by force."[40] Machiavelli's revival of the Roman ideas of *virtus* and citizenship relied on the individual's (i.e., male's) own abilities to master the circumstances he finds in the world. Moreover, this mastery was itself contingent—it neither depended on God's will nor was its success guaranteed by following any objective system of knowledge and laws.

Machiavelli's writing became associated over the next two centuries with a distinctly secular and "modern" attitude toward politics and government. By liberating the political will from its medieval religious and traditional restrictions, his writings allowed explorations of the way states could actually maintain and enhance their power. Reflections on the state in the Machiavellian mode could become reflections of the state itself, on how to efficiently order its affairs to maximize its power. This way of thinking about the political realm as embodying a distinctive, even ruthless spirit of political intrigue and action came to be called Machiavellism or, alternatively, "reason of state."[41]

Science for the Benefit of Mankind

A third aspect of late medieval life that led to the emergence of the modern territorial state was the development of a new attitude toward knowledge in general. Increasingly, knowledge and science came to be seen as having intrinsic value that satisfied human curiosity about the basic makeup of the Earth and the heavens, and as means that should be used to improve the material condition of humankind. The renewal of curiosity about the natural world and the practical applications of that knowledge challenged the traditional presumptions about the nature and purposes of knowledge.

As we discussed in the previous chapter, the Catholic Church during the Middle Ages held a monopoly on advanced knowledge. This allowed the Church to define the standards of truth and the proper uses of science. To the medieval Church, knowledge was important because it led people to know God and therefore directly affected how people could live a good, moral life. Knowledge was to lead to a spiritual awakening and purification of the soul. Thus, knowledge was closely linked to religion through its role in teaching people how to "know and love God."

While knowledge remained connected to the moral life throughout the medieval period, links between scientific knowledge and the moral life became more indirect. "Modern" science did not tell people what the moral life was, but it could be an important tool for accomplishing specific tasks and solving specific problems, such as how to build bigger ships to meet the demand for more goods, or how to count populations accurately so that taxes could be more efficiently collected. Rather than being limited to the Church and a hierarchy of knowledges that defined God's will as supreme and the unity of the human world as part of God's plan, knowledge became "technologized"; that is, it became an instrument to be used by those who wielded power in order to accomplish specific tasks or solve certain problems.

This new use of knowledge would have two important effects. One was to produce among human beings a sense of power and control over the natural and social worlds. The second was to produce a sense among human beings that knowledge of the natural and social worlds was of intrinsic value because it could lead to a better, more comfortable, and "civilized" way of life. By the early sixteenth century, this new attitude would be reflected in the emergence of a new genre of literature, the *utopia*. These fictional narratives described a perfected social order that could be produced by applying scientific knowledge. Among the most popular of such works were *Utopia* (1516) by Thomas More (1478–1535) and *The City of the Sun* (1623) by Tommaso Campanella (1568–1639). The most influential in promoting the secular and political power of science was *New Atlantis* (1627) by Francis Bacon (1561–1626), which proposed a government based on a scientific technocracy.

Summary

This chapter has described both continuities and discontinuities between the elements of the medieval state, the precursor to the modern territorial state, and the feudal and Roman worlds out of which it grew. Central elements of the modern territorial state, such as large standing armies and professional administrations, reemerged in the medieval period, roughly from the eleventh through the fifteenth centuries. By examining elements of the new language of politics that emerged in medieval monarchies, we have illuminated how the modern, territorial state was made possible by both its past and the contingent history in which it operated.

Notes

1. Charles Tilly, *Coercion, Capital, and European States, A.D. 990–1990* (Cambridge, MA: Basil Blackwell, 1990); Brian M. Downing, *The Military Revolution and Political Change: Origins of Democracy and Autocracy in Early Modern Europe* (Princeton, NJ: Princeton University Press, 1992); Bruce D. Porter, *War and the Rise of the State: The Military Foundations of Modern Politics* (New York: Free Press, 1994); Richard Bean, "War and the Birth of the Nation-State," *Journal of Economic History* 33 (March 1973): 203–221.

2. Samuel E. Finer, "State- and Nation-Building in Europe: The Role of the Military," in Charles Tilly (ed.), *The Formation of National States in Western Europe* (Princeton, NJ: Princeton University Press, 1975): 102–108.

3. Lynn White Jr. *Medieval Technology and Social Change* (Oxford: Oxford University Press, 1962).

4. For details, see Maurice Keen, *Medieval Warfare: A History* (Oxford: Oxford University Press, 1999).

5. On the military revolution, see Clifford J. Rogers, ed., *The Military Revolution Debate: Readings on the Military Transformation of Early Modern Europe* (Boulder, CO: Westview Press, 1995).

6. Phillippe Contamine, *War in the Middle Ages* (Oxford: Basil Blackwell, 1980), 119–165.

7. Anthony Giddens, *The Nation-State and Violence* (Berkeley and Los Angeles: University of California Press, 1985), 114–115.

8. Janice E. Thompson, *Mercenaries, Pirates, and Sovereigns: State-Building and Extraterritorial Violence in Early Modern Europe* (Princeton, NJ: Princeton University Press, 1994).

9. John Keegan, *A History of Warfare* (New York: Vintage, 1993), 14.

10. William H. McNeill, *The Pursuit of Power: Technology, Armed Force, and Society Since A.D. 1000* (Chicago: Chicago University Press, 1982), 117.

11. Norman Davies, *Europe: A History* (Oxford and New York: Oxford University Press, 1996), 519.

12. Joseph A. Schumpeter, "The Crisis of the Tax State," in Richard Swedburg (ed.), *The Economics and Sociology of Capitalism* (Princeton, NJ: Princeton University Press, 1991): 102–108; Michael Mann, "State and Society, 1130–1815: An Analysis of English State Finances," in Maurice Zeitlin (ed.), *Political Power and Social Theory: A Research Annual,* vol. 1 (Greenwich, CT: JAI Press, 1980), 165–208.

13. Schumpeter, "The Crisis of the Tax State," 106.

14. Ibid.

15. Ibid.

16. Joseph R. Strayer, *Feudalism* (Princeton, NJ: Van Nostrand, 1965), 61–68.

17. Joseph and Frances Geis, *Life in a Medieval Castle* (New York: Harper & Row, 1979).

18. Joseph R. Strayer, *On the Medieval Origins of the Modern State* (Princeton, NJ: Princeton University Press, 1970), 28.

19. Ibid.

20. Ibid., 29.

21. Ibid., 33–34.

22. Gianfranco Poggi, *The Development of the Modern State: A Sociological Introduction* (Stanford, CA: Stanford University Press, 1978), 77–79.

23. Strayer, *Feudalism,* 67.

24. Poggi, *The Development of the Modern State,* 60–67.

25. Ernst H. Kantorowicz, *The King's Two Bodies: A Study in Medieval Political Theology* (Princeton, NJ: Princeton University Press, 1957).

26. Jean Bodin, in *Six Books of the Commonwealth* (1576), is credited with being the first to investigate sovereignty theoretically in reference to the depersonalized state. The imagery in which the state is rendered a "body politic" is most vividly deployed in Thomas Hobbes's *Leviathan,* ed. Richard Tuck (Cambridge: Cambridge University Press, 1991), wherein he describes the sovereign as an "Artificiall Soul" (p. 9) and "Mortal God" (p. 120).

27. William E. Connolly, *Political Theory and Modernity* (Oxford and New York: Basil Blackwell, 1988), 20.

28. St. Thomas Aquinas, *Summa Theologica,* in *St. Thomas Aquinas on Politics and Ethics,* trans. and ed. Paul E. Sigmund (New York: W. W. Norton, 1988): 46.

29. St. Thomas Aquinas, *On Kingship,* in *St. Thomas Aquinas on Politics and Ethics,* trans. and ed. Paul E. Sigmund (New York: W. W. Norton, 1988).

30. Jean Bethke Elshtain, *Public Man, Private Woman: Women in Social and Political Thought* (Princeton, NJ: Princeton University Press, 1981), 74–78; Diana Coole, *Women in Political Theory: From Ancient Misogyny to Contemporary Feminism,* 2d ed. (Boulder, CO: Lynne Rienner Publishers, 1993), 48–51.

31. Coole, *Women in Political Theory,* 72.

32. Adam B. Seligman, *The Idea of Civil Society* (New York: Free Press, 1992).

33. See J. H. Hinsley, *Sovereignty,* 2d ed. (Cambridge: Cambridge University Press, 1986), 82–88; Quentin Skinner, *The Foundations of Modern Political Thought,* vol. 1, *The Renaissance* (Cambridge: Cambridge University Press, 1978), 16–22.

34. Hinsley, *Sovereignty,* 83.

35. Skinner, *Foundations,* 8–12.

36. Ibid., part 1.

37. Sheldon Wolin, *Politics and Vision: Continuity and Innovation in Western Political Thought* (Boston: Little, Brown, 1960), 198.

38. Niccolò Machiavelli, *The Prince and the Discourses,* ed. Max Lerner (New York: Random House, 1950), 4.

39. Wolin, *Politics and Vision,* chapter 7.

40. Machiavelli, *The Prince and the Discourses,* 94.

41. Still the most important chronicle of this tradition is Frederich Meinecke, *Machiavellism: The Doctrine of Raison d'Etat and Its Place in Modern History,* trans. Douglas Scott (New Haven, CT: Yale University Press, 1962). For an interpretation of its importance in the development of political economy, see Albert O. Hirschman, *The Passions and the Interests: Political Arguments for Capitalism Before Its Triumph* (Princeton, NJ: Princeton University Press, 1977), 33–35.

PART 2

THE MODERN TERRITORIAL STATE

In Part 1, we saw how kings were able to take advantage of their territory-wide obligations to defend the realm and provide justice in order to construct uniform, centrally administered systems of law, taxation, weights and measures, coinage, etc. These states more and more regularized and homogenized social and economic life within their domains, making the extraction of the human and material resources necessary for fighting war with large armies possible. Rival forms of politico-military rule (e.g., city-states) began to fade as serious competitors, leaving the territorial state as the dominant form of politico-military rule within the geographical space of Europe. In Part 2 we discuss the various forms that the territorial state has taken within Europe. Chapter 4 addresses absolutist states, Chapter 5 discusses liberal states, Chapter 6 presents the idea of antiliberal states, and Chapter 7 examines what we call managerial states. In these chapters, we will show how the construction of the territorial state and the construction of a system of territorial states in Europe took place synchronically.

4

The Absolute State:
Sovereignty Unbound

The modern territorial state took several centuries to become established. In this chapter, we discuss the first form the territorial state took in Europe, from roughly the sixteenth to the eighteenth centuries, and focus on how territorial sovereignty was imagined and instituted. Specifically, we look at the transformation of political structures, the rise of capitalism, and the transformation of the relation of state to capital. The emphasis is on the transformation of political space, in thought and practice, into an idea of territoriality that linked the local to the national in ways that broke with the traditions of medieval Christendom. After painting each of these transformations in rather broad strokes, we turn to two specific case histories that show how sovereignty was instituted in two early modern states, England and France.

The Emergence of Sovereign Territoriality

The catalyst for the transformation of the heteronomy of the medieval period was the crisis of Christianity known as the Reformation and the religious violence and wars it spawned.[1] The Reformation was a revolt against the Catholic Church by those who considered it corrupt, more concerned with maintaining its power and privileges than with guiding the spiritual salvation of Christendom. At first, reformists were members of the clergy, such as the German monk Martin Luther (1482–1546). But soon the reform religions, such as Lutheranism, Presbyterianism, and Calvinism, spread throughout Europe, especially among the bourgeoisie, but also among some of the nobility. Reformers, known as Protestants (from the "protests" against Charles V at the Diet of Speyer in 1529), argued that salvation depended on faith alone. Protestant religious practice emphasized the private, personal relationship between the individual person and God. A personalized relationship, they argued, obviated the need for the Catholic Church's liturgy, sacraments, and official hierarchy of priests, bishops, and pope. Indeed, Protestants argued that the Catholic Church's statues and

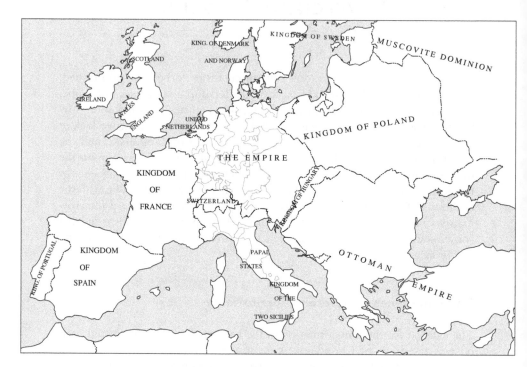

Europe at the Peace of Westphalia, 1648

images of its saints amounted to false gods; some even viewed the Catholic hierarchy, including the pope, as the Antichrist. Moreover, Protestant sects taught that if a ruler commits impious acts or undermines "true" religion, the people over whom rule was exercised had a right and duty to resist.

The Catholic Church tried to suppress Protestantism with military force by encouraging monarchs who remained loyal to the Church to attack those who had converted to one of the new Protestant religions. Fighting between Catholic and Protestant monarchs was ended by the Treaty of Augsburg (1555), which recognized Protestantism as one of the two religions that could be practiced within Europe, the other being Catholicism. The Treaty of Augsburg recognized the right of the monarch to establish the religion of his realm. The monarch's choice was binding on his subjects and those who did not accept his choice were obliged to worship in secret or emigrate. The Treaty of Augsburg "enhanced the powers of state rulers within the Holy Roman Empire and directed growing attention to those states as discrete territorial units."[2]

The Treaty of Augsburg was soon violated, however. States began to advance the religions of their rulers by attacking states whose rulers professed the opposite faith. These wars, known as the Thirty Years' War (1618–1648), began in German-speaking kingdoms, principalities, and dukedoms and pitted Catholic and Protestant rulers against each other. The fighting was extremely bloody because the combatants thought they had God on their side and that the enemy was the instrument of Satan. It is estimated that about one-third of the population of German-speaking Europe died as a result of the fighting. Eventually, exhaustion and the desire to end the bloodshed and the resulting economic devastation led to a new concern with peace in Europe. Peace treaties, signed at Münster by Catholic kings and estates and Osnabrück by Protestant kings in 1648, known collectively as the Peace of Westphalia, sanctioned the division of Europe into Catholic and Protestant states.

The Peace of Westphalia recognized the principle of state sovereignty and enshrined the concept of secure and universally recognized state borders in law. It accepted the principle of nonintervention in the territorial space of other states for any reason. After the treaty was signed, Europe experienced a period of peace and stability that helped normalize the principle of state sovereignty. From this point onward, a commitment to the right of individual rulers to exercise absolute control within their own territory took hold and the territorial state began to "crowd out competing conceptions of how power might be organized to the point where the sovereign territorial [state] became the only imaginable spatial framework for political life."[3]

The treaty also encouraged further development and use of diplomacy; that is, the art and practice of conducting relations among states through embassies and ambassadors, which had begun in the sixteenth century. Modern diplomacy, with its concepts of extraterritoriality and diplomatic immunity, reflected a new sense of estrangement in Europe. Increasingly, the political "other" was conceived of as a state, with a specific geographic location, rather than heretical religious group, a rival noble family, or a person of inferior rank. Gaining knowledge about and communicating with other states required different norms, rules, and formal institutions than did overcoming the estrangement from heretics or rival nobility. The new institutions of diplomacy, then, both presupposed the sovereignty of territorial states and helped to further their entrenchment into a system of states.[4]

The ideal of territorial sovereignty arose, then, in good part as a historically contingent resolution of a spiritual crisis of Christianity. By sanctioning the division of Christendom into sovereign territorial states, the Peace of Westphalia also consolidated and gave a new political form to Europe. After Westphalia, an interstate society was gradually created that had at its core a commitment to the right of individual rulers to control all matters within their own territories. Europe as a political identity began to take hold; that is, the term "Europe" increasingly was used to refer to an imagined political space defined by a system composed of states and an international society with its own body of law (international law) that regulated relations among them. The peoples outside Europe came to be understood not only as non-Christian "others" but as extralegal peoples who were not governed by the same rules of the international society of Europe, which had enormous consequences for colonial and imperial policies. Estrangement of European peoples from themselves becomes a double estrangement, simultaneously religious and political. A third estrangement, through colonialism, was also in the making. European states would come to be seen as more economically and culturally advanced than the non-European peoples they conquered and colonized, about which we will say more in Part 3.

Representing Territorial State Sovereignty

The Peace of Westphalia created a problem: how to imagine and represent a combined religious, moral, and political authority in a secular, earthly entity confined within territorial borders. Finding a solution was imperative given that these territorial entities were created by conventions and agreements, which gave some measure of peace to the Europe of religious wars.

The first and predominant solution to this crisis of the representation of territorial authority was to imagine the state as a symbolic body, a "body politic." Such a discursive practice had two notable sources. First, locating authority in a symbolic body had a long history and resonance in

Christianity and was recognizable by both Protestants and Catholics. Christians located authority in the human world in the body of Christ, who, as the Son of God, had a dual nature. He was both flesh and blood and ethereal at the same time, that is, "man and God." Second, legal discourses during the Middle Ages had similarly endowed the body of the king with a special significance and dual nature. Political factions in the early modern state, in spite of their differences, could appeal to the fiction of the king's two bodies. One side emphasized the tradition of the divine right of kings, in which the king's authority was traced through the patriarchal lineage of Adam, the first male given authority over other men and women by God. The other side appealed to the king's body as a collective body composed of his subjects.[5]

The latter, which was to have lasting influence, was developed in England, for example, by Thomas Hobbes (1588–1679) in *Leviathan* (1650). For Hobbes, the basis of the state, which he called a commonwealth, was the interest of individual subjects in securing their own peace and protection. He hypothesized that without a sovereign, people lived in a "state of nature" characterized by a war "where every man is Enemy to every man," which made "the life of man, solitary, poore, nasty, brutish, and short."[6] According to Hobbes, individuals living in a state of nature created a sovereign power to defend themselves "from the invasion of Forraigners, and the injuries of one another, and thereby to secure them in such sort, as that by their owne industrie, and by the fruites of the Earth, they may nourish themselves and live contentedly." Hobbes saw the sovereign as a unity of the wills of the individual subjects who composed it: "The only way to erect such a Common Power . . . is, to conferre all their power and strength upon one Man, or upon one Assembly of men, that may reduce all their Wills, by plurality of voices, unto one Will." Moreover, he argued that to create this sovereign, one consents to a "social compact," a promise on the part of all individual subjects to "authorise and give up my Right of Governing my selfe, to this Man, or to this Assembly of men, on this condition, that thou give up thy Right to him, and Authorise all his Actions in like manner."[7] Blending the religious and legal conceptions of the symbolic body, Hobbes describes the sovereign as an "Artificiall Soul" residing in the "Artificiall Man," which is the commonwealth,[8] or, alternatively, as a "Mortall God."[9]

This new way of imagining and representing the sovereignty of the state had two primary effects. First, it rendered the state more abstract and enacted the dualistic structure (inside/outside) of the Westphalian settlement. The sovereign treated his subjects inside the territory as a collective being, a population to be regulated and molded for the good the state. At the same time, it mediated their estrangement from those outside (who were increasingly presented as threats), which required the internal organization of the subjects by the sovereign. The head/soul (sovereign) needed to organize, coordinate, and regulate the physical body (subjects, territory) to protect it from the outside.

The second effect of the new way of imagining sovereignty was to deepen the patriarchal domination of women. The state, or collective body, comprised a robust public life in which war, intrigue, and the pursuit of wealth were reserved largely for men. States now protected something increasingly referred to as "society." Society came to refer to a private, interior world, first in the court life among the courtiers of the king, and then in the social world of art, high culture, and fashion, which was generated by the court, and through which capitalism was rapidly spreading throughout the population.[10] Increasingly, the state depended on a private sphere in which male subjects were socialized to participate in public activities, such as owning property, serving in the state bureaucracy, or fighting in the army—activities reserved for men. In this private sphere, men learned to be *individuals,* to cultivate their particular talents, which could then be appropriated and used by the sovereign.

Rather than being viewed as individuals whose status resulted from personal abilities, achievements, and wealth, as was the case for men in public life, women continued to be understood as products of nature, better suited to the private than the public sphere. The functions of this private sphere, such as nurturing and caring for children, giving emotional support, and developing personal habits of hygiene, increasingly came to be associated with a new norm of "femininity," which was held in opposition to the public world's "masculine" characteristics, such as competing in business, gaining a rational education, and exercising governing power.[11]

Changes in the basic idea of the family, then, were crucial components of the new sovereign states. The family became bound up with a new idea of privacy. The family became the institutionalized form of the private sphere; here men developed their individuality and here, too, they cultivated their usefulness to and participation in the body politic. Spaces such as the bedroom, in which, during the medieval period, it had been the custom to entertain important guests, became private enclosures from which outsiders were excluded. Women came to be seen as belonging "naturally" in this private space. This prevented them from becoming individuals themselves and rendered them aides to the development of men's individuality.

Reimagining Political Space

The early modern state reimagines political life and sovereignty within territorial boundaries.[12] We have seen various ways in which states at different times imagined the boundaries and key components of political space.

Classical republican city-states, such as those of ancient Greece and Rome, considered the state as an association of human beings that provided for the common good. Politics properly took place in cities because this was where citizens met to discuss common needs and make common decisions. Because the republic meant the association of citizens, territorial boundaries were less important. Cities were separated from other cities by open areas rather than by fixed boundaries. Political space was associated with the specific place in which citizens met to debate and decide about laws and the common good. This classical republican idea of political space was manifested in the city-states of northern Italy during the Renaissance and still informs some elements of modern states.[13]

Nevertheless, the republican imaginary of political space is not the predominant one in modern states. Modern states are defined in terms of sovereignty and territorial boundaries. Political space is not the specific place in which citizens meet to debate and decide political matters, but refers to the area inside the territorial boundaries under the state's control. Politics comes to be associated less with the debating and deciding of the common good and more with securing borders and maintaining the territorial integrity and sovereignty of the state. The political space of the modern state becomes something to be pacified, administered, and defended.[14]

Unlike republican theories of political space, which refer to the specific place where politics occurs, and includes all the specific attributes of that place (especially its people, with their distinctive culture and traditions), political space in modern states is more general. It refers to territory that states control. This idea of political space draws on the concepts of space that were invented in Euclidean geometry during the early modern period.[15] Space was increasingly seen not as separated places having little to do with one another, but rather as a continuous field, a singular and empty space. Political space for the modern territorial state, then, in principle, included the entire planet, and was seen to enclose particular political spaces on the planet that particular states could pacify, administer, and defend effectively. The political ordering and governance of specific places was contingent, not natural or sacred. In this way of imagining political space, the type of government a state has is less important than its being a state. Whereas the modern state can be designated in various ways, its designation simply as a state, that is, as an entity that exercises administrative control over a specific territory with fixed and secure borders, becomes predominant.

Not tied to place, state sovereignty could become an abstract and general model; it could be transplanted, and sometimes reconfigured, to suit different locales. Being based on such a generalized model allowed particular states to expand into the space outside, and permitted the state form to be exported via European colonialism and imperialism. By the end of the nineteenth century, as we will see in Part 3, the entire planet came to be divided into separate states. This was made possible by the new idea of the planet as space filled by the contingent organizations of territorial states, rather than the naturally differentiated spaces of ancient or medieval conceptions, or the non-Western conceptions of space, which either sacralized place, as did the Chinese and Mayan Empires, for example, or which considered human societies as embedded in their natural environment, as did the native peoples of North America, for example. Other forms of political life, such as tribes, traditional empires, and republican city-states, were no longer recognized as legitimate ways of organizing and practicing politico-military rule.

The new conception of political space enabled the development of new principles of hegemony in the European world order. Claims to power and influence in the European world order shifted from claims of leadership within Christendom or claims to inheritance of the Holy Roman Empire to the command of secular space and time in order to enhance territorial stability and wealth. This required the ability to integrate principles of territorial authority (how successful states were at centralizing authority and power) with the forces of capitalism. As the latter developed, the conditions of hegemony within the European world order changed, altering the fate of states within the system as a whole.

Perhaps the first state able to achieve this modern hegemony was that of the Dutch, who, during the first half of the seventeenth century, achieved independence from the Spanish Habsburgs and formed a republic. As we will see in Part 3, the Dutch state became an important colonial power. It was also able to establish dominance within the trading system that developed from the influx of wealth from the Americas. The Dutch state did so as the premier commercial power, dominating the European banking industry, something the Spanish failed to do even though they probably brought more wealth into Europe than did the Dutch. Amsterdam became the leading banking center of Europe, the hub through which much of Europe's colonial wealth passed.

In the first half of the seventeenth century, hegemony in the European world order came primarily from the mastery of commercial capitalism, the funding of new ventures that required a secure state in which commerce played a dominant role. By the second half of the seventeenth century, France would become the dominant power, combining colonial possessions with its vast agricultural resources at home. As Louis XIV succeeded in centralizing state power, markets developed and capital shifted into France. The principles of hegemony shifted from commercial to mercantile, that is, hegemony came to require developing markets that integrated local production with trade and colonial possessions. France, being the largest and most populous state in Europe at the time, excelled under these conditions once the territorial state solidified.

The conditions that would allow for the mastery of space and time in Europe would begin to shift again in the eighteenth century. As French power declined, in part because the military ambition of Louis XIV led to an overextension of the state and eventual defeat in a series of wars both in Europe and in the colonies, it appeared that no single power achieved hegemony in the European world order. At the Peace of Utrecht (1715), the idea emerged that European stability depended upon a balancing of power among major states. Following the Newtonian idea of the world as comprised of physical systems that operated according to mechanical laws, the balance of power was seen as a mechanical system: once one state seemed to be gaining preeminent power, others would naturally come together to defeat its ambitions. Each state could, then, legitimately seek to maximize its power without threatening the existence of other major states (also, the independence of less powerful states could legitimately be sacrificed as necessary to the mechanical balancing of major powers). The mastery of space appeared to be a result of natural forces working through individual states. War appeared to be natural, and hence was considered legitimate and legal, insofar as its aim was the rational pursuit of state policy.

This construction of the European order as a space managed by a natural, meaning mechanical, balancing of state power lasted a little more than a century. In the nineteenth century, on the heels of the second industrial revolution—especially the introduction of steam power and the development of factory-based production—the English would assert a new hegemony. Significantly, the space over which the European world order was expanding, and the English were best situated to take advantage of the new situation. Hegemony in the European world order remained the ability to master secular space through the integration of capitalism with territorial state power.

Economy and State / Public and Private

Territoriality and the new imaginary of political space that constituted it broke sharply with the past. They made possible both an intensification of internal consolidation by the state and the modular extension of the state to the rest of the world. In order to understand the different forms the state took in this period, we need to look at the reconstitution of economic life and its relation to the state.

In medieval states, economic accumulation was still largely considered the province of corporate groups, especially the nobility who owned the land, from which the greatest amount of wealth derived, and the bourgeoisie, whose guilds regulated manufacturing and commercial activity in the towns. During the sixteenth and seventeenth centuries, fundamental changes occurred in economic activity and the way it was understood and envisioned. Two developments were crucial.

First, the type of wealth characteristic of the bourgeoisie—that involving manufacturing and trade—became more and more important. Mobile property such as money and the financial instruments necessary for trade, as well as those commodities produced for the local market, accounted for an increasing proportion of the state's wealth. These commercial practices were developed first and most fully in the city-states of northern Italy, as well as the Hanseatic cities on the north coast of Germany, but eventually spread throughout Europe. They spread especially to states such as the Netherlands and England, which depended on long-distance trade because local supplies of important goods, such as wheat, grain, wood, and wine, had been exhausted or had to be imported.

The second development, closely connected to the first, was the general acceptance of the principle of individual ownership of property. Property came to be seen as a right of the individual, not the corporate group, and thus the individual was allowed to buy and sell it at will.

Early modern states attempted to use these new economic conditions of mobile and individual property in policies called "mercantilism" by eighteenth-century economists.[16] The specific ways they did so had much to do with the development of different forms of the state. It should be remembered, however, that an economy based on private property (i.e., capitalism) and the modern state developed together, each intertwined with and required by the other. Only later, at the end of the eighteenth century, would a science of political economy emerge that tried to disentangle them.[17]

Mercantilism assumed that a state's wealth was based on the amount of gold and silver it could accumulate and that the quantity of these precious metals that one monarchy accumulated was an equivalent loss by another. States therefore wanted to colonize lands rich in gold and silver, and export as many manufactured goods as possible. By exporting as much as possible and minimizing imports, states gained what economists call a favorable balance of trade. To make sure that exports exceeded imports, states levied tariffs (i.e., taxes) on imports in order to keep foreign goods out and subsidized the development of domestic industries by granting them monopolies, or by founding the industries themselves.[18]

Such policies created a mercantile sector of the economy that related differently to the rest of the state's economy, depending on the circumstances of the particular state. Two broad types of economic structure can be distinguished.

In certain states the landed nobility continued as the dominant economic power. Most wealth within these states derived from land ownership, which largely remained in the hands of the nobility. The private sector consisted primarily of "petit bourgeoisie," i.e., shopkeepers and small manufacturers engaged in local markets. The portion of the private sector that engaged in long-distance trade and large commercial ventures was small, in part because of the relatively undeveloped financial sector, especially banks.[19] The result was that the revenues generated by the mercantile sector—consisting largely of enterprises created and chartered by the king to control specific aspects of long-distance, colonial trade, especially joint-stock companies, or to engage in large manufacturing enterprises—did not filter through the general economy to generate further growth of the private sector.

In other states, such as England and the Netherlands, a substantial private sector engaged in long-distance trade and large-scale manufacturing, which utilized newly invented machines and the factory system. Indeed, in these states, the private sector now predominated over the landed nobility. Such ventures were facilitated by highly developed financial industries (banking and credit).[20] Joint-stock companies chartered by the state controlled much of the colonial trade, but given the relatively large private commercial sector and the financial industries, its profits were circulated through this sector and fed further growth. This economy created a very different situation for the state than was the case in those states where the landed nobility remained predominant.

Absolutism

The specification of monarchy as the only legitimate form of the state by the Peace of Westphalia encouraged the development of absolutism within the European states-system. The word "absolutism" (from the Latin *absoluta,* meaning unbound) usually refers to rule by an all-powerful, all-embracing monarch who faces no checks or control on his power. The absolute monarch rules his realm directly through a staff of administrative officials whom he has rendered totally dependent upon him. The assembly of estates has been "put to sleep" by the Crown; that is, it has been suppressed and is no longer consulted by the king. Moreover, local entities have been brought under the direct authority of the Crown. Power is exercised without the concurrence of the estates, and the monarch has become absolute territorial sovereign. Monarchical absolutism was generally justified by the theory of "divine right of kings."[21]

Absolutist monarchies as a form of the early modern state are usually counterposed to parliamentary monarchies—that is, to a form of the early modern state in which the estates have won the struggle for power with the Crown and the king's ability to rule his realm on his own has been reduced or eliminated completely. In place of the feudal constitutional order of joint or mixed rule, an assembly embodying the estates, called a "parliament" (from the French verb *parler,* meaning to speak), has defeated the king and become the center of territorial sovereignty.[22] However, we believe that the dichotomy between absolutist monarchies and parliamentary monarchies is a false one. In our view, both are varieties of absolutism.

Recall that the military revolution that took place from the fourteenth to the sixteenth centuries, and transformed the feudal host into the standing army of infantry and artillery, led to the creation of an incipient, centralized governing apparatus and practices realized primarily for the purpose of directly extracting from the realm the men, money, and matériel needed to fight wars.[23] War and preparing for war generated a great struggle in all medieval realms between the Crown, on the one hand, and the estates, on the other. This great struggle evolved in two main directions: one was toward the Crown, which became the absolute territorial sovereign to the exclusion of the estates; the other was toward the estates, which became the absolute territorial sovereign at the expense of the Crown.

Varieties of the Absolutist State

Which of the two institutions, Crown or estates, became the absolute territorial sovereign in a particular emerging territorial state depended on the outcome of the struggle between the two. The outcome of this struggle was conditioned by the contingent "situational factors" of the monarchy in question—factors such as the realm's geographical position with respect to rival monarchies, the starting condition of the realm, the personal strength of individual kings, and the ability of the estates to resist.[24]

The way these situational factors and the starting condition of the realm have influenced the instituting of absolute sovereignty can be seen in the following brief comparative histories of early state formation in England and France. In England, contingent situational factors, such as the insularity of the realm, its small size, its early centralization by conquest, and the importation of feudalism, allowed the estates to win the struggle for absolute territorial sovereignty. In France, on the other hand, contingent situational factors, such as the realm's indigenous feudalism, strong regionalism, and its geographical location near emerging rival kingdoms (especially Spain), allowed the Crown to win the struggle for absolute territorial sovereignty.

England: An Absolutist Parliamentary State

In 1066, William, Duke of Normandy (ruled 1066–1087), invaded England and defeated the Anglo-Saxon king Harold at the Battle of Hastings. William the Conqueror, as he is known, imported feudalism from France.

He distributed among his Norman barons the choicest lands in the kingdom as fiefs. The barons had to supply a certain quota of knights, whom they supported by dividing their fiefs among their vassals. Thus, a feudal hierarchy was imposed, which gave rise to a struggle between the Crown and the baronage as each attempted to increase its power against the other.

William was a strong king who did not hesitate to jail great barons and assert his right to appoint bishops and abbots. To finance his court, he did not hesitate to extract heavy taxes. When William died in 1087, his eldest son inherited Normandy as a separate dukedom, and a younger son, William Rufus, inherited England. Rufus, who was unpopular with the Church because he was satirical and also homosexual, ruled until he was murdered in 1100. He was succeeded by Henry I (ruled 1100–1135), who persuaded the barons to accept him as king provided he would stop the objectionable practices of his brother, which included charging unreasonable taxes and forcing widows to remarry.

Henry restored Normandy to his realm and developed a central administration and an efficient financial system. The kingdom was divided into shires, to each of which he assigned a reeve recruited from the lower ranks of the feudal hierarchy. His shire-reeves, or sheriffs, were made to appear before the barons of the exchequer to pay the revenues they had collected for the king. Henry's heavy-handed rule resulted in a series of revolts by the baronage, which he was able to put down.[25]

When Henry died in 1135, he left no male heir. As a result, a dynastic war broke out among rival claimants to the throne. During the strife, the barons were able to build much local autonomy by promising support to the claimant who offered the most extensive privileges. Thus, when Henry II (ruled 1154–1189) ascended the throne in 1154, the kingdom, which reached from Scotland to the Pyrenees and included half of today's France, had been pulverized and divided into numerous powerful baronies. Henry fought these barons and took away many of the lands and privileges they had gained during the previous fourteen years of turmoil. Henry II's sons, Richard I (ruled 1189–1199) and John (ruled 1199–1216), continued to expand the power of the Crown at the expense of the barons. Richard, the Lion-Heart, was a crusader who taxed his realm to the utmost to pay for his campaigns in the Holy Land. John, who faced high inflation, taxed the realm inordinately for his wars in Scotland, Wales, and Ireland, violated laws, and demanded frequent scutage (payments of money in lieu of military service). John's actions resulted in a baronial revolt. The barons demanded a return to the laws of Henry I, which recognized the rights of the nobility and limited the powers of the Crown. On June 15, 1215, John accepted the demands of the barons and drafted a document called the Magna Carta, sealed at Runnymede, in which he agreed not to levy taxes that had not been approved by an assembly of the barons. After the Magna Carta, the barons gained the upper hand in their struggles with the Crown. They forbade the king's sheriffs from entering their lands, took possession of his courts, and usurped the powers of his local administrators.[26] Rather than being a victory for the liberty of the common people, as it is often claimed today, the Magna Carta was actually a victory for England's powerful barons.

Henry III (ruled 1216–1272), who needed money and troops, expanded the Great Council to include two knights from the shires, two leading citizens from the cities and towns, and the clergy. He consulted this "Model Parliament"—which was divided into two chambers, the House of Lords and the House of Commons—when he levied taxes, especially for fighting wars. The financial exigencies of fighting wars strengthened Parliament rather than the king, however, because it was able to exchange approval of tax requests for extensions of parliamentary rights and privileges. The power of Parliament was strengthened greatly during the Hundred Years' War (1337–1453) by granting the king's request for money to fight the French king over conflicting dynastic claims in exchange for the right to meet regularly, to control royal ministers, and to examine the Crown's accounts.[27]

The wars against the Irish, Welsh, and Scots extended the territorial boundaries of the English monarchy and had an important influence on the military defense of the realm. As with medieval monarchies elsewhere, the feudal host of heavy cavalry was the core of the king's army. However, wars against the Welsh and Scots, who were able to defeat mounted cavalry thanks to rough terrain and guerrilla tactics, encouraged the English to incorporate more foot soldiers into their armies. These foot soldiers were recruited by the barons, under whose control they remained as local militias. This meant that the English Crown was not able to build a strong army under its direct control. Moreover, the Crown had come to depend upon Parliament for the money to fight wars. The lack of a centrally controlled standing army was not a problem, however, for the survival of the realm because England was an island kingdom and was not directly threatened by the increasingly centralized and powerful monarchies on the Continent. What efforts the Crown made to strengthen its military capacity went into the navy, upon which it came to rely to defend the realm.[28]

During the reign of Henry VIII (ruled 1509–1547), the Crown sought to strengthen itself by forming an alliance with the landed gentry, a group of farmers below the nobility who were becoming rich thanks to the gradual commercialization of English agriculture. Henry regularly sought approval for his taxes and his policies, one of the most important being the reformation of the Catholic Church in England. Henry separated the English Church from Rome, made himself its head, and confiscated the property and lands of the great monasteries and convents. During this period, the House of Commons became the focus of the gentry's power.

Despite increasing military involvement in wars with other centralizing monarchies, especially France and Spain, the English Crown did not become absolute during the reigns of the two strongest rulers of the House of Tudor, Henry VIII and his daughter, Elizabeth I (ruled 1558–1603). Parliament remained a force to be reckoned with. No large standing army was created. To a great extent, the ranks of England's army were filled with mercenaries and freebooters, who were demobilized and sent home at the end of a war. Emphasis was placed on the navy, which was, in large part, composed of privateers—that is, ships belonging to private owners authorized by the Crown to conduct hostilities in its name.[29]

The Crown's wars were paid for, in part, by selling Crown lands, confiscating Church property, and borrowing money abroad. Additional money came from taxes granted by Parliament. Parliament became a steady source of revenue for the Crown. Thus warmaking, even during the period of strong Tudor monarchs, was conducted within the limitations of England's feudal constitutionalism. Moreover, a small standing army and reliance on privateers for a navy meant that the English Crown did not need a large, centralized bureaucratic apparatus of direct rule. Parliament was strengthened by granting the Crown the money it requested in exchange for the recognition that certain forms of taxation were illegal.[30]

Eventually, Parliament became so strong as an independent institution that it was itself able to go to war against the Crown. This war, known as the English Civil War (1642–1648), was precipitated by a breakdown of the agreement between king and Parliament concerning taxation. Charles I (ruled 1625–1649) needed money to put down rebellions in Scotland and Ireland, which Parliament was unwilling to grant. Charles imposed taxes to pay for his military campaigns without Parliament's consent. Parliament responded with the Petition of Right (1628), which restated its traditional right to be consulted. Charles answered by dissolving Parliament and attempting to rule alone; Parliament then took up arms against the Crown. The king's army was small, poorly equipped, and irregularly paid. Moreover, Charles did not have an administrative structure through which he could extract the financial and human resources to support his army. He had to rely, instead, upon donations from wealthy supporters and proceeds from the sale of land seized from the supporters of Parliament. Parliament's army was also small, but it was well supported by funds raised from the sale of confiscated royal property as well as forcibly collected taxes. Owing to its superior ability to raise revenues necessary to support the army, Parliament won the war and abolished the monarchy. Charles was beheaded in 1649, and England became a republic.[31]

After the war, the unity of the Parliamentarians collapsed into factionalism and backstabbing, which ushered in the rule of Oliver Cromwell (ruled 1649–1660). During the Protectorate, as Cromwell's rule is called, Parliament continued to sit and exercise its right to approve war subsidies, however. Despite disagreements with Parliament, Cromwell was committed to it as an institution and to the concept of the gentry's representation.

The Protectorate was unstable, and in 1660 the monarchy was restored. When Charles II (ruled 1660–1685) of Scotland became king, he attempted to circumvent Parliament. Cromwell's "New Model Army" was demobilized, leaving only a small force. Charles was succeeded by his brother James II (ruled 1685–1688), a dedicated absolutist, who also attempted to rule without Parliament by relying on loans, increased customs revenues, and the taxation of religious dissidents—in other words, by relying more and more heavily on the wealth generated by the private sector. This continued to increase the power of the bourgeoisie and to limit the power of the monarchy. The result was a strengthened Parliament.

James was opposed by Parliament and driven into exile. A new dynasty was founded when Parliament installed William III (ruled 1688–1702), of the Dutch House of Orange, on the throne. In the Act of Settlement (1689), William accepted the crown on terms set by Parliament. The ouster of James II and the installation of William, which is known as the Glorious Revolution (1688–1689), demonstrated the absolute power of Parliament and the utter futility of any monarch's challenging its authority. Parliament had become without question the sovereign of the emergent modern English state. Over the next two centuries, the power of the Crown continued to decline and that of Parliament to increase, so that by the eighteenth century absolute sovereign power had been completely acquired by Parliament.[32]

France: An Absolutist Monarchical State

When Hugues Capet (ruled 987–996) was chosen to be the king of West Francia, that portion of Charlemagne's empire that had been ruled by his son Louis, the entire kingdom, except for a small royal demesne called the Île-de-France around Paris, was in the hands of six great barons: the count of Flanders, the duke of Normandy, the duke of France, the duke of Burgundy, the duke of Aquitaine, and the count of Toulouse. The new king's power was severely limited by these powerful barons.[33] Although early Capetian kings, such as Philippe I (ruled 1060–1108) and Louis VI (ruled 1108–1137), increased the size of the royal patrimony, the kingdom remained for the next two centuries a loose aggregation of baronies protected by feudal limitations on the king's power.

Philippe II (ruled 1180–1223) was the first of four late Capetian kings who centralized and expanded royal power. He reconquered Normandy from the English Crown in 1204 and later annexed Brittany, Anjou, Maine, Touraine, and Poitou to his directly ruled domain. Philippe supervised local courts and made alliances with the bourgeoisie against the nobility. Many towns were given charters, and trade was encouraged by granting privileges to merchants.[34]

Philippe's son, Louis VIII (ruled 1223–1226), gained portions of Aquitaine and Languedoc. His son, Louis IX (ruled 1226–1285), also known as St. Louis, did not extend the Crown's territory but centralized its power. Although he respected the rights and privileges of the nobility, Louis did not tolerate feudal infringements on royal authority. He suspended the baronial courts and replaced them with his own and gradually established a common law for the realm. The third powerful king, Philippe IV (ruled 1285–1314), extended the boundaries of his kingdom to the Atlantic in the west, the Pyrenees and Mediterranean in the south, the Alps in the east, and the Rhine in the north; this established the present territorial dimensions of the contemporary French state.

Initially, the administration of the kingdom was simple. Officials of the king's household managed the affairs of the realm. The steward had general supervision over the demesne. The king's constable and marshal, who cared for his horses, commanded his knights in battle. Since the time of Hugues Capet, royal lands were looked after by officials called *prévôts*, who collected revenues, performed judicial functions, and maintained peace. As the kingdom expanded it was divided into bailiwicks and a *bailli* (bailiff) was assigned to each. The baillis, who represented the royal presence, controlled various prévôts, sat as judges, and carried out police functions. Prévôts and baillis were recruited from the lower nobility and bourgeoisie. The French monarchy continued to centralize under Philippe IV's descendants, and by the beginning of the fifteenth century it had an extensive administrative system in place supported by a regular tax called the *taille*.[35]

Like other medieval monarchs, Philippe convoked an expanded *curia regis* (royal court) called the Estates General (in medieval fashion, this was composed of clergy, nobility, and bourgeoisie) that gave advice on major decisions affecting the realm and approval for the taxes he levied. Unlike the English Parliament, however, the Estates General did not evolve into a strong institution capable of resisting the demands of the king. It was convoked only when the king wished for it to meet, and usually only during an emergency. Because each estate met separately in Paris and Toulouse, the Estates General was easily manipulated by the king's lawyers. Using his own administrators, the king was easily able to bypass the Estates General and forge direct links with the *pays d'états,* or local assemblies. Later, the

Crown was able to destroy these local centers of power and replace them with its own centralized, bureaucratic apparatus to extract resources in order to make war and maintain a large standing army.

French kings continued to rely on the feudal host for military defense long after the superiority of the infantry had been demonstrated. Disastrous defeats of French cavalry during major battles of the Hundred Years' War at Crécy (1346), Poitiers (1356), and Agincourt (1415), where six thousand French knights were annihilated by a small English force armed with long-bows and pikes, did not bring about military modernization. After watching English armies march across France and defeat French knights during the Hundred Years' War, the French Crown decided to modernize its military. In 1439, the Ordonnance sur la Gendarmerie created a regular military force composed of cavalry, artillery, and infantry units armed with long-bows. Although this initiative gave the Crown a stronger and more reliable military force, discipline and training were lacking. In order to pay for these units, which were garrisoned and supplied locally, the Crown levied a uniform tax without the approval of the *pays d'états*. The uproar that result-ed forced the king to negotiate a series of complicated taxes with each *pays d'états*. Although some early French kings occasionally resorted to raising taxes without the consent of the *pays d'état,* at no point in the early history of the French state was the power of the *pays d'états* destroyed.[36]

This situation began to change during the reign of Louis XIII (ruled 1610–1643). Louis's finance minister, Cardinal Richelieu (1585–1642), realized that the armed forces were the backbone of the king's power within the realm and beyond. In 1626, he ordered the destruction of all private fortresses and forbade the construction of fortified private dwellings. In that same year, he created a standing army of twenty thousand soldiers under a disciplined chain of command and with regularized pay, uniforms, arms, and quarters provided by the king. Richelieu also created a royal navy of thirty ships, fortified French harbors, and established arsenals. In order to support the army and navy, both of which rapidly grew in size, Richelieu reorganized the bureaucracy and imposed stringent taxes. These taxes were directly collected by thousands of administrative agents, called *intendants,* who were loyal solely to the Crown. The intendants supervised local administration, finance, justice, law enforcement, and the conscrip-tion of troops. These measures, and even more stringent ones applied by Richelieu's successor as finance minister, Cardinal Mazarin (1602–1661), taken in order to fight a war against the Spanish Habsburgs, resulted in a rebellion of the nobility, known as the Fronde (1648–1653). The Frondeurs sought to restore feudal rights and privileges against the Crown, but were crushed.[37]

The policies of Richelieu and Mazarin allowed Louis XIV (ruled 1643–1715) to establish monarchical absolutism in France. Louis, who believed that he had been ordained by God to rule France with absolute power, centralized all the functions of government at his palace at Versailles. He personally chaired the meetings of the councils that managed provincial affairs, taxation, expenditures, and major policies, and involved himself in every detail and decision. Louis XIV became known as the "Sun King," around whom the realm revolved. In 1661, the supreme practitioner of mercantilism, Jean Baptiste Colbert (1619–1683), became minister of finance and proceeded to organize the entire economy of France to serve the state, and especially its industrial sector. He issued detailed standards for manufacturing, established new industries protected by tariffs, and created state monopolies financed at public expense. He provided scientific and technical education, kept wages low, abolished all internal tariffs, improved France's network of roads and canals, and expanded the navy to protect French commercial interests abroad. Under Louis's minister of war, the Marquis de Louvois (1641–1691), the army was expanded to well over a hundred thousand well-disciplined men equipped with the latest weapons.[38]

French monarchs ignored the Estates General after 1440 and eventually abandoned the policy of frequent convocations. From 1484 until 1560, the Estates General did not meet. In the words of one scholar, "After having battled over three centuries to achieve . . . sovereignty vis-à-vis foreign and domestic rivals, by the late 1400s the kings of France were not prepared to share that sovereignty with the Estates General."[39] The Estates General stopped being called in 1614. The Crown had centralized itself sufficiently by that time and no longer needed the consent of the Estates General for the extraction of revenue. Thus the monarchy excluded the estates of the realm from any role in governing the kingdom. The nobility had been rendered useless and the rising bourgeoisie of industrialists, merchants, and professionals were cut off from any significant involvement in the affairs of the realm. The Crown had become beyond all question the embodiment of absolute sovereignty in the early modern French state.

Summary

The early territorial state, developing roughly from the late sixteenth through the eighteenth centuries, pioneered a political organization based on a new understanding of sovereignty. Fundamental ideas of a unified, indivisible state ruling over people within a given territory emerged and took shape. Economies came to be envisioned as spaces within states in which wealth is produced, and wealth became the object of state control in order to build large armies and, in some cases, navies. Contingent situational factors encouraged the institution of the sovereign as either an absolutist parliament or an absolutist monarchy within the European states-system, the latter being, by far, the most prevalent.

Notes

1. On the importance of the Protestant revolt for the rise of the current global order of sovereign states, see Daniel Philpott, *Revolutions in Sovereignty: How Ideas Shaped Modern International Relations* (Princeton, NJ: Princeton University Press, 2001).
2. Alexander B. Murphy, "The Sovereign State System as Political-Territorial Ideal: Historical and Contemporary Considerations," in Thomas J. Biersteker and Cynthia Weber (eds.), *State Sovereignty as Social Construct* (Cambridge: Cambridge University Press, 1996): 86.
3. Ibid., 91.
4. On modern diplomacy as a new form of estrangement, refiguring the idea of who the political "other" and enemy was as a state, see James Der Derian, *On Diplomacy* (London: Basil Blackwell, 1987).
5. Ernst H. Kantorowicz, *The King's Two Bodies: A Study in Medieval Political Theology* (Princeton, NJ: Princeton University Press, 1957).
6. Thomas Hobbes, *Leviathan,* ed. Richard Tuck (Cambridge: Cambridge University Press, 1991), 89.
7. Ibid., 120.
8. Ibid., 9.
9. Ibid., 120.
10. For an account of this in England, see Neil McKendrick, John Brewer, and J. H. Plumb, *The Birth of a Consumer Society: The Commercialization of Eighteenth-Century England* (Bloomington: Indiana University Press, 1985).
11. There is now a large literature on the development of the distinction between a public and private sphere in the seventeenth and eighteenth centuries. See especially Carole Pateman, "The Fraternal Social Contract," in *The Disorder of Women* (Stanford, CA: Stanford University Press, 1989); Jean Bethke Elshtain, *Public Man, Private Woman* (Princeton, NJ: Princeton University Press, 1981), chapter 3.
12. This section owes much to Benedict Anderson, *Imagined Communities,* rev. ed. (London and New York: Verso Press, 1991), and Henri Lefebvre, *The Production of Space,* trans. Donald Nicholson-Smith (Oxford: Basil Blackwell, 1991).
13. For a discussion of the continuing influence of republicanism on international relations, see Nicholas Onuf, *City of Sovereigns: Republican Themes in International Thought* (Cambridge: Cambridge University Press, 1998).
14. On the importance of surveillance and pacification to the spatial construction of sovereignty, see Anthony Giddens, *The Nation State and Violence* (Berkeley and Los Angeles: University of California Press, 1985).
15. See Alfred W. Crosby, *The Measure of Reality: Quantification and Western Society, 1250–1600* (Cambridge: Cambridge University Press, 1997).
16. It should be remembered that this term was originally a pejorative one coined by advocates of free trade in the latter half of the eighteenth century.
17. This argument is made convincingly with respect to property rights, the state, and the states-system by Kurt Burch, "The 'Properties' of the State System

and Global Capitalism," in Stephen J. Rosow, Naeem Inayatullah, and Mark Rupert (eds.), *The Global Economy as Political Space* (Boulder, CO: Lynne Rienner Publishers, 1994): 37–59.

18. On mercantilism see Fernand Braudel, *The Wheels of Commerce: Civilization and Capitalism 15th–18th Century*, vol. 2 (New York: Harper & Row, 1979), 542 ff. Also see Benjamin J. Cohen, *The Question of Imperialism* (New York: Basic Books, 1973).

19. See John U. Nef, *Industry and Government in France and England, 1540–1640* (Ithaca, NY: Cornell University Press, 1964).

20. For the case of the Netherlands, see Violet Barbour, *Capitalism in Amsterdam in the 17th Century* (Ann Arbor, MI: University of Michigan Press, 1963).

21. Emile Lousse, "Absolutism," in Heinz Lubasz (ed.), *The Development of the Modern State* (New York: Macmillan, 1964): 43–48.

22. On the parliamentary state, see David Judge, *The Parliamentary State* (London/Newbury Park/New Delhi: Sage Publications, 1993).

23. See Charles Tilly, *Coercion, Capital, and European States*, A.D. *990–1990* (Cambridge, MA: Basil Blackwell, 1990).

24. This idea of "situational factors" influencing state trajectories was first articulated by the German scholar Otto Hintze at the turn of the nineteenth century. See his lecture "Military Organization and the Organization of the State," in Felix Gilbert (ed.), *The Historical Essays of Otto Hintze* (New York: Oxford University Press, 1975). Its most recent iteration is in Brian Downing, *The Military Revolution and Political Change: Origins of Democracy and Autocracy in Early Modern Europe* (Princeton, NJ: Princeton University Press, 1992), and Thomas Ertman, *Birth of the Leviathan: Building States and Regimes in Medieval and Early Modern Europe* (Cambridge:Cambridge University Press, 1997).

25. Otto Hintze, "The Emergence of the Democratic Nation-State," in Heinz Lubasz (ed.), *The Development of the Modern State* (New York: Macmillan, 1964): 65–71.

26. Sidney Painter, *The Rise of the Feudal Monarchies* (Ithaca, NY: Cornell University Press, (1951), chapter 2.

27. Ertman, *Birth of the Leviathan,* 167.

28. Bruce D. Porter, *War and the Rise of the State: The Military Foundations of Modern Politics* (New York: The Free Press, 1994), 79–83.

29. Janice E. Thompson, *Mercenaries, Pirates and Sovereigns: State-Building and Extraterritorial Violence in Early Modern Europe* (Princeton, NJ: Princeton University Press, 1994), chapter 2.

30. Downing, *The Military Revolution,* chapter 2.

31. Carl J. Friedrich and Charles Blitzer, *The Age of Power* (Ithaca, NY: Cornell University Press, 1957), chapter 6.

32. Norman Davies, *Europe. A History* (Oxford and New York: Oxford University Press, 1996), 631.

33. Painter, *The Rise of the Feudal Monarchies,* chapter 1.

34. Hendrick Spruyt, *The Sovereign State and Its Competitors* (Princeton, NJ: Princeton University Press, 1994), chapter 5.

35. Ibid.

36. Downing, *The Military Revolution,* chapter 5.

37. Friedrich and Blitzer, *The Age of Power,* chapter 5.

38. Ibid.

39. Ertman, *Birth of the Leviathan,* 93.

5

The Liberal Constitutional State: Sovereignty Popularized

From the sixteenth century, states in Europe came to take for granted that their survival depended on absolute control over a bounded, territorial space. Sovereignty was imagined as the unifying "soul" inscribed on the landscape and population within the state's territory, which was protected, and extended, by a large military and industrializing economy under the control of the absolute sovereign, whether crown or parliament.

In order to institute sovereignty, territory had to be conquered and pacified and local nobles and other independent sources of politico-military power, such as cities and towns, had to be brought into the centralizing orbit. Absolutist monarchical states, then, inscribed sovereignty on the territories they ruled through the grid of bureaucratic and administrative units that linked local jurisdictions to the central monarchy. In states in which the parliament emerged as absolute sovereign, the struggle to institute territorial sovereignty focused more on the juridical, legalistic struggles over forms of property rights. Although these states also developed bureaucracies, including a military, in order to link the local to the central state, this institutional grid meant something different for state sovereignty. Facing a different configuration of social power in which the state much earlier came to depend on the bourgeoisie for its revenue and was forced into compromises with it, parliamentary states eventually subordinated the state apparatus and crown to a parliament or similar governing body.

In the eighteenth and nineteenth centuries, developments in capitalism and reactions to absolutism (both in absolutist monarchies and absolutist parliamentary states) combined to produce a new imaginary of sovereignty and a new form of the state. We call this new formation the "liberal constitutional state," at the center of which is a new imaginary of sovereignty as inhering in the people. The focus of this chapter is on the way liberal states arose out of the dilemmas faced by early modern states, especially the dilemma of procuring the resources needed to make war and managing the expanding capitalist economy while maintaining the legitimacy of state power.

The Paradox of Popular Sovereignty

As the modern state came to be more highly developed, the problematic of instituting sovereignty shifted. Sovereignty came to be seen as inhering in the population of a territory, and not in the ruler (the king) or ruling assembly (parliament). This new imaginary of sovereignty, which came to be called "popular sovereignty," had roots in the republican theories of the Renaissance, especially those of Machiavelli, which described the common good of the state as the necessary outcome of political power. In seventeenth-century England, the republican idea of the common good was combined with, and transformed by, arguments that individual subjects had a prior right to private property. This led to the association of the interests of the state with the protection and furtherance of the property of its subjects.[1]

Sovereignty could be represented as "popular," that is, as inhering in the population of the state, in two primary ways. One was as a possession of the people, as a utility, a tool for the protection of their property and their private lives. This was the idea enacted by the Glorious Revolution (1689) in England. The other representation of popular sovereignty was as the expression of the collective, or general, will of the people. This was the idea formulated most clearly by the eighteenth-century French-speaking Swiss philosopher Jean-Jacques Rousseau (1712–1778), whose ideas would influence the French Revolution. The American Revolution would oscillate between both, and come to rest in the Constitution of 1789 with the former, more conservative version.[2] In both cases the meaning of the state's population shifted from being an object of administration by the state apparatus to being an almost organic entity endowed with a separate being and will of its own.

Both versions of popular sovereignty positioned the sovereign as protector of a separate private sphere consisting of the market economy and the sphere of private conscience. Therefore, both were inseparable from the gendered structure of individualist and capitalist societies. In the imaginary of popular sovereignty, the state was conceived as a creation of a preexistent people either as its useful property or as its expression. The "people" was constituted as prior to the state primarily via two processes and institutions: the economy, in which private property was produced, and the family, in which the rational individuals who authorized the sovereign were nurtured. Both were by law and custom the preserves of men, as we discussed in the previous chapter. Owning and managing private property were considered male pursuits. Innovation and competition were thought to require physical and mental toughness, attributes coded as masculine. The world of private property was opposed to a sphere of love, nurturing, and tenderness in the family, a sphere associated with the feminine.

States based on an imaginary of popular sovereignty continued to perform those functions performed by the early territorial states. Armies needed to be raised. Class conflicts between the bourgeoisie and landed nobility, and increasingly between the bourgeoisie and the working class (i.e., the class of laborers dependent on wages), needed to be mediated. States based on popular sovereignty remained dependent on their ability to impose taxes, put tariffs on imports, and otherwise extract economic resources to make war.[3]

States based on the idea of popular sovereignty developed an idea of politics as police power to regulate the population and maintain order. Police power was needed to regulate the working classes and those caught in the often painful and unsettling transition from rural peasant to wage laborer. Police power also kept the inequalities of the capitalist economy from erupting into open social conflict. The "science of the police," as political science was often called during the eighteenth century, encompassed the regulation of the social habits of the population to ensure that people conformed to the model of the rational individual, necessary to the functioning of the private property economy and the private family. Maintaining order meant not only doing what the bourgeoisie expressly considered to be in its economic interests, but also the state's intervening in the direction of everyday life to ensure those social habits of behavior that would lead to civil and economic order.

In short, the institution of sovereignty as popular sovereignty created a new realm of individual freedom that weakened the absolutist state in favor of the individual, while paradoxically subjecting the individual to new forms of power, exercised by the state and others and aimed at molding and regulating public behavior. Behavior came to be watched, catalogued, measured, anticipated, calculated, and managed.[4] Rather than weakening the state to the point of near disappearance, the interpenetration of capitalism and the state and the new imaginary of popular sovereignty made possible the expansion of state power, although in new forms.

Liberal Constitutionalism

From the late seventeenth century, attempts to reform the absolutist state to make it protective of private-property rights and responsive to the freedom of individuals to pursue profit in the market became popular, both among intellectuals and the bourgeoisie. By the nineteenth century, this reformist movement would be called "liberalism," and its defenders would be called "liberals," a term first used to refer to the party of the bourgeoisie in early nineteenth-century Spain. By the middle of the century, it had spread throughout Europe, becoming a name adopted by major bourgeois political parties.[5]

Liberal ideas circulated not through religious channels or through official state-sanctioned media, but through the new commercial markets of civil society, primarily in the political pamphlets and books made possible by combining the technology of the printing press with the increasing wealth of the middle class. Public opinion was created by the emerging newspapers and magazines, such as *The Spectator* and *The Tattler,* published by two English liberals, Joseph Addison (1672–1719) and Richard Steele (1672–1729). On the European continent, especially, liberal ideas circulated through the coffeehouses, salons, and Masonic lodges frequented by the middle class and in the scientific associations in which intellectuals published and otherwise circulated their writings. The most important of these was the initiative in France of the *Encyclopedia,* a massive publishing project under the direction of the French philosopher and intellectual Denis Diderot (1713–1784), which brought together in a unified set of volumes all the latest knowledge of natural and human sciences. In some places (the German states and Scotland, for example), universities played an important role in developing and spreading liberal ideas.[6]

Liberalism developed in opposition to dogmatic religion, arguing that all forms of knowing, including religious knowledge, should be subjected to rational (i.e., reasoned) forms of discussion and debate. To be a "subject"—increasingly used to refer to individuals not only in a political but also in a moral sense—was to be an agent who acted rationally. Liberals set out self-consciously to reform the state so that it would support the private world of the individual in civil society, which they understood as the voluntary social interactions and organizations of rational individuals. They did so not only for economic reasons but for moral reasons as well. In Enlightenment liberalism, the economic and moral were intertwined. Liberalism developed a distinctive form of ideology that accepted the state only insofar as it could be justified by a rational discourse appealing to universal standards of human nature and justice.

By positing a universal rational knowledge as the basis of truth, liberalism solved one of the most vexing problems of the early modern territorial state: that is, how to make war and effectively exercise power, yet, at the same time, maintain the willingness of the people to provide the state with the necessary human and economic resources to do so. In return for subordinating the individual to the rules of a reason that would maximize productivity and social wealth, which the state could then appropriate for its military and other purposes, the state would be subordinated to the universal laws of reason that would limit its power. In this way, liberalism, by promoting an ideology based on universal principles, made room within the sovereign state for capitalism and civil society, and for state sovereignty within capitalism and civil society.

To see how liberalism and the liberal state emerged out of the absolutist state, it is necessary to look briefly at the relation between politics and morality. During the religious wars of the seventeenth century, absolutist monarchies sought to resolve moral conflicts politically—that is, by distinguishing morals from politics and subordinating the former, especially in the form of religious beliefs, to the latter by granting to the state the power to compel moral behavior and religious belief. As we have seen, the creation of the states-system after the Peace of Westphalia depended upon this relation of morals to politics. The state and the states-system followed the same philosophical logic. Although morality was considered a matter for the individual subject's conscience (i.e., his or her inward belief), the absolutist state compelled that inward belief in the name of an established religion.[7] Public order was the supreme good, and private conscience and religious morality were to be subordinated to it.[8]

Against absolutism, the philosopher and political writer John Locke (1632–1704), in his *Letter on Toleration* (1689), articulated a position that would later come to define liberalism. In this pamphlet, Locke accepted the idea that morals are a matter of individual conscience and that they should be determined by reason and not by custom, nature, or political power. Counter to the logic of the absolutist state, Locke wrote that toleration is a universal good that states should accept and that should guide their acceptance of the rule of law. Locke's point was that the state, rather than reigning supreme over the individual conscience, as the absolutist would argue, should be subordinated to the universal principles of reason that govern the private conscience.[9]

Religion, Locke argued, should not dictate laws for the state, which exists in Locke's view "for the procuring, preserving, and advancing" of the individual's "life, liberty, health and indolence of body; and the possession of outward things, such as money, lands, houses, furniture, and the like."[10] Neither should the magistrates of the state "forbid the preaching or professing of any speculative opinions in any church, because they have no manner of relation to the civil rights of the subjects."[11]

The Liberal State as a Rights-Based State

By subordinating the territorial state to universal principles derived by reason, individual subjects and the civil society they circulated in came to be seen as existing independently of and *prior to* the state. This meant that subjects came to be seen in the liberal state as bearers of certain rights, which accrued to them as autonomous individuals. To justify this, many liberal thinkers drew initially on the tradition of natural rights, as when the drafters of the U.S. constitution argued that all individuals were endowed by "their Creator" with "inalienable rights to life, liberty and the pursuit of happiness." Specifically, two rights, which Locke alluded to in his *Letter on Toleration*, were most important to liberals: the right to private property and the right to be protected from arbitrary and unfair treatment by the state. Each of these requires brief mention.

The general right to private property entailed, first, the right to secure possession of one's belongings, which was based on the belief that individuals had a natural right to choose how they wanted to live their lives by selecting their own occupation, religion, associates, leisure-time activities, and so forth. Second, it entailed the right to private property, which included the right to alienate one's possessions, that is, to be able to buy and sell property at will. Third, the general right to private property entailed the right to accumulate as much wealth as one wished, so long as one did so through buying and selling or other legal activities.

In effect, natural rights supported a capitalist market society, that is, a society in which the economic market is paramount. Adam Smith (1723–1790), the Scottish philosopher and political economist, developed the theory of the market and its implications in his book *The Wealth of Nations* (1776). In this work, Smith introduced the idea that the market was self-regulating. Smith's liberalism is based on the assumption that human beings are rational creatures who should be permitted to develop their inherent capacities to the fullest. Moreover, he assumed that all are born with "the propensity to truck, barter, and exchange one thing for another."[12] All barriers to the individual's inherent ability to achieve his or her capacities must be removed. Doing so would encourage people to act according to reason, and subordinate their passions by subjecting them to the rule of rational self-interest. In *The Wealth of Nations,* Smith argued that the economic restrictions of mercantilism retarded economic growth and with it the general welfare of the subjects because it restricted individual economic freedom.

Smith argued that an economy free of state interference and monopoly would produce prosperity efficiently if the law of supply and demand were allowed to operate unfettered by state controls. Efficient producers would prosper and inefficient ones would fail. He believed that the "unseen hand" of the market, that is, the rational calculations of a myriad of individual consumers making their buying decisions based on economic self-interest, would automatically produce economic growth and prosperity for all. This presumed harmony of interests extended to the international economy, which Smith did not explicitly distinguish from the domestic economy, although nineteenth- and twentieth-century liberals would. If states were left free to trade without any tariff barriers, everyone subject to the world capitalist economy would benefit and a general peace would prevail among states. Or so liberals argued.

The liberal state, then, is in one respect a "minimal" state; that is, it is deliberately structured not to be itself a threat to the "natural right" of property ownership, which is the ultimate justification for the dominant position of the bourgeoisie within the state. Participation is restricted by property-owning requirements to eliminate a threat to the bourgeoisie's control of the state from economically less advantaged groups from below.[13]

The second right that liberals considered inalienable was the right to protection from arbitrary and capricious treatment by the state. Being free of the arbitrary and capricious state power characteristic of the absolutist states meant first and foremost the application of the principle of the rule of law. The theory that a state was legitimate only when it was subordinated to the rule of law, and not the rule of men unrestrained by law, went back to the ancient Greek and Roman idea of a republic. For Greek political philosophers such as Aristotle and Plato, and for the Roman statesman and philosopher Cicero, states were to be ruled by the laws made by citizens. The rule of law for them was justified because citizens themselves made the law. The aim of politics was to ensure that those citizens who were best able to make the laws actually ruled, although republican philosophers differed on how this condition could best be met. This idea was revived by the civic republican tradition in the Renaissance, whose most famous theorist was Machiavelli (see Chapter 3).

In the civic republican tradition, the rule of law was grounded in the idea of the public good. That is, the rule of law was justified because it served the public benefit, and any state that did not respect the rule of law would, in the long run, work against the public good and lead itself to a general decline. States governed according to the rule of law, this tradition believed, would be secure, prosperous, and less inclined to factionalism, civil war, and general violence than states in which rulers could impose a personal and arbitrary authority. This republican tradition provided considerable ammunition in the struggle against the absolutist state.

Liberalism defended the rule of law, but did so on different grounds. It supported the rule of law because it would protect citizens best from arbitrary and capricious personal rule and leave individuals the most freedom to pursue their own private lives and, especially, to trade and accumulate wealth and property. That is, liberalism grounded the rule of law negatively: the law should rule not because it promotes the public good but because it allows individuals the greatest freedom by protecting their private interests.

Liberals recognized that the law might itself treat individuals unequally or might contradict some of their rights; to prevent this, liberalism committed to the equal treatment of individual subjects. Liberals reduced all subjects to a common denominator, an abstract concept of the person that eliminated his or her particular differences, the so-called "abstract individual." To liberals, being protected from arbitrary and capricious power and authority meant that the state had to treat all individuals as essentially the same. That is, no natural attributes of birth, such as social class, sex, or race, should matter in the way individuals were treated. Much of liberal political theory during the twentieth century has been concerned with defining these extralegal principles on which the rule of law is seen to rest.

Liberal Constitutionalism

Liberals believed that the best way to preserve individual rights and establish the rule of law was to limit the state by a constitution. Two forms of constitutionalism appeared among liberals. One was based on the doctrine of the "ancient" constitution, which maintained that there were certain legal principles that had been established over a long period of time, many centuries, that could be deduced from the history and customary law of a people. The most famous proponent of this notion of constitutionalism was the "conservative" English thinker and politician Edmund Burke (1729–1797), who famously argued that the English constitution was the manifestation of an ancient partnership between the dead, the living, and generations not yet born. He saw the English constitution as the embodiment of the English people down through the ages. Ancient constitutionalism referred to the constitutionalism of the medieval period when monarchs were not absolute, their power being limited by the complex web of feudal duties and obligations that compelled them to exercise politico-military rule jointly with the estates of the realm. Liberals who believed in ancient constitutionalism fought for a limited or constitutional monarchy. In his book *Reflections on the Revolution in France* (1790), Burke defended the principle of limited monarchy against the excesses of the French Revolution and the English monarchy in particular as the epitome of this form of politico-military rule.

The other form of constitutionalism was based on the doctrine of the written constitution drafted by the people. This form of constitutionalism, unlike ancient constitutionalism that relies on historical, mystical, or religious beliefs, is based on rational, moral, and philosophical arguments. Liberals of this persuasion believed that all human beings possessed the capacity to reason and could, therefore, acertain the unchanging moral order of the universe ordained by God, which was manifested in natural law. They argued that rational human beings could contemplate natural law and discern for themselves that they possessed rights based on their common humanity exclusive of their particular social and political situation.

John Locke, who, as we saw above, argued that rational human beings are autonomous creatures capable of making informed choices and acting responsibly, was the most famous proponent of this view. He argued that the state should be restricted to regulating the general conditions under which rights-bearing, independent, rational individuals could exercise their power to make informed economic, social, and political choices with the minimum of restrictions. To create such conditions, the state had to be limited by a written constitution that divided its politico-military power among three separate branches of government (legislative, executive, and judicial) and elevated the concept of individual rights above those of the state. Such a constitution was seen as a contract between a preexisting people living in a state of nature and the state, and which could be broken if the state exceeded its authority and began to violate individual rights. In this conception of liberal constitutionalism, no individual is obliged to obey the state unless he or she has consented personally to its authority.

Liberalism and Democracy

It should be noted that liberals were not, at first, democrats in the modern sense of that word.[14] Liberals came to accept democracy only reluctantly, because it was the best way to protect individual liberty from the growing power of the state.[15] This was the argument of utilitarians such as Jeremy Bentham (1748–1832) and James Mill (1773–1836). For these liberals, the state was needed to maintain order and defense, as John Locke had argued, and in general to promote a condition of "the greatest happiness of the greatest number," the main principle of utilitarian philosophy. Utilitarians did not argue against the state, but for a state in which reason, in the sense of the efficient matching of means to ends, ruled. This sort of state would continue to exercise considerable power, especially police and military power, and would continue to promote a rational society, especially by providing education for all, even if it had limited power to regulate economic activity.

In his *Essay On Government* (1820), James Mill averred that the main end of politics was to permit people to become rational and mature individuals. This can be done, he argued, only when they are able to make decisions that affect their own lives. Even though a wise and benevolent absolute ruler might make better decisions than individuals could make for themselves, a limited representative state would be better, he argued, because individuals would be responsible for their own mistakes. Therefore, some form of representative state would be better than an absolute monarchy, even a benevolent one.

The liberal idea of democracy, or "liberal constitutional democracy" as it has come to be called, advocates democracy not as a value in itself but as a way of checking the power of the state while subjecting it to rational debate among citizens. The most powerful defense of liberty of thought and discussion can be found in John Stuart Mill's (1806–1873) essay *On*

Liberty (1859). In this essay, Mill, who was James Mill's son, argued that the real threat to liberty came from irrational citizens who unquestioningly followed social norms and prejudices. A rational and well-educated public was the best guarantee against the state's becoming too powerful and violating individual rights. Indeed, when Mill did advocate a universal franchise in his *Considerations on Representative Government* (1861), he coupled it with a system of weighted voting so that those who were highly educated and commercially successful, which he took to be evidence of their rationality, would cast more votes.

Liberals at first believed that the right to vote and to hold office should be restricted to those individuals who owned a certain amount of property. Such restrictions were justified by the belief that the ability to decide political issues in an enlightened and critical manner was present only in individuals who owned property. Thus, when liberals gained power, the right to vote was restricted to property owners.

Under pressure from the working classes and from women in the suffragette movements, liberals eventually began to accept the so-called universal franchise, but they always did so only when they were sure that the workers had accepted the principles of the capitalist economy. John Stuart Mill was one of the first liberals to argue for the vote not only for the working classes but also for women. But nineteenth-century liberals such as Mill in England and Alexis de Tocqueville (1805–1859) in France worried about the general trend toward equality that democratization represented in modern states. They believed that this would lead to the coming to power of mediocrities or poorly educated individuals who could be easily persuaded to support antiliberal policies.

Although women began to agitate for the franchise in the nineteenth century, women's suffrage in most liberal states was not granted until the twentieth. Even after having been enfranchised, women still faced barriers that prevented the equal exercise of their formal rights. Some barriers were legal, such as laws restricting the autonomy of married women and their rights to own property independently of their husbands. Some were the persistence of customs and social prejudices regarding motherhood, women's bodies, and their "proper" roles in the family; these barriers prevented women from being considered citizens with the same rights as men.

Mary Wollstonecraft (1759–1797), a philosopher who shared liberalism's commitments to the rational development of individuals, exposed many of these prejudices, as well as how the state promoted them by denying equal education to women. She argued that only through a system of education in which men and women were educated equally and in a culture that was blind to gender difference would a truly free society be realized. Mill and his wife Harriet Taylor extended Wollstonecraft's argument in *On the Subjection of Women* (1869), which attacked the laws that restricted women's roles and positions.

Varieties of the Liberal State

During the eighteenth and nineteenth centuries, liberals challenged monarchical and parliamentary absolutists for control of the emerging European territorial states. These struggles mark the beginning of the third great transformation of society that produced the current global order of states in which the only legitimate form of the state is one based on some version of popular sovereignty. In Europe in general, the rise of liberalism with its idea that sovereignty flowed from "the people," challenged and gradually defeated the notion, enshrined at Westphalia, that sovereignty was invested in a monarch or parliament.

Liberalism flourished in Britain and its colonies in North America primarily because Britain had the largest bourgeoisie of all European monarchies, thanks to its early industrialization and the extensive commercialization of its economy. Liberalism spread more easily in Britain, too, because the absolute parliamentary state that had emerged out of the struggle between the Crown and the estates proved easier to capture than did the absolutist monarchies in Europe. On the European continent, liberals had to overcome greater resistance (deeply entrenched absolutism, powerful centralized state administrations, and pronounced militarism), all results of the constant danger of war that existed on the continent. Absolutists were not definitely defeated and were able to resist the imposition of the liberal state for a considerable time. This resulted in prolonged and often bloody struggles between liberals and absolutists in these realms, as well as a European-wide war known as the Napoleonic Wars (1804–1815). Although this war was won by the monarchies of the Quadruple Alliance (Britain, Austria, Prussia, and Russia) at Waterloo in 1815, liberals continued the struggle and were eventually, over the course of the nineteenth century, successful in instituting popular sovereignty as the only basis on which a state could be legitimately based.

Liberalism supported the rise of Britain's hegemony in the European world order. Remember, as we discussed in the previous chapter, that hegemony involved integrated mastery of territorial space with the terms of wealth production in capitalism at a particular time. We saw in Chapter 4 how the Dutch were able to achieve hegemony in the European world order in the first half of the seventeenth century, when that order encompassed primarily Europe and its colonies. Integration of the colonies into the European world order at that time was in an early stage. Mercantilism allowed the French state to rise in power because it was able to coordinate its colonial wealth and its domestic, primarily agricultural, economy. Throughout the eighteenth and into the nineteenth century, the European world economy expanded to encompass more and more of the planet, becoming more and more a "world" economy. Mastery of this expanding space required vaster resources as well as greater organizational and managerial power. Liberalism, with its faith in science and rationality and its emphasis on private property and individualism, worked with industrialism to give the British the edge in this new space during the nineteenth century.

Britain: A Liberal Parliamentary State

After the English Civil War and the Act of Settlement, which forbade monarchical absolutism in Britain, two factions struggled for control of the state within Parliament based on personal, regional, religious, and family loyalties. One faction was known as the Whigs (meaning "cattle thieves" in Scots-Gaelic) and favored the gentry's commercial interests and such Protestant sects as the Methodists, Baptists, Presbyterians, and Congregationalists because they did not conform to the hierarchy and liturgy of the Anglican Church, the established Church of England. The other faction was known as the Tories (meaning "Irish papist outlaws") and favored the interests of the traditional aristocracy and the Anglican Church. During this period, seats in Parliament were controlled by powerful families and many were openly bought and sold.[16]

In the early 1800s, demands by Britain's growing bourgeoisie for an end to the practice of buying and selling of seats for admission to Parliament resulted in reforms in the way that members of Parliament were chosen. The first reform was the Great Reform Act of 1832, which extended the franchise to 14 percent of the adult males, and made it possible for the Whigs, who thereafter became known as Liberals, to come to power. Note that the Reform Act conceded the right to vote only to those who had already accepted the tenets of liberalism, the new bourgeoisie. The Liberals were supported by the commercial and industrial bourgeoisie and adherents of the nonconformist Protestant sects, who favored minimal interference into economic and social life. Tories, who became known as Conservatives, were supported by the traditional aristocracy and adherents of Anglicanism, who favored an absolutist monarchical state that would interfere with economic and social life to protect people from their irrational impulses.

The Reform Act of 1867, which doubled the electorate by reducing property-owning restrictions for voting, allowed portions of the working class to cast ballots for the first time. The Reform Act of 1884 provided for a secret ballot and created universal male suffrage. These reforms co-opted not only the bourgeoisie but also segments of the emergent working class to pursue political aims through Parliament. Britain was thus peacefully and gradually transformed into a liberal parliamentary state based on the defense of private property, individual liberties, religious equality, and universal male suffrage.[17]

The United States: A Liberal Federal State

A received truth of American politics is that the United States does not constitute a state.[18] The Founding Fathers never used the word when speaking or writing about the new state that they were creating. Instead, they called it either a "government," a "republic," or a "union." When they used the term "state," they were referring to one of the constituent states of the new entity or to Britain. The founders were also compelled to avoid the term to more easily gain ratification for the new constitution among those for whom the term "state" conjured images of the all-powerful absolutist monarchist states of Europe. Despite the Founding Fathers calling it something else, a state was, in fact, what they created. Moreover, its purpose was not fundamentally different from that of the absolutist states of the day, including the extraction of resources in order to maintain a standing army.[19] The format of the state was, however, different because the Founding Fathers were imbued with liberal ideas about rational knowledge, toleration, natural rights, the rule of law, equality, and a free-market economy.

The movement for independence began as a protest against the extra taxes levied on the colonies by the British Parliament to cover extraordinary expenses incurred during the French and Indian Wars (1755–1763) and to pay for western garrisons to protect settlers against continuing attack by Native Americans. These new taxes included the Sugar Act of 1764 and the Stamp Act of 1767, which required that revenue stamps be affixed to all legal and printed documents. These taxes affected the two groups in colonial society with the most extensive commercial interests: New England merchants and southern planters. Using the slogan "No taxation without representation," New England merchants and southern planters formed an alliance with shopkeepers, artisans, and small farmers to protest the new taxes and boycott British-made goods. In response, the British Parliament rescinded the new taxes; the New England merchants and southern planters, now satisfied, sought to calm a situation that had exposed the more radical elements of colonial society: shopkeepers, artisans, and small farmers. Mobilized over taxes, these elements asserted that British power maintained an unjust colonial economic and social structure; they began to agitate for independence, a state the New England merchants and southern planters did not want.[20]

In 1773 the British granted a monopoly on the export of tea to the East

India Company; this ended a lucrative trade for New England merchants. Colonial merchants sought to persuade the British to rescind the Tea Act. Meanwhile, the radicals, led by Samuel Adams (1722–1803), who hoped to goad the British to take action that would alienate the New England merchants and southern planters, dumped tea from East India Company ships into Boston Harbor. After the Boston Tea Party, as this event is known, the British Parliament took harsh measures: the port of Boston was closed to commerce, the colonial government of Massachusetts was changed, persons accused of criminal acts were taken to Britain for trial, and movement west was restricted; this last measure especially aggravated southern planters, who were in constant need of new land for their main crop, cotton. A cycle of provocative actions by the colonists and harsh retaliation by the British resulted in the convening of the First Continental Congress in 1774. Delegates from all the colonies attended and called for a complete boycott of British goods and, prodded by the radicals, considered the possibility of independence from Britain.[21]

The Declaration of Independence (July 4, 1776), written by Thomas Jefferson (1743–1826) and adopted by the Second Continental Congress (1776), began by stating the tenets of liberalism: natural law, social contract, inalienable rights, popular sovereignty, and limited government. These were followed by a list of grievances the colonial elite harbored against the British. By the end of the following year, the colonists declared independence and adopted a written constitution, the Articles of Confederation and Perpetual Union, which stayed in force until March 1789. The Articles created a confederal state—that is, one in which the central government enjoys only those powers the constituent member states are willing to give it. There was no national-level executive, and laws passed by the Continental Congress were to be executed by the member states. Although the Continental Congress could declare war, make peace, ratify treaties, coin or borrow money, and regulate trade with Native Americans, it could neither levy direct taxes nor regulate commerce among the member states. There was no standing army and each state maintained its own militia.[22]

The Articles of Confederation did not, then, create a state strong enough to promote the economic interests of New England merchants and southern planters. The newly independent states competed with one another for foreign commerce, and European states treated each state of the confederation as a sovereign state. At the same time, the influence of radicals in the Continental Congress and the legislatures of certain states, such as Pennsylvania and Rhode Island, increased, threatening dominant economic interests. Faced with these threats, the Virginia state legislature called a conference of state leaders, which met in 1786 in Annapolis, Maryland, in order to organize a subsequent conference to revise the Articles of

Confederation. In the meantime, Daniel Shays (1747?–1825), a former Revolutionary War army captain, led a rebellion of debt-ridden farmers against the State of Massachusetts to prevent foreclosures on their land. Although Shays's Rebellion (1786), as this event is known, ended peacefully when fourteen of the captured rebels were eventually pardoned and the state legislature met some of their demands, it demonstrated the weakness of state militias and the growing influence of the radicals.

A conference was convened in May 1789 in Philadelphia for the purpose of revising the Articles. All states except Rhode Island sent a delegation.[23] The fifty-five delegates, representatives of New England merchants and southern planters, agreed upon the broad ideological principles on which the new state should be based. As adherents of liberal principles, they wanted a new state capable of promoting commerce and protecting property from radical state legislatures.[24]

The constitution produced by the convention in Philadelphia brought into being a state strong enough to promote commerce and protect private property, but not to become itself a threat to commerce and property as radical state legislatures had become. To accomplish both power and protection, the central government was separated into coequal legislative, executive, and judicial branches. The legislative branch (Congress) was subdivided into two houses: the Senate, appointed by state legislatures to six-year terms, staggered such that only one-third of the Senate would be appointed every two years, and the House, directly elected for two-year terms.[25]

Power and protection were also accomplished by dividing governmental responsibilities between the central government and the constituent state governments. A strong, but not too strong, central state was imposed upon the preexisting states, which had been autonomous from one another under the Articles of Confederation and as colonies of Britain. The Constitution of 1789 rescinded the right of the preexisting states to maintain armies in peacetime, and gave the central state the power to conduct foreign policy and command the army as well as the militias (if called into national service). To Congress, the Constitution granted the right to declare war, to call the state militias into national service, and to appropriate money to support the armed forces. In addition, Congress was given the responsibility of assisting commerce by making "internal improvements," such as building roads, bridges, and canals, creating a national currency, controlling patents, collecting tariffs, and providing subsidies. To the preexisting states were given the power to make law in a host of areas, including property, banking, business, family, public health, education, crime, elections, local government, occupation, and land use.

To ratify the new Constitution, it was necessary that a bargain be struck with those who believed that, despite separation of powers and federalism, the state was still too strong and might still threaten economic interests and individual rights. A Bill of Rights was adopted in 1791 in the form of amendments to the original document. In spite of the guarantee of individual rights to all persons, the Constitution maintained the "Three-Fifths Compromise," which stipulated that five slaves would be counted as three persons for purposes of apportioning seats in the House of Representatives.

Thus, the purpose of the liberal federal state built by the drafters of the Constitution was to strengthen the central government ("form a more perfect Union") and create a single army ("provide for the common defense"), while at the same time making certain that the new state itself could not be easily taken over by radical forces.

France: A Liberal Republican State

The establishment of a liberal state was relatively easy in the former colonies of British North America, which were dominated by the commercial classes. The colonies never had a peasantry or nobility in the European sense. There was no deeply entrenched Catholic Church, and no traditional landed nobility. This was not the case in Europe, where, as was shown in Chapter 4, strong absolutist monarchies supported by the Catholic Church had been built. In France, liberals had a difficult time gaining control of the state and were not immediately successful. Although French liberals were able to overthrow the monarchy, a long and difficult struggle between liberals and conservative absolutists ensued in the years following the French Revolution. Even after successfully gaining control, the resultant liberal republican state retained many aspects of the previous absolutist state, especially its centralized, unitary character.

As was shown in the previous chapter, the statemaking process in France resulted in the most absolute monarchy for its day in all of Europe. In 1789, Louis XVI (ruled 1774–1792) summoned the Estates General, its first meeting since 1628, to gain support and consent for new taxes to pay debts associated with France's recent war with Britain in North America. The nobility and the clergy refused the king's request and challenged his authority by demanding a say in the governance of the realm in exchange for the relinquishment of their immunity from taxation. This challenge to the king's authority encouraged the third estate, that is, the bourgeoisie, which was already very heavily taxed, to make their own demands. The third estate declared itself the only true representative of the French people. Rioting and protests broke out in Paris and on July 14, 1789, a mob stormed the Bastille prison. Rioting and civil unrest soon spread to the rest of France; an attempt to form a constitutional monarchy was unsuccessful and France was proclaimed a republic in 1792. Louis was tried and executed as a traitor on January 21, 1793.

Although in Britain and the United States civic republicanism had been transformed in ways supportive of property and capitalist commercial interests, in France a more radical republicanism gained influence and circulated in political writings, theater, music, opera, and scientific circles. French radical republicans, who were called "Jacobins" (from the name of their meeting place, a former Dominican convent), placed the claim of equality for all citizens—an implicit element of liberal claims of individual rights, which moderate liberals more responsive to the concerns of the property-owning bourgeoisie avoided—above all else, even the protection of private property. Drawing liberalism toward radical individualism, the Jacobins promulgated the Universal Declaration of the Rights of Man (August 26, 1789) and abolished provincial administrative units of monarchical France as well as serfdom and noble privileges. Important Jacobin leaders such as Maximilien Robespierre (1758–1794) and the Marquis de Sade (1740–1814) combined radical individualism with an intense commitment to republican freedom and independence; they argued for a widened sphere of individual liberty that would encompass all aspects of individual life, not only property ownership but also moral and sexual life.[26] Although France was declared a republic in 1792, the stiff resistance of the nobility and the clergy prevented liberals from gaining full control of the French state. Moreover, France was invaded by surrounding monarchical states, which saw the survival of the new French republic as a direct challenge to the concept of monarchical sovereignty.

In order to deal with these threats, the republic ordered universal conscription (*levée en masse*) in August 1793. At the same time, all of France's economic resources were placed under the authority of the new republican government, called the Directory. These two actions were truly radical: for the first time, an army of citizen-soldiers loyal to the nation was raised and supported by mobilizing the vast resources of an entire national economy, which as we will see later, had a transformative impact on the European states-system. To compensate for its weakness at home, the republican regime waged war against its absolutist, monarchical enemies abroad. As the cost of these wars in terms of blood and treasure began to rise, rioting against the new republic began; France plunged into turmoil. Internal disorder, military threats from abroad, and rising sentiments for a return to strong centralized rule encouraged Napoléon Bonaparte (1769–1821), the republic's most successful general, to seize dictatorial power in 1799.

Napoléon sought to unify France around the liberal ideals of the revolution—*liberté, egalité, fraternité* (liberty, equality, and brotherhood)—and to restore order. Between 1799 and 1804, he reorganized the state's central administration, provided France with a constitution and a uniform legal system called the Code Napoléon (1804), and expanded territorial administration. He placed *préfects* under the absolute control of the central govern-

KING. OF
SWEDEN
KING. OF DENMARK
AND NORWAY
RUSSIAN
EMPIRE
UNITED KINGDOM
OF GREAT BRITAIN
AND IRELAND
KING. OF PRUSSIA
GRAND DUCHY
OF WARSAW
CONFEDERATION
OF THE
RHINE
AUSTRIAN
EMPIRE
FRENCH
EMPIRE
SWITZERLAND
KING. OF
ITALY
ILLYRIAN PROVINCES
KINGDOM
OF
SPAIN
KING. OF PORTUGAL
OTTOMAN
EMPIRE
KING. OF
NAPLES
KING. OF
SARDINIA
KING. OF
SICILY

Europe, 1812

ment in charge of the eighty-three *départements* into which France had been divided by the previous revolutionary government. Napoléon also revived the Conseil d'État, which since the time of Louis XIV had been composed of salaried counsellors—lawyers and administrators—who worked under the direction of the king.

Napoléon sought not only to unify France but to unify Europe around French liberalism, which he attempted to do by force. He declared himself emperor of France in 1804, raised an army of six hundred thousand men, and, from 1804 to 1815, invaded and defeated monarchies across Europe, from the German principalities to Portugal. Defeated initially in 1814 and then again at Waterloo in 1815, Napoléon was banished from France to St. Helena in the South Atlantic, where he died in 1821.

A constitutional monarchy was begun in whose parliament a number of political groups appeared that fought a seesaw battle for control of the French state. On one side were the Royalists, conservative members of the aristocracy, who fulminated against the French Revolution and sought to reestablish the monarchy and to restore the prerogatives of the Catholic Church. On the opposite side were the Jacobins, or radical liberals, who continued to fight for a secular, egalitarian republic. Numerous moderate liberal groups took positions between these two.

The constitutional monarchy of Louis XVIII (ruled 1815–1824) and Charles X (ruled 1824–1830) was overthrown by Louis Philippe (ruled 1830–1848), who reestablished absolutism. In 1848, liberals overthrew the monarchy once again and established France's Second Republic, which lasted only until 1851. During this short period, France was governed by a popularly elected president and a unicameral parliament. The Second Republic was overthrown in 1851 by Louis Napoléon, the nephew of Napoléon Bonaparte, who established the Second Empire, which he ruled as Napoléon III from 1851 to 1870, when his armies were defeated by the Prussians.

In the wake of Napoléon III's defeat, liberals established the Third Republic in 1871, which lasted until Germany invaded France in 1940. The Third Republic had a two-house legislature. The Chamber of Deputies was elected by universal male suffrage and the Senate by indirect election by local notables. In liberal fashion, the terms of office were staggered: senators served longer than deputies and their age requirements were higher. The executive was divided between a president and a council of ministers headed by a prime minister. The president appointed all members of the council, including the prime minister, but it was collectively responsible to the legislature. The president was elected by a joint meeting of the two houses of the legislature for a seven-year term of office and was given the power to dissolve the legislature, a traditional monarchical prerogative. This basic format was carried over to the Fourth Republic, which was organized in 1945 and lasted until 1957, when it collapsed under the weight of the Algerian crisis, and to the present Fifth Republic, which was established in 1958 by General Charles de Gaulle (1890–1970).

Summary

In this chapter we have concentrated on the formation of liberal constitutional states. Liberalism's ideas of popular sovereignty were manifested in different ways under different circumstances to transform absolute monarchical and parliamentary states into ones more readily able to resolve the problem of the mutual dependence of sovereign and subject. Liberalism established the conditions under which the property of the bourgeoisie could be protected and expanded while maintaining the state's ability to mobilize for war and provide public justice. It is important to recognize that liberalism also created opportunities for opposition movements to create a space in which working classes, women, slaves, and religious and racial minorities could organize politically and claim access to and otherwise challenge the basic organization of the state. The way liberal states have been transformed in the late nineteenth and twentieth centuries will be discussed in the next two chapters; its role in the globalization of the European states-system will be discussed in Part 3.

Notes

1. On this discursive transformation, see John Pocock, *The Machiavellian Moment* (Princeton, NJ: Princeton University Press, 1975).
2. For an interpretation of the American Revolutionary period as moving from a more radical interpretation of popular sovereignty more consistent with Rousseau to one more compatible with a capitalist order and the writings of John Locke, see Sheldon Wolin, *The Presence of the Past: Essays on the State and the Constitution* (Baltimore, MD: Johns Hopkins University Press, 1989).
3. Charles Tilly, *Coercion, Capital, and European States, A.D. 990–1990* (Cambridge, MA: Basil Blackwell, 1990), 99–101.
4. See Pasquale Pasquino, "Theatrum Politicum: The Genealogy of Capital—Police and the State of Prosperity," in Graham Burchell, Colin Gordon, and Peter Miller (eds.), *The Foucault Effect: Studies in Governmentality* (Chicago: University of Chicago Press, 1991): 105–118.
5. See the "Introduction" to E. K. Bramsted and K. J. Melhuish (eds.), *Western Liberalism* (London: Longman Group, 1978). For the connection between Enlightenment ideals and capitalism, see C. B. Macpherson, *The Political Theory of Possessive Individualism* (London: Oxford University Press, 1962); and for a somewhat different view, see Albert O. Hirschman, *The Passions and the Interests: Defenses of Capitalism Before Its Triumph* (Princeton, NJ: Princeton University Press, 1977).

6. On the emergence of bourgeois civil society, see Jürgen Habermas, *The Structural Transformation of the Public Sphere*, trans. T. Burger and F. Lawrence (Cambridge, MA: MIT Press, 1989).

7. For a graphic illustration of how the compelling of belief was central to order in the absolutist state, see Michel Foucault's recounting of the execution of Damian by the eighteenth-century French state, which comes at the beginning of his book *Discipline and Punishment,* trans. Alan Sheridan (New York: Pantheon, 1977). The state did not simply set out to punish Damian but to put him through an elaborate and tortuous ceremony of public execution in order to exact from him public remorse and a public confession of his sin and renewed religious faith. In the liberal state, on the contrary, punishment and the judicial practices did not set out to compel inward faith through the spectacle of punishment in public. Punishment of criminals, including executions (where they remained legal), became private and were conducted behind closed doors as the liberal state took hold in the nineteenth century. Indeed, the liberal state aimed at disciplining people through the promotion of regimens of normality to prevent people from committing crimes in the first place and by reforming criminals when they do commit crimes.

8. See Reinhart Koselleck, *Critique and Crisis: Enlightenment and the Pathogenesis of Modern Society* (Cambridge, MA: MIT Press, 1988).

9. Locke's argument raised one of the most important issues of seventeenth-century philosophy and politics. The absolutist state compelled the individual subject to believe in those religious and moral principles that the state deemed necessary to impose to keep order. Locke's argument rendered this practice illegitimate, subordinating the sovereign to the universal principles of reason and morality that guided the individual conscience. If the state could compel neither inward belief, one of the important arguments in the *Letter on Toleration,* nor blind obedience to the sovereign, what would ensure that people would obey the sovereign, especially if their conscience might tell them that the sovereign was acting immorally and, therefore, should not be obeyed? As Hobbes had earlier argued, subjects might view the sovereign as immoral and illegitimate whenever the sovereign did something that went against their private interests. This question has haunted liberal theory ever since. Locke answered by restricting the principle of toleration to religious believers. Atheists, he said, could not be trusted to act morally and, therefore, the state had to tolerate any religious system in its subjects, but it did not have to tolerate atheism. He argued that reason confirmed the existence of God and that all rational men and women therefore would accept some version of Christianity. This was a position others such as René Descartes (1596–1650) and Blaíse Pascal (1623–1662) had argued more thoroughly. But it represented a belief in the consistency of reason and faith that many liberals during the late eighteenth and early nineteenth centuries would reject, whereas others, such as the writers of the U.S. Constitution, would continue to accept it.

10. John Locke, *A Letter Concerning Toleration,* introduced by Patrick Romanell (Indianapolis, IN: Bobbs-Merrill, 1955), 17.

11. Ibid., 45.

12. Adam Smith, *An Inquiry into the Nature and Causes of the Wealth of Nations*, vol. I, ed. Edwin Cannan (Chicago: University of Chicago Press, 1976), 17.

13. Gianfranco Poggi, *The Development of the Modern State: A Sociological Introduction* (Stanford, CA: Stanford University Press, 1978), 119–125.

14. On the relationship between liberalism and democracy, see Norberto Bobbio, *Liberalism and Democracy* (London: Verso Press, 1990). See also C. B.

Macpherson, *The Life and Times of Liberal Democracy* (Oxford: Oxford University Press, 1977).

15. See Macpherson, *The Life and Times*, and David Held, *Models of Democracy* (Stanford, CA: Stanford University Press, 1987).

16. Stanley Rothman, *European Society and Politics* (Indianapolis, IN: Bobbs-Merrill, 1970), 314–315.

17. David Judge, *The Parliamentary State* (London and Newbury Park, CA: Sage Publications, 1993).

18. See, for example, Seymour Martin Lipset, *American Exceptionalism: A Double-Edged Sword* (New York: W. W. Norton, 1996).

19. Bruce D. Porter, *War and the Rise of the State: The Military Foundations of Modern Politics* (New York: The Free Press, 1994), 243–244.

20. Theodore J. Lowi and Benjamin Ginsberg, *American Government: Freedom and Power,* 3d ed. (New York and London: W. W. Norton, 1994), 27–30.

21. Ibid., 31.

22. Ibid., 32–33.

23. Ibid., 33–35.

24. Charles A. Beard, *An Economic Interpretation of the Constitution of the United States* (New York: Macmillan, 1913).

25. Changed to direct popular election by the Seventeenth Amendment.

26. For a reading of the relationship of the Marquis de Sade to republicanism and liberalism, see William E. Connolly, *Political Theory and Modernity* (Oxford: Basil Blackwell, 1988), 68–85.

6

The Antiliberal State: Sovereignty Particularized

The focus of this chapter is the dilemma faced by liberal states as their economies became increasingly industrialized. In certain states, such as the United States and Britain, where liberals came to power with little difficulty, and where liberalism heavily influenced the organization and governing practices of the state, a form of the state has emerged in the twentieth century in which the distinctions between state and civil society are maintained but combine in subtle ways to manage jointly the social, economic, and political life within it. This "managerial" state will be the subject of Chapter 7. In other states, two distinct varieties of the antiliberal state emerged: the progressively centralized communist state, which abolished the distinction between state and civil society, and the "reactionary modernist" fascist state, which combined capitalist modernization (i.e., belief in technological and scientific progress linked to utilitarian goals of organization, efficiency and productivity) with a reactionary imaginary of the *volk,* or "people," as constituting a historically homogeneous and "pure" nation.

Industrializaton, Modernity, and the Crisis of Liberalism

Remember that one aspect of liberal thought was a belief in rationalism, especially scientific thought. Liberals believed that science would transform the world for the better by producing new technologies to make life more comfortable. Liberals also believed that science would perfect human morals and social life by providing a critique of all irrational belief systems and by eliminating all arbitrary power. The transformation of the world for the better through science was to be realized by giving free rein to individual initiative and acquisitiveness in civil society and by rationalizing the state and society, that is, subordinating government to the rule of law and reducing politics to rational administration.[1]

The tremendous increases in industrial production and trade that took place from the middle to late nineteenth century appeared to liberals to be the realization and validation of their belief in the progressive power of rationality. Liberals tended to attribute such progress to rational individuals, rather than to the state, which they tended to view as a neutral protector of the private sphere of individuals rather than as a progressive force.

Industrialization was, however, a double-edged sword. On the one side, it produced an abundance of material goods, while on the other, it produced profound misery. One economist and social theorist, in summarizing the impact of the Industrial Revolution, puts the problem thus: "There was an almost miraculous improvement in the tools of production, which was accompanied by a catastrophic dislocation of the lives of the common people."[2] Catastrophic dislocation was widely evident in the cities in which much industrial production took place, and to which increasing numbers of people looking for work moved. Cities were dark, dirty, dangerous, and congested. The living and working conditions of the "proletariat," the label given to the working class in the nineteenth century (from the French *proles*, meaning the lowest economic class), were extremely bad. Workers, including children, were paid very low wages and were compelled to work long days, often fifteen hours or more. They lived in crowded, dilapidated housing without heat or plumbing. Their food was extremely poor; this, together with the long hours of work in unhealthy conditions, made them susceptible to debilitating, chronic illnesses for which medical care was scarce and expensive, if available at all. Women were placed in especially difficult circumstances. After working in factories or doing "piecework" (i.e., work paid by the number of items produced, not by the hour) at home to supplement their husband's or father's inadequate pay, they, and their unmarried daughters, had to perform hours of backbreaking household work for which they were not compensated.

Eventually, workers began to demand a living wage and better working conditions as well as a share of political power. At the beginning of the nineteenth century, the protest of the proletariat was manifested in a more or less militant campaign for the right to vote, which would give the proletariat some measure of indirect control over industrial capitalism by allowing it a voice in the affairs of the state. Early suffragette and feminist groups often took a leading role in such campaigns.[3] Workers supported liberalism's commitment to individual equality and its emphasis on procedural democracy. Early feminists, such as Mary Wollstonecraft, were drawn to its emphases on individual merit and universal education; they argued that these were the prerequisites for the emancipation of both women and men.

Nevertheless, liberal parties and politicians tended to become more apologetic of industrial capitalism in the nineteenth century and unwilling to go beyond modest political reforms. Liberalism came to understand industrialization in exclusively economic terms. That is, liberals thought that the free market would solve all the social problems created by industrialization. They assumed that the horrendous social dislocation, gross inequalities of wealth, and urban squalor that it produced would be dealt with by the "trickle-down" effect, which would spread wealth from the rich to the poor by the judicious application of minimally intrusive reforms. They also thought that the market would create a harmony of interests among all peoples engaged in global trade, which would put an end to war. For liberals, the state's role was limited to facilitating the workings of the free market by providing the people with the education they needed to make the industrial market economy prosper, guaranteeing the individual the right to accumulate private property, and encouraging economic competition by preventing monopolies. This way of thinking failed to address the social and political concerns of workers, and liberals began losing their support.

Feminists also turned away from liberalism because the men who controlled liberal parties generally refused to extend to women the individual rights and respect their ideology promised. Feminist theories came to emphasize instead the cultural customs, traditions, and institutions (such as the nuclear family) that reinforced even liberal men's sense of their superiority over women.

Radical Working-Class Movements

By the end of the nineteenth century, the proletariat turned to movements that sought to take direct control over industrial capitalism by overthrowing the liberal state and making all industry, business, and agriculture the property of the proletariat rather than the original owners. These movements were animated by ideologies, such as socialism, anarchism, and utopianism, that rejected, in often provocative ways, the managerial and rationalized forms of industrial capitalism. Anarchists, such as Mikhail Bakunin (1814–1876) and Pierre-Josèphe Proudhon (1809–1865), called for direct action to violently disrupt the social and political processes of industrialization. The Luddites, a semiorganized group of workers opposed to the way industrialization continually put workers out of work, broke into factories and smashed machines.

Various humanistic utopian socialists, most significantly Comte de Saint Simon (1760–1825), Francois-Charles Fourier (1772–1837), and Robert Owen (1771–1858), developed socialist and communal alternatives to industrial life, sometimes creating experimental communities based on Christian or humanitarian values. The latter were often romanticist attempts to return to a pure, pristine, and humane human essence in harmony with nature, now obscured by industrialization.

By far the most influential radical theory was that of Karl Marx

(1818–1883), a German philosopher, economist, journalist, and political organizer. Modern capitalist economies, he argued, forced the majority of the population to live under conditions in which they were powerless. Factory owners and finance capitalists owned the means of production, and workers had nothing but their bodies to sell. Wages were set by a market over which capitalists had complete power. Marx described the social effects of the production and consumption cycle of industrial capitalism as "alienation," a process in which "the worker becomes a slave of the object" he or she produces. Specifically, "the object produced by labour, its product, now stands opposed to it as an *alien being*, as a *power independent* of the producer."[4] More generally, in his *Communist Manifesto* (1848), Marx characterized the general effects of the rapid changes brought about by industrial capitalism in the following way:

> Constant revolutionizing of production, uninterrupted disturbance of all social conditions, everlasting uncertainty and agitation distinguish the bourgeois epoch from all earlier ones. All fixed, fast-frozen relations, with their train of ancient and venerable prejudices and opinions, are swept away, all new-formed ones become antiquated before they can ossify. All that is solid melts into air, all that is holy is profaned, and man is at last compelled to face with sober senses, his real conditions of life, and his relations with his kind.[5]

To Marx, the dependence of life on the circulation of commodities meant a life of enormous uncertainty, constant change, and the extreme exploitation of workers by owners of capital. But, in Marx's interpretation, industrial capitalism also opened up the possibility for people to organize and take control of the changes occurring in the areas that mattered most—the productive relations that, Marx argued, in reality governed their lives.

Marx's critique of industrial capitalism was powerfully attractive to industrial workers because it blamed their economic plight not on themselves as individuals, as did the liberals, but on the capitalist mode of production. It appealed to some feminists because it traced the patriarchal domination of men over women to the structures of industrial capitalism, and promised that with the overthrow of capitalism, men and women would not just be politically equal, as liberal feminists argued, but equal in all aspects of life.[6]

The role of the state posed difficult questions for Marx's analysis. Although he never wrote a systematic treatise on the state, Marx began to develop an account of the capitalist state through his criticism of the idealist German philosopher, Georg Friedrich Hegel (1770–1831). Hegel had posed fundamental criticisms of the liberal conceptions of man and state. Unlike liberals, Hegel saw the state as an active agent of change; indeed, he saw the state as it had emerged in Europe as the supreme manifestation of the rational nature of human beings. For Hegel, the state embodied the spirit of human history and the realization of a rational society. He argued that liberalism's belief that separate, abstract individuals using only their own initiative could produce a rational and just society was mistaken. For Hegel, the liberal constitutional state realized only a truncated version of human reason, one based on instrumental calculations of self-interest and the alienation of men from other men. A fuller realization of reason was embodied in a modern state in which men gave self-conscious direction to the organization of their shared ethical and social life. The state, to Hegel, represented an ethical unity; sovereignty became the medium between particular human communities and the universality of the human spirit. Therefore, the realization of human freedom was to be found in the struggles among sovereign states, leading eventually to the victory of the sovereign power that represented the most free and rational ethical life, that is, the state in which all forms of arbitrary power had been eliminated. Such a state was, for Hegel, the parliamentary state with a highly developed professional bureaucracy that administered justice fairly and universally.

Although Marx shared Hegel's rejection of liberalism's idea that the individual in civil society was the agent of human progress, he rejected Hegel's idealist view of the state, and with it Hegel's entire conception of, and allegiance to, state sovereignty. For Marx, the agent of historical change was "class conflict," not the conflict between sovereign states, as it was for Hegel. Marx argued that the political order was a reflection of the class holding power. Under capitalism, the bourgeoisie created a state that promoted its needs and power. Police power kept the subordinate class of workers in check and was needed to keep order in the context of the misery and destitution caused by capitalism; the state's economic agencies ministered to the capitalist order, providing necessary infrastructure; its judicial system secured the rights not of everyone but of property owners; its wars opened markets and secured investments abroad. In a communist system, Marx argued, the state would become unnecessary: eliminate class conflict and the need for a coercive apparatus would likewise disappear. Sovereignty, then, for Marx was a myth, a form of "false consciousness"; that is, it led people to believe their society was rational, fair, and free when it was in reality a historical creation that served the particular interests of the capital-owning class.

Antiliberal and Antisocialist Ideologies

The first to resist liberalism's individualism and progressive rationalism were conservatives, that is, those who defended the monarchical state, the aristocracy, and the established church, whether Catholic or Protestant. In

Britain, conservatives rallied behind Edmund Burke, who, as mentioned in the previous chapter, defended the principle of constitutional monarchy in general and the British monarchy in particular against the excesses of the French revolution.[7] In France, as was discussed in Chapter 5, royalists sought to resurrect the monarchy and to restore the privileged position of the Catholic Church, which they were able to do from 1815 until 1871, except for the brief period of the Second Republic (1848–1851). In the German-speaking kingdoms and principalities, conservatives came to see the state itself as the embodiment of national culture and tradition.[8] Conservatives were no better than the liberals at dealing with the dislocations and social miseries of industrial capitalism, however.

Conservatives and some workers began to turn to fascist movements, which had arisen in the 1920s in many European states that were suffering the dislocations of capitalist industrialization. Fascism, a word coined from the imperial Roman symbol of authority (a bundle of sticks bound around two axes, or *fasces*), arose as an ideological antidote to the class warfare called for by socialism. It rejected liberalism because it thought that rational individualism and bourgeois civil society weakened the state. Fascists accepted industrialization and used science and technology to serve the needs of state power.[9] It appealed to those of the population who felt left out and exploited by rapid industrialization: the small farmer, shopkeepers, and some elements of the proletariat. It also drew support from the owners of big businesses and industrialists who were seeking a way to control the proletariat. It called for the creation of a single movement led by a single, charismatic leader possessed of natural gifts of "body and spirit . . . believed to be supernatural, not accessible to everybody."[10]

Varieties of Antiliberal States

Industrial capitalism conditioned the organization and governing practices of states in the twentieth century. All twentieth-century states became more highly centralized and organized, using science to rationalize administration and intensify their power to control society. The organizational form a particular state took depended on its history, especially the way in which challenges emerged to absolutism and liberalism. Two prominent states in the twentieth century explicitly rejected liberalism and sought to construct an alternative solution to the problems of industrialization; these were the Soviet communist state in Russia and the fascist state in Germany. Our consideration of Germany and Russia as antiliberal states takes issue with accounts of these two states that separate them into two different types, one "authoritarian" (Germany) and the other "totalitarian" (Russia), and which ignore how their particular histories of statemaking and the problems of industrialization have influenced their twentieth-century forms.[11]

Russia: A Soviet Communist State

Russia's absolutist past set the conditions that allowed the emergence of the antiliberal Soviet communist state. An absolutist monarchical state had developed around the principality of Muscovy (Moscow), which, with the help of the Orthodox Church, was able to gain independence from the Tartars by the fourteenth century. During the principate of Ivan III, the Great (ruled 1462–1505), Moscow gained control over the neighboring Russian-speaking principalities, as well as its own nobility, and formed a powerful absolutist state.[12] Centralization continued under Ivan IV, the Terrible (ruled 1533–1584), who first used the title czar (Russian for Caesar), and Czar Alexei (ruled 1645–1676), who enserfed the Russian peasantry.[13] Peter the Great (ruled 1689–1725), an energetic, ruthless, and cruel czar, strengthened Russia's army and navy by borrowing military technology from European states, especially Sweden, Holland, Britain, and France, and by employing Western European technical experts in various departments of government. During Peter's reign, the bureaucracy was streamlined and the Orthodox Church was subordinated to the authority of the Crown by making it into a governmental department. The state promoted trade, education, literature, science, and the arts. Peter also conquered Ukraine and acquired a stretch of the Baltic coast, where he built his capital city, Sankt Petersburg (St. Petersburg; later Petrograd, then Leningrad in 1924, and back to Sankt Petersburg in 1991).

Russian absolutism was eventually challenged by an emerging intelligentsia that pushed for a liberal constitutional monarchy. This challenge was encouraged by Russia's defeat in the Crimean War (1853–1856), which undermined the position of those who argued that a tyrannical absolutism was the key to Russia's military successes and future survivability as a state.

In response to this agitation and Russia's defeat in the Crimean War, Czar Alexander II (ruled 1855–1881) introduced a number of reforms that he hoped would satisfy the demands of the intellectuals. Alexander abolished serfdom and initiated a system of local self-government under assemblies (*zemstvos*) chosen by a restricted franchise with limited powers at the provincial and municipal levels. He also reformed the judiciary to make it more independent of the Crown, and expanded the freedom of the press and that of academic inquiry at the universities. At the same time, however, the czar's agents prevented Russian workers from creating unions, and ruthlessly crushed strikes. This attempt to impose liberalism from above by an absolutist monarchy collapsed when terrorist activities by revolutionary groups persisted. The czar responded by rolling back his reforms, censoring the press, and clamping down on the universities. These repressive measures only served to antagonize his opponents, who increased their terroristic activities. In 1881 the czar himself was killed by a bomb thrown under his carriage by a group who opposed absolutism.[14]

Alexander III (ruled 1881–1894), Russia's penultimate czar, believed that more repression was the monarchy's only salvation. Therefore, he clamped down on the discontented even harder than had his father. When he died of natural causes in 1894, he bequeathed to his son, Nicholas II (ruled 1894–1917), the most repressive and absolute monarchy in Europe. Industrial development lagged behind the economic powerhouses of Germany, Britain, the United States, and Japan. Much of Russian industry was controlled by foreigners, under contracts with the monarchy, and Russian capitalists often invested their profits abroad. Together, these limited the development of the bourgeoisie, who were portrayed as being in league with the czar as agents of foreign powers. Owing to the ruthlessness of the czar's regime, and the negative view held by many workers and peasants of the bourgeoisie, antiliberal political programs had gained considerable room for development. Thus, the particular version of absolutism that grew in Russia established the conditions that made the experiment with a progressively centralized, communist state possible.

The Soviet communist state emerged in the context of World War I (1914–1918) and on the heels of failed attempts to transform a ruthless absolutist state into a liberal state in the second half of the nineteenth and early twentieth centuries. The war devastated Russia, as it did other states in Europe. During 1914–1916, over 2 million Russian soldiers were killed or wounded. The war imposed a heavy strain on the economy, which was industrially weak compared with other major powers in Europe. The economy eventually collapsed, and strikes broke out in Petrograd in 1916. Troops sent by the czar refused to suppress the strikers, and Nicholas abdicated on March 15, 1917.

To develop war industries and to fight the war, much of the population had been mobilized, either as soldiers or as workers in the heavy industries necessary for the war effort. This politicized the population, especially the urban working classes, which increased in size and importance as elements of the rural peasantry moved to the cities to take industrial jobs.

The absolutist monarchy could not sustain itself in the context of an increasingly politicized population that demanded justification for state policies and even a say in governing. Indeed, after defeat in the Russo-Japanese War (1905), the czar experimented with a parliament, called the Duma, which failed. With the Duma, the czar attempted to mediate the maintenance of the old regime with the new demands of middle-class bourgeoisie and the working classes, both of which became mobilized in political parties. Although the Duma was divided into two houses—an upper house appointed by the czar from the nobility, the Orthodox Church, universities, and provincial councils, and a lower house elected from a fairly broad franchise—it failed to contain the political energies provoked by Russia's military losses and an industrializing economy.

The Bolsheviks (meaning majority in Russian), one of the working-class parties led by Vladimir Ilyich Ulyanov (later known by his revolutionary pseudonym, Lenin, 1870–1924), took power on November 6, 1917, after a brief attempt by liberals and social democrats to establish a government. Their support came in part from radicals in the working class in important cities such as Moscow and Petrograd. But they drew more general support from other sectors of the population by promising, and delivering, a separate peace with Germany, thus ending Russia's involvement in World War I. The Bolsheviks called for a social and political revolution that would create a society based on equality through collective and national ownership and direction of the economy. All citizens were to have jobs; the nobility was to be abolished and land given to those who worked it; private ownership of industry was to be eliminated along with the vast inequalities of wealth, status, and influence it had produced.

In part to respond to counterrevolutionary activity, in part to consolidate power against rival liberal and left factions, and in part to defend against invasions from outside powers (the United States, with British backing, invaded Siberia in 1919), the Bolsheviks established a political structure that consolidated power in the party leadership. The party was built on the *soviets* (committees), ad hoc groups that sprang up in 1917 in order to coordinate the strikes of the workers, soldiers, and peasants. The soviets elected representatives to the national councils, which would elect party leadership and set and oversee state policy.

The second national congress in January 1918 established the Central Committee of the Communist Party as the state's chief executive body and promised an impressive list of political and social rights, which were extended only to the working class.[15] In January 1924, after their victory in the civil war and the reconquest of territory originally comprising the Russian Empire, built up by the czars, a new constitution was promulgated that extended this state structure into a federal Union of Soviet Socialist Republics (USSR). The supreme governing body was the Congress of Soviets, which was divided into a Council of the Union chosen on the basis of population, and a Council of Nationalities composed of delegates from each union, autonomous republic, and province. The Congress of Soviets selected a Presidium, which handled its business between sessions, and a Central Committee, which directed the activities of the federal ministries. Despite having created a formal state structure, real decisional power rested with the Communist Party, especially the Politburo and Central Committee. Decisions were taken according to a procedure known as democratic centralism, which allowed for full discussion of an issue but required absolute obedience to the decision once taken.

Democratic centralism established a strategy of state construction that was modernist, that is, based on the same progressive character of science, technology, and rationalism that lay behind industrialization. Modernists sought a vantage point and vision from which they could see and understand the entire social world as a whole, and put tremendous faith in large-scale organization directed from a central point to manage and coordinate the social world. The Soviet communist state located it in the state apparatus itself. The state would manage progress—scientific, economic, political, social, and moral—directly rather than relying on a bourgeois civil society.

Therefore, the entire Soviet economy, except for individual households, was directed and administered by the State Planning Commission for the USSR (GOSPLAN). GOSPLAN determined production targets, wages, and prices. It determined what consumer goods (refrigerators, cars, clothes, etc.) would be produced, and where they would be produced. The goods produced were sold in state-run stores at prices fixed by the plan. These stores were often out of stock because GOSPLAN emphasized heavy industry and military production at the expense of consumer goods for the individual Soviet citizen. The state also provided a vast array of social and medical services. From the 1920s, Soviet citizens were guaranteed unemployment insurance, free medical care in state-run clinics and hospitals, old-age pensions, and disability pay. Housing, although often in short supply and poorly constructed, was provided at low rents.

The political structure of the state together with the modernist ideology allowed the general secretary of the Communist Party to adopt extraordinary power. Iosif Vissarionovich Dzhugashvili (later known by his revolutionary pseudonym, Joseph Stalin [1879–1953]), who became secretary-general in a power struggle after Lenin's death in 1924 and held this position until his own death in 1952, ruled the Soviet state with a ruthless despotism reminiscent of the czars. In 1934, after the assassination of his likely successor, he unleashed a reign of terror over the Soviet Union lasting until 1938, during which time he purged the Communist Party of the Soviet Union (CPSU) and the army of "unreliable" elements and arrested ordinary citizens for "antistate" activities. The state secret police became omnipresent. Millions lost their lives by execution or overwork in labor camps in Siberia.[16]

Stalin was followed in 1953 by Nikita Krushchev (1894–1971), a reformer who appealed to the humanitarian aims of communism. He was ousted by conservatives in the top organs of the party in 1964 because of his disclosures about Stalin's reign of terror, his proconsumer, antimilitary policies, and the humiliation caused by his retreat during the Cuban missile crisis. This ushered in approximately twenty years of conservative, bureaucratic rule. Leonid Brezhnev (1906–1982) was designated secretary-general in 1965 and ruled the Soviet Union until his death in 1982. Brezhnev was cautious and conservative and governed in a consensus-building, bureaucratic style. During his years as secretary-general, the Soviet state became increasingly corrupt, the activities of its political class resembling those of the Mafia. He was replaced in 1982 by Yuri Andropov (1914–1984), who died the following year of cancer. Andropov was followed by Konstantin Chernyenko (1911–1985), who died from emphysema in 1985. In 1985, Mikhail Gorbachev (b. 1931) became what subsequent events would prove to be the Soviet Union's last secretary-general.

Gorbachev, who was influenced by the reforms of the Khrushchev years, instituted a comprehensive reform program that included democratization, public openness (*glasnost*), and restructuring (*perestroika*). Restructuring involved a radical decentralization of control and management of the economy to the level of factories and limited private ownership of retail stores and services. By democratization, Gorbachev meant reducing the monopoly over political power held by the CPSU, which involved the introduction, in 1989, of free elections for some seats in a new national legislature called the All-Union Congress of Peoples' Deputies. Public openness meant ending censorship of the media and arts.[17] His strategy was to introduce a civil society independent of the state while maintaining the political monopoly of the CPSU.

This strategy unleashed powerful social forces that ripped the Soviet state apart in 1991. Disengaging civil society from the party apparatus left the way open for numerous possibilities. One was a nonstatist form of socialism, which anti-Soviet radicals in East Germany and (in the mid-1960s) Czechoslovakia had explored. The Czechoslovakia experiments under Alexander Dubček (1921–1992) were ruthlessly suppressed by Soviet armies in 1968. Western European and, especially, U.S. intervention in post-Soviet Russia has led to another possible trajectory: a liberal state with a civil society dominated by a capitalist economy fed largely by foreign capital and directed by international financial organizations.

Germany: A Fascist State

Although Germany developed an antiliberal state in the twentieth century, it did so out of a very different geostrategic position and according to a different history of state formation from that of Russia. However, several similarities exist: both states absorbed civil society and in both the state came to be identified with a single political party. Also, both committed unspeakable cruelties against their subject populations and those in neighboring states whom they defined as enemies. But the German fascist state embodied a personalized rule driven by an ideology of ethnic purity and exclusion, which looked to the past for its identity and glory. The fascists rejected the present in favor of an eternal past, whereas the Bolsheviks tried to remake the present into a more rational and egalitarian future.

The particular history of absolutism and liberalism in the formation of the German state set the terms for the emergence of the fascist state in the 1930s. Most important was the dominance of Brandenburg-Prussia, one of a multiplicity of small city-states, minor kingdoms, duchies, and principalities that had come into existence in the German-speaking area of Europe since the time of Charlemagne's Holy Roman Empire. By the seventeenth century, Prussia, under the leadership of a powerful monarchy descended from the last grand master of the Teutonic Knights, Albrecht von Hohenzollern, and a landowning military aristocracy called the Junkers, became dominant by building a powerful absolutist state. In Prussia, like nowhere else in Europe, war made the territorial state and the state, once formed, made war.[18]

Prussia, a German-speaking tribal area that had been forcibly Christianized by the Teutonic Knights, did not evolve as England had into a state dominated by its parliament. Surrounded by strong neighbors— Sweden to the north, Russia to the east, and France to the southwest—and lacking protective geographical features such as mountain ranges, marshlands, or open ocean, the Prussians built an efficient military machine in support of a strong, centralized state. The relation of the landed nobility to the state also made possible their unconditional military service. As one historian put it: "Nowhere did the cult of mechanical military obedience . . . so come to permeate the landowning class."[19]

The first attempt to build such a state was taken during the Thirty Years' War, when Friedrich Wilhelm, the Great Elector (ruled 1640–1688), imposed a tax to support a small army without the approval of the Ständestaat. Members of the Ständestaat, the Prussian estates, who disapproved, were arrested and imprisoned. After the war, such draconian measures were abandoned and feudal constitutionalism reasserted itself. The second attempt, and the decisive one, was taken during the First Northern War (1655–1660), which involved Poland, Sweden, and Prussia, when Friedrich Wilhelm was able to persuade the Ständestaat to agree to a standing army. As the war progressed, he proclaimed his right to raise taxes without the approval of the Ständestaat and to use his army to collect them. Under Friedrich III (ruled 1688–1713) and Friedrich Wilhelm I (ruled 1713–1740), known as the drillmaster of Europe, the Crown continued to strengthen itself against the Ständestaat, which declined in power and importance.

The decline of the Ständestaat was paralleled by the rise of the king's bureaucracy and increased centralization. The major institution in this process of centralization was the Generalkriegskommissariat, or General War Commission, which came to control all aspects of the recruitment and maintenance of the army. It created a three-tiered administrative structure that penetrated local government and was run from a central office in Berlin, the capital of Prussia. It collected taxes, administered justice, and controlled the police. Under the Generalkriegskommissariat, Prussia was gradually militarized. The Junkers formed the officer corps of the army and their peasants were forced into its ranks. The harshness of the state-building process in Prussia was aggravated because the region was economically backward and the population small. The economy was one of large estates owned by the Junker aristocracy upon which a multitude of landless peasants scratched a living from very poor soils. There was almost no bourgeoisie. Unity and identity with the state were fostered through respect for military virtues: obedience, discipline, and heroism. Victories in battle justified continued heavy taxation to support a strong military.[20]

The building of a strong, centralized, militarized state and the concomitant glorification of martial values inclined Prussia toward aggressive actions against surrounding states. Under Friedrich II the Great (ruled 1740–1786), the Prussian state fought and defeated the Austrians, Poles, Czechs, and the Russians. In 1806, Napoléon invaded the German-speaking kingdoms and principalities. He defeated the Austrians at Austerlitz (1805) and the Prussians at Jena (1806). Within eighteen months, all the other smaller German principalities were defeated and occupied by French troops.

The French Revolution had stimulated the development of liberalism in Germany, and, at first, many intellectuals and liberals welcomed Napoléon's invasion, which they viewed as an agent of progress against the absolutist regime. Note, however, that German liberalism was distinctive, and critical of its British and French versions. As was the case with British and French liberals, Immanuel Kant (1724–1804), the most important German philosopher of the Enlightenment, opposed the absolutist state, but in a way that argued for a cosmopolitan republican state governed by the rule of law. Kant viewed reason as dictating moral imperatives and laws to men and women rather than seeing it as primarily the instrumental calculation of self-interests. For Kant, reason did not guarantee that states would be governed by the rule of law and would eschew arbitrary power, but it opened the possibility of a state that would function positively within a moral society. Therefore, Kant's liberalism was more sensitive to the role of the state in modern life, even if it considered the state as something of a Faustian bargain (i.e., a pact with the devil).[21]

The defeat and six-year occupation of the German states by the French stimulated the creation in 1815 of a confederation of thirty-nine of these entities. It was reasoned that defeat and occupation by a foreign power could be avoided if German states were united into a single state. The idea of a unified German state was also fed by the historical and political philosophy that developed in Enlightenment Germany. Having rejected the individualism of English and French liberalism, German political philosophy contained a strong romanticist streak in which the social order was viewed as a living, organic unity in time and space that fed on a common language and common folk traditions, as in the work of Johann Gottfried von Herder (1774–1803).[22] Over the next century, the German state came to be associated with its own unique German *kultur,* or culture. Liberalism was associated by many Germans with foreign states, especially Britain and France, and was seen as having been imposed on German culture.

During the 1840s, the demand for more than a confederation was raised by German liberals, who were increasingly supported by the bourgeoisie. The overthrow of the monarchy and the establishment of the Second French Republic (1848–1851) by French liberals touched off popular disturbances in Vienna, the capital of Austria, and Berlin, as well as in other German cities. Too weak to suppress these uprisings, the rulers of these states agreed to the liberals' demand for the election of a constituent assembly, which was given the task of writing a constitution for a unified German state. This effort eventually failed because of disputes about which German-speaking entities were to be included.

Prussian victories in wars against Denmark (1864), Austria (1866), and France (1870–1871) assured Prussia's status as the most powerful German-speaking state. Prussia forcefully brought together less powerful German-speaking states into an empire led by Wilhelm I (ruled 1861–1888) of Prussia, who proclaimed himself its *kaiser* (Caesar, in German), or emperor. Although the empire-wide parliament, called the Reichstag, was elected on the basis of universal male suffrage, placating the liberal demand for representation, the real decisions affecting the functioning of the empire were made in the Bundesrat, which was composed of delegates from the *länd* (state) governments and presided over by the chancellor. The Reichstag was limited to dealing with nonessentials.[23]

The creation of universal male suffrage stimulated the development of German political parties. The first party to appear was the Social Democratic Party (SPD), which was founded in 1875 and became officially socialist in 1891. The SPD grew very rapidly. In 1877, it received 9 percent of the vote cast for the Reichstag; by 1890 its share of the vote was 20 percent; and by 1903 it had soared to 32 percent, which made it the largest party in the German Empire (1871–1918). By 1907, the SPD counted over 1 million dues-paying members and had a close relationship with Germany's trade unions, whose leaders had assumed key positions within the party.

Otto von Bismarck (1815–1898), chancellor of Prussia from 1862 and the empire's chancellor under Wilhelm, attempted to suppress the party, though without success owing to the party's disciplined political organization and its strong support among the proletariat. Therefore, he attempted to attract workers away from the SPD by passing a series of laws that met the SPD's demands for the health, safety, and retirement of workers. In 1883, he passed a law that insured workers against sickness; in 1884 a law was passed that insured against accidents; and in 1889 a law provided for disability insurance and old-age pensions. Bismarck's strategy did not work, however, and workers continued to flock to the SPD.[24]

The German Empire created by Bismarck was defeated in World War I, which led to the transformation of Germany into a liberal constitutional state called the Weimar Republic (1919–1936). The Weimar Republic was imposed by the Allies upon a Germany that was deeply divided between liberals and socialists, who supported it, and conservatives, who preferred the old imperial state. This division made it difficult for the Weimar Republic to govern effectively and prevented it from dealing with the serious economic problems Germany began to experience in the 1920s: soaring inflation and massive unemployment brought on by the excessive war reparations that had been imposed on Germany by the Allies, and the worldwide economic depression. Saddled with an ineffective state, Germans began to be drawn in large numbers to parties that sought to destroy the Weimar Republic. One of these parties was the German Communist Party, which had been formed in 1919 by radical members of the SPD who supported the Russian Revolution. The other was the National Socialist German Workers' Party (NSDAP) or Nazi Party, led by Adolf Hitler (1889–1945), which was a virulently racist and anti-Semitic fascist party.

In the 1932 elections, the Nazis became the largest party in the Reichstag. The Nazis and the Communists, who had come in third, formed an anti–Weimar Republic majority, which made it impossible for the pro-republic parties to form a stable government. As Germany's economic crisis continued, widespread rioting and street clashes between Nazis and Communists became a regular occurrence. Encouraged by conservative parties and many agrarian and industrial leaders, the president of the republic, Paul von Hindenburg (1925–1934), named Adolf Hitler chancellor on January 30, 1933.

Once in power, Hitler proceeded to overthrow the Weimar Republic from within and erect in its stead an antiliberal and antisocialist state (the Third Reich) to be united by its love for the Fatherland, and promised to protect Germany from the evil machinations of "lesser" races (especially Jews), "decadent" Western democracies, and "subhuman" Marxists. The Nazi Party did not recognize the constitution or any law save the will of the Führer. The Nazis destroyed the federal structure of the Weimar Republic and centralized all political and administrative power in Berlin, the capital of the Third Reich. Jews were expelled from the civil service and Nazi Party members were placed in key administrative positions. The Reichstag was abolished and land governments were merged with national ministries. The governors of the länder, which were now, in effect, administrative units of the central state, were Nazi *gauleiters* (party leaders) appointed by Hitler. The judiciary was purged of "non-Aryan" judges and centralized under the Reich ministry of justice. Special People's Courts, dominated by Nazi Party members, were established to try those accused of political crimes. A vast secret police network, which included the Geheimestaatspolizei (Gestapo) and the Schutzstaffel (SS), was created.[25]

Under the Nazis, the state massively intervened into civil society. Hitler developed numerous public-works projects in order to create jobs and achieve full employment; married couples with children were given family allowances; free holidays were provided for low-paid workers at state-run resorts; and factories were placed under state direction, if not ownership, as was agriculture. As fascism considered the economy to be at the service of the state, workers and employers were required to join a single corporation called the National Labor Front, controlled by the Nazi Party, which regulated working conditions and wages. Independent unions were abolished, and strikes were outlawed. Professionals, such as lawyers and doctors, were required to join guildlike organizations under Nazi Party control.[26]

In order to create the "Master Race," the Nazis instituted a policy of sterilization and extermination of what they considered to be undesirable elements of the German population: the incurably ill, the feebleminded, homosexuals, Gypsies, and especially Jews. Jews and others were systematically rounded up and put into work or extermination camps, where millions died, subjected to scientifically sophisticated techniques of mass murder and genocide. The roundups and exterminations were so routinized and bureaucratized that they appeared to the participants as "normal." In her famous accounts of the trial of Adolph Eichmann (1906–1962), a former camp commandant who escaped justice until 1961, Hannah Arendt described the process as the "banality of evil."[27]

Hitler's belief that Germany needed *lebensraum* (living space), which he sought to get from, in his view, the "racially inferior" Slavic peoples to the east, proved to be the Nazi state's undoing. In 1939 Hitler invaded Poland, an act of aggression that started World War II. Germany's defeat by the Allies in 1945 brought an end to the Nazi fascist state. After the war, Germany was occupied and partitioned by the victors into zones controlled by the United States, France, Britain, and the Soviet Union. The Soviet Union was given land from Polish territory in the east for which Poland was compensated by giving it German territory, and from which Germans were expelled. Berlin, which was well within the Soviet zone, was itself divided into U.S., French, British, and Soviet zones of occupation. In 1949, the British, French, and U.S. occupiers merged their zones into a new liberal democratic state, the Federal Republic of Germany (West Germany), with its capital in Bonn. In response, the Soviets transformed their zone of occupation into a new communist state called the German Democratic Republic (East Germany), with its capital in East Berlin. Thus, two rival German states existed until 1990, when the German Democratic Republic collapsed and was absorbed by the Federal Republic and a single German state was created.

Summary

In the nineteenth century, the relationship of the state to key features of modernity, especially industrialization, came under question. The traditional ways in which absolutism and liberalism had institutionalized sovereignty did not permit the newly industrialized state to play the role it was increasingly called upon to play. In this chapter, we discussed the emergence of antiliberal forms of the modern territorial state that abolished civil society in order to help the state meet the challenges posed by industrialization. The next chapter examines the emergence of another form of state, the managerial state, which sought to relegitimate liberalism and capitalism in light of the increasing role of the state in modern life.

Notes

1. Sheldon Wolin, *Politics and Vision: Continuity and Innovation in Western Political Thought* (Boston: Little, Brown, 1961).

2. Karl Polanyi, *The Great Transformation: The Political and Economic Origins of Our Time* (Boston: Beacon Press, 1957), 33.

3. Heinz Lubasz, ed., *The Development of the Modern State* (New York: Macmillan, 1964), 8–9.

4. Karl Marx, *Economic and Philosophical Manuscripts*, in T. B. Bottomore (ed. and trans.), *Karl Marx: Early Writings* (New York: McGraw-Hill, 1964): 122–123. Emphasis in the original.

5. Karl Marx, *Manifesto of the Communist Party,* in Robert C. Tucker (ed.), *The Marx-Engels Reader,* 2d ed. (New York and London: W. W. Norton, 1978): 476.

6. The implications of Marx's theory for feminism were developed by his collaborator, Frederick Engels, in *The Origin of the Family, Private Property and the State* (New York: International, 1942). Originally published in 1884.

7. On Burke, see Stephen White, *Edmund Burke* (Beverly Hills, CA: Sage Publications, 1994).

8. On conservatism in general, see the classic essay by Karl Manheim, "Conservative Thought," in Kurt H. Wolff (ed.), *From Karl Manheim* (Oxford: Oxford University Press, 1971): 132–222.

9. See Jeffrey Herf, *Reactionary Modernism: Technology, Culture, and Politics in Weimar and the Third Reich* (Cambridge: Cambridge University Press, 1984).

10. Hans H. Gerth and C. Wright Mills, eds., *From Max Weber* (New York: Oxford University Press, 1958), 245.

11. Perhaps most influential of these was Carl J. Friedrich and Zbigniew Brzezinski, *Totalitarian Dictatorship and Autocracy* (Cambridge, MA: Harvard University Press, 1965).

12. Hugh Seton-Watson, *Nations and States* (Boulder, CO: Westview Press, 1977), 79–80.

13. Ibid., 80.

14. Stanley Rothman, *European Society and Politics* (Indianapolis, IN: Bobbs-Merrill, 1970), 99.

15. These and the following details on the organization of the Soviet state and the Communist Party are from Rothman, *European Society and Politics*, 416–434 and 557–566.

16. Alexander Solzhenitzen, *The Gulag Archipelago, 1918–1956* (New York: Harper & Row, 1975).

17. Jorgen S. Rasmussen and Joel C. Moses, *Major European Governments*, 9th ed. (Belmont, CA: Wadsworth, 1995), 485–499.

18. This and the following paragraphs on the case of Prussia follow Brian M. Downing, *The Military Revolution and Political Change: Origins of Democracy and Autocracy in Early Modern Europe* (Princeton, NJ: Princeton University Press, 1992), chapter 6.

19. Perry Anderson, *Lineages of the Absolutist State* (London: New Left Books, 1974), 227.

20. Downing, *The Military Revolution*, chapter 6.

21. Hans Reiss, ed., *Kant's Political Writings* (Cambridge: Cambridge University Press, 1970).

22. See Robert T. Clark Jr., *Herder: His Life and Thought* (Berkeley and Los Angeles: University of California Press, 1969).

23. Arnold J. Heidenheimer and Donald P. Kommers, *The Governments of Germany,* 4th ed. (New York: Thomas Crowell, 1975), 12.

24. Ernest Barker, *The Development of Public Services in Western Europe 1660–1930* (Hamden, CT: Archon Books, 1966), 75–76.

25. Rothman, *European Society and Politics,* 695, 737.

26. Heidenheimer and Kommers, *The Governments of Germany,* 23.

27. Hannah Arendt, *Eichmann in Jerusalem: Report on the Banality of Evil* (New York: Penguin Books, 1963).

7

The Managerial State: Sovereignty Rationalized

In this chapter we argue that the formal organizational characteristics, internal operations, and basic purpose of the state have been converging, especially since the nineteenth century,[1] to produce a singular form of the state that we call the "managerial state." The managerial state, like the Soviet and Nazi antiliberal states, seeks to solve the problems of industrial capitalism but does so by continuing to rely on liberal ideology to frame its subjects' understandings of the state and civil society. However, liberal ideology does not describe the actuality of the politico-military power of the managerial state. Rather, liberal ideology hides the actual operation of state politico-military power, making it appear that managerial states have no state at all or have, at most, a very weak one. In the managerial state, the economy and civil society are not absorbed by the state's bureaucratic apparatus.[2] Rather, in the managerial state the boundary between "the government" and "society," although distinct at the level of ideology, is actually blurred because state power is diffused throughout society. In this way, in the words of one scholar, the managerial state "assumes responsibility for the entire condition of contemporary society—the condition of the air, the food and water; the relationships its citizens must be involved in; the habits they develop; their education; and their ability to make a living."[3]

Rationalizing the State

In the nineteenth century, states began to develop mechanisms and strategies to gain some control over the contingencies of industrialization. One way to do so was to develop a knowledge of industrialization and its consequences; such knowledge facilitated direction and control. New social sciences—economics, sociology, political science—developed based on the idea that industrialization and societies in general comprised systems or structures; that is, they were wholes that were more than the sum of their parts. The individual parts could be understood and made somewhat predictable by understanding the laws of the whole. Systems came to be seen as coordinated through "instrumental rationality"; that is, reason came to be seen as the efficient application of means, or the invention of new ones, to a given end. The end was given by the nature of the system: war/victory; economy/prosperity; polity/democracy. Viewing what were complex sets of contingent events as integral wholes that could be planned, gave to those in power a new sense that the effects of industrialization could be mitigated and their outcomes controlled. In short, the rationalization of knowledge about politics and society helped to make the managerial state possible. What this meant for politics was that the state came to be seen as the coordinator of all of the complex systems that were said to compose society, such as the economy, government, class structure, and value system. Intervention in each subsystem was limited to coordinating them with the others in managing the whole of the state.

The greatest theorist and critic of the way this new form of knowledge transformed the state was the German historian, legal scholar, and sociologist Max Weber (1864–1920). Weber saw the rationalization of the state as inevitable because of the breakdown of the status-based solidarity of feudalism and the emergence of the industrialized and urbanized states of the late nineteenth century. The most important aspect of this development for Weber was the advance of bureaucracy because of its purely technical superiority over other methods of administration. Bureaucracy broke down the complex functions of organizations, such as governments and large corporations, into individual decisions, all coordinated in terms of laws and the instrumental rationality of the whole. According to Weber, compared to other types of social organization, bureaucracy is the most efficient means of exercising control over a large number of human beings.[4]

Bureaucracy (from the French *bureau,* meaning desk or office) refers to the sum of individuals who are engaged in administering the public services that must be rendered each day if a state is to survive. As was discussed in Chapter 3, bureaucracy was developed by medieval monarchs in order to extract directly the men, money, and matériel necessary to fight wars and maintain a standing army. The first administrators, or civil servants, were from the king's household—his steward, reeves, chancellor, and constable—who collected his revenue, provided his justice, and maintained his peace. Gradually, two parallel sets of hierarchically organized institutions (financial and legal), staffed by individuals trained in the law and accounting, came into being. Within these institutions, clerks and scribes developed and preserved routine ways of drafting orders and issuing instructions. Thus a group of individuals appeared who spent their entire working lives in the service of the king. The development of a staff of full-time judges, lawyers, tax collectors, clerks, and scribes gave the medieval king not only the ability to rule his realm directly without the assistance of the aristocracy, but also the ability to bypass the estates.

Initially, those who occupied positions within the developing administrative structures regarded their offices as private property that they owned outright, derived income from, and bequeathed to their heirs. In other words, offices were hereditary. During the nineteenth century, a gradual rationalization of the administrative organization in every major European state took place, and the idea that such offices were private property gave way to the notion that they were public positions to be filled on the basis of ability and training. This rationalization involved organizational reform and the creation of a merit system for recruiting administrators. The idea developed that all of these offices and functions were related to one another in a complex system, a bureaucracy, and that state sovereignty was, in part at least, dependent on the ability to coordinate and manage these complex systems of relations. For this, a scientific knowledge of the laws of bureaucratic systems was necessary.

For Weber the bureaucratic system was efficient because it rationalized human interactions in the following ways. First, it depersonalized them; that is, it treated all interactions without regard to the personal characteristics of the actors, such as gender, age, race, appearance, and ethnicity.[5] Second, it neutralized them; that is, it eliminated all emotional feelings of love, hate, desire, envy, and so forth from nonfamilial human interactions. Third, it universalized them; that is, it disregarded social position, privilege, status, rank, and so on in personal interactions. Fourth, it qualified them; that is, it eliminated friendship and family connections in interactions involving hiring and promotion. Finally, it organized them; that is, it arranged human interactions into a series of offices and roles with clear lines of domination and subordination between them.[6]

To Weber, bureaucratization and rationalization were systems of social control whose historical roots reached back to the Protestant Reformation.[7] Although he was interested in questions of why they developed, much of his work explained how they worked as systems of domination, not why they came about. Although Weber's use of a methodology of ideal types may have led him to overstate the coherence and consistency of the bureaucratic system, and to ignore ways in which bureaucracies drew on noninstrumentally rational forms (e.g., personal loyalty, social prejudices), his idea that rationalization and bureaucratization constituted forms of subjectivity distinctive to the modern state and society, and legitimated the state on a new basis, is extremely important. The modern political subject has come to be constituted through the rationalizing systems of bureaucratic domination.

The managerial state, then, appeared to represent progress toward a political order free of domination because it was based on the rule of law and liberal ideals of individual rights and freedoms, but it came to exercise its control through familiar institutions and routine practices. In other words, the subject population of the managerial state came to accept domination by the state and willingly complied with it insofar as the state was perceived as legal and rational—that is, had been constructed by some rational procedure of which the subject was himself or herself a part.[8] This was a far cry from the medieval state in which domination was accepted by reference to the personal status or position of the order-giver.

Weber was convinced that the rationalization and bureaucratization of both state and civil society were necessary and inevitable. However, rather than a new realm of freedom, as liberals saw these processes, they represented for Weber a new mode of domination that gave the state, and other bureaucratized and rationalized organizations such as economic corporations, tremendous powers of control. According to Weber, modernizing the state and society comes with significant costs. While rationalization eliminates personal and emotional elements such as love, hate, and desire from human interactions, it also results in widespread disenchantment and alienation manifested in various kinds of antibureaucratic activities and resistance, ranging from grumbling about "red tape" to violent attacks on administrative offices.[9]

Rationalization also separates means and ends, so that the determination of the latter was removed from rational judgment. For Weber, this amounted to the impoverishment of human spirituality and moral life. In a famous essay, he argued that modern science, for all its methodological sophistication and explanatory power, could never justify the choices it had to make about the ends to which society ought to use its knowledge. The spiritual and moral guidance human beings once took from religion and culture was thoroughly disempowered by the rationalization and disenchantment of the world. What was left was an "iron cage," a neat, highly structured, law-governed, objective order that, by seeking to eliminate contingency, eliminated much of the human spirit that made life worth living.[10]

Managing Citizenship

As the managerial state has expanded in the twentieth century, individual citizens have increasingly come to be treated less as bearers of rights, as in liberal states, and more as efficient contributors to and consumers of the outcomes of bureaucratic state practices. In the managerial state, the political consciousness of the citizen becomes that of the rational consumer, who looks at the state through the lens of a utilitarian calculus of costs and benefits. Taxes, for example, come to be seen less as necessary contributions to the public good and more as the price of government services. The managerial state becomes the "producer" of public "goods" ("good" slipping in meaning between a normative "good"—what should be done—and a "good" in the sense of a commodity) that are "sold" to the citizenry through the industrialized mass media. As will be shown in Chapter 9 (on nationalism), one of the most important political "goods" that the state "sells" to the public is a set of images of a homogeneous national identity sufficient to establish the individualized consumer/citizen as part of a unified, political, and moral community.

As we saw in regard to the liberal state, political information circulated in a public sphere consisting of newspapers, magazines, clubs, scientific societies, commercial book publishing, and so on.[11] Although the liberal public sphere was never as egalitarian or rational as it is often presented, liberal citizenship presupposed the "marketplace of ideas" that managerial states transform in important ways.[12] Although the marketplace of ideas continues to exist in managerial states, technology and the industrialization of media industries and the concentration of ownership have reconstituted the way information is circulated. Political information is increasingly managed and mediated by (1) political parties, which are interested primarily in winning elections; (2) industrial capitalist media, which are interested primarily in profit; and (3) state bureaucracies, which are concerned with producing rational outcomes.

In the liberal state of the late nineteenth and early twentieth centuries, political information and imagery were mediated by political parties in which organized elites set out interpretations of the state's needs and shared goals according to class affiliation, political ideology, or other group identities. As the industrialization of the mass media has increased during the twentieth century—especially through radio and television, which reach subjects in the "privacy" of their own homes—political parties have declined as mediators of political information and interpreters of political needs.

With the decline of parties, the public character of political discussion and debate has also declined. People in managerial states receive their information and interpretations of politics as spectators outside the forums for political discussion and debate, such as union or party meetings or civic organizations, through which citizens used to receive much of their political information. In the managerial state, political information and images are produced and circulated as industrial products like soap and cars. To be successful as capitalist corporations, television and newspapers must reach wide audiences and, therefore, seek to present images and information tailored to the "average" consumer of information. Increasingly, the attitude prevails that one can be a good citizen and gain the knowledge one needs to vote by "keeping up with the news," but not by actively engaging in political activity and debate; this attitude has routinized the citizen as a consumer and has caused political values and ideologies to become merely images to be consumed rather than subjects of political discussion.

The blurring of the distinction between the state and civil society is apparent in this industrialized construction of the citizen as consumer of media-presented information. The media are both public and private. Although the state does not own and directly control the media, it does intervene to limit and at times direct the way in which information is presented. This is clearest in times of war, as was the case recently with the U.S. military's manipulation of information about the Gulf War and the invasion of Iraq.[13] Election campaigns that take place primarily through the media adopt the same kinds of strategies for controlling the images of candidates, devising and strategically placing advertisements, and controlling the timing of statements. The aim of these efforts is to manage the electorate by carefully regulating, according to the expert knowledge of professional media consultants, the images and information it consumes.

This new language of citizenship appears to reinvigorate a republican political imaginary insofar as information about government and society is made more widely available in the public media. But this mode of publicity actually deepens the passivity of citizenship, even as it allows some citizens to become more well-informed about public affairs. The language of citizenship in managerial states maintains the appearance of popular sovereignty while allowing room for the autonomous operations of bureaucratic and managerial structures under conditions in which the mediations of citizenship and power are opaque to most citizens. One is either "inside" the system, the "insider" being a government official, a lobbyist, or some other functionary privy to and presumed to be knowledgeable about the inner workings of the system, or "outside," a consumer of the outcomes of a system that appears as an opaque box. Moreover, even those inside the state are subordinated to the logic of spectatorship.

In other words, in the managerial state, citizenship is constructed in a new way. Most citizens must be outside the governing apparatus of the state for it to function smoothly according to the criteria of bureaucratic and instrumental rationality. Citizens who do manage to move inside participate only in those specific areas in which they can claim some special competence or some proprietary interest, such as lobbyists and "special interest groups." The managerial state must unify this distribution of insiders and outsiders, making them all appear as members of a single, territorial community. It does so through association with the "nation," a ritualized performance that invokes an abstract, imagined community created through public imagery in the mass media.

Managing Capitalism

Perhaps the most important change that undermined the social conditions of the liberal state and encouraged the formation of managerial states was the reorganization of the capitalist firm, which brought about a shift in the form of capitalist individualism. Prior to the second half of the nineteenth century, the dominant form of organization of capital was the individual firm, that is, the business owned by an individual, a family, or a small partnership. In most cases, those who owned the business participated directly in it. From the point of view of enhancing profits in an industrial system, however, this individualist organization was quite restrictive. It limited the amount of capital that could be invested to that owned by the individual owner or family. It also entailed considerable risks for the owner: if the business went bankrupt or was sued, the personal assets of the individual owners were at risk.

By the end of the nineteenth century, first in the United States and then throughout the industrial capitalist world, the individualist entrepreneur was replaced by the corporation. Incorporation was a highly useful tool that overcame the limits of individual or family ownership. Unlike the latter, the "corporation as a form severs the direct link between capital and its individual owner."[14] Risk of failure and loss of capital were now borne not by the owners but by the corporation. This made possible vast combinations of capital.

One cultural historian of the post–Civil War United States describes the new economic form of capitalism this way:

> The corporation embodied a legally sanctioned fiction, that an association of people constituted a single entity which might hold property, sue and be sued, enter contracts, and continue in existence beyond the lifetime or membership of any of its participants. The association itself was understood as strictly contractual, not necessarily comprised of people acquainted with each other or joined by any common motive other than profit seeking.[15]

He goes on to assess the cultural significance of the idea of the corporation as follows:

> With the corporate device as its chief instrument, business grew increasingly arcane and mysterious, spawning new roles intermediary between capital and labor, in middle management, accounting, legal departments, public relations, advertising, marketing, sales: the entire apparatus of twentieth-century corporate life was developed in these years and clouded the public perception of the typical acts of business. Organization and administration emerged as major virtues, along with obedience and loyalty. At the same time the rhetoric of success continued to hail the self-made man as the paragon of free labor, even as the virtues of that fictive character grew less and less relevant.[16]

The idea of the corporation—the large hierarchical and bureaucratically organized combination of capital—would become the standard organization of private property and production during the twentieth century in managerial states; in some, however, the corporations were direct arms of the state and in others they were owned and managed by private capital. In many states, corporations were owned, either entirely or in significant parts, by foreign capital.

The corporation allowed forever greater concentrations of capital, which dramatically increased productive capacity. During the first half of the twentieth century, a new social system emerged in which workers were increasingly seen as consumers of the products of the industrial economy. Workers increasingly came to be seen as individual consumers whose identities as human beings were tied to the products they consumed, as participants in a consumer culture.[17] The creation of a corporate form of capital created the conditions in which the United States would rise to global hegemonic power in the twentieth century.

In the early twentieth century, the industrialist Henry Ford (1863–1947), founder of the Ford Motor Company, pioneered a new social system for an industrial economy. This system has become known as Fordism, and describes the network of political, economic, and social relations that dominated managerial states increasingly from the 1930s to the 1970s.

In his automobile factories, Ford improved techniques for mass production to the point where he could produce large numbers of identical automobiles at greatly reduced cost. The first automobile to be so produced was the Model T, which was the first "world car," a standardized product that would appeal to "ordinary" people everywhere. Of course, the "ordinary" person who needed or wanted his or her own automobile had to be created, in part through advertising but also through changing the rules of industrial society. Ford realized that he could improve profits by selling these cars to the very workers who produced them. This meant paying higher than subsistence wages, contrary to the norm of nineteenth-century capitalist firms. In effect, Fordism amounted to a class compromise in which workers accepted loss of control in the factories in return for sufficient wages to live a comfortable, private life. Of course, this only applied to workers in some factories and in industries in which higher wages could be wrested from often intransigent employers. Fordism was in practice inequitable, creating divisions within the working class. Nevertheless, after World War II, and in part because of the war, the Fordist construction of the worker as consumer became the norm that determined the aspirations of even the poorest workers. For liberals, Fordism came to be seen as a worthy system of industrial relations, which the state should and could manage by manipulating economic policies. To Marxist critics, Fordism, although it produced certain isolated gains for some workers, entrenched the alienation of the industrial capitalist system deep into social life and relegitimized the domination of the bourgeoisie over industrial society.[18]

In the Fordist compromise, workers became consumers who compensated for the loss of control over their work with consumption of material goods during leisure time. Increasingly, workers would be represented by labor unions—representation that led to increased wages, safer and better working conditions, and a shorter workweek. Unions and workers would turn to the state to guarantee the gains won in organized labor struggles. In return for legalizing unions and for the state's acceptance of its role as guarantor of labor's hard-won gains, unions gave up the aspirations of socialist and more radical workers' movements to redirect investments toward social needs rather than corporate profit, or democratizing control over the factories. Essentially, mid-twentieth-century labor unions, especially in the United States, accepted the class compromise of Fordism, and organized the patriotism and support of workers for a form of the state that managed the Fordist industrial system.[19]

Fordism became entrenched in the U.S. economy during the 1930s as an antidote to the Great Depression, and in the 1940s as a facilitator of the massive war production needs of World War II, during which vast numbers of people had participated as either workers or soldiers. After World War II, the consumer aspect of Fordism became deeply entrenched. This was in part for the economic reason of absorbing the tremendous productive capacity that the war had produced, and in part for political reasons: to control and pacify workers and soldiers whose expectations had been heightened by participation in the war. The state came to function as the instrumentally rational guarantor of the Fordist class compromise and the consumer society.

Managing Gender Relations

One result of Fordism was that responsibility for ensuring the well-being and continued prosperity of the economy was transferred to the state. The working class looked to the state to cement the gains it had won through unionization and collective bargaining with private capital. Private capital looked to the state to oversee the general conditions of accumulation of wealth in the national economy, managing the money supply through its treasury and central bank, regulating the stock market, ensuring competition by regulating monopolies, and providing or guaranteeing investments in infrastructure such as roads, ports, electrical grids, and telephone systems. Of particular importance was the state's role in providing general security and stability through the police, the courts, the prisons, and the social services (at home) and through military interventions (abroad) to stabilize opportunities for investment and trade.

Fordism also depended on a particular division of work between men and women. Early on, Ford required that workers in his automobile factories maintain a stable, healthy, and traditional family life. By this he meant that women would care for the children and do housework while men worked in the factory for wages (of course, women were not paid for their work), and that the family would go to church regularly and would avoid alcohol and drugs. Antisocial or disruptive behavior, even in "private" life, could be cause for dismissal from the factory. Although unions were able to fight and defeat many of the social restrictions placed on male workers, they left the division of labor between men and women intact.

The family, then, played a distinctive role in Fordist economies and in the regulation of the industrial citizen. It provided the "private" infrastructure of emotional support and organized consumption that kept men happy at work and, above all, self-disciplined. That is, they were disciplined to support the family, a responsibility that they accepted because of the services women provided for them outside the factory by taking care of household work, raising children, planning family consumption, and providing sexual and emotional satisfaction.

World War II, paradoxically, deepened this divide; managing the division of labor between men and women became an important part of the managerial state. This was paradoxical given that during the war, as men went to fight, women took up industrial jobs. Rosie the Riveter became the symbol of a generation of women who ably demonstrated that they possessed the strength, intelligence, and character to do the "hard work" of mass industrial production, despite the contention of Fordist ideology that they were naturally unsuited to do so.

After the war, government programs guaranteed returning soldiers their old jobs and required women to return to "private" life. These programs not only managed the supply of workers by ensuring against the massive unemployment that might be expected to follow the demobilization of millions of soldiers, but they also reinstituted the structure of Fordist discipline. Government programs to aid education also helped manage the labor supply, giving male workers the skills for the next generation of industrial jobs by providing ex-soldiers with grants to attend college in programs such as the G.I. Bill in the United States. The return to domesticity in the larger culture of the 1950s and 1960s can then be seen as a strategy within the context of managerial states, which blended elements of state and civil society together in a diffuse network of regulatory power.

To accomplish their objectives, twentieth-century managerial states have come to rely increasingly on experts in economics, law, psychology, organizational science, and various substantive areas of public policy. For women, this meant the promotion of scientific approaches to "home economics" and the inclusion of this subject for girls in public schools. This has led not only to the retaining of professionals and experts within a state's own bureaucracy, but also to the development of close interconnections between experts in private industries and in universities, whether public or private. Lawyers still dominate in government positions, as Max Weber argued they would in modern states,[20] but to manage late capitalist industrial economies, states have generated networks of experts and bodies of expertise that cut across the boundaries of state and civil society.

Managing the Economy

Under some circumstances, the managerial state would intervene directly in the industrial capitalist economy by nationalizing industries that failed as private enterprises, but provided the public goods the system as a whole needed (for example, railroads and utilities); by subjecting private corporations to environmental regulations; by providing social services; and by energizing the economy with spending on the military. In some cases the state would manage the economy indirectly by adding incentives and disincentives to the tax code or by passing tariffs or subsidies to favor some industries or forms of investment over others. The specific strategies used depended on situational factors in specific states, such as the history of bureaucratization within them; the roles of war and the military in the development of state institutions; the strength, ideology, and character of political parties and unions; and the relative position of the national economy in the world economy.[21]

Even states that continued a strong ideology of economic liberalism, and professed allegiance to nonintervention by the state in markets, developed into managerial states. In France and Germany, some of the institutions created to direct mercantilist economies provided fertile ground for the growth of managerialism. In both cases, the state took responsibility for developing the infrastructure and pioneered national systems of education, in part to produce well-trained civil servants with managerial and engineering expertise.

Both France and Germany have gone through periods when certain industries were nationalized, that is, taken over and managed by the state. In the nineteenth century, the German state continued to industrialize by importing British machinery, then the most advanced in the world, and British technicians to train German workers in its proper operation. During the period of the German Empire, industries owned by the nobility, such as breweries in Bavaria, porcelain factories in Meissen and Berlin, and cigarette manufacturing facilities in Strasbourg, were nationalized. Agriculture and mining also came under state regulation and control during this period.[22] After World War II, the West German state denationalized certain industries, relaxed economic controls, and gave market forces (supply and demand) more significance. Nonetheless, the West German state continued, and continues, to intervene very actively in economic life. Subsidies were made available in order to encourage postwar reconstruction, especially in housing. Tax exemptions were given in order to increase savings and reduce personal consumption. The state subsidized the production of fertilizer and controlled certain agricultural prices by regulating imports and exports. In general, the approach was and continues to be state intervention in order to manage market forces to achieve specific ends.

In France, nationalization occurred after World War II and continued into the 1980s, when U.S.- and British-inspired neoliberalism (see Chapter 12) began to influence even the socialists away from state ownership of industry and toward more indirect forms of market management using tax and fiscal policies. In the late 1940s and early 1950s, the railroads, electricity production, telephone communications, petroleum production, aircraft manufacturing, and some automobile manufacturing were taken over by the state because state ownership was seen as necessary for economic development or, as in the case of the Renault automobile manufacturer, a punishment for collaborating with the Vichy regime during the war. After the war, national economic planning was introduced.[23]

It was not until the twentieth century that active state regulation and management of the economy began in Britain. As will be shown in Part 3, during the nineteenth century, Britain dominated the world economy as the strongest and most innovative capitalist economy. Liberal economic policies were a crucial factor in its dominance. During the 1920s, when Britain no longer dominated the world capitalist economy, the price of coal began to be regulated and industries were encouraged by tax-abatement schemes to locate themselves in economically depressed areas. During the 1930s, John Maynard Keynes (1883–1946), an economist teaching at Cambridge University, argued that the Great Depression could be overcome, and economic depression in general be prevented, if the state actively intervened by using monetary and fiscal policy to encourage economic growth. The key to economic growth, he argued, was full employment to be attained by careful management of markets.

After World War II, the British state began to nationalize certain industries, such as coal, steel, electricity, and transportation; institute a series of economic development councils that offered technical and financial incentives to key industries; and use Keynesian-inspired monetary and fiscal measures to attain full employment. Systematic economic planning was introduced in the 1960s with the establishment of the National Economic Development Council, which brought together representatives from government, industry, and labor to monitor the performance of the economy, consider plans to foster economic growth, and agree upon methods to improve economic performance. Other measures were taken to improve economic productivity and managerial efficiency. In essence, the British state guides a largely privately owned economy by manipulating market mechanisms.[24]

In the United States, where liberalism has also had a significant impact, state management of the economy developed out of different historical conditions than those in Britain. In important ways, the growth of managerialism in the United States owes much to direct mobilization for war by a state whose ideology and geographical location inclined it to avoid a large permanent military force, at least until after World War II.[25]

The necessity of mobilizing economic resources in order to fight the Civil War (1860–1865) and reconstruct the South after the war marks the first significant intervention of the U.S. state into the economy. From 1860 to 1877, the state became a major purchaser of iron, textiles, shoes, and meat. The state established and operated its own manufacturing facilities for clothing, pharmaceuticals, foodstuffs, and firearms. The state also instituted the first U.S. income tax, as well as other taxes, including excise, luxury, and inheritance, during this period in order to supplement revenues from customs duties.[26]

Several acts of Congress passed during the Civil War were designed to encourage industrial growth and westward expansion. The Homestead Act of 1862 gave land in the western states to those who were willing to settle and farm it. The Morrill College Act of the same year granted land for the building of universities dedicated to the improvement of agriculture and mining. The Immigration Act of 1864 allowed millions of immigrants to flood into the United States in order to provide labor for the new factories serving its rapidly industrializing economy. The Union Pacific and Central Pacific Railroads were founded as federally chartered companies and given land in the West in order to construct a transcontinental railroad.[27]

During World War I, the U.S. state intervened in the economy in order to boost the production of war matériel. It regulated industries, imposed price controls, and involved itself in labor disputes. It set up a complex of boards and agencies that mobilized U.S. workers and industry for the war effort. The income tax, which had been abolished after the Civil War, was revived and made permanent with the passage of the Income Tax Amendment in 1913. The War Industries Board regulated industrial production according to wartime needs.[28]

After World War I, the state did not significantly intervene in the economy until the Great Depression of the 1930s. Faced with the collapse of the economy, Franklin D. Roosevelt (1882–1945), who had been elected president in 1932, initiated a program called the New Deal, which sought to revitalize the economy by stimulating aggregate demand through government spending on public works and other types of projects. The National

Industrial Recovery Act of 1933 established the National Recovery Administration and the Works Progress Administration, which, by means of price supports for agricultural products, bulk purchasing of manufactures, regulation of credit and interest rates, monetary controls, and jobs programs (which built roads, bridges, dams, schools, libraries, and houses), stimulated the economy to recover from the Depression.[29]

During World War II, the U.S. state again intervened in the economy in order to mobilize it for the production of war matériel. Throughout the war, the executive branch held unfettered control over the economy. The Office of War Mobilization, the Office of Price Administration, and the Office of Economic Stabilization together managed the economy by controlling prices, wages, rents, and profits, and by rationing consumption.[30]

After the war, the U.S. state relaxed its grip on the economy but did not release it completely. As in other managerial states such as Britain, France, and Germany, state management of the economy has become permanent. The principal tools for this task were Keynesian-inspired monetary and fiscal policies and a host of regulatory agencies and commissions, such as the Federal Trade Commission and the Interstate Commerce Commission. The state also subsidizes major sectors of the economy, such as agriculture.[31]

As the dominant power on the Western side of the war, the United States engaged in massive military spending—which took the form of contracting for weapons from private arms producers. During the Cold War, military spending became a form of economic management, not unlike the way military spending during World War II had helped to pull the economy out of Depression. The arms race during the Kennedy administration in the early 1960s and under President Ronald Reagan in the early 1980s became the main engine of economic growth and spurred technological development in the economy as a whole. A policy of military Keynesianism, which blurred the lines between state and civil society by generating a military-industrial complex, remains central to managing the U.S. economy.

Managing Welfare

One of the most significant areas of state management of industrial capitalism is social welfare. Welfare programs such as health insurance, social security, unemployment insurance, and aid to the poor are important tools used by the state to manage prosperity and maintain public order. These programs are often used to channel money to consumers to ensure sufficient aggregate demand for the mass-produced goods of industrial corporations, and to redirect labor to the new jobs that the economy requires. They are also important components of the management of general social order by disciplining recipients of aid through stipulating program requirements and by ameliorating and confining the worst effects of the dislocations of the capitalist marketplace.

Concern for the welfare for the entire subject population did not, however, begin with the managerial state. Such programs paralleled the development of the state in Europe. During the medieval period it was the duty of the Catholic Church to assist the poor and to provide education, which it did primarily to educate its own priesthood. Over time, these responsibilities and many others were gradually shifted to the state. Three epochs in the process of transference can be identified. The first includes the period before the Industrial Revolution, when the primary concern was poverty among the rural peasantry. The second epoch begins with the Industrial Revolution, about 1750, and lasts until the beginning of the twentieth century; during this epoch, the social and economic problems created by industrialization and urbanization were addressed. In the third epoch, which began in the early decades of the twentieth century and extends to the present, the state has taken on the responsibility of maintaining the education, health, and safety of the entire subject population.[32]

In the first epoch, the state sought only to rescue the rural poor from destitution. The most developed system for providing "poor relief," as it was called, appeared in England during the Tudor period (1536–1603). During this time, several poor relief acts were passed by Parliament. Under these acts, every destitute person was to receive relief and each parish was to raise money in order to pay the indigent an allowance to supplement their meager wages. Poor relief programs were administered by county justices of the peace. By the end of the eighteenth century, this system of poor relief came under heavy criticism because it depressed rural wages and reduced the mobility of the poor, who could not seek better employment elsewhere without losing their allowances. Therefore, Parliament passed the Poor Law Amendment Act (1834), which removed poor relief from the justices of the peace and gave it to elected local boards operating under central authority. In 1929, the English Parliament passed an act that abolished poor relief and replaced it with a system of public assistance administered by county councils.

In France, until the French Revolution, the king relied upon the Catholic Church to provide poor relief through its hospitals, outdoor relief centers, and other charitable foundations. The king provided bread (*pain du roi*) to the beggars and vagabonds of Paris, and each of his intendants was permitted to use a small share of the king's revenues to aid the poor in their *généralités*. The French Revolution abolished the charitable foundations of the Church and the royal revenues; hence poor relief fell to the new local authorities (*départements* and *communes*) created by the revolutionary government. *Préfects* of the *départements* were required to deal with rural destitution and, after Napoléon seized power, undertook many public-works projects, such as building roads, in order to provide jobs for the rural poor. In 1871 the French National Assembly passed a law that required each *département* to provide public assistance to all who were unable to work because of old age, mental illness, or sickness.[33]

During the second epoch, the idea that the state's responsibility to provide poor relief as a temporary concession to the indigent, working poor was replaced with the idea that the state could regulate its workers by providing a panoply of social services. The new conditions that caused this change in thinking were industrialization, urbanization, and modern warfare. It began to be recognized that beyond the rural worker's basic right to life, which poor relief laws recognized, workers of a state's population had to be provided a minimum standard of health and physical well-being. This recognition was connected to the necessity of maintaining a healthy subject population for the dual purposes of providing recruits for the armed forces and boosting morale.[34] Thus, the state began to concern itself with standards of sanitation in the new industrial towns, to regulate the conditions of employment in the new factories, and to guarantee a decent standard of subsistence by insuring against sickness, unemployment, and old age. These programs were designed to discipline or otherwise minimize the restlessness of workers and the poor as a first line of defense, so to speak, against radical political parties and movements as well as general social disorder, which would disrupt the industrial economy.

The first such regulation was initiated in Britain. In the nineteenth century, Parliament passed the Factory Act (1833), which created a system of factory inspection. The Mine Regulation Act of 1842 protected miners; the Factory Act of 1847 limited the workday to ten hours; the Merchant Shipping Act of 1876 protected merchant seamen; and the Regulation of Railways Act of 1889 protected railroad workers. In 1848, Parliament passed the Public Health Act, which guaranteed minimum levels of sanitation in places of work and in dwellings.[35]

The first system of insurance against sickness, unemployment, and old age was started in Germany. In the 1880s, German Chancellor Bismarck pushed a series of laws through the Reichstag that he hoped would destroy the Social Democratic Party by making the state responsible for the provision of social insurance for the working class. The first of these laws, which insured workers against sickness, was passed in 1883. Workers paid two-thirds of the cost and their employers the other one-third. These premiums were collected and paid by special insurance societies approved and regulated by the state. A second law, which insured workers against accidents, was passed in 1884. Premiums for this insurance were paid by employers, who were permitted to form industrial associations to collect the premiums and pay claims. The third and last law of this series was passed in 1889 and insured workers against invalidity and old age. Workers

and employers contributed equally to this fund, and the state made a contribution to the pension ultimately paid.[36]

The German system spread to other industrializing European states. In
Britain, Parliament passed the Workmen's Compensation Act in 1897,
which required that employers insure employees against the dangers of
their employment. In 1908, the Old Age Pensions Act introduced a pension
system paid for entirely by the state for workers over the age of seventy
who were unable to support themselves. In 1909, Parliament passed the
Trade Boards Act, which established a minimum wage for workers in jobs
that did not provide trade union representation. In 1911 the National
Insurance Act introduced a health insurance scheme to which workers,
employers, and the state paid equal premiums. This act also provided for
unemployment insurance in certain industries such as iron founding and
shipbuilding.[37]

Social insurance for workers advanced much less rapidly in France.
The first such act was not passed until 1905, when pensions were provided
by the state for the aged poor and incurably ill. In 1910, the National
Assembly passed the Old Age Pension Act, which provided pensions for
wage earners from a fund contributed to by employees, employers, and the
state. In 1913, the National Assembly passed an act that gave aid to families with more than three children in order to encourage population growth
and to fight a high infant mortality rate.

In the United States, the advent of social insurance was even slower
than in France. Although perhaps as much as 30 percent of workers had
workmen's compensation insurance required by different states, only 2 percent had old-age insurance in 1915. Not until the depths of the Great
Depression did the U.S. state introduce accident, unemployment, and old-
age insurance for wage earners. Industrial accident insurance was introduced in 1930. The Social Security Act of 1935 introduced retirement and
unemployment insurance. In 1950, the portion of the Social Security Act
that provided aid to blind and needy children became an aid-to-children
program called Aid to Families with Dependent Children, which paid benefits to one parent in a family where children were beneficiaries. In the same
year, aid was extended to the totally disabled. In 1972, a uniform federal
system of Supplemental Security Income was set up for the aged, blind, and
disabled.[38]

In the third epoch, the idea that the state's responsibilities were to provide social services to the working class was replaced with the notion that
the state was responsible for insuring the health, safety, and retirement of
the entire subject population. Again, the aim was to discipline and regulate
the poor, to limit the political development of radical movements, and to
promote general social order.

In Britain the Widows, Orphans, and Old Age Contributory Pensions

Act of 1925 created a new social insurance scheme and extended unemployment insurance to cover most wage earners. A series of housing acts gave the state the responsibility of constructing housing. In 1928, France passed a compulsory social insurance law that gave sickness, maternity, invalidity, and old-age insurance to all citizens. During the Weimar Republic in Germany, unemployment insurance was expanded.

After World War II, in Britain the Family Allowance Act, which paid weekly benefits to families with two or more children under the age of fifteen, was passed by Parliament. In 1946, the National Insurance Act was passed; it provided substantial coverage for sickness and unemployment as well as maternity benefits, widows' allowances, and retirement pensions for the entire population. The National Assistance Act, which was passed in 1948, required local governments to make accommodations available for the old, the infirm, and those in need of a place to live. Finally, also in 1948, the National Health Service was created; this placed all health services (private, local, and national) under the authority of the state and made it freely available to the entire subject population.[39]

After World War II, the French state also strengthened and rationalized its social insurance scheme such that the vast majority of its subject population became covered by social insurance paid for by contributions from employers and employees. French social insurance covers sickness, disability, retirement, widowhood, and death. It also includes generous benefits for families. The larger the family, the greater the benefits. An additional allowance is paid to families if the mother does not work. In addition, large families receive income tax rebates, reduced fares on public transportation, and increased pensions. France also provides an extensive system of hospitals, orphanages, retirement homes, and asylums. Although the French state does not have a national health service, it does contribute to an individual's medical expenses under a fee reimbursement plan. Patients are free to choose their physicians, and the state insurance system reimburses the patient for 80 percent of the bill.[40]

The German state has also broadened its coverage since the end of World War II. Social security legislation passed in 1954 allowed retired persons to maintain the standard of living they enjoyed during their working years by indexing pensions to reflect earnings and taking inflation into account. The Federal Unemployment Office makes payments and grants low-interest loans to workers to cover travel expenses incurred during their searches for new jobs, moving expenses, interview expenses, vocational retraining, and counseling. Since 1959, German construction workers have received subsidies from employment offices, known as "bad weather money," for rainy, snowy, or subzero winter days. In 1996, these payments were replaced with a system guaranteeing workers 75 percent of their gross pay per hour for inclement days during the months from November to

March. Germany continues to provide health insurance through the system established by Bismarck in the 1880s, although it was overhauled in 1955. The scheme is still supported by joint contributions from workers, employers, and the state, and is still administered by welfare funds that pay the physicians of the patients' own choosing.[41]

The U.S. state did not introduce health insurance until 1964 with the passage of the Medicaid program, which provides joint federally and state-funded health insurance for the poor, and the Medicare program, which provides federally funded insurance for the elderly that covers hospitalization and subsidized outpatient care.[42] In 2003, Congress passed a controversial prescription drug plan. Unlike European states, the U.S. state still does not provide health insurance for the general population.

Contemporary liberals consider welfare programs as entitlements, that is, as programs justified in part because they are equally available to all citizens as individuals regardless of race, class, or gender, and in part because they are seen as providing the prerequisites for all persons in the society to live a dignified life. All persons, liberals argue, are entitled to receive adequate medical care, to avoid destitution, to be able to provide for their own and their family's economic well-being, and to receive unemployment compensation when they are thrown out of work through no fault of their own. Entitlements, for liberals, then, are legitimate functions of the state in an industrial economy. But the liberal ideology does not fully recognize the extent to which these programs intervene in the recipient's private life. In other words, liberals want to maintain a clear and inviolable distinction between state and civil society and between public and private; but these programs actually blur this distinction. Conservatives who challenge the legitimacy of these programs also promote a sharp distinction between civil society and the state, public and private, which does not accord to the realities of welfare programs.

In practice, the management of social services for the poor, the elderly, or the unemployed involves the state deeply in the regulation of people's everyday lives. Moreover, in spite of the attempts to maintain the universality and equality of entitlement programs, wealthy and privileged groups have been able to avoid the more intrusive forms of intervention entailed by them. Feminists have recognized the disciplinary aspects of social services most clearly.

Women and men become subjects of the state's management of social services in different ways and to different extents.[43] This is especially the case in states, such as the United States, where women have been relatively unsuccessful in obtaining child-care programs, maternity leave, and equal pay for equal work, all of which would help make them equal to men in the public world of civil society and the world of work. Although all social service programs require recipients of benefits to conform to certain rules, some programs intervene into the private lives of their recipients more intrusively than do others. To receive unemployment insurance, for example, one of the few social service programs in which men participate more than women, one must actually be looking for work, going to school, or enrolled in a job-training program to receive compensation. But the state relies on the recipient to provide evidence; it does not send an agent of the state out to follow the individual around to see if he is actually looking for work or going to school.

On the other hand, the programs in which women participate in greater numbers than men often subject recipients to far more state scrutiny and intrusion into their lives. Single mothers receiving state aid for their children may be required to live with their parents, and those receiving food stamps are limited in the choices of what they can buy with them. More significant, women in these programs are often subjected to constant surveillance by social workers and other agents of the state, such as the police, who have the power under some circumstances to take children from their mothers. These programs fall disproportionately on women because of the traditional prejudices and social structures that see women as primarily responsible for the home and "private" life. As we mentioned above, these customary prejudices were an important part of Fordism. In practice, the man's private life in managerial states is more inviolable than is the woman's. The poor, which often includes high numbers of racial and ethnic minorities because of prejudice and structural inequalities in the provision of education and work opportunities, are also often subjected to intrusive forms of state intervention that blur the lines of public and private.

Managing Politics

As we discussed above, the managerial state reconstitutes citizens according to a logic of insiders and outsiders, and relocates sovereign unity and indivisibility in the nation. This political distribution is managed by the formalization and routinization of procedural democracy.

The principal way that people participate in politics in the managerial state is through regular elections, which channel participation away from unpredictable, disruptive, and spontaneous forms of participation such as demonstrating, rioting, and throwing bombs. Elections "domesticate" and pacify participation and transform it into a routine, peaceful public activity. Through rules that (1) regulate the composition of the electorate and (2) transform voters' choices into electoral outcomes, the managerial state controls when, where, how, and which individuals will participate.

From the early nineteenth century in the United States, for example, the composition of the electorate was regulated by property-owning and tax-paying requirements, poll taxes, literacy tests, and franchise laws that denied women, blacks, and youths the right to vote. Although these restrictions have been abandoned in the twentieth century, the inconvenience and expense of registering to vote (furnishing proof of identity, residency, and citizenship, and taking time off from work to appear at the registrar's office) still regulates the composition of the electorate by depressing the electoral participation of the poor and poorly educated. Thus, in the United States, personal registration skews the electoral process in favor of better-educated, higher-income people.[44] Recent reforms, such as "Motor-Voter" registration, which allows people to register to vote when they obtain a driver's license or automobile registration, have made voter registration easier but still have not significantly increased voting by the poor.

In the managerial state, elections are increasingly understood as electoral "systems." Elections make sense, and are made sense of by the press and the academic discipline of political science, as part of a rational system of rules and regulations, the aim of which is to produce predictable outcomes. Crucial to regulating this system is the manipulation of the outcomes of elections by regulating the way in which individual votes will be translated into seats in a representative body. Two sets of regulations are crucial to managing this system: (1) those that establish the criteria for winning and (2) those that define the electoral districts.[45]

There are two ways to regulate winning. One is to award victory to the candidate who receives either a plurality or a majority of the ballots cast. Another is to award victory to competing political parties in rough proportion to the votes each has received of the ballots cast. For example, a party that received 40 percent of the vote would receive about 40 percent of the seats in the representative body. Systems of proportional representation are advantageous to small and weak social groups; majority and plurality systems are advantageous to large and powerful groups. This is because in an election to a representative body, proportional representation reduces the number of votes that a political party must receive in order to win seats, and majority and plurality rules increase that number. Thus, the choice of the rules that regulate winning will have a substantial impact on the number and nature of the political parties within the state.[46]

Britain and the United States both manage the participation of their subject populations through regular elections for representative bodies such as Parliament, Congress, state legislatures, and city and county councils. Elections for Parliament must be held every five years, and elections for one-third of the Senate and the House of Representatives of the Congress every two years. Neither state controls the composition of the electorate through property-owning requirements, poll taxes and the like, although in the United States, residency requirements of varying amounts of time are still used by individual states.

The composition of the electorate is regulated primarily through personal registration laws, especially in the U.S. state, where the political parties are weak. Winning has been regulated by the use of plurality electoral systems, which favor large, powerful groups and have produced two dominant political parties both in Britain and the United States. Although other parties exist in both states, they have had difficulty surviving—especially in the United States, because the electoral system and state laws create difficulties for "third-party" candidates attempting to gain access to the ballot. In the United States especially, the outcomes of elections can be influenced by gerrymandering (manipulating the geographical boundaries of districts in order to increase one outcome over another), named after an early nineteenth-century governor of Massachusetts, Elbridge Gerry (1744–1814), who allegedly redrew the lines of a district in the shape of a salamander in order to increase the vote for his party. Because different distributions of voters among districts produce different outcomes, those who control the lines of the districts are able to manipulate the results. Gerrymandering has been used extensively in the United States to dilute the voting strength of racial minorities.[47]

The French and German states have also managed political participation by regulating the composition of the electorate and manipulating the transformation of voters' choices into electoral outcomes. In the nineteenth century, both used property-owning and tax-paying requirements and restricted the franchise to men. In the twentieth century, the franchise has been granted to all individuals over eighteen years old, who are, by law, required to register. From 1871 to 1958, France used proportional representation, which produced ten to twenty parties, none of which was large enough to win a majority of seats in the National Assembly. When Charles de Gaulle came to power in 1958, he changed the electoral law to a majority system that requires a second ballot if no candidate, including in elections for the presidency, receives a majority on the first ballot.

Germany has used both plurality and proportional systems. During the Weimar Republic, proportional representation was used, which produced a plethora (about forty) of small parties. During the Third Reich, only one party was permitted, the Nazi Party, and no elections were held after 1933. After World War II, the German state instituted a combined plurality-proportional electoral system. One-half of the seats in the Bundestag are elected by plurality from single-member districts and one-half by proportional representation.

The trend in managerial states has been toward fewer large parties that do not differ much from one another in terms of ideology.[48] Such catchall parties seek to capture as many voters as possible by appealing to prudent administration, managerial ability, technical expertise, or personal morality, as well as appealing to what is good for the "nation" or "the people" as a whole.

Thus, elections in the managerial state have become ritualistic confrontations between candidates and parties who claim to be able to manage the state more effectively and efficiently than their opponents, rather than occasions for serious public debate and discussion about pressing issues. Increasingly, parties control their images by employing the marketing techniques of consumer manipulation used in commercial advertising in order to mobilize or demobilize voters. Public-opinion polling is also used extensively. Recent trends in such management of participation have produced significant political disenchantment among voters and a general apathy toward public affairs, which is reflected in marked declines in the percentage of eligible voters who actually vote in all managerial states.

Summary

In the managerial states of the twentieth century, the relation of subject and sovereign has been reconstituted, and the state has developed new powers of surveillance and social control. One of these new forms of control stems from the relocating of sovereignty in the nation, an imagined community of all citizens within a particular territory. Part 3 discusses nationalism and the nation as part of modern state practice and the spread of the state as the hegemonic form of political organization throughout the world. Part 4 examines the question of whether the recent trends toward neoliberalism— a revival of economic liberalism in the context of a globalizing capitalist economy—are transforming the managerial state or whether this trend can best be understood as a retooling of managerialism in an era of globalization. It also examines recent promptings that seem to be changing the managerial state into a post- (or hyper-) managerial form.

Notes

1. See Raymond Grew, "The Nineteenth Century European State" in Charles Bright and Susan Harding (eds.), *State Making and Social Movements: Essays in History and Social Theory* (Ann Arbor: University of Michigan Press, 1984). See also Alan S. Milward, *The European Rescue of the Nation-State* (Berkeley and Los Angeles: University of California Press, 1992); Giandomenico Majone, "The Rise of the Regulatory State in Europe," in Wolfgang C. Müller and Vincent Wright (eds.), *The State in Western Europe: Retreat or Redefinition* (Newbury Park, CA: Frank Cass, 1994): 77–133; Richard Rose, "On the Priorities of Government: A Developmental Analysis of Public Policies," *European Journal of Political Research* 4 (1976): 247–289; Robert Solo, *The Positive-State* (Cincinnati, OH:

South Western Publishing Co., 1982); Wendy Wheeler, *A New Modernity* (London: Lawrence & Wishart, 1999), especially chapter 4; James C. Scott, *Seeing Like a State: How Certain Schemes to Improve the Human Condition Have Failed* (New Haven, CT: Yale University Press, 1998); Bernard S. Silberman, *Cages of Reason: The Rise of the Rational State in France, Japan, the United States, and Great Britain* (Chicago: University of Chicago Press, 1993).

2. Giandomenico Majone, "The Rise of the Regulatory State in Europe," in Wolfgang C. Müller and Vincent Wright, eds., *The State in Western Europe: Retreat or Redefinition* (Newbury Park, CA, and Great Britain: Frank Cass, 1994), 77–101.

3. Szymon Chodak, *The New State: Etatization of Western Societies* (Boulder, CO: Lynne Rienner Publishers, 1989), 17.

4. Henry Jacoby, *The Bureaucratization of the World* (Berkeley and Los Angeles, CA: University of California Press, 1973), 147–149.

5. This claim has been challenged by feminist scholars who argue that the instrumental rationality, historically situated in male positions in society and reinforcing values and norms considered by Western states to be masculine, has rendered bureaucracies as gendered institutions in which women occupy lower-level, subordinate jobs while men occupy the more authoritative, higher-level positions. See especially Kathy Ferguson, *The Feminist Case Against Bureaucracy* (Philadelphia, PA: Temple University Press, 1984).

6. Hans H. Gerth and C. Wright Mills, eds., *From Max Weber* (New York: Oxford University Press, 1958).

7. Max Weber, *The Protestant Ethic and the Spirit of Capitalism*, trans. Talcott Parsons (New York: Scribner's, 1958).

8. Robert A. Solo, *The Positive State* (Cincinnati, OH: South-Western, 1982), 26.

9. Jacoby, *The Bureaucratization of the World*, 181–190.

10. Max Weber, "Science as a Vocation," in Hans H. Gerth and C. Wright Mills (eds.), *From Max Weber* (New York: Oxford University Press, 1958).

11. On the liberal public sphere, see Jürgen Habermas, *The Structural Transformation of the Public Sphere* (Cambridge, MA: MIT Press, 1990).

12. On this, see "Introduction: Habermas and the Public Sphere," in Craig Calhoun, *Habermas and the Public Sphere* (Cambridge, MA: MIT Press, 1992).

13. See John R. MacArthur, *Second Front: Censorship and Propaganda in the Gulf War* (New York: Hill & Wang, 1992).

14. Harry Braverman, *Labor and Monopoly Capitalism: The Degradation of Work in the Twentieth Century* (New York: Monthly Review Press, 1974), 258.

15. Alan Trachtenberg, *The Incorporation of America: Culture and Society in the Gilded Age* (New York: Hill & Wang, 1982), 83.

16. Ibid., 84.

17. Stuart Ewen, *Captains of Consciousness: Advertising and the Social Roots of the Consumer Culture* (New York: McGraw-Hill, 1976).

18. Braverman, *Labor and Monopoly Capitalism*.

19. Mark Rupert, *Producing Hegemony: The Politics of Mass Production and American Global Power* (Cambridge: Cambridge University Press, 1995).

20. Weber, "Politics as a Vocation."

21. On the Asian version of the managerial state, see David Martin Jones, "Democratization, Civil Society, and Illiberal Middle Class Culture in Pacific Asia," *Comparative Politics* 30 (January 1998): 147–169.

22. Stanley Rothman, *European Society and Politics* (Indianapolis, IN: Bobbs-Merrill, 1970), 734–745.

23. Ibid., 760–768.

24. Ibid.

25. Bartholomew H. Sparrow, *From the Outside In: World War II and the American State* (Princeton, NJ: Princeton University Press, 1996), 1.

26. Bruce D. Porter, *War and the Rise of the State: The Military Foundations of Modern Politics* (New York: The Free Press, 1994), chapter 7.

27. Ibid.

28. Ibid.

29. Ibid.

30. Ibid.

31. Ibid.

32. Ernest Barker, *The Development of Public Services in Western Europe 1660–1930* (Hamden, CT: Archon Books, 1966), 68–70.

33. Ibid., 70–73.

34. On the influence of war on the development of social services, see Richard M. Titmuss, *Essays on the Welfare State,* 2d ed. (Boston: Beacon Press, 1963), chapter 4.

35. Barker, *The Development of Public Services,* 73–74.

36. Ibid., 75–78.

37. Ibid.

38. Robert T. Kudrle and Theodore R. Marmore, "The Development of Welfare States in North America," in Peter Flora and Arnold J. Heidenheimer (eds.), *The Development of the Welfare State in Europe and America* (New Brunswick, NJ: Transaction Books, 1981): 91–107.

39. Barker, *The Development of Public Services.*

40. Rothman, *European Society and Politics,* 767–768.

41. Ibid., 772.

42. Kudrle and Marmore, "The Development of the Welfare States," 94.

43. On women in the welfare state, see Nancy Fraser, "Women, Welfare, and the Politics of Need Interpretation," in Nancy Fraser, *Unruly Practices: Power, Discourse and Gender in Contemporary Social Theory* (Minneapolis: University of Minnesota Press, 1989); Iris Marion Young, *Justice and the Politics of Difference* (Princeton, NJ: Princeton University Press, 1990); Susan Okin, *Justice, Gender and the Family* (New York: Basic Books, 1989). See also Seth Koven and Sonya Michel, eds., *Mothers of a New World: Maternalistic Politics and the Origins of Welfare States* (London: Routledge, 1993).

44. Theodore J. Lowi and Benjamin Ginsberg, *American Government: Freedom and Power,* 3d ed. (New York: W. W. Norton, 1994), 416–423.

45. Ibid.

46. Ibid.

47. Ibid.

48. Otto Kircheimer, "Germany: The Vanishing Opposition," in Robert A. Dahl (ed.), *Political Oppositions in Western Democracies* (New Haven, CT: Yale University Press, 1966).

PART 3

GLOBALIZING THE TERRITORIAL STATE

In Part 3 we discuss the second and third great transformations: the extension of the idea of the territorial state to areas of the globe beyond Europe via European expansionism and the eventual division of these non-European areas of the globe into separate sovereign territorial states by the forces of nationalism. In Chapter 8 we discuss the various manifestations of European expansionism and the resultant colonial empires established across the globe from the fifteenth to the nineteenth centuries. Chapter 9 deals with the rise of nationalism and the way it created a range of challenges to European supremacy across the globe using the territorial state as the instrument of this challenge. In Chapter 10 we show how non-European states created by European colonization have sought to institute their territorial sovereignty through various forms of reflexive state formation.

8

The Colonial State: Sovereignty Expanded

As we discussed in Chapter 3, the idea of sovereign political space depended on a new way of envisioning the world as a whole: as an infinite, empty
space. The globe consisted of an infinite landscape given to men, and sec-
ondarily to women, to use to satisfy their needs and realize their purposes
and wants. Over about four centuries European states carved this space into
empires, jurisdictions, and spheres of influence over which each claimed
absolute sovereignty. The legitimacy to rule within a territory was bound up
with the recognition of that right by other states, who claimed the same
sovereign rights over different territories, as well as the right to participate
in practices of diplomacy. The existence of territorial states was deeply
implicated in the construction of a world order that was economic and cultural as well as political and military. Indeed, it is impossible to understand
the development of modern states without taking into account the way
European states constructed an interconnected global order by means of
conquest, trade, religious conversion, and diplomacy. In this chapter, we
look at the territorial state as it was implicated in the construction of a global grid of imperial possessions. In the next two chapters we turn to the
emergence of states within this grid.

European Imperialism

"Imperialism" refers to the process of "expanding a state's power and
authority by territorial acquisition or by extending political and economic
domination and control over other peoples."[1] By acquiring territory beyond
their borders, European states produced the first global system of contiguous and interconnected empires extending across oceans and continents.
The planet was thus enclosed in a grid of European colonial possessions.
Very few portions of the non-European areas of the globe escaped
European imperialism. Huge swaths of territory—all of the Americas,
Australia and New Zealand, most of Africa and the Middle East, and por-
tions of Asia—were incorporated within the European imperial system.

Those areas that escaped direct European conquest—China, Persia (Iran), Japan, Korea, Siam (Thailand), and Abyssinia (Ethiopia)—were eventually reconstructed by indigenous elites using the state as it had emerged in Europe as the basic model and incorporated into the globalizing system of nation-states largely on European terms.

Typically, discussion of European imperialism begins with the voyages of discovery (1400–1600) by Europeans along the coast of North Africa, out into the Atlantic Ocean, and beyond. Actually, European expansion began much earlier. It is important to recognize that expansion overseas was essentially a continuation of Europe's internal expansion. Europe's warrior society of the feudal period aggressively pushed outwards the boundaries of its domains. The feudal politico-military practice of governing, which was discussed in Part 1, was spread by conquest and dynastic marriage from the Frankish core of Europe to the peripheries of the continent and to the British Isles. The Normans conquered and colonized England, Wales, Scotland, Ireland, and southern Italy, as well as the island of Sicily. Burgundian knights were a major force in the reconquest of the Iberian Peninsula. Teutonic Knights conquered and Germanized the Prussians, after which they conquered and converted the Livonians. These conquests resulted in the political homogenization of Europe around feudal institutions. They were not the creation of patterns of regional subordination and dependence associated with modern imperialism, however. Frankish culture and politico-military governing practices were spread by individual knights who replicated feudal institutions as they conquered the peripheries of Europe. Thus, internal European expansion took place by a process of individualized "cellular multiplication" rather than according to an overall imperial plan organized and carried out by a centralized state.[2]

The primary reason for the internal expansion of Frankish politico-military practices was hunger for land. The knights who conquered and settled the peripheries of Europe were usually land-hungry second and third sons who were forced to find their own land in distant regions because the eldest son had, according to the law of primogeniture, inherited the family fief. A general scarcity of fiefs and an overpopulation of warrior-knights developed in the core of Europe during the eleventh century and sparked a scramble for new hereditary fiefs in areas of Europe not yet touched by feudalism. Thus the rise of a class of fiefless knights created expansionary pressures in the original Frankish core, which resulted in the spread of feudal institutions to the peripheries of Europe.[3]

Such expansionary pressures, combined with religious fanaticism and the desire for booty and trade, resulted in Europe's first attempt at external expansion, the Crusades. From the eleventh through the thirteenth centuries, European warrior kings engaged in a papally orchestrated holy war against the Muslim peoples of the eastern Mediterranean in order to establish and maintain hegemony over the holy sites of Christianity in Palestine. Four Christian feudal "states"—the County of Edessa, the Principality of Antioch, the Kingdom of Jerusalem, and the County of Tripoli—were carved out and held for about two hundred years (1099–1291). They were protected by the crusading military orders of the Knights of the Hospital of St. John of Jerusalem (Hospitallers), which was created in 1099 after the First Crusade; the Poor Knights of Christ and the Temple of Solomon (Templars), which was organized in 1118 to protect pilgrims to Jerusalem; and the Knights of the Hospital of St. Mary of the Teutons in Jerusalem (Teutonic Knights), who, finding that they could not compete with the Hospitallers and Templars, joined the crusade against the Prussians in 1230. Palestine was eventually reconquered by Muslim armies led by Salah al Din (Saladin) (1138–1193), the great Muslim ruler who had unified Egypt and Syria in 1187.

The Crusades, and the religious differences they reinforced, helped to give rise to an increasingly European cultural identity that understood the world as divided between Christian and non-Christian civilizations, cultures, and religions. This imaginary was reinforced by the rise of the Ottoman Turks, a Muslim people who overthrew the Byzantine Empire in 1453. As one historian says: "From the Renaissance onwards . . . European political thinkers in the age of Absolutism repeatedly sought to define the character of their own world by opposition with that of the Turkish order, so close and yet so remote from it; none of them reduced the distance simply or mainly to one of religion."[4]

The voyages of discovery, then, can be seen as Europe's second external expansion. This second expansion was linked to the first. It can be seen as a continuation of the Crusades by the emerging medieval monarchical states. In addition to religious fanaticism and the deep-rooted pugnacity of European society, this second external expansion was driven by a need for more land. By the fifteenth century, European agricultural production had reached its maximum output, given the level of technology and arable land available. At the same time, the advent of large standing armies, brought about by the military revolution discussed in Chapter 3, sharply increased the revenue requirements of medieval monarchs. More land, which had not yet been replaced by commerce as the primary source of wealth, was needed to expand agricultural production in order to increase revenue.[5]

The emergent territorial states, each with its own economic base and centralized political institutions, were the chief vehicles for Europe's second external expansion. Unlike China, where a single politico-military authority prevailed over the entire empire, limiting Chinese expansionism, no such overreaching authority existed in Europe. But this did not lessen the impact or culturally specific character of European imperialism. European states, although independent entities, were linked together

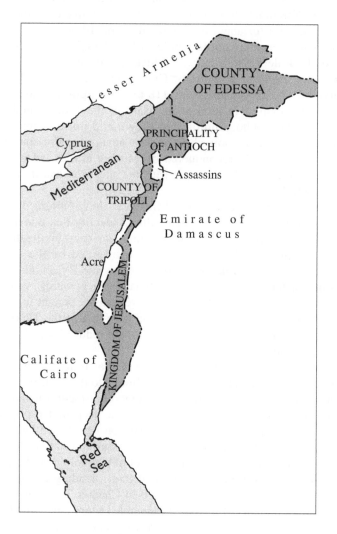

The Crusader States, 1200

through an interlocking system of politico-military rivalry. This situation was historically unique and engendered a vast global quest among rival European territorial states for political, economic, and military power. In other words, the "European dynamic," the politico-military competition among Europe's emergent territorial states, which had been heretofore confined to the European continent, began to spill over into the oceanic sphere in the early fifteenth century. This resulted in the partitioning of the globe into European colonial empires and spheres of influence.[6] A major consequence was the transference of the idea of the state to non-European areas of the globe through colonial rule.

Before European Hegemony

Before discussing Europe's second expansion in more detail, we need to discuss briefly the global economic situation before European hegemony.

Europe, after a period of isolation following the disappearance of the Roman Empire, had gradually become integrated into an economic system of exchange that stretched across Eurasia from northeastern Europe to China. This economic system involved merchants, traders, and producers operating from key cities who exchanged agricultural goods (mainly spices) and manufactures (mainly silk cloth and other textiles). During the Middle Ages, Europe was the least developed of the regions of the Eurasian world economy and China the most advanced. Neither Europe nor China was dominant over the other. Although linked together by sea-lanes and overland caravan routes, Europe and China were distinct from each other in terms of language, religion, and culture. This trading system was composed of three major commercial regions: Western Europe, the Middle East, and the Far East. The Americas, the Pacific Islands, Japan, and the Antipodes (Australia and New Zealand) existed independently of this system.[7]

Western Europe formed a region bound together by three trading networks, each with its own center. The first was the Champagne fairs, which were held in the east-central French cities of Lagny, Provins, Troyes, and Bar-sur-Aube. These cities had year-round commodities markets established by local counts who wanted to make profits and become independent of their overlords. They rented halls, stalls, and stables to traders for whom they provided protection and safe conduct. Fair guards appointed by the counts policed the fairs, heard complaints, enforced contracts, collected fines, and punished cheating. Six fairs were held annually. They started in one city and moved to another, in a predictable circuit, according to religious feast days.

The second network was in Flanders, where favorable soils and terrain for sheep raising, and an ancient tradition of weaving, resulted in Europe's first major industry: woven woolen textiles. Ghent and Bruges were the two key commercial and financial centers of this network. The third was northern Italy, which linked the western European region to the rest of the world trading system through the port cities of Genoa, commanding the western Mediterranean, and Venice, commanding the eastern Mediterranean. These port cities were linked to the Champagne fairs by overland routes and to the Middle East through the Kingdom of Jerusalem in Palestine. Shipping and shipbuilding had become major industries in these cities, especially Venice, which built ships to carry Crusaders and their equipment to the Holy Land. Long-distance trade between Flanders and the Italian port cities was dominated by Italians, who introduced banking, credit, and bookkeeping into Europe. The major items of trade were spices and silks from the Far East.[8]

The Middle East was the core of the Eurasian economy in the thirteenth century. It connected the western European region to China by way of three routes. A northern route, called the Silk Road, went eastward from the Kingdom of Jerusalem via Constantinople across the Asian landmass to China. A central route connected the Mediterranean with the Indian Ocean via Baghdad and the Persian Gulf. A southern route linked Alexandria and Cairo to the Red Sea, which was linked to the Arabian Sea and the Indian Ocean.[9]

The Indian Ocean formed a region between Western Europe and the Far East that was divided into two sailing circuits. In the western portion, Muslim shipowners sailed from the Arabian Peninsula to the Malabar Coast (the southwest coast of India). The eastern portion was dominated by Hindu shipowners who sailed from the Malabar Coast to the Straits of Malacca. These two circuits were produced by the natural forces of the monsoons, which created two sailing seasons, west to east in the spring and summer, east to west in the autumn and winter. Arab traders were the intermediaries between the western Mediterranean and India, and Indian traders were the intermediaries between India and the Straits of Malacca. Trade beyond the Straits of Malacca was dominated by Chinese shipowners. The Malabar Coast was the central exchange point, where the western European region via the Middle East and the Far Eastern region via the Straits of Malacca converged.[10] When the three routes through the Middle East fell under the control of the Seljuk Turks, Europeans began to seek a new route to India.

Europe's Second Overseas Expansion

Europe's second overseas expansion succeeded because of political and technological developments as well as the religious zeal, economic greed, and military adventurism with which it was pursued. Advances in maritime technology, especially the magnetic compass, the astrolabe (an instrument for observing the position of celestial bodies), and *portolanos* (maps that provided a picture of the Earth more in conformity with reality than previous maps) enabled sea captains to find their positions in open ocean and encouraged voyages out of the sight of land. The oared galleys of Roman design, which had evolved in the relatively placid waters of the Mediterranean, were replaced by the more maneuverable lateen-rigged caravels, which had greater cargo capacity and could sail efficiently across expanses of rough, open ocean, with or against the wind.[11] These new maritime technologies shifted the geographical locus of power and economic accumulation from the Mediterranean Sea to the Indian and Atlantic Oceans, and to the general exploitation of the wealth of Asia and the Americas. They opened vast new opportunities for the accumulation of wealth and expansion of the European state's power in both its domestic and international spaces.

The first thrusts outward from Europe were made by the Genoese, who sailed out of the Mediterranean through the Straits of Gibraltar and into the Atlantic Ocean in order to establish a sea route from Genoa to Flanders. The Genoese were eventually successful in diverting the overland trade between northern Italy and Flanders onto their own ships and thus ruined the economic viability of the Champagne fairs, which went into economic decline and closed.

In the fifteenth century, the Genoese were replaced by the Portuguese and Castilians. Of the two, the Portuguese led the way owing to their geostrategic location on the southern edge of the European landmass, their experience in long-distance maritime trade, and their strong and centralized monarchical state.[12] The first Portuguese discoveries were the Madeira Islands in 1419 by Gonçalves Zarco, and the Azores Archipelago in 1427 by Diogo de Silves. Both island groups, uninhabited when they were discovered, were quickly colonized. Madeira, initially a source of timber, later became one of Europe's chief sources of refined sugar. These discoveries and the profitable trade in sugar that they created encouraged additional voyages into the Atlantic and along the western coast of Africa. After 1460, the pace of exploration slowed, resuming only after the pope settled a conflict between the Portuguese and the Castilian Crowns over which monarchy had the right to explore Africa and the Atlantic. The Treaty of Alcoçaves (1479), which settled the dispute, gave the Portuguese a monopoly of fishing, trade, and exploration along the coast of Africa and allowed the Castilians to keep the Canary Islands.

The Portuguese, therefore, devised a plan for opening a sea route to India, with the Crown taking 20 percent (the "Royal Fifth") of the profits of these explorations, which it conducted in secret in order to safeguard Portugal's lead in maritime technology and geographical knowledge. In 1483, Diogo Cão discovered the Congo River and sailed south as far as 22 degrees south latitude. In 1487, Bartolomeu Dias (c. 1450–1500) rounded the Cape of Good Hope. In 1497, Vasco da Gama (c. 1460–1524) left Lisbon with a large fleet and sailed up the east coast of Africa to Mombassa, where he secured the services of an Arab pilot who guided him across the Indian Ocean to the Malabar Coast of India in 1498, thereby circumventing the Seljuk Turks.

Following da Gama's voyage, the Portuguese sent large fleets to Asia on a regular basis. One of these, led by Pedro Álvares Cabral (1468–1520), accidentally discovered Brazil in 1500. Afonso de Albuquerque (1453–1515), who was made viceroy of India in 1509, extended Portuguese hegemony by defeating the Turks, Malays, and Moghuls. He captured the port cities of Ormuz and Muscat from the Arabs and built forts in Sumatra, Timor, the Malaccas, and Ceylon. His captains sailed to the mouth of the Mekong River in Vietnam and arrived on the coast of China at Canton, and then Japan, in 1542. Portugal had established its hegemony in Asia and control of the entire spice trade to Europe.

When Christopher Columbus (1451–1506), sailing for Spain, landed in Lisbon in 1493, the Portuguese king laid claim to his discoveries in the Americas, arguing that they were his under the terms of the Treaty of Alcoçaves. The Spanish appealed to the pope, who drew an imaginary line on the globe 100 leagues (about 1,000 miles) west of the Azores and granted to Spain all discoveries west of that line and to Portugal all discoveries east of it. The Treaty of Tordesillas was signed in 1494 and allowed Portugal to maintain control of the sea route around Africa to India and to keep Brazil.

Columbus made several additional voyages to the "New World," during which he found no gold or spices. Other Europeans followed, such as the Florentine Amerigo Vespucci (1454–1512), who explored the southern coast of South America to Patagonia; the Castilian Vasco Nuñez Balboa (1475–1519), who crossed the isthmus at Panama and sighted the Pacific Ocean in 1513; and the Portuguese Ferdinand Magellan (c. 1480–1521), who in 1519 found the strait at the southern tip of South America that now bears his name and sailed up the west coast and into the Pacific and to the Philippine Islands. Magellan's voyage, completed by one of his captains, was the first to circumnavigate the globe and, in the process, found the westward sea route to India sought by Columbus. However, Magellan's strait was never used as a regular channel of trade with the East.

Globalizing European International Society

The expansion of European monarchical states spread European society throughout the world. The processes through which European political, economic, and cultural norms and practices became the norms for all states and peoples made those states into what they became, about which we will say more in Chapter 10.

As we discussed in previous chapters, some states became hegemonic within the European world order by integrating their mastery of territorial space with the prevailing conditions of capitalism. Now we discuss how the order, composed of territorial mastery and capitalism, expanded into a global order.

By the hegemony of European society, we mean not only the dominance of specific actors or institutions, but the routinization of specific sets of social relations through which peoples inside and outside Europe were integrated into the European imperial system. The principles of these social relations were economic (private property and capitalism), political (rule associated with the territorial state, especially pressures of militarization), and cultural (Christianity and humanism). The specific processes of European expansion and the encounters with non-European peoples were multilayered and multifaceted experiences that fundamentally changed both conqueror and conquered alike.

Economic gain, military and diplomatic competition, and religious mission all provided important motives for the expansion of early European monarchical states. It is important to remember that developments inside and outside Europe were closely connected. English and Dutch advances in weaving produced cloth, not only for home markets but for foreign trade; the development of credit instruments in Venice and other Italian port cities was motivated by foreign trade, as were numerous important technologies. Sovereignty inside became dependent upon conquests outside; that is, the ability to realize the sovereign identity European territorial states claimed for themselves came to depend upon the colonial possessions over which they exercised control.

Sovereignty inside European states, then, became dependent upon denying sovereignty to other peoples. Imaginaries of non-European peoples were constructed (through travel literature, for example) that justified treating non-Europeans as not worthy of sovereignty. It is important to recognize that these imaginaries constructed what was meant to be "European" as well, which marginalized groups such as Gypsies, Jews, and Muslims living in Europe. Europeans considered non-European peoples either as inferior by nature or as primitive and unable to take on the responsibilities of sovereignty. What Europeans did not question was the universality of the sovereign state and their right to spread it throughout the world. They generally failed to recognize, however, that this portended violence toward peoples within as well as outside Europe. European lawyers and statesmen came to understand the international society being created as a global *civitas,* a global city or "republic of all mankind."[13]

This way of thinking was justified by liberal political theorists such as John Locke, for example, who argued that being civilized meant recognizing the institution of private property as the foundation of moral and political order. This principle was, moreover, the result of universal, human reason. God gave the Earth to men for their use and comfort, Locke argued. Because dividing the Earth into private property made it more productive, and hence more useful to human material life, it was justified by a rational and religious morality, Moreover, since private property, in Locke's argument, derived from individual labor, it was ethically valuable, since it directed human effort into an activity of general benefit to human beings. Therefore, peoples who did not recognize the foundational role of private property could legitimately have their land expropriated by those who would put it to productive use, thereby expanding its potential to serve the human material good.[14]

The dualistic political and moral structure generated by the way European statesmen, lawyers, and clergy came to imagine non-European "others" can be seen in slavery. Long after slavery was outlawed in Europe, European states continued to promote it in their colonies and supported it in world trade. Even after the slave trade was outlawed, colonial states continued to use economic strategies not unlike slavery.[15] Europeans used coercive labor discipline in their colonies long after such practices had generally disappeared in Europe, having been replaced by wage labor.

In large part, the reasons for continuing forced labor were economic. Slavery and other directly coercive labor regimes produced extremely large profits. These practices also persisted and were legitimated, even when they were not so economically profitable, in part, for geopolitical reasons, especially the politico-military competition among European states. Colonies came to be regarded by European states as pawns in strategic and economic competition with other European states. Therefore, keeping order and creating allies among colonized peoples led to treatment of those peoples that would be unacceptable toward Europeans.

By the nineteenth century, colonialism also took on a certain psychology in which the colonies were portrayed and treated according to paternalistic attitudes and practices. Regularly, native peoples were associated simultaneously with paternalistic possession and with the feminine in European culture. Colonized peoples were often seen as children in need of the domination of the colonial master. One scholar has shown how, in India, the experience of colonialism masculinized the subcontinent's traditional culture by accentuating the character traits, attitudes, and practices associated with male dominance over women that had been secondary within traditional India.[16] In this paternalistic psychology, race and gender overlaid each other.

The dualistic structure created by the hegemony of European society can also be seen in diplomacy. As we discussed in earlier chapters, the institutions of modern diplomacy first emerged primarily in the struggles over Italy during the late fifteenth and early sixteenth centuries, when institutions of diplomacy developed as a strategy to gain information and influence about the motives and movements of rival city-states and potential allies. The papacy was the initial object of such strategies, given its central position in the network of Italian city-states, over which Spain, France, and the Habsburg Empire (later the Austro-Hungarian Empire) struggled during this period. As a result of this struggle, European states created the institutions of resident embassies, extraterritoriality, and congresses of states to produce treaties. These became the central institutions of modern diplomacy among states.

But diplomatic practices with regard to non-European peoples emerged in a somewhat different way and created similar tensions with the system of diplomacy, as had developed in Europe. First, Europeans did not initially understand the languages of the peoples they encountered. Also, because non-European peoples did not organize their societies around the principles of private property, especially with respect to land, misunderstandings and miscommunication frequently occurred. Usually in such cases, either Europeans assumed that indigenous peoples understood what the Europeans meant by treaties and agreements (assuming that certain behaviors by the natives constituted agreement with the Europeans on their terms), or they simply imposed their "agreements" on them. This can be seen in the way Europeans went about giving their discoveries European names as a way of taking possession of them.[17]

The dualism in the European-created global order is exemplified by an early weapon of mass killing, the machine gun.[18] Invented during the nineteenth century, the machine gun seemed to European militaries to violate all the norms of war (as the crossbow had been considered during the Middle Ages), which they still considered a noble enterprise in which soldiers were to conduct themselves honorably and to demonstrate their valor on the battlefield. The machine gun was simply a weapon for mass slaughter, and many types of machine guns were invented. In 1862, the American Richard Jordan Gatling (1818–1903) patented a machine gun that could reliably fire two hundred rounds per minute. Although not used in the U.S. Civil War, the Gatling gun was used extensively against Native Americans during the conquest and colonization of the West by the U.S. state. During the 1860s and 1870s, various European states and the Ottoman Empire bought Gatling guns and used them, together with various types of machine guns invented by others, in their colonies, especially in Africa. Here, racism intersected with the other behaviors of colonialism. It is helpful to quote from one history of the machine gun in Africa:

The Colonization of Latin America

Whatever the general causes, or the personal motives of the individual colonizers, the whole ethos of the imperialist drive was predicated upon racialism. Attitudes to the Africans varied from patronizing paternalism to contempt and outright hatred, but all assumed that the white man was inherently superior to the black. . . . Clearly, working from such a theory of human development, it was easy, even natural, to go on to regard superior military technology as a God-given gift for the suppression of these inferior races.[19]

Emergence of European Colonial Empires

In the Americas, the Spanish organized a series of conquests of native peoples and empires into an imperial administrative system. Balboa, the first *conquistador* (conqueror), achieved hegemony over the indigenous Americans of the isthmus by military force, terror, and diplomacy. Hernando Cortéz (1485–1547) conquered the Aztecs of Mexico by military force and diplomacy (1519–1521), establishing his capital at Mexico City, the former Aztec capital. Francisco Pizarro (1475–1541) defeated the Incas in 1532 and established his capital in Lima, not Cuzco, the Inca capital, which was too high in the Andes for Europeans to live comfortably. Hernando de Soto (1500–1542) explored and conquered the U.S. Southeast (Florida), and Juan Vásquez de Coronado (1525?–1565) explored and conquered the U.S. Southwest. Conquests were aided by the spread of epidemic diseases carried by the European conquerors. Smallpox, measles, influenza, and typhus wiped out 95 percent of many Native American populations because they had no natural immunities to such diseases.[20]

In addition to having established themselves on land, the Spanish were able to create a monopoly of seaborne trade between the Americas and Europe, much as the Portuguese had done between Portugal and India. These trade monopolies were eventually challenged by other European monarchical states during the latter part of the sixteenth century. England, under Elizabeth I, tried to break the Spanish monopoly, but was unsuccessful. In 1604, the English signed a peace treaty with Spain (the Treaty of London) that recognized Spain's right to dominate the Caribbean trade in exchange for England's right to colonize coastal areas of North America. Although the eastern seaboard of North America had been originally explored in 1534 by a Genoese, Giovanni de Verrazzano (1485?–1528), and a Breton, Jacques Cartier (1491–1557), in 1536, both of whom were sailing for the king of France, the area was colonized by the Dutch and the English in the 1600s. Settlement was encouraged by the English because it was the only way to prevent the Spanish from challenging their claims. The English were able to dislodge the Dutch from the city of New Amsterdam (renamed New York) and to establish a string of settlements along the coast.[21]

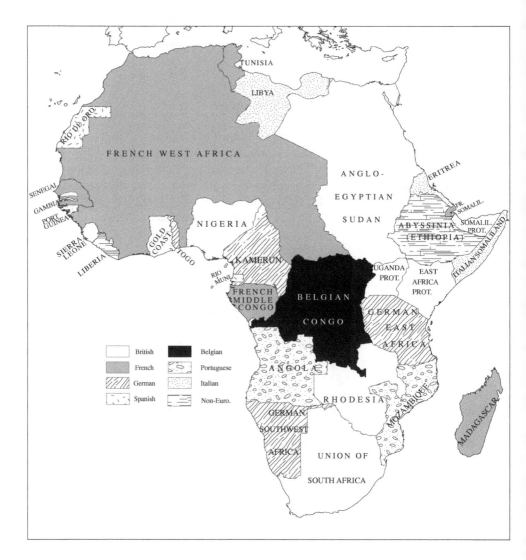

Africa, 1914

In the Far East, the seaborne empire established by the Portuguese was challenged by the Dutch, who sought to create an alternative trade in spices by controlling both the supply and the shipping. The Dutch began to acquire territory in the East Indies (especially on the island of Java) and founded a colony at the Cape of Good Hope in 1652, which functioned as a way station for Dutch ships involved in the spice trade. The Dutch established a direct trade, controlling the source and carrying the spices to Europe by sailing a southerly route around the Cape of Good Hope. Gradually, the Dutch replaced the Portuguese and the spice trade shifted from the Red Sea and Persian Gulf to the area around the Straits of Malacca. A Dutch captain, Abel Tasman (1603?–1659), charted New Zealand and Australia in 1642–1643. By the early seventeenth century the Dutch had become, arguably, the dominant colonial power on the globe, in part by using their advanced capitalist financial institutions.[22]

In Brazil, the Dutch challenged the Portuguese-controlled market for brazilwood (which was used for dying cloth) and sugar, which had been brought by the Portuguese from Madeira. In 1623, the Dutch invaded Brazil and captured Bahia; in 1643 they occupied Pernambuco. However, in 1645, Portuguese settlers rebelled against the Dutch and had expelled them by 1654.[23]

Despite having had its coast explored very early by Europeans, Africa remained relatively isolated from the emerging European colonial system until the 1800s. In Africa, a plethora of large and small tribal societies existed side by side and interacted with one another. Like the indigenous systems in the Americas, these societies had their own histories of war, conquest, and peaceful coexistence. For several hundred years after the beginning of Europe's second external expansion, Europeans and Africans had contact with each other only along the coasts. The Portuguese established trading forts at various places, where they traded for gold and slaves. Africa was first integrated into the emerging colonial global order when the demand for labor increased dramatically in the Americas, where labor-intensive crops such as sugar, cotton, and tobacco were being grown on ever-expanding plantations. In the 1780s, the decade when the greatest number of slaves were taken from Africa, 88,000 Africans per year were carried across the Atlantic. One-half of these went to the Caribbean, one-third to Brazil, and the remainder to the English colonies in North America.[24] Many thousands perished en route because of the horrible conditions under which slaves were transported.

During the 1800s European adventurers, Christian missionaries, and explorers began to penetrate the interior of Africa. Africa's isolation was finally ended in the latter decades of the nineteenth century, when global rivalries among the major European territorial states led to the penetration, pacification, and occupation of the African hinterland. A dispute between

Portugal and the king of Belgium over ownership of the mouth of the Congo River led to a conference in Berlin in 1884–1885, known as the Berlin Conference, at which France, Britain, Portugal, Spain, Germany, and Italy presented colonial claims. They negotiated among themselves and, without regard to the wishes of Africans or knowledge about boundaries among African tribes, partitioned Africa among the attending states. The boundaries they mapped at the Berlin Conference became the boundaries of their colonial possessions in Africa. The doctrine of effective occupation, advanced at the conference, impelled what has come to be called the "scramble for Africa." Europeans, using military force, began to penetrate the interior in order to conquer and pacify African peoples; thus they could effectively occupy their colonial claims. Conquest was quickly followed by occupation and the establishment of colonial administration. Within a couple of decades, all of Africa was enclosed within a colonial grid.

In addition to Africa and the Western Hemisphere, other parts of the globe were enclosed within the grid of European imperial domination. As the Portuguese were displaced from the Straits of Malacca and Sundra by the Dutch, the East Indies became a Dutch colony. The instrument of colonization was the Dutch East India Company, which built forts at various places. The company used military means to take and hold several of the archipelago's islands and to dominate the Straits of Malacca. The company's rule was consolidated over Java. In the 1800s the Dutch government began to penetrate the interior of the islands, then known as the Netherlands Indies. The process of enclosure was complete by 1909. Plantations were laid out and planted with coffee, sugar, tea, tobacco, indigo, cinnamon, and cotton.[25]

British and French rivalries in Asia and Southeast Asia brought about the enclosure of other areas. The British East India Company occupied India in 1700 and controlled it until 1857, the year of the Sepoy Rebellion, when the British government took it over from the company. Threats from the French encouraged the British to invent a pretext to start a war with the king of Burma in order to occupy his kingdom; the occupation was completed in 1852. The Dutch, who had replaced the Portuguese in Malaya, were themselves replaced by the British; the most important place occupied was Singapore, an island at the tip of the Malayan Peninsula that was easy to defend and gives easy access to the Straits of Malacca. Malaya was initially administered by the East India Company, and later by the British India Office. The French conquest of Vietnam began in 1857, with Saigon becoming the site of the new colonial government after its capture in 1859. Vietnam, Cambodia, and Laos were ruled as French Indochina. The Philippines, long a colony of Spain, became a colony of the United States after Spain's defeat in the Spanish-American War (1898–1899).[26]

China and Japan were never directly colonized by the European states.

Japan was able to isolate itself from direct foreign control, about which we will have more to say in Chapter 10. China, on the other hand, although not occupied, was forced to conclude a number of treaties, known as the "Unequal Treaties," which effectively denied Chinese sovereignty by allowing the major European states to establish spheres of influence over large sections of Chinese territory along the southern coast.

The United States, itself the creation of British imperialism, expanded its sovereignty westward, enclosing and destroying indigenous peoples in the process. In 1803, it bought the Louisiana Territory from Napoléon and in 1819 acquired Florida from Spain. The Republic of Texas, which had broken away from Mexico, was admitted to the Union in 1845. During the Mexican-American War (1846–1848), the United States seized what is now the U.S. Southwest and California. After the Civil War, the United States bought Alaska from Russia, and after the Spanish-American War in 1898 it acquired Puerto Rico and the Philippines. The United States also seized Hawaii, Guam, and other Pacific islands.

The Middle East was incorporated into the global order after World War I, when it was the empire of the Ottoman Turks. At its height in the seventeenth century, the Ottoman Empire included the Middle East, the Balkans, North Africa, and parts of southern Russia and Ukraine. After World War I, the empire, which had fought on the German side, was replaced by the Turkish Republic in 1923, and its Middle Eastern provinces were given to France and Britain to administer under League of Nations mandates.

Colonial Rule

Europeans expanded their sovereignty by extending their principles and practices of administration, which were based on their conceptions of colonies as their private property, and on their imaginary of the non-European peoples they took it upon themselves to rule.

Portuguese sovereignty penetrated inland only in Brazil, where Portugal established fifteen captaincies; these were ruled by individuals who received hereditary delegation of royal jurisdiction and a percentage of the royal tithes and rents in return for securing and settling horizontal strips extending indefinitely inland from the coast. In the rest of their empire, the Portuguese were content to occupy outposts on the coasts. They established a viceroyalty at Goa from which they extended a network of outposts throughout the Indian Ocean and Straits of Malacca. It was from such coastal settlements that Portugal was able to dominate the sailing routes of the Indian Ocean until challenged by the Dutch.

The Spanish, on the other hand, expanded their sovereignty by constructing a territorial rather than maritime empire. Unlike the Portuguese, who were content to confine themselves to the coasts, the Spanish sought to impose themselves on land and people. Once the exploration and conquest of the Americas were completed, Spain set up a centralized administrative structure. Spain's absolutist governing practices were then transferred to Spanish possessions in the Americas. The empire in the Americas was initially divided into two viceroyalties, New Spain (Mexico) and New Castile (Peru); each was headed by a viceroy, who ruled in the king's name. Viceroys, who were without exception born in Spain, were instructed to enforce colonial law, maintain order, and collect revenue. They were assisted by advisory and judicial bodies known as *audiencias*. Audiencias were established at Santo Domingo, Mexico City, Panama, Lima, Guatemala, New Galicia, and Bogotá. They were further subdivided into territorial units administered by an *alcalde,* who handled legal matters, and a *corregidor,* who executed colonial law and collected taxes.[27]

The Spanish system was highly centralized, and little colonial self-government was allowed. All important decisions were made in Madrid. The wealth produced by the colonies in the Americas encouraged Spanish absolutism at home because it gave the Crown an independent source of income that allowed the king to ignore his own estates (*cortes*) when money was needed to pay for his armies and wars.

The expansion of British sovereignty took a different form. British possessions along the eastern seaboard of North America were of three types: Crown colonies, which were owned by the king and governed by an appointed governor; property colonies owned by individuals such as Lord Baltimore and William Penn, who appointed their own governors and high officials; and charter colonies owned by joint-stock companies, which elected their own governors and officials. Eventually, the Crown made all the British colonies in North America into Crown colonies; their governors and high officials were appointed by the king. These colonies were then grouped together under a governor-general. The British colonies were the only colonies in the Americas where locally elected assemblies played a significant part in the governance of the colony. This was a result of Parliament's new power as a governing institution in Britain.[28]

The joint-stock company was a common method of British and Dutch imperial conquest and administration. Privately owned mercantile companies, such as the British East India Company, Hudson's Bay Company, the Royal Africa Company, and the Dutch East India Company, were granted full sovereign powers. In addition to the monopoly on trade in a given region or commodity, these companies were allowed to function as if they were states: they raised armies, built forts, made treaties, waged war, governed, and minted money. They fought wars against non-European native peoples in the name of trade. The Dutch East India Company, from its birth in 1602, had as its objective the capture of the spice trade in nutmeg, cloves, pepper, and cinnamon. It later fought a five-year war in the Malaccas in order to suppress a revolt of local people that had broken out in 1649 over the Dutch policy of uprooting trees to control the production of cloves. Eventually, the Dutch East India Company, from its stronghold in Djakarta, acquired territorial control throughout the entire East Indies archipelago. In effect, the company became a colonial state. The British East India Company took Bengal by military force in 1764. It fought four wars with the rulers of Mysore in 1769, 1780, 1790, and 1799, who after their defeat became dependent on the company. After three wars between 1775 and 1817, the company established its rule over Maranthas. Nepal was conquered between 1814 and 1816. The company took the Punjab and Burma in the Anglo-Sikh Wars (1848–1852) and the Anglo-Burmese Wars (1824–1826), respectively. By the 1830s, practically all of India was under the direct control of the British East India Company.[29]

Although Portugal, Spain, and France used mercantile companies to further their imperial ambitions, the companies chartered by these states were for all intents and purposes state-run enterprises, not joint-stock companies organized by private commercial interests. The French Crown forced its merchants, bankers, and financiers to invest in its various East India companies. Eventually, all such companies were taken over by the state and their colonial holdings were integrated into the administrative structure of the imperial European state.[30]

In Africa, colonial rule reached its apogee. By the time of the so-called scramble for Africa, the doctrines of colonial administration of non-European peoples had been developing for five hundred years. At the end of the nineteenth century, the European state had acquired the administrative capacity to extract resources and coerce its subjects well beyond that of the early monarchical states, which had carried out the initial phases of European expansion. Thus, the subjugation of Africans was more systematic and exploitive than the subjugation of other peoples had been.

By the end of the nineteenth century, there existed basic premises about how colonial states should be organized and administered; these were ruthlessly applied to Africa. The first was effective occupation. This premise, which originated in the sixteenth century (when the English and French were challenging Spanish and Portuguese imperial claims in the West Indies based solely on the doctrine of "discovery," and reaffirmed at the Berlin Conference), required that a colonial claim be occupied physically in order for the claim to be valid. Effective occupation extended the principle of sovereign territoriality to the colonies. The second was economic self-sufficiency. This premise required the colony to generate enough revenue to pay the costs of its administration and development. The third premise was metropolitan advantage; colonies always had to be of some use to the

European state, be it economic or political. The fourth was beneficence. It was assumed that the colonial state was beneficial for the subjugated African peoples within it. This assumption was based on the universal belief that colonialism, no matter how oppressive, was better than the "savagery" and "barbarism" of African peoples. The fifth premise was permanence; that is, it was assumed that the colonial state would last forever.[31]

Two methods of colonial administration developed in Africa. One was indirect rule, which used existing African rulers to administer the colony, especially in places where there was a clear pattern of African hierarchical authority that acquiesced to European conquest and made no demands. Indirect rule was favored by the British, who saw it as an inexpensive way to administer their colonies, and a means to avoid the social and political disruption that would be caused if indigenous institutions were destroyed.[32]

The other method of colonial administration was direct rule, which removed existing African rulers and substituted European administrators in their stead or made the African chief a part of the colonial administrative hierarchy. This method was favored by the other colonial powers, especially France, which minimized the importance of existing African institutions and attempted to incorporate local chiefs into the administrative apparatus. The incorporation of indigenous chiefs and the minimalization of existing African institutions was motivated by the more "positive" imperial mission of the European states that employed direct rule. The French, Italians, Portuguese, Belgians, Spanish, and Germans maintained the fiction that their colonies were an integral part of their states. This positive imperial mission was mostly favored by the French, who sought to create black Frenchmen out of their African colonial subjects and never contemplated giving them independence.[33]

Whether ruled indirectly or directly, the most important premise of colonial rule in Africa was economic self-sufficiency. Because indigenous African economies were not monetarized, the labor of African peoples had to be converted into cash in order to meet the financial needs of the colony. This was done by forcing Africans into the money sector of the colonial economy created by the imperial power.

Africans were forced into the money sector in several ways. First, a tax, which had to be paid in cash, was levied on each hut or individual. In order to earn the money to pay hut or head taxes, Africans had to work for a period of time in the European sector of the colonial economy. Such taxes, which became routine in the 1920s throughout Africa, were the chief source of colonial revenue and increased in amounts as more and more Africans were incorporated into the money economy. Second, Africans were forced into work gangs to build colonial outposts, roads, bridges, and railroads, and into portage gangs to carry supplies. The colonial authorities justified such forced labor by arguing that work was an ennobling obligation required of every able-bodied African male. Third, colonial officials forced Africans to grow cash crops, such as peanuts, cotton, coffee, tea, and palm oil, on their own land or by forcing them to work on European-owned plantations that grew such crops. Thus, African farmers were coerced into devoting a certain amount of their own land and labor to the raising of cash crops for export, often to the detriment of the production of food for themselves, a pattern that continues today throughout the world economy.[34]

Summary

In this chapter we discussed the way in which the idea of the territorial state was extended to non-European areas of the globe and how those areas were constructed into a world-wide system of European colonial possessions and spheres of influence. At the beginning of the twentieth century, the global order was one of sovereign territorial states within Europe and European colonial empires beyond. In other words, the state and colonial empire were simultaneously legitimate forms of politico-military rule. In the next two chapters we discuss how this dual global system was transformed into the present homonymous global order in which the territorial state is the only acceptable form of politico-military rule.

Notes

1. Steven L. Spiegel, *World Politics in a New Era* (Fort Worth, TX: Harcourt Brace, 1995), 185.
2. Robert Bartlett, *The Making of Europe: Conquest, Colonization and Cultural Change, 950–1350* (Princeton, NJ: Princeton University Press, 1993), 46–51. See also John Gillingham, "An Age of Expansion c. 1020–1204," in Maurice Keen (ed.), *Medieval Warfare: A History* (Oxford: Oxford University Press, 1999).
3. Bartlett, *The Making of Europe*.
4. Perry Anderson, *Lineages of the Absolutist State* (London: New Left Books, 1974), 397.
5. Immanuel Wallerstein, *The Modern World System: Capitalist Agriculture and the Origins of the World Economy in the Sixteenth Century* (New York and London: Academic Press, 1974), 50–51.
6. John A. Hall and G. John Ikenberry, *The State* (Minneapolis: University of Minnesota Press, 1989), chapter 3; Paul Kennedy, *The Rise and Fall of the Great Powers: Economic Change and Military Conflict from 1500 to 2000* (New York: Random House, 1987), 31.
7. Janet L. Abu-Lughod, *Before European Hegemony: The World System A.D. 1250–1350* (New York: Oxford University Press, 1989), 33–38.
8. Ibid., part 1.
9. Ibid., part 2.

10. Ibid., part 3.

11. This discussion of early European expansion is based on J. H. Parry, *The Age of Reconnaissance: Discovery, Exploration and Settlement, 1450 to 1650* (Berkeley: University of California Press, 1963).

12. For details on Portugal's expansion, see C. R. Boxer, *Four Centuries of Portuguese Expansion, 1415–1825: A Succinct Survey* (Berkeley and Los Angeles: University of California Press, 1972).

13. For a discussion of the language in which early modern international law and political philosophy framed the "global city," which argues for the appropriateness of the terms "republic" and "city," see Nicholas Onuf, *City of Sovereigns: Republican Themes in International Thought* (Cambridge: Cambridge University Press, 1998).

14. See Locke's discussion of property in the *Second Treatise of Government*, chapter V in Peter Laslett (ed.), *John Locke: Two Treatises of Government* (Cambridge: Cambridge University Press, 1960). For the interpretation of Locke's argument as justifying colonialism, see James Tully, *Strange Multiplicity. Constitutionalism in an Age of Diversity* (Cambridge: Cambridge University Press, 1995), 71–78; Uday S. Mehta, "Liberal Strategies of Exclusion," in Frederick Cooper and Ann Laura Stoler (eds.), *Tensions of Empire: Colonial Cultures in a Bourgeois World* (Berkeley: University of California Press, 1997), 59–86.

15. On the British case of forced labor in Kenya, for example, see Roxanne Lynn Doty, *Imperial Encounters* (Minneapolis: University of Minnesota Press, 1996). On the Portuguese, see James Duffy, *A Question of Slavery: Labour Policies in Portuguese Africa and the British Protest, 1850–1920* (Cambridge, MA: Harvard University Press, 1967).

16. On this overlap of race and gender in European colonialism, see the Indian scholar Ashis Nandy, *The Intimate Enemy: Loss and Recovery of Self Under Colonialism* (New Delhi: Oxford University Press, 1983). For an argument that a similar psychology spread to Latin America through twentieth-century mass culture, see Ariel Dorfman, *The Empire's Old Clothes: What the Lone Ranger, Babar, and Other Innocent Heroes Do to Our Minds* (New York: Pantheon Books, 1983).

17. Tzvetan Todorov, *The Conquest of America: The Question of the Other*, trans. Richard Howard (New York: Harper & Row, 1984).

18. This paragraph follows John Ellis, *The Social History of the Machine Gun* (Baltimore, MD: Johns Hopkins University Press, 1975).

19. Ibid., 80.

20. See Jared Diamond, *Guns, Germs, and Steel: The Fates of Human Societies* (New York and London: W. W. Norton, 1997).

21. J. H. Parry, *The Establishment of European Hegemony, 1514–1715*, 3d ed., rev. (New York: Harper Torchbooks, 1959).

22. See C. R. Boxer, *The Dutch Seaborne Empire, 1600–1800* (London: Penguin Books, 1965).

23. Ibid.

24. On slavery, see Michael L. Conniff and Thomas J. Davis, *Africans and the Americas: A History of the Black Diaspora* (New York: St. Martin's Press, 1994).

25. Boxer, *The Dutch Seaborne Empire*.

26. This and the ensuing paragraphs follow Spiegel, *World Politics in a New Era*, 202–208.

27. Charles Gibson, *Spain in America* (New York: Harper Torchbooks, 1966), chapter 5.

28. Parry, *The Age of Reconnaissance*, 266–270.

29. Janice E. Thompson, *Mercenaries, Pirates and Sovereigns* (Princeton, NJ: Princeton University Press, 1994), 32–41.

30. Ibid., 33–34.

31. Crawford Young, *The African Colonial State in Comparative Perspective* (New Haven, CT: Yale University Press, 1994), 95–99.

32. Richard Hodder-Williams, *An Introduction to the Politics of Tropical Africa* (London: George Allen & Unwin, 1984), 33–44.

33. Ibid.

34. Young, *The African Colonial State,* 125–128.

9

The Nation-State:
Sovereignty Reimagined

Through imperialism European states transferred the idea of the state to non-European parts of the world, which laid the foundation of the present global system of sovereign territorial states. A strong congruity exists between the boundary lines of the present system of sovereign territorial states and the boundaries of the administrative units of the European colonial empires, most of which were fortuitous and arbitrary markers of the limits of European conquest. Thus, non-European peoples acquired the state as an institutional artifact of colonialism.

A main force that transformed the world of sovereign states in Europe and European colonial empires outside of Europe into the current world of independent territorial states was nationalism, which arose in connection with popular sovereignty and liberalism, and generated independence movements in the European colonial empires. Nationalism began to connect states to "nations" by inscribing the sovereign territorial state as the dominant form of political organization throughout the world and by generating a variety of particular experiences of nationhood within them, depending on specific historical situations. In short, nationalism re-formed the state as it had appeared in Europe and transformed the world of colonial empires into the present global grid of sovereign nation-states.

Imagining Nationhood

Originally, the word "nation" (from the Latin *natio,* meaning birth or place of origin) was a derogatory term that referred to groups of foreigners from the same place whose status was below that of Roman citizens. During the Middle Ages, the word was used to designate groups of students from the same geographical locations attending Europe's medieval universities. Because students from the same regions often took sides as a group against students from different regions in scholastic debates, the word "nation" came to mean an elite community of scholars who shared an opinion or had a common purpose.[1]

As was discussed in Chapter 3, the medieval state was stratified into the estates of the realm and other corporate groups that did not see themselves as belonging to a common people. Medieval monarchies were ruled by kings and nobles who spoke languages and lived lives that were quite different from those of the ordinary people over whom they ruled. This was also true of the clergy. The kings and nobles of the medieval monarchy had a common outlook and culture that they shared with the kings and nobles of other monarchies, despite the dynastic wars they fought against each other. The ordinary people took no part in ruling, which was the affair of the king and nobility, often spoke different languages from them and the clergy, and strongly identified with their locales. The medieval state was culturally and linguistically heterogeneous. Its subjects did not share a common monarchy-wide identity. In the words of one historian,

> Medieval Europeans were conscious of belonging to their native village or town, and to a group possessing a local language whose members could communicate without recourse to Latin or Greek. They were aware of belonging to a body of men and women who acknowledged the same feudal lord; to a social estate, which shared the same privilege; above all, to the great corporation of Christendom.[2]

During the early sixteenth century, the word "nation" began to be applied to a whole population of people from a particular geographical locale rather than to a student elite. Entire populations were elevated and made into the bearer of sovereignty, the basis of political solidarity, and the ultimate object of loyalty. One's national identity, therefore, came from being a member of a certain people, which was defined as homogeneously distinct in language, culture, race, and history from other peoples. Thus, "nation" came to have its contemporary meaning: "a uniquely sovereign people readily distinguishable from other uniquely defined sovereign peoples who are bound together by a sense of solidarity, common culture, language, religion, and geographical location."[3]

Scholars once thought that national identity was a natural human emotion and that the world was fundamentally divided into nations based on common primordial cultures, languages, religions, and histories. These scholars saw nationalism as the awakening of long-dormant feelings of national identity. In this understanding of nationalism, the nation is awakened by its irrepressible desire for freedom, self-determination, and a state of its own.[4]

Such "Sleeping Beauty" views of nationalism have served the function of justificatory ideologies. On the contrary, we follow recent scholars who view nations not as natural and primordial but as historically constructed; that is, imagined, and createded.[5] We view the nation as more or less consciously invented in order to create the cultural, sociological, and psychological conditions necessary to increase the politico-military power of the sovereign territorial state. The development of a full-blown national identity that overrides regional, class, and religious loyalties requires the systematic effort of the state. Creating a sense of nationhood requires the breakdown of the individual's attunements to local languages and cultures in order to create a common national culture (language, values, norms of behavior) that inculcates in the state's subject population a common national frame of reference across space (i.e., territory) and time (i.e., a single national history). Therefore, initially, the creation of a nation was closely connected to the needs of the territorial state.

During the eighteenth and nineteenth centuries, the territorial state was increasingly "nationalized," that is, the construction within them of nations bound together by imagined bonds of common language, culture, and history began "at the very time in which Europe was torn apart by the War of the Atlantic, that is the visceral struggle between Britain and France during the long eighteenth century. . . . States were forced to extract historically unprecedented amounts from their societies."[6]

Creating a common national identity enabled states to raise huge armies without creating a threat to the state itself from these armies. Remember that medieval warfare was small-scale, episodic, and limited. It was conducted by temporary coalesences of mounted and heavily armored aristocratic warriors who fought over lands and castles. Remember also that three technological innovations (longbow, pike, and gunpowder) revolutionized medieval warfare and transformed armies from small contingents of mounted aristocratic warriors to large bureaucratic organizations composed of many thousands of infantrymen. The great cost of such armies encouraged the development of the institutions and processes of the modern territorial state. More and more war was monopolized by the state. Also remember that initially the ranks of these large armies were filled with mercenaries and the dregs of society (petty thieves, drunks, misfits) who were often forced into military service as an alternative to prison. Consequently, early infantry-based armies were composed of men who had to be constantly watched over and coerced so that they would not desert or turn their weapons against their officers.[7]

This problem was solved with the nationalization of the state, which took place first in France and then spread to other states. The French Revolution formally fused the idea of the nation to the state. Article 3 of the Universal Declaration of the Rights of Man, which was written by French revolutionaries, declares that sovereignty resides with the people, not the monarch. This declaration heightened feelings among the French population that they were a unique people that had liberated itself from the tyranny of absolute monarchy. The French Revolution vastly increased the willingness of civilians and soldiers to endure huge sacrifices in the service of the state, which was now seen as the instrument of the people. Physical coercion was no longer necessary to fill the ranks of the army and keep soldiers on the battlefield during combat. Hence, revolutionary France was able to field very large armies composed of highly motivated troops who were fighting not for themselves but for the nation. War and nationhood were expressly linked in 1792 at the Battle of Valmy in northeastern France when a "ragtag French army under fire from the much better trained and better equipped Prussian infantry, held its ground to the revolutionary battle-cry of 'Vive la Nation' [to which] Goethe, who was present at the battle, [declared] . . .that 'this date and place mark a new epoch in world history.'"[8]

The peoples that the French defeated and occupied in the Napoleonic Wars, such as the Germans, Russians, Spanish, and Portuguese, grew to hate the French invaders, which sparked feelings of national consciousness among occupied peoples. Resisting French occupation became an affair of the people themselves and was encouraged by aspiring nation-makers who used it as a way of mobilizing their people and increasing the politico-military power of their states.

Initially, kings were reluctant to encourage nationalist sentiments, because they could subvert the existing monarchical order. Already, in the seventeenth century in England, claims of "the rights of Englishmen" by the gentry and commercial class were used to establish the supremacy of Parliament against the king. In the North American colonies, rising national sentiment was linked to challenges to the supremacy of the central monarchy and even led to calls for independence. However, kings gradually learned how to separate nationalist feelings from liberalism's claims of popular sovereignty. Therefore, states could remain monarchies and still retain sentiments of national identity, and armies loyal to the monarchical state for which they fought could be fielded.

Gradually, the rise of nationalism began to transform the legitimating principle of the state and the emerging global system of states. After Westphalia, the legitimating principle of the territorial monarchical state was "divine right of kings." Subjects of such states were loyal to their king and his state. With the rise of nationalism, the legitimating principle becomes "national self-determination," that is, the right of a nation to have its own state and determine its own affairs. Hereafter, a state's legitimacy is based on the extent to which it is seen as a manifestation of the will of the people.[9]

Nations and Intellectuals

The architects of nationalism were intellectuals, the articulators and disseminators of ideas, who began to imagine and propagate the idea of a historically unique people conjoined to its own state.[10] Nationalism was a central element of the liberal public sphere, which we discussed in Chapter 5. Although the creation and sustaining of a nation required the systematic activities of the centralized territorial state, the specific characteristics of a particular nation materialized out of the preoccupations of a small number of educated elites. Nationalist intellectuals often painted a heroic picture of the nation's past and present and hid the inequalities, exploitation, and patterns of domination and subordination that the creation and maintenance of a state inevitably involved.[11]

Intellectuals in general had become important with the rise of "discursive literacy"; that is, the general ability to read and write and the development of printing, which made mass-produced books, magazines, and newspapers widely available, created an audience for the discussion of ideas among the general population.[12] Early forms of nationalism appeared in the arts, such as opera, which became a popular form of entertainment throughout Europe during the eighteenth century.[13]

Nationalism was, then, an important element in the rise of mass markets. Initially, at least, it was compatible with, and even partly responsible for, the spread of the liberal state, inscribed, as it were, as a central element of the "marketplace of ideas." It is as difficult to imagine the nation emerging without the creation of a mass market in literature, news, and culture as to imagine the mass market emerging without symbols of national identity through which its products could be sold.

Moreover, the nations envisioned by nation-imagining intellectuals, the vast majority of whom have been men, have been invariably gendered and representations of nationhood have been ordered around binary conceptions of masculinity and femininity, such as "Uncle Sam" in the masculinized U.S. version, and "John Bull" in the British. In feminized versions, women are praised and revered as objects to be protected, but not as equally participating citizens. Women appear as mistresses, rape victims, "pinup girls" on patriotic calenders, wives, girlfriends, and daughters waiting dutifully at home. In these versions, women are a subordinated and disempowered national commodity needing protection. In masculinized versions, women appear as conquerors and soldier-heroes, such as "Marianne" in the French version. Both types of representations of nationhood marginalize women from public roles and limit their contribution to maintaining the family and educating the children.[14]

By the middle of the nineteenth century, intellectuals across Europe were defining nationalism as the highest human value. Nationalism became an ideology in its own right. Its basic tenet was the idea that a state should share a common culture and be governed only by individuals of the same culture. The invention of a nation required hard scholarly work: dictionaries of national languages had to be compiled; a body of national poetry, literature, theater, music, opera, painting, and popular festivals had to be created; and, most significant, a distinction was necessary from other national cultures as well as "deviant" cultures within the state that resisted identity with the nation as intellectuals had fashioned it. National rituals, symbols, and insignia, such as flags, seals, and commemorations of heroic events, had to be designed. Although the task of inventing the nation rested with intellectuals, it was in good part through propaganda and systematic political education by the state that the local identities of the subject population were shifted to the newly imagined nation.[15]

Types of Nationalism

It is useful to distinguish different types of nationalism in order to show how nationalism helped generate and undergird different states. Three different types can be distinguished: liberal nationalism, ethnic nationalism, and anticolonial nationalism. We will discuss each of them in turn.

Liberal Nationalism

As we saw above, the Enlightenment imaginary of liberalism and popular sovereignty, along with the French Revolution and its aftermath, were crucial catalysts for the development of nationalism, both in Europe and in Europe's overseas colonies. Although not all nationalists were liberals, liberal intellectuals began to organize nationalist movements. In certain cases, liberal movements demanded changes in such extant absolutist states as France, Portugal, and Spain. In others, they demanded the creation of new unified states based on liberal principles where none had previously existed, as in Germany and Italy. In still others, they demanded independence from a colonial power and the formation of a republic, as in the Americas. Thus, initially, nationalism went hand in glove with the spread of liberalism.

Liberal nationalism bases its appeal on loyalty to a set of political ideals and institutions. Inclusion within the nation is determined by birth or long-time residence within the nation's territory. Some knowledge of the nation's language and its political institutions may be required to gain citizenship.[16]

Liberal ideas spread from Europe to the Spanish, Portuguese, and British colonies in the Americas, where they were accepted by educated, locally born elites. When combined with local conditions and circumstances, they produced nationalist movements. The first nationalist movement for independence was born in the thirteen British colonies along the eastern seaboard of North America. As we discussed in Chapter 5, a colonial elite composed of locally born, prosperous New England merchants and southern planters, who had been strongly influenced by the principles of liberalism and were strenuously opposed to the taxes that had been levied on their commercial interests by the British Parliament, took the opportunity created by the war in the Atlantic and organized a movement for independence that produced the first new sovereign states in the Western Hemisphere: Massachusetts, Rhode Island, New York, Pennsylvania, Maryland, Virginia, and the rest of the original thirteen colonies.

Although the Constitution of 1789 brought these states together into a single federal state, it took nearly a century more for the U.S. "nation" to be created. From the founding to the Civil War, ordinary people of the United States primarily identified with their respective states or regions. It was only after the Civil War that individuals became loyal to a national political community beyond their states and began to think of themselves as Americans. This American identity was bound up with Protestant ideals of an exceptional people with a unique mission in the world, which in turn convinced Americans they had the right to conquer the entire continent.[17] Eventually, this new nation-state itself became an imperial power that imposed its sovereignty across the landmass of North America and beyond: to Puerto Rico in the Caribbean Sea and to certain islands in the Pacific Ocean, such as Hawaii, Guam, and, eventually, the Philippines.

As described in Chapter 8, Spain's colonial holdings in the Americas were divided into viceroyalties, which were subdivided into *audiencias.* Viceroys were always *peninsulares,* individuals born in Spain, and *audiencias* were staffed by locally born administrators of Spanish descent known as *criollos* (creoles). Gradually, the elongated shape, variation in topography and climate, and communications difficulties of Spain's vast land-based empire imparted to the criollo elite in each of its audiencias a sense that they were inhabiting distinct communities. Encouraged by the success of the independence movement in the British colonies to the north, criollo elites formed a broad movement for independence from Spain.[18]

Discontent with and resentment against Spain was mostly economic. The colonies were a source of gold and silver and were a market for Spain's manufactured goods. Both markets were monopolized by Spaniards, who overcharged for imports and underpaid for exports. The spark that ignited rebellion was struck by Carlos III (ruled 1759–1788), who in an effort to modernize the administration of the empire introduced new senior officials from Spain, whose task was to execute colonial policy more efficiently and improve the collection of taxes. The better-educated criollo elite resented the new administrators and were particularly aggrieved by the policy of

The Latin American States

promoting the importation of goods manufactured in Spain by Spanish merchants to the detriment of goods locally produced.[19]

Napoléon's occupation of the Iberian peninsula (between 1807 and 1810) encouraged criollos in Caracas, Buenos Aires, Bogotá, Santiago, and Mexico City to take up arms against Spain. Unlike the short, relatively bloodless war fought by the North American colonies, the war for independence from Spain lasted twenty years and produced heavy casualties. The war was not a united effort by a single army. Rather, it was fought by various armies commanded by regional leaders such as Simón Bolívar (1783–1830), who liberated most of the viceroyalty of New Granada; José de San Martin (1778–1850), who liberated the viceroyalty of La Plata and, with the help of Bernardo O'Higgins (1778–1842), defeated the Spanish in the audiencia of Chile. San Martin and Bolívar also liberated the viceroyalty of Peru. Numerous uprisings against Spain in the viceroyalty of New Spain, beginning in 1810, resulted in Mexico's independence in 1824. These events sparked the creation of the United Provinces of Central America in 1823, which separated into five independent states—Costa Rica, Guatemala, Honduras, Nicaragua, and El Salvador—by 1838. When the wars for independence were over, all that remained of the Spanish empire in the Americas were Cuba, Puerto Rico, and Santo Domingo in the Caribbean.[20] In its stead were fifteen new sovereign territorial states, the boundaries of which conformed very closely to the empire's original administrative subdivisions.

The commitment of the criollo elite to the ideals of liberalism was limited, however, by its social conservatism, which was based on its fear of insurrection from below. The criollo elite governed large Native American and slave populations that, if imbued with liberal values and mobilized politically against Spain, would have in all likelihood revolted against criollo domination as well. The massive and bloody Indian revolt led by the Inca descendant Tupac Amurú (1742–1781) in 1780, and the slave rebellion led by Toussaint l'Ouverture (1743–1803) in 1791 on the Caribbean island of Santo Domingo, which created the new state of Haiti, were very much in the minds of many criollos as they challenged Spanish rule. Therefore, nationalist movements in Latin America vigorously avoided mobilizing nonelites, a pattern of politics that continues to this day in the states of the region.[21]

In contrast to Spanish America, the nationalist movement in Portugal's only colony in the Americas, Brazil, remained unified. A territory-wide mentality was present among the colonial elite because the Portuguese required their locally born administrators to circulate throughout Brazil, which prevented them from developing a strong identification with a particular locale. Unity was also favored by the displacement of the Portuguese Crown to Brazil during the invasion and occupation of Portugal

The Unification of Italy, 1859–1924

by Napoléon's armies from 1807 to 1810. After the Portuguese, with British help, expelled the French from Portugal, the Portuguese king stayed in Brazil until 1820. When the king finally departed for Portugal, he left his son Pedro behind to rule Brazil as regent. Pedro, who because of his long years in Brazil had been imbued with the liberal nationalism of the local elite, decided not to return to Portugal. On September 7, 1822, he declared Brazil independent and made himself constitutional emperor, Pedro I (ruled 1822–1831). Brazilian independence was recognized by Portugal and no war of independence was necessary. Brazil became a republic in 1898.[22]

In Europe, liberal nationalism animated the creation of a new sovereign state, Italy, and played a role in the creation of another, Germany. We have already seen in Chapter 6 that the German-speaking region of Europe was fragmented into a multiplicity of small kingdoms, principalities, duchies, and free cities. The defeat and occupation of these entities by Napoléon's armies produced a reaction by German intellectuals, who began to demand a unified German state that would be able to defend itself against foreign foes and be based, paradoxically, on the liberal principles that the French had helped to spread. For German liberals, the demand for unity could not be separated from the demand for political rights. Because nationalism and liberalism were intertwined, German kings and princes initially resisted the demands for unity and discouraged feelings of national consciousness from developing among subject populations. This resistance was overcome to some degree during the early nineteenth century, however. The accession to the Prussian throne of Friedrich Wilhelm IV (ruled 1840–1861), who was sympathetic to nationalism and liberalism, and the establishment of the short-lived Second French Republic (1848–1852), encouraged the formation of liberal governments in a number of German states.

As we also discussed in Chapter 6, the dream of a unified German constitutional monarchy failed, having been disabled by the dispute between those who wanted a greater Germany that would have included all the German-speaking territories of the Habsburgs, and those who were satisfied with a lesser Germany, which would have excluded Austria. Germany was eventually unified by Bismarck, the Prussian chancellor, in 1870, who proclaimed Germany an empire.[23] Nationalism in Germany became increasingly antiliberal and exclusionary, considering Germans to be a unique people defined by race and culture.

The Italian movement for national unity was, like the German, the result of foreign occupation. At the Congress of Vienna (1815), which concluded the Napoleonic Wars, the victors placed the many small Italian-speaking kingdoms, principalities, duchies, and city-states of the peninsula under Austrian rule and protection. Owing to the presence of French troops in Italy during the Napoleonic Wars, liberal ideas had spread among Italian

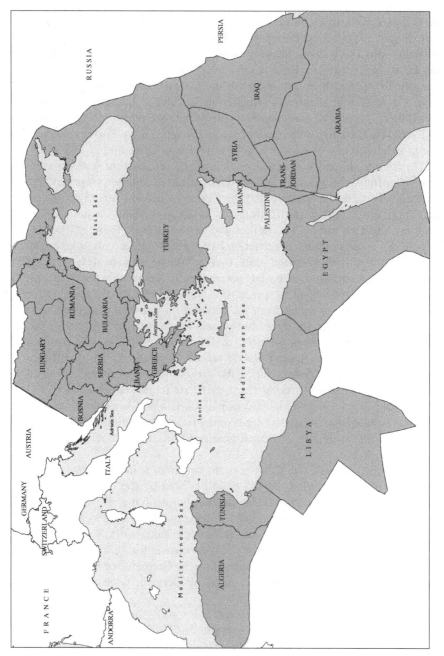

The Decline of the Ottoman Empire, 1699–1923

intellectuals and professionals. An Italian nationalist movement, organized primarily by liberals, began to agitate against Austrian domination and for the creation of a unified Italian state. A series of insurrections against the Austrians and for a unified constitutional state took place during the 1820s and 1830s. These were successfully suppressed by Austrian troops. In 1848, inspired by the Second French Republic, Italian liberals were able to persuade the rulers of several of the peninsula's kingdoms and duchies (Naples, Piedmont, Tuscany, and the Papal States) to grant constitutions. A liberal uprising in Vienna (the capital of Austria) that same year sparked liberal uprisings and rebellions against foreign rule along the length of the peninsula, which, after achieving some military success, were again eventually suppressed by the Austrians. During the next twenty years, Austrian hegemony over the peninsula waned and a unified Italian state was created, with French assistance, by Piedmontese armed force and diplomacy. The Risorgimento (Resurgence), as Italy's unification is known, did not, however, produce the republic desired by the liberals, but a constitutional monarchy instead.[24]

Ethnic Nationalism

In contrast to liberal nationalism, "ethnic nationalism" bases its legitimacy on a common language, religion, and shared historical experience and/or myth of shared kinship, which are used as criteria to include and exclude individuals from the nation. Ethnic nationalism appeared within the great multilingual and polyethnic empires of the Ottomans, Habsburgs, and Romanovs during the nineteenth century, and was made possible by a notable increase in literacy as well as by industrialization, which destroyed traditional ways of life and caused a massive movement of people from the countryside to the cities.[25] Pasts were imagined and reimagined as singular cultures. Religion, language, and history were fused together in the minds of nationalist intellectuals, who made their respective communities within these empires appear to constitute primordial nations deserving of their own sovereign states.

Within the Ottoman Empire (1453–1918), Greek, Bulgarian, Albanian, Romanian, Armenian, and Serbo-Croatian-speaking intellectuals, along with merchants, priests, teachers, and university students, became interested in their own languages. They wrote dictionaries and began to publish poetry and histories of their communities, creating a national identity among the literate elements of these communities. Eventually, such sentiments were transformed into a political demand for independence. Many achieved success, however, only when forces outside of the empire intervened on the side of the nationalists. Thus, Greek intellectuals who had demanded an independent Greece as early as 1798, and had instigated numerous uprisings in subsequent years, were eventually successful in 1828 thanks to Russian intervention. Bulgarian Orthodox priests, who were, in effect, nationalists in ecclesiastical robes, achieved a separate Orthodox Church, with a Bulgarian-speaking exarch (an Eastern Orthodox bishop) as its head, after a decade of effort. A nationalist uprising in 1876 was savagely put down by the Turks. Two years later, Russia went to war with the Ottomans, which resulted in the creation of the sovereign state of Bulgaria.[26] The empire was finally dissolved by the Allies after World War I, the Ottomans having sided with imperial Germany and the Austro-Hungarian Empire. Turkey, the core of the Ottoman imperial territory, became a sovereign state in 1923. The Middle Eastern provinces of the empire were placed under British and French control and were ruled under mandates granted by the newly organized League of Nations.[27]

The Austro-Hungarian Empire, which had been gradually built up from the Middle Ages by the Austrian branch of the Habsburg family through war and dynastic marriage, was a polyglot realm that stretched from Gibraltar to Hungary, and from Sicily to Holland. Within it, the idea of nationality was officially rejected, the unity of the empire being maintained by the principle of loyalty to the emperor, who was seen as above ethnic differences. In 1784, a decision to conduct all of the empire's official business in German instead of Latin suddenly placed non-German-speaking intellectuals from among the Czech, Slovak, Hungarian, Polish, and Italian communities at a disadvantage with regard to social, economic, and political advancement within the imperial system. This disadvantage engendered nationalist movements throughout the empire.

The strongest nationalist movement was in the Magyar (Hungarian)-speaking provinces, where a Magyar language movement was already well developed. Budapest, with its university and parliament, was the center of intellectual and political life. There, Hungarian nationalists agitated for a public education system in which instruction would be in Magyar. In the 1830s and 1840s, the Hungarian parliament passed laws that made Magyar the language of government, administration, and public instruction within the province. Defeated by the French in 1859 and the Prussians in 1866, the emperor was forced to relax his rule, and in 1867 Hungary essentially became a semisovereign state within the empire, hence the name Austro-Hungarian Empire.[28]

Nationalist forces representing other ethnic communities steadily gained ground within the empire. The assassination of the heir to the Austro-Hungarian throne, Archduke Franz-Ferdinand (1863–1914), while on an official visit to Sarajevo, the Bosnian capital, by a Serbian nationalist in June 1914 precipitated World War I. After being defeated by the Allies, the Austro-Hungarian Empire was broken up into five sovereign states: Austria; Hungary; Poland; Czechoslovakia, which brought together Czechs and Slovaks; and Yugoslavia, which was composed of Slovenians, Croatians, Bosnians, Serbians, Montenegrans, and Macedonians.

The overthrow of the czar in Russia, the turmoil caused by the Bolshevik revolution of 1917, and the subsequent civil war, created conditions that permitted a number of territories within the Russian Empire to become independent states: Finland; the Baltic states of Latvia, Lithuania, and Estonia; Georgia; and Ukraine. The last two were reincorporated into the Soviet Union after the victory of the Bolsheviks in the civil war, as were the Baltic states with Hitler's consent in 1940.

Anticolonial Nationalism

A third type of nationalism, "anticolonial" nationalism, bases its legitimacy on the idea that colonies are unjust and a violation of the principle of "national self-determination." Anticolonial nationalism challenged the legitimacy of the European colonial empires and was instigated by Western-educated intellectuals and leaders in the colonies, with support from certain anticolonial states, such as the United States and the USSR, and the United Nations, which, as an organization, was committed to colonial independence.[29] Independence was often granted without the need for armed struggle, although there were many exceptions. For thirty years or so after the end of World War II, a flood of new sovereign states appeared on the globe in Asia, Africa, and the Middle East, which transformed the global order.

The legacy of World War II and the subsequent Cold War enabled the achievement of independence by many colonial states. First, European states had been weakened significantly by the war, making maintenance of colonial empires expensive and logistically difficult, especially against increasingly organized nationalist opposition. Second, the determination of the United States to rebuild a capitalist world economy favorable to its own economic expansion led it to support independence, provided the new states would remain open to U.S. influence and investment. The hegemonic position of the United States in the world economy enabled it to informally dominate postcolonial states. When nationalists threatened to forge real independence in states that the United States considered economically or strategically important, it installed more compliant indigenous rulers, often through direct military intervention.

Third, nationalism in colonial states itself was a "derivative discourse."[30] That is, having originated among Western-educated elites in the colonies, it was reflexively incorporated into the local experience. This resulted in political programs among the nationalists that sought to build states along the lines of European models. Hence, nationalist revolutionaries sought to build states suited to the conditions of their own societies and cultures as they saw them, but usually within the territorial boundaries and conceptual parameters of the states-system established by Europeans during colonization.

Creating independent states in colonial areas according to nationalist programs involved a particular dilemma that led to attempts to produce highly centralized states. On the one hand, newly independent states had to ensure their autonomy from former colonial powers and to counter attempts both to reassert the direct colonial control and to assert more informal dominance that would render independence and sovereignty moot. This led not only to a central role for the military in the new states, but to politico-military strategies needed to confront the often overwhelming military forces of the former colonial powers. Insurgencies, which included political organization of sympathetic civilians, charted not only new rules of military engagement but also conditioned new forms of state power. The most significant such case was in Vietnam, where nationalists first defeated French attempts to reassert colonial control after World War II, and then U.S. attempts to impose de facto control over a nominally independent state. Once imagined, the nation had to be promoted and maintained against alternative imaginaries of social and political life that did not self-consciously stake the future to a centralized nation-state or participation in a world order of nation-states.

In Asia the first colony to become independent under these terms was British India, where Mohandas Gandhi (1869–1948) became the first post–World War II nationalist leader to attract a mass following. Educated in London in law, he initially practiced in South Africa, where he organized the Indian community against British racial policies. Upon returning to India in the 1920s, he began to agitate for independence. Using campaigns of nonviolent, passive resistance, hunger strikes, and peaceful protest marches rooted in a particular blending of Hindu and Western ideas and practices, his movement forced the British to quit India in June 1948. As a parting gesture of colonial power, and in an attempt to limit widespread ethnic bloodshed, which the British had earlier encouraged in order to divide Hindus and Muslims, the British partitioned India into two new states: the northwest and most of Bengal in the east becoming Pakistan, led by its own nationalist leader, the Western-educated Muslim lawyer Muhammad Ali Jinnah (1876–1948), and the remainder becoming India.[31]

In Southeast Asia, nationalist movements appeared in the British colonies of Burma (now Myanmar), which was granted independence in 1948, and Malaya, which contained a sizable Chinese population that had immigrated to the colony during the nineteenth century and had concentrated itself in the city of Singapore. The Chinese were linguistically and culturally distinct from the indigenous Malays, spawning two rival nationalist movements that nevertheless cooperated with each other in ousting the

British in 1957. Independent Malaya did not initially include Singapore, which remained under British rule. But six years after independence, in 1963, a new and larger state was created, called Malaysia, which included Singapore and two former British territories on the island of Borneo. This arrangement lasted only until 1965, when the city of Singapore, led by Lee Kuan Yew, seceded and became an independent state.

The forerunners of the nationalist movement in the Philippines were Spanish-educated liberal intellectuals who lobbied for the Philippines to become a regular province of Spain and for certain civil liberties and reforms of the civil service. The leading light among this group, known as the Propagandist, was José Rizal (1861–1896), a physician, sculptor, novelist, and poet. His execution in December 1896, after being falsely accused by the Spanish of leading an armed uprising, sparked rebellions in several provinces, which the Spanish suppressed. The nationalist uprising continued after the United States defeated Spain in 1898 and took control of the Philippines. Fighting between the United States and Filipino rebels lasted from 1899 until 1901, when the nationalist leader Emílio Aguinaldo (1869–1964) was captured. The United States began to prepare the Philippines for independence, ensuring that an independent regime would be favorable to U.S. interests. Although progress toward independence was interrupted by Japanese occupation from 1942 to 1944, the Philippines became a sovereign state on July 4, 1946.

In the Dutch East Indies several small nationalist groups appeared in the 1920s, led by Dutch-educated Javanese. The most outstanding of these was Ahmed Sukarno (1901–1970), who was imprisoned by the Dutch but released by the Japanese when they occupied the Dutch East Indies during World War II. After the war, the efforts by the Dutch to restore their rule were vigorously resisted. Sukarno established a stronghold on the island of Java and defeated Dutch attempts to reunify the islands. Indonesia, including all the islands of the Dutch East Indies, became independent in 1950.

The nationalist movement in French Indochina began among French-educated Vietnamese intellectuals between World War I and World War II. Encouraged by the Vichy regime in France, the nationalists resisted the Japanese occupation of Indochina in 1940. The leader of this resistance was Ho Chi Minh (1890–1969), who had been educated in France and had lived many years in various European states and the United States. When the Japanese were defeated, the Vietminh, as the Vietnamese nationalist movement was known, were in a strong position, especially in the north, which they controlled. The French hoped to create a federated Indochina composed of Vietnam, Laos, and Cambodia. Negotiations failed to produce an agreement, however, and in December 1946 the Vietminh attacked French military forces.

After seven years of war, which culminated with the defeat of the

French at Dien Bien Phu, an international conference, which met in Geneva in 1954, granted independence to Cambodia and Laos, and divided Vietnam at the seventeenth parallel. This division produced two rival governments in Vietnam: a communist one in the north, led by Ho Chi Minh and supported by China and the Soviet Union, and an authoritarian one in the south, led by Ngo Dinh Diem (1901–1963) and supported by the United States. Although the Geneva Conference called for reunification of north and south in an internationally supervised election, this election was never held because of the active opposition to it by the southern government, which was almost certain to lose. In 1958 the Vietcong, a southern communist and nationalist group wanting unification, rebelled against the government of the south, whose armed forces were lavishly supported by the United States. In 1964, fearing a collapse of the southern government, the United States sent its own armed forces to Vietnam. Despite a massive military effort, the United States was unable to defeat the combined forces of the Vietcong and the North Vietnamese. In 1973 the United States abandoned the southern government, and two years later, in 1975, the whole of Vietnam became independent under the government of the north, which had successfully linked communism to the idea of Vietnamese nationhood.

In Africa south of the Sahara, nationalism was influenced by pan-Africanism, a movement initiated by well-educated blacks from the West Indies, such as Marcus Garvey (1887–1940), George Padmore (1902?–1959), and the black U.S. scholar and academic W.E.B. DuBois (1868–1963). Pan-Africanism encouraged pride in African heritage and organized a number of conferences in the 1920s, which brought together African-American and African intellectuals, writers, poets, and painters to discuss common concerns. Aimé Césaire, a poet from Martinique, developed the concept of Négritude around which an impressive literature and poetry developed in French-speaking colonies. The sixth Pan-African Conference held in Manchester, England, in 1945 was attended by many African intellectuals, such as Kwame Nkrumah, Jomo Kenyatta, and Léopold Sédar Senghor, who were destined to lead nationalist movements in their respective colonies.

In 1945, three independent states existed in Africa south of the Sahara: Ethiopia, Liberia, and South Africa. Ethiopia had never been colonized; Liberia had been founded in the 1840s as a haven for freed U.S. slaves; and South Africa, which had come under British hegemony at the beginning of the nineteenth century, had been granted independence in 1931. It was subsequently led by a minority, racist government of elite descendants of Dutch colonizers, until 1993.

The first effective African nationalist movement in the postwar period appeared in the Gold Coast, a British colony that had a relatively large class of well-educated Africans. The movement for independence in the Gold

Coast was led by Kwame Nkrumah (1909–1972), who, inspired by Gandhi in India, launched a campaign of civil disobedience and passive resistance in 1950. Nkrumah's movement won the elections held in 1951 called for by constitutional reforms instituted by Britain in 1949; these reforms had allowed the Gold Coast to prepare itself for independence by becoming internally self-governing. In March 1957 the Gold Coast became the first African colony to become an independent state, and its name was changed to Ghana.

Within a few years, nationalist movements in other British African colonies achieved independence. In Nigeria, three regional and ethnic nationalist movements had appeared: one founded by Nnamdi Azikiwi (1904–1996) with support from educated Ibos in the colony's southeast; another, founded in 1951 by Chief Obafemi Awolowo (1907–1987), drew support from the Yoruba people in the west; and the third was supported by the Muslim Hausa-Fulani people, located in the north. In October 1960 Nigeria became independent as a federal state. Additional British colonies in West Africa followed: Sierra Leone in 1961 and The Gambia in 1965.

In the East African British colony of Kenya the nationalist movement was blocked by resistance from a large European settler population, which owned large plantations situated on land taken from the Kikuyu people. The nationalist movement, founded by educated Kikuyus such as Jomo Kenyatta (1894–1978), who had earned a doctorate in anthropology in Britain, began to agitate for the return of their lands. In 1952 a Kikuyu uprising, known as Mau Mau, broke out. The resulting crackdown led to the imprisonment of Kenyatta, a ruthless policy of repression, and the forced resettlement of native peoples into British-controlled villages. Such "pacification" continued until 1959, when Kenyatta was released from prison; he became president of a newly independent Kenya in 1963. The other British colonies in East Africa also achieved independence: Tanganyika, which the British had taken over from Germany after World War I, became independent in 1961 under the leadership of Julius Nyerere, a Western-educated Methodist minister; Uganda followed in 1962.

British colonies in southern Africa included three territories—Northern Rhodesia, Southern Rhodesia, and Nyasaland—which had been joined in 1953 in the Central African Federation. A substantial number of European settlers in the Rhodesias bitterly opposed the African nationalist movements that had sprung up. In Nyasaland, where there were few white settlers, the U.S.-educated physician Hastings Banda won widespread African support. Despite white resistance, Britain yielded to the demands of the African nationalists: Nyasaland and Northern Rhodesia became the sovereign states of Malawi and Zambia, respectively, in 1964.

Southern Rhodesia remained a colony and the African nationalist leader, Joshua Nkomo, was jailed. The whites in Rhodesia, from whose name "Southern" was dropped, were determined to maintain themselves in power, whereas the British government insisted on independence under African majority rule. In November 1965 the leader of the white community, Ian Smith, unilaterally declared Rhodesia independent from Britain and under white rule. The British and the international community imposed economic sanctions, which lasted for eleven years. At the same time, African nationalists, now led by Robert Mugabe, took up arms and waged a low-grade guerrilla war against the white minority regime from sanctuaries in the newly independent states of Tanzania, Zambia, and Malawi. Finally, in September 1976 the Smith government capitulated and agreed to constitutional revisions designed to give Rhodesia an African government within two years. In 1980 Robert Mugabe became president of the independent state of Zimbabwe.

In the Congo, little had been done to prepare the African population for independence, which had never even been contemplated by the Belgians. By the end of the 1950s there was only a handful of university-educated Africans in the colony. In 1959, riots organized by various nationalist groups broke out. The Belgian government reacted by attempting to prepare the colony rapidly for independence. Elections were quickly held for rural and town councils. In 1960 the Belgians hastily granted the Congo its independence, but the Congo fell into civil war as various nationalist leaders, aided and abetted by rivalry among the European states, fought to gain control of the central government. Eventually, Joseph Mobutu (1930–1997), the commander of the Congolese armed forces, achieved ascendancy over the others and in 1965 changed the former Belgian colony's name to Zaire.

Although the French never considered independence for their African colonies, the situation after World War II made their position untenable. During the 1950s, elections were held for assemblies in the eight territories of French West Africa: for a territory-wide assembly located in Dakar and for deputies to the French National Assembly in Paris. In 1958 the French offered the territories of French West Africa the choice of complete independence or membership in a new confederation of French-speaking states tied to France. Initially, only the territory of Guinea accepted the offer; it became independent in 1958. By 1960 six additional territories—Senegal, Mali, Niger, Upper Volta (now Burkina Faso), Benin, and Côte d'Ivoire—followed Guinea's lead and became independent. Mauritania, the eighth territory, chose independence as well, although formal recognition was delayed by a claim by Morocco that it had been historically part of Moroccan territory. Togo, a former German colony governed by France under League of Nations and United Nations mandates, was given independence in 1960. The island of Madagascar, which became the Malagasy Republic, and the four territories of French Equatorial Africa, which became Chad, Central African Republic, Congo, and Gabon, were also given independence in 1960. Cameroon, also a former German colony governed by the French under League of Nations and United Nations mandates, was also granted independence in that year.

Portugal was the last European imperial state to leave Africa. Portugal steadfastly clung to the doctrine that its colonies in Africa were an integral part of Portugal and refused to contemplate independence. Nationalist movements led by well-educated African elites sprung up in every Portuguese colony. Faced with Portuguese intransigence, these movements had to take up arms in order to achieve independence. In Mozambique, the U.S.-educated college professor Eduardo Mondlane (1920–1969) led the armed nationalist struggle from sanctuaries in Tanzania until he was killed by a letter bomb sent by the Portuguese secret police in 1969. His death did not deter the African nationalists, who continued the struggle. In Angola, three rival elite-led nationalist movements sprung up, each drawing support from different ethnic groups. One was led by Agostinho Neto, and was supported by the well-educated intelligentsia in the capital city of Luanda; another was led by Holden Roberto and was supported by the Bakongo people; and the third was led by Jonas Savimbi and supported by the Ovimbundu. All three movements waged war against the Portuguese and each other from safe havens in neighboring Zaire and Zambia. In Portuguese Guinea the nationalist movement was led by the agronomist Amílcar Cabral (1921–1973). His assassination by the Portuguese in 1973 did not deter the nationalists, who continued the armed struggle under new leadership.

Despite the commitment of two hundred thousand troops, the Portuguese were not able to stamp out the independence movements. Eventually, war-weariness in Portugal and discontent within the armed forces resulted in the overthrow of the authoritarian civilian government in Lisbon on April 25, 1974. Portugal's new democratic government granted independence in 1975 to Guinea (Bissau), Mozambique, and Angola. Angola was plunged into a civil war as fighting continued among the above-mentioned rival nationalist movements, which, aided and abetted by outside states, continued despite the imposition of twelve thousand Cuban troops from late 1975 to May 1991, and several truces brokered by the Portuguese. A ceasefire was signed in 2002 that finally ended the war.

All but a handful of the newly independent African states contained a medley of different ethnic groups lumped together into new political units, the boundaries of which paid no heed to indigenous ones. The only cases where the territorial boundaries of the new African states conformed to the traditional boundaries of ethnic groups were Swaziland, Lesotho, and Botswana, all three of which had been British colonies and achieved their independence in 1967, 1966, and 1966, respectively. One new state, Somalia (1960), which had been an Italian colony, also contains only one ethnic group; this group, the Somalis, also live in neighboring Ethiopia and Kenya.

In Africa north of the Sahara and in the Middle East, only Iran (Persia) had never been colonized and only the Kingdom of Saudi Arabia, Egypt, and Iraq, which we will examine in more detail in the next chapter, had achieved independence between World Wars I and II, the last two under treaties with Britain that greatly restricted their sovereignty. Since the rise of nationalism in North Africa and the Middle East, there have been two positions regarding the meaning of the Arab nation. One position argued that the Arab state's authority derives from the Arab nation that surrounds it, that is, from a single pan-Arab nation that transcends the territorial state borders imposed by Europeans after World War I. The other position holds that Arab nationalism could be manifested within each of the territorial states imposed by Europeans.[32] The idea of a pan-Arab nation was strongest in Syria, Iraq, and Egypt. During this period, pan-Arab nationalism was intensified by the conflict between Arabs and Jews in Palestine, caused by the Balfour Declaration of 1917, which had called for the establishment of a Jewish homeland in Palestine, and where Jewish immigration from Germany was on the rise because of Hitler's anti-Semitic policies. Arabs saw their lands being taken and given to European settlers. With the outbreak of World War II, Arab nationalists looked to the antiliberal fascist states of Italy and Germany as future liberators. In the immediate postwar period, pan-Arab nationalism became even stronger owing to the partitioning of Palestine by the United Nations into two states, one Jewish and the other Arab. The Arabs rejected this decision and attacked the Jewish state of Israel when its independence was proclaimed in 1948. When the Israelis defeated the Arabs, an armistice was concluded in 1949 under United Nations auspices. The Arabs never accepted this settlement and refused to recognize Israel, which they attacked again in 1967 (the Six-Day War) and 1973 (the Yom Kippur War).

The first defeat of the Arabs by Israel accelerated the spread of pan-Arab nationalism. In Egypt, the Free Officers Movement led by Lieutenant Colonel Gamal Abdel Nasser (1918–1970), who supported pan-Arabism, toppled King Farouk in 1952. In North Africa in the early 1950s, the French attempted to stop the spread of Arab nationalism by taking repressive measures. In 1951 they arrested Tunisian nationalist leaders and in 1953 they deposed Morocco's sultan, who was sympathetic to the pan-Arab cause. As these measures did not bring about the desired results, the French were forced to grant independence to Tunisia and Morocco in 1956. In Algeria, which the French considered to be an integral part of France, an insurrection led by the nationalist Ben Bella broke out in 1954. A savage guerrilla war, intensified by the presence of nearly a million French settlers, many of whom had been born in Algeria, raged until 1958. Algeria was granted independence in 1962.

Since the defeat of the Arab states by Israel in 1967, pan-Arab nationalism has faded and the conception of nationalism consistent with the European-imposed territorial division of the Arab world took hold among Arab nationalists, such as the late King Hussein of Jordan. More and more, Arab nationalism is no longer seen in pan-Arab terms and the Arab states have come to accept each other's sovereignty, although the rise of organizations such as al-Qaeda suggests that the pan-Arab nationalism is not yet dead and has resurfaced in religious form.[33]

Summary

Nationalism (liberal, ethnic, and anticolonial) was the motive force behind the second and third great transformations of global society. Liberal nationalism transformed the territorial monarchical state into the nation-state. Ethnic and anticolonial nationalism transformed the global order of states in Europe and empires outside of Europe into the present global order in which the nation-state is the only legitimate form of politico-military rule. Thus, the territorial nation-state has extended to all the land surfaces of the Earth. No other form of politico-military rule has achieved such universality. In the next chapter we will see how non-European nationalists have attempted to institute politico-military rule in their states.

Notes

1. Liah Greenfeld, *Nationalism: Five Roads to Modernity* (Cambridge, MA: Harvard University Press, 1992), 4.

2. Norman Davies, *Europe: A History* (Oxford and New York: Oxford University Press, 1996), 382.

3. Ibid., 7–8.

4. Hans Kohn, *The Idea of Nationalism: A Study of Its Origins and Background* (New York: Macmillan, 1944). See also John A. Armstrong, *Nations Before Nationalism* (Chapel Hill: University of North Carolina Press, 1982); Anthony D. Smith, *The Ethnic Origins of Nationalism* (Oxford: Basil Blackwell, 1986).

5. On this view of nationalism, see Benedict Anderson, *Imagined Communities: Reflections on the Origins and Spread of Nationalism* (London: Verso Press, 1983); Ernest Gellner, *Nations and Nationalism* (Ithaca, NY: Cornell University Press, 1983); Geoff Eley and Ronald G. Suny, eds., *Becoming National: A Reader* (New York: Oxford University Press, 1996), especially the introduction.

6. John A. Hall, "Nationalisms: Classified and Explained," *Daedalus* 122 (summer 1993): 6.

7. John J. Weltman, *World Politics and the Evolution of War* (Baltimore, MD: Johns Hopkins University Press, 1995), 36–45.

8. Rogers Brubaker, *Nationalism Reframed: Nationhood and the National Question in the New Europe* (Cambridge: Cambridge University Press, 1996), 1.

9. Rodney Bruce Hall, *National Collective Identity: Social Constructs and International Systems* (New York: Columbia University Press, 1999).

10. Liah Greenfield, "Transcending the Nation's Worth, *Daedalus* 122 (summer 1993): 47–62.

11. Patrick J. Geary, *The Myth of Nations: The Medieval Origins of Europe* (Princeton, NJ: Princeton University Press, 2002).

12. On the importance of "discursive literacy," see Michael Mann, "The Emergence of Modern European Nationalism," in John A. Hall and I. C. Jarvie (eds.), *Transition to Modernity: Essays on Power, Wealth and Belief* (Cambridge: Cambridge University Press, 1992): 137–165; and on the social and political importance of mechanical printing, see Lucien Febvre and Henri-Jean Martin, *The Coming of the Book: The Impact of Printing 1450–1800* (London: New Left Books, 1976).

13. By the middle of the nineteenth century, opera, in the hands of Wagner in Germany and Verdi in Italy, who were both active in promoting national unification, became a central tool of nationalist movements, especially among the commercial middle classes.

14. Geoff Eley and Ronald Grigor Suny, "Introduction: From the Movement of Social History to the Work of Cultural Representation," in Geoff Eley and Ronald Grigor Suny (eds.), *Becoming National: A Reader* (Oxford: Oxford University Press, 1966): 26. See also Andrew Parker et al., eds., *Nationalisms and Sexuality* (New York: Routledge, 1992). For the development of the dual imagery of representations of woman and the nation in Western political theory, see Jean Bethke Elshtain, *Women and War* (Chicago and London: University of Chicago Press, 1987).

15. See Eugin Weber, *Peasants into Frenchmen: The Modernization of Rural France, 1870–1914* (Stanford, CA: Stanford University Press, 1976).

16. Yael Tamir, *Liberal Nationalism* (Princeton, NJ: Princeton University Press, 1993).

17. See Sacvan Bercovitch, *The American Jeremiad* (Madison: University of Wisconsin Press, 1978).

18. Hall, "Nationalisms," 9–10; Anderson, *Imagined Communities,* 50–65.

19. Hugh Seton-Watson, *Nations and States: An Inquiry into the Origins of Nations and the Politics of Nationalism* (Boulder, CO: Westview Press, 1977), 201.

20. Ibid., 196–226.

21. Hall, "Nationalisms," 9.

22. J. G. Merquior, "The Patterns of State-Building in Brazil and Argentina," in John A. Hall (ed.), *States in History* (Oxford: Basil Blackwell, 1986): 264–288.

23. Seton-Watson, *Nations and States,* 89–101.

24. Ibid., 102–110.

25. On the importance of industrialization for nationalism, see Ernest Gellner, *Nations and Nationalism* (Ithaca, NY: Cornell University Press, 1983).

26. Seton Watson, *Nations and States,* 143–191.

27. Ibid.

28. Ibid.

29. Daniel Philpott, *Revolutions in Sovereignty: How Ideas Shaped Modern International Relations* (Princeton, NJ: Princeton University Press, 2001), 153–167.

30. Partha Chatterjee, *Nationalist Thought and the Colonial World: A Derivative Discourse* (Minneapolis: University of Minnesota Press, 1986).

31. The details on the Indian nationalist movement and those below on Asia, Africa, and the Middle East are from Seton-Watson, *Nations and States*.

32. Michael Barnett, "Sovereignty, Nationalism, and Regional Order in the Arab States System," in Thomas Biersteker and Cynthia Weber (eds.), *State Sovereignty as Social Construct* (Cambridge: Cambridge University Press, 1996): 148–189.

33. Daniel Philpott, "The Challenge of September 11 to Secularism in International Relations," *World Politics* 55 (2002): 66–95.

10

The Postcolonial State:
Instituting Sovereignty

The territorial boundaries of the vast majority of non-European states were defined by the imperial states of Europe as they colonized the planet. The anticolonial nationalist movements led by Western-educated indigenous elites promised a reversal of external domination, a recovery of the past, and a chance to construct an independent future. In their drive toward independence, indigenous nationalist elites in non-European states either accepted the institutions of direct rule imposed by the colonial power or created their own. In effect, indigenous elites used the instruments of direct rule as they had been imposed by Europeans to reimagine the state in order to achieve economic independence and political sovereignty within a global system of states.[1]

Against Modernization Theory

Outside Europe, nationalism was bound up with programs to transform colonies into modern sovereign states. This entailed viewing indigenous peoples as living in "traditional" societies and European peoples as living in "modern" societies. Modernization theory developed in U.S. and European social science to explain the process of transformation from traditional to modern societies. Traditional societies were defined as those characterized by small villages, subsistence agriculture, simple social structures, and particularistic behavior. Modern societies were defined as those characterized by cities and towns, commercial agriculture, industry, complex social structures, and universalistic behavior. Modernization theory held that the transition to "modernity," the condition of being modern, would recapitulate the European experience. It was supposed by scholars of modernization that the former colonies would undergo the same developmental processes that European states had experienced, and would, eventually, end up looking much like them.[2]

This way of understanding modernization assumes that the political structures of all societies, given sufficient time, will evolve into a state.

Further, it assumes that the original European states had reached the end of this evolutionary process. The end point toward which all non-European societies were supposedly evolving, albeit at different rates, was the industrialized, democratized, urbanized, bureaucratized, and culturally cohesive nation-state of Europe. Such a view is, first of all, ahistorical; that is, it sees the creation of the state as a universal, inevitable evolutionary process rather than the politico-military solution to a particular crisis situation at a given time and place: medieval Europe.[3] Second, such a view is ideological in two ways. First, it hides from view, and implicitly justifies, the power, violence, exploitation, and racism through which Europeans imposed the state in non-European areas. Second, it considers the state's positive features as a gift of rationalist European civilization to the non-European world, and its negative features as the result of the inability of non-European peoples to live up to advanced European standards. Again, the result is to justify a global order that either eliminates or co-opts non-European ways of life, transforming them so that they reinforce the European imposed global order.

As we have shown in Parts 1 and 2 of this book, the idea that there exists an inevitable, inherent, standard series of stages or crises through which all states must pass grossly distorts the European state-making experience. We saw that the original states emerged from a more or less common feudal and medieval basis, but owing to different situational factors, different outcomes of political struggles within them, and different pressures and influences from other states, they followed different trajectories that resulted in different forms of the state. In similar fashion, the state imposed on non-European peoples has been taken up and reworked by indigenous elites according to particular circumstances and conditions.

Modernization theory's effect as a discipline of knowledge about states is to mark non-European states as always lagging behind the more "advanced" states of Europe. This reinforces the dualistic political and moral structure of European-created international society, although in a way that allows for a degree of independence of those states, but which "regulates" their sovereignty. That is, this way of thinking about non-European states encourages and sanctions behaviors that limit the sovereignty of non-European states, both by European states and by indigenous elites seeking to "modernize" them. This is not to deny that many non-European states, especially postcolonial states, have been ruled by ruthless civilian dictators and military strongmen. It is to say, however, that modernization theory prejudges these states by declaring such regimes as normal, natural, and even necessary in the "young" or "politically immature" states outside of Europe.[4] Paradoxically, then, modernization theory sanctions intervention by "more advanced" or "more developed" states while simultaneously justifying military regimes and dictatorships, with all their horrors and cruelties, as necessary to these "undeveloped" states.

Reflexive Development

The formation of states outside of Europe must be understood not in terms of a presumed universal process of modernization exemplified by the original European states, but rather in terms of how the sovereign state as a political form of politico-military rule was imposed and constituted *reflexively* by contending elites as they sought to construct states in the context of the encounter between European and non-European peoples.[5] In addition, we must take into account the global system of states, as well as the world economy, both of which have pressured non-European states to develop in specific ways. European states, and the global order their colonial activities generated, influenced and controlled developments within non-European areas of the globe. Sovereignty, then, in non-European states has been both contested within and limited from the outside.

Some states outside of Europe were created by the mass migrations of Europeans to non-European areas of the globe, such as in North and South America, Australia, and New Zealand. In these states, the local peoples, such as the Iroquois and other tribes in North America, Incan peoples in South America, Mayan peoples in Mexico, and Aborigines in Australia, became what we can call internal exiles—"others" within a territory that was ruled by a state that kept them out by pushing them off the land they occupied. Other states outside Europe were made according to two different but not unrelated reflexive processes.[6]

The first such method of reflexive state formation was by direct conquest of non-European peoples and their domination by European states. In this situation, the idea of the state was directly imposed on tribal, often nomadic, peoples whose politics were not oriented to a formalized, territorial space. Direct conquest created new politicized territorial spaces within which complex social hierarchies based on race (white over black), religion (Christian over "pagan"), and ethnicity (tribe over tribe) generated new relationships of domination and submission. Nationalist elites in these directly created and dominated states sought to reverse the hierarchies of dominance and submission through independence. However, nationalist elites in such states were not able simply to reject the state imposed by direct conquest and return to some precolonial past.[7]

The second method of reflexive state formation in non-European areas of the globe was by external inducement. In this situation, states developed from indigenous systems of politico-military rule in areas that were never directly conquered by European states. Externally induced states, such as Japan (which we will discuss further below), were produced through the ability of certain non-European peoples, for various reasons, to resist direct European hegemony and survive into the present by adopting the institutions and practices of the European state and grafting them to indigenous systems of rule.[8]

Instituting Sovereignty in Non-European States

For European states, the right of one state to be sovereign implied the right of all others to be sovereign as well. The states-system invoked background understandings of freedom, autonomy, rights, and equality, which were taken to be universal even as they justified and authorized the dominance of particular states.[9] This meant that the gaining of sovereignty by non-European states was, in effect, a direct challenge to European global domination. The right to self-determination, then, although an important constitutive rule of the sovereign state and states-system, created a significant dilemma: the global system has come to operate simultaneously on the universal principles of sovereignty for all states and the regulation of that sovereignty either by the common rules of the system or by more powerful states. European states (including the United States) have sought to regulate the sovereignty of non-European states as a condition of the latter's independence. Non-European states, although nominally independent, have been continuously subjected either to direct military intervention or to a panoply of less dramatic measures to ensure that they developed and maintained a particular form of sovereignty that followed the prevailing norms of the European-created system.

We have already mentioned the role of modernization theory in such regulation. More important, the integration of non-European states into the world capitalist economy also regulates their sovereignty. It has opened non-European states (as we will see in Chapter 11), and increasingly all states, to surveillance in order to ensure compliance with the norms and principles of capitalism as set by the international economic system. It has also subjected them to daunting pressures to manage their economies and societies in ways consistent with integration into the world capitalist economy, such as conditioning loans on the adoption of deregulatory policies and reduced state subsidies and social benefit programs. Non-European states are the objects of enormous data gathering and analysis. The World Bank annual development reports, for example, are used as the basis for aid and investment decisions by European states, banks, major corporations, and investors. Subject states are constrained to do what is necessary to produce "good" reports in order to encourage investment and to enable broader access to markets for their own exports. The regulation of sovereignty through the global capitalist economy has increasingly become the case for all states.[10]

From the non-European point of view, instituting sovereignty required constant wariness against direct European military intervention designed to structure sovereignty to the former colonial power's liking, and/or toward the global agencies of the regulation of sovereignty, such as the World Bank, International Monetary Fund, the United Nations, and foreign-aid programs.[11] It should be kept in mind, first, that for many of the former colonial states the "outside" pressures from European states were already "inside" at the time of independence. That is, the act of colonization established boundaries and created state institutions that constrained and conditioned the sovereignty of postcolonial states at the outset of independence. Bureaucracies and militaries, which were initially formed as direct appendages of colonial rule, remained the backbone of the state apparatus after independence. Military advisers from the former colonial power often remained after independence to train the armies and police of the new states.

Second, nationalist leaders generally accepted both the basic principles and outlines of the European concept of territorial sovereignty, leading them to institute sovereignty within the territorial borders arbitrarily established by the colonial powers and to comply with the norms of an international states-system that limited their sovereignty. Third, economies of the newly independent states usually remained dependent upon the economy of the former colonial power, which controlled the value of their money, provided the markets for their exports, supplied investment capital, and owned much of their land and national assets.

It should also be kept in mind that sovereignty was contested, actually and potentially, by numerous forces within these states themselves. The identity of these forces depended upon the history and circumstances of the particular state. In some cases, conservative and reactionary nationalists sought to revive precolonial kings or emperors as heads of modern states. As we will see, this was the case in Japan, where during the nineteenth century Japanese nationalists influenced by the Prussian model sought to build a militaristic state that looked back to a presumed glorious imperial past. In many non-European states, nationalist leaders imported Western models of the state (usually antiliberal but on occasion liberal), which they sought either to meld with or to replace indigenous forms of politico-military rule. It should be remembered that "local traditions" had already been modified and reconstituted by colonialism, as, for example, in the spread of Christianity, which fused with native religions.

The efforts of nationalist elites to create sovereign states were contested, then, both by forces that sought to construct the state differently from those in power and by numerous forces that resisted the imposition of sovereignty altogether, preferring indigenous forms of social and political organization. And, of course, these internal struggles were not isolated from "outside" influences that limited and regulated sovereignty: powerful states sought to influence the outcome of these struggles in part by manipulating what remained of the colonial structures, such as the Church, the military, civil service, landowner organizations, and corporations, and in part by giving military, financial, and diplomatic aid to various factions in local power struggles.

One of the most important factors in these power struggles has been "ethnicity." Ethnicity as we are using the term should not be taken to mean "tribe." Rather, ethnicity is an identity that people adopt under the disruptive condition created by the imposition of the colonial state, the most important being urbanization. Under these conditions, ethnicities based on languages, race, and religion are constructed by nationalist leaders and compliant followers in order to organize political power within the context of the colonial state. After independence, ethnicity has continued to provide alternative identities around which political life is organized.

Therefore, competition among contending elites for control of the state apparatus of politico-military power came to be organized around imagined ethnicities, with different leaders drawing their support from particular groups whose solidarity they constructed and played upon. Thus, control of the postcolonial state has been fiercely contested by strong individuals connected by patron-client networks to particular ethnic groups. These struggles to control the state and the concomitant ability to extract resources for oneself and one's supporters from the enclosed subject population, fragmented into rival ethnic groups, has created much turmoil in non-European states, especially those created by direct European conquest. This turmoil has legitimized military rule as well as the frequent intervention of former colonial powers in the name of "stability."

Under such circumstances, a written constitution generally plays a different role in instituting sovereignty than it does for European states, but not because non-European peoples are too immature or politically undeveloped to appreciate constitutionalism, as modernization theory once argued.[12] Rather, this differing role was due to the distinctive historical circumstances that condition the emergence of non-European states. In Europe, constitutions establishing the basic institutional form of the state served to unify the subject population in time and space, as the U.S. Constitution did for the diverse colonial society of southern planters, New England merchants, yeoman farmers, and urban artisans. Because the modern European nation-state emerged in the context of developing capitalism, constitutions served as focal points of national unity by providing the framework of laws that, above all, stabilized commercial relations and reinforced the political and social order necessary to a market economy. In many states, however, especially postcolonial states, the constitution does not perform the same function. In such states, the linkages between local and national were not established primarily by capitalist markets.

In so-called patrimonial states,[13] for example, individuals seek to acquire power through "patronage" (from the Latin *patron,* or a person chosen as a special guardian or protector)—that is, through connections with strong individuals and a particular family, clan, tribe, village, or region within the state. In many non-European states, the political links between local and national are made by "patron-client networks" through which powerful politicians in the capital city (patrons) have close personal connections to less powerful politicians (clients) among certain families, clans, tribes, or villages. The relationship between the patron and clients is reciprocal. Patrons receive political support from their clients in exchange for access to government jobs, contracts, assistance with the state's bureaucracy, and government spending programs.[14] Clients provide loyalty and political support.

In such states, then, the tremendous power and authority of the state is manifested in the personal rule of the strong leader. It is significant that such a form of rule establishes spatial linkages and identities that do not necessarily conform to the territorial boundaries of the state, especially of those drawn by European colonial powers; that is, tribal, clan, ethnic, racial, religious, and other such networks and identities either do not fill completely or they overflow the borders of states. It should also be noted that personal rule and the patron-client networks it engenders have become political forces only as the result of the imposition of the state from outside and are not a given consequence of indigenous peoples' being organized into families, clans, or tribes.[15]

It is not surprising, then, given the historical circumstances of their emergence, that non-European states have often been ruled by the military. The military was the strongest institution in most non-European, postcolonial states at the time of independence. The military and the police were the European institutions of direct rule and thus had been in existence for an extended period prior to independence; parliaments, presidencies, and prime ministerships were usually created only on the eve of independence. Moreover, the military was reasonably well trained, well equipped, and well versed in the techniques of controlling civilians and putting down rebellion. The strength of the military as an institution was also enhanced by the fact that it was often supported with training and equipment from European states (usually the former colonial power). The military has often been able to establish itself as the "real" unifier of the nation, as the necessary bulwark against the outside interference of European states.

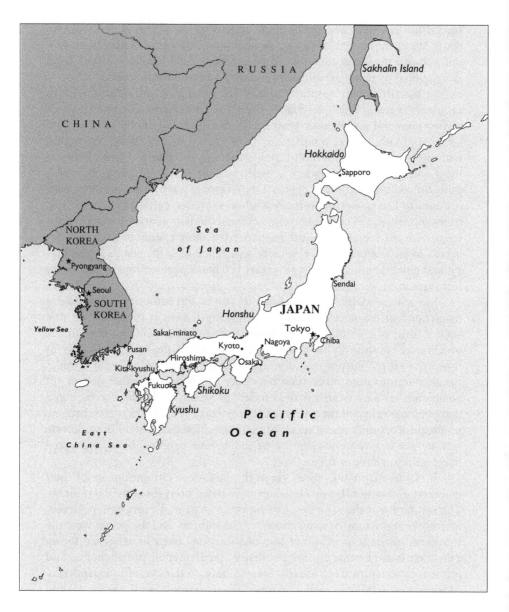

Japan

Varieties of Reflexive State Formation

We now turn to three cases of reflexive state formation—Japan, Iraq, and the Congo—in order to show in detail how their sovereignty was instituted, regulated, and conditioned by the imposition of the European states-system, including the world capitalist economy, as well as by resistance from indigenous cultures and political struggles among rival elites.

Japan: Externally Induced State Formation

The Japanese archipelago consists of four main islands: Honshu, which is the largest; Kyushu and Shikoku to the south; and Hokkaido to the north, as well as numerous smaller islands. The original inhabitants of these islands were the Ainu, an ancient Caucasoid people. The Ainus were gradually displaced to the northern island of Hokkaido by successive waves of Mongoloid peoples, who entered the islands from the Asian mainland through the Korean peninsula. Governance among them was clan-based. Each clan consisted of a number of households that claimed to have descended from a common chieftain. Eventually, one of these chieftains, Yamato, became dominant over the others.[16]

In the fifth century A.D., Japan fell increasingly under the influence of imperial China. Chinese religion, Buddhism, and the Chinese system of centralized territorial rule were imported. The chieftain of the dominant clan was proclaimed emperor, and a bureaucracy selected according to competitive examination was created to assist him in governing. Centralization was resisted by the chieftains of the clans, especially the richest and most powerful. Gradually, large areas of the archipelago fell under the rule of powerful chieftains, who gathered around themselves groups of armed retainers who helped protect their domains. These armed retainers eventually formed a warrior caste, known as the samurai, which rendered faithful service to the chieftains in return for payments of rice. The samurai, not unlike the warrior nobility of the European feudal "state," developed a code of conduct, called *bushido*, which emphasized good deeds, bravery, and unswerving loyalty.

Japanese feudalism sparked a long period of civil war among powerful chieftains. Finally, in 1600, Tokugawa Ieyasu (ruled 1603–1616) won a decisive victory and became the most powerful chieftain in the Japanese archipelago, and assumed the title shogun, or military governor. From 1603 to 1867, the Tokugawa family ruled Japan as military dictators. The family itself directly controlled about 25 percent of the archipelago's land; the other 75 percent was ruled by the Tokugawa shogun's vassals. Although Japan was theoretically governed by the emperor, his position was purely ceremonial. Actual rule was in the hands of the shogun and his vassals, each assisted by armed retainers of samurai.

In the 1500s the Japanese began to encounter Europeans. Portuguese explorers contacted Japan in 1542 and were quickly followed by Jesuit missionaries. When the Tokugawa shogunate was established in the 1600s, contact between Japanese and foreigners, primarily Europeans but also Chinese, was forbidden, except for carefully regulated trade at the port of Nagasaki. The shogunate's policy of isolation was based, first, on the fear that Christianity, which was seen as a subversive doctrine, would spread if Europeans were allowed to enter Japan in large numbers and, second, on the fear that certain of the shogun's vassals could become powerful enough to challenge his dominance if they had access to European military technology.

The strategy of isolation succeeded for about a hundred years. However, chronic financial difficulties eventually weakened the shogunate. The currency was debased and taxes were raised in order to raise revenue. Gradually, the situation of small farmers became precarious as more and more rice had to be given to the shogun's tax collectors. Riots became common.

By the middle of the nineteenth century, Japan was under great pressure by European states—such as Britain, Russia, and the United States—that wanted to topple the shogunate and enter the archipelago. The shogunate faced a difficult dilemma. It could no longer resist the European states, which possessed superior military technology; therefore, it signed treaties with Russia, Britain, France, and the Netherlands, states that regulated trade and diplomatic relations. For this the Tokugawa shogun was castigated by primarily low-ranking samurai from western Japan, assisted by certain nobles from the imperial court and by wealthy merchants. When the shogun was overthrown in 1868, governing authority returned to the Emperor Meiji. Although the Meiji Restoration, as the overthrow of the shogunate is called, transferred authority back to the emperor, he remained a ceremonial figurehead. Those who toppled the shogunate moved the emperor's court from Kyoto to the palace of the Tokugawa shoguns, established Tokyo as the capital, and thus strengthened the central government.

The young samurai who led the Meiji Restoration realized that Japan's survival as an independent entity depended upon the formation of a European-style national state. They made the decision to learn the secrets of European military and economic superiority. They imagined a state with a well-trained army and navy equipped with the best modern weapons available and supported by a modern industrial economy. Soon after the restoration, Japan's new elite began to invite European experts to Japan to teach new industrial and military techniques, and Japanese students were sent abroad to acquire European scientific and engineering knowledge. Railroads were constructed and a telegraph system was created. Factories were set up and strategic industries were subsidized. Schools and universities were built and compulsory education was decreed. A banking system was established. A conscripted standing army that replaced the samurai was created. The state was reorganized: feudalism was abolished and, inspired by France's centralized system of internal administration, the Japanese archipelago was divided into prefectures. A standard coinage was adopted and internal barriers to trade, a legacy of feudalism, were eliminated. A legal code and a system of courts were copied from those of European states.[17]

The resources needed to build a European-style state were extracted by borrowing and from taxing the subject population, especially farmers. Farmers began to resist the heavy burden of taxation, which they saw as primarily benefiting the urban industrial sector, and resorted to armed uprisings. The restoration elite responded by suppressing these uprisings militarily, jailing the leaders, and censoring newspapers. The ruling elite eventually struck a bargain, promising to grant a constitution and establish a parliament. A commission was sent to Europe to study constitutions and returned most impressed with imperial Germany. With the assistance of Prussian advisers, a constitution was drafted in 1889. It created a legislature, called the Imperial Diet, composed of a House of Peers and a House of Representatives, the numbers of which were chosen by a very small electorate defined by high tax-paying status. It met for the first time in 1890.

If Japan was going to compete successfully with its European rivals, a sense of nationhood also had to be developed. A national imaginary was created by nationalizing certain Japanese institutions and practices, especially those focusing on the emperor, as well as Buddhist ethics. In 1890 a law was passed that called upon all subjects to practice filial piety, to be loyal to the emperor, to obey the law, and to offer oneself to the state.[18]

By the end of the nineteenth century, the Meiji elite had built a European-style state with Japanese characteristics. Evidence of the Meiji elite's success came in 1904–1905, when Japan defeated Russia, the first time in modern history that a non-European state had defeated a European one. This victory enhanced the prestige of the military, which, during the 1930s, began to play a major role in Japanese politics. The military took indirect control of the state and launched a massive military buildup in order to counter the effects of the worldwide economic depression. They justified these policies by pointing to threats from other states to Japan's geostrategic position in northeast Asia, such as U.S. efforts to choke the flow of oil to Japan. The Japanese state thus became expansionist. The eventual result of this expansionism was defeat in World War II and occupation by the United States, a consequence that, ironically, the state-building project from its beginning was designed to avoid.

After World War II, the United States forced upon the Japanese a constitution that eliminated much of the military and gave the United States access to military bases on Japanese soil. Under the tutelage of the United States, the Liberal Democratic Party has dominated Japanese politics and succeeded in developing a managerial state in which large corporations oriented toward economic control of world consumer markets work closely with state technocrats, especially the Ministry of Technology and Industry, to manage an export-led economy. Within major companies, workers are guaranteed a job for life in return for nearly absolute loyalty to the company, but the majority of the work force is subject to the precariousness of the world capitalist economy. Wages remain fairly low, although the state, together with major corporations, provides significant social benefits, and consumer markets are tightly restricted to limit imports.

Japan has become one of the most powerful states in the current world order. It remains such even though it has experienced a prolonged recession and banking crisis beginning in 1989–1990 with the inflation in land prices and the collapse of the stock market. The Japanese system of on-time production, which increases flexibility and innovation in manufacturing while reducing costs, along with collective forms of labor management in which responsibility is spread to teams of workers, continue to be models for firms seeking to compete in the global economy. While reforming the banking industry, Japan's current reformist prime minister, Junichiro Koizumi, seems to be preserving an industrial policy in which the state and leading corporations coordinate closely.

With the end of the Cold War, new opportunities and concerns have arisen for the Japanese state. Investment has increased in Russia, and the regional economy has become more complex. Japan, which is still the second-largest economy in the world, is facing increasing competition from South Korea and China. Moreover, while at present the United States' security commitments remain intact, there is increasing disagreement over how best to guarantee Japanese security. While the United States has pressured the Japanese to change their constitution to allow the Japanese state to contribute militarily to global security operations, such as the war in Iraq, it has resisted; a majority of the population remains in favor of retaining the constitutional provision (Article 9) that prohibits Japan from either developing nuclear weapons or sending military force abroad. As competition and tensions rise in the Asia/Pacific region, and as Japan commits itself to multilateralism and is wary of U.S. unilateralism in world affairs, the Japanese state may be at a crossroads at which significant decisions will affect its basic structure and role in the world.

Iraq: State Formation by Semi-Direct Conquest

Until the end of World War I, the territorial space that eventually became Iraq existed as three administrative regions of the Ottoman Empire. In 1916, Britain conquered these and other districts, dismantled Ottoman administration, and substituted their own system of indirect colonial rule developed in India. The British governed Iraq through tribal *shaykhs*, or chieftains, who, in exchange for grants and privileges, collected taxes and maintained law and order.[19]

In 1920 the League of Nations assigned the mandate for Iraq to Britain, sparking a revolt among the shaykhs that the British put down by force. The British decided to end indirect rule through the shaykhs and imposed a provisional government made up of Iraqis friendly to them, which they replaced in 1921 with a constitutional monarchy. The British selected Faysal (ruled 1921–1933), the third son of Sharif Husayn of Mecca, which is in Saudi Arabia, not Iraq, to be king. Faysal, after a well-managed plebiscite produced a 96 percent approval rating for Britain's choice, was enthroned on August 27, 1921. Relations between Britain and the new Iraqi monarchy were formalized in a treaty that allowed the British to be closely involved in Iraqi internal affairs. An Iraqi army was established with the advice and assistance of British officers, and British advisers were placed in the government's ministries. Military and other types of aid were provided. Although a parliament was created, political life revolved around the king, a foreign monarch dependent upon the British, who wanted their supporters in the king's cabinet and parliament, and Arab politicians, who had no deep roots in constituencies outside of parliament, except to tribal shaykhs, and who formed parliamentary coalitions based on personal ties.

In 1929 negotiations between the Iraqi and British governments produced the Anglo-Iraq Treaty, which would remain in effect for twenty-five years. According to the terms of this treaty, the British were to promote Iraq's membership in the League of Nations, provide help to the Iraqis if attacked, maintain close cooperation in foreign affairs, be allowed to maintain two air bases on Iraqi soil, and continue training and equipping the Iraqi armed forces.

The political instability engendered by Faysal's death in 1933 led to a military coup d'etat in 1936, which was carried out by Bakr Sidqi, an Arab nationalist officer influenced by European fascism who favored an efficient authoritarian state strong enough to reverse British domination. A series of coups followed from 1937 until 1941. Elements of the indigenous officer corps had become the main site of Iraqi nationalism and resistance to the British. They jockeyed for power with pro-British governments until the British occupied Iraq militarily after a coup by a group of profascist nationalist officers in March 1940.

Iraq

Under a new treaty in 1947, British troops were withdrawn and the two air bases were returned to Iraq, although the armed forces were still to be armed and trained by the British, who would also still have a say in Iraqi defense planning. Widespread demonstrations against the new treaty led to a declaration of martial law and to the installation of a pro-British military government in 1952. Arab nationalist opposition to the government went underground and spread within the army, which had become dissatisfied with the pro-British elite. On July 14, 1958, the Iraqi army overthrew the Hasimite monarchy and, on July 14, the pro-British government.

The coup was engineered by Abd al-Karim Qasim and Abd al-Salam Arif, members of the Free Officers Movement, which opposed the British-installed monarchy and its foreign policy. After a power struggle between Qasim and Arif, another coup was staged by Arab nationalist army officers. They were supported by the Ba'th Party, which had originated in Syria, was strongly pan-Arab, and advocated radical social change. Initially, moderates led by Arif in the Revolutionary Command Council (RCC), as the new government was called, took control of the state in a bloodless coup in November 1963. After a period of weak rule and growing social discontent, a strong group of military men and Ba'thist politicians deposed Arif in July 1968. After this coup, the Ba'th Party established a one-party state.

An internal power struggle for control of the state ensued between civilian and military Ba'thists, eventually won by one of the civilian leaders, Saddam Hussein. On July 16, 1979, Hussein became secretary-general of the Ba'th Party, chairperson of the RCC, commander in chief of the armed forces, and president of the republic, all of which were approved by a newly elected national assembly in which delegates were either loyal Ba'th Party members or favorable to Ba'th Party principles.

The conditions of Ba'thist rule are complex. It should be remembered that Iraq was a legacy of borders imposed on a variety of groups that the British forcibly integrated into a state. Colonialism generated two fundamental forces, not only in Iraq but throughout the Middle East, that defined the possibilities and limits of sovereignty. One was Arab nationalism, a multilayered movement that politicized an ethnic identity as an anticolonial force. It emerged in part among army officers who sought control of the armed forces against the colonial advisers and officers, as well as complicitous procolonial generals. This aspect gave Arab nationalism a statist form. More generally, Arab nationalism became an anticolonial force in reaction to colonial domination of the regional economy, especially oil, and the formation of the state of Israel in Palestine by the British, the League of Nations, and European Zionists. These together politicized Arabism in complex ways.

The other force, by no means completely separate from but not reducible to Arab nationalism, was Islam. In Iraq, Islam had developed considerable complexity, offering different forms that could be translated under conditions of colonialism into various political movements. Within Iraq, sharp divisions between Shiites (primarily in the south) and Sunnis threaten to break the state apart. In the north, the Kurds have struggled for their own sovereign state, often with significant aid from foreign powers. At times, colonial powers used Islamic clerics to bolster their domination. On the other hand, Islam provided a moral and spiritual basis, as well as a well-established social organization, for the political mobilization of the poor and oppressed. In some forms, Islam saw in colonial domination a threatening modernizing and secularizing trend. Other forms of Islam embraced modernization. Note that neither Arab nationalism nor Islam pointed unambiguously to the nation-state as the most appropriate form of political organization.

Hussein reconstituted the state in Iraq by successfully manipulating these political forces, sometimes through repression, sometimes through accommodation. Initially drawing on the Ba'thist ideology of radical social reform, based in a largely secular, socialist program although tailored to the conditions of Arab societies, and pan-Arabism, which called for close alliances among Arab states, he buttressed his control over Iraq's formal institutions through a vast network of kinship and personal ties built up since he joined the Ba'th Party in 1957. This, in good part, insulated the state apparatus from the conflicting social and political pressures of rival political forces, nationalist and Islamic.[20]

Iraq's position in the world economy and the states-system also conditioned state sovereignty. The British had established an economy in Iraq that was dependent on oil exports, which the British controlled first through direct ownership and then through its monopoly of technology for extracting and refining the oil. It also, along with giant U.S. (and one Dutch) oil companies, controlled the markets. Economically, this severely constrained the Ba'thist Party's programs of social reform. Also, the type of state organization Hussein created, dependent on networks of personal contacts and loyalties, funneled money into the personal bank accounts of Hussein and his ministers. Lacking the industrial base to build and maintain an advanced military, Iraq remained dependent on European powers and on playing off the superpowers during the Cold War. Considerable sums were used to purchase weapons from abroad, which entailed taking on debts to foreign banks. From the end of the Cold War to the United States' invasion of Iraq in 2003, Hussein struggled to hold Iraq together as a secular, centralized state.

From 1980 to 1988, Iraq fought a devastating war with Iran, in part over concerns that Iranian support for Iraqi Shiites would upset the religious balance Saddam Hussein had been able to establish. Also, Iraq's only access to the Persian Gulf was through the Shiite region of Iraq. In this war,

Iraq was supported by the United States. The war also involved Hussein's concern to maintain a leading position for Iraq in the Middle East, especially among Arab states, that he saw being threatened by the rise of (non-Arab) Iran. This Arab-Persian conflict also has a long history and has conditioned the development of states in the region. Whatever the motives, however, the war devastated Iraq and made Hussein's domestic balancing act among different groups more difficult.

One of the issues that prompted the war was the persistent sense of the Iraqi state that its limited access to the Persian Gulf (a legacy of the colonial creation of Iraq as a state) was threatened. Without such access, control of its oil economy was weakened, as it would lose leverage against other Gulf states that could more easily control access to the Gulf and hence weaken Iraq in the region. Iraq's other main line of export for its oil was a pipeline through Syria, which likewise raised concerns about the vulnerability of its oil economy. This was an important concern leading to Iraq's invasion of Kuwait, with apparent acquiescence, if not tacit support, from the United States. This set in motion the chain of events that led to the U.S. invasion of Iraq in 2003 that resulted in Hussein's removal from power by the Americans, preceded by more than ten years of devastating sanctions imposed by the international community, and the policing of Iraqi airspace by coalition forces throughout the 1990s.

However, little if anything structurally in Iraq has changed, although the United States did support the formation by the Kurds in the north of a de facto independent state. While this de facto state had the appearance of being democratic, it has in fact been run by competing Kurdish warlords. The United States seems committed to imposing a liberal democratic state on Iraq, or, more cynically, imposing a regime open to foreign investment that will comply with the neoliberal hegemony in the world order. It remains unknown whether either of these efforts will succeed. Given our analysis of the historical formation of the Iraqi state, we are skeptical.

Congo: State Formation by Direct Conquest

The area of Africa now occupied by the state known as the Republic of Congo was settled over many centuries by small bands of Bantu-speaking peoples who engaged in subsistence agriculture. They encountered Pygmy peoples who lived by hunting and gathering. Later, non-Bantu-speaking peoples penetrated the area from the north and settled on the fringes of the tropical rainforest. Except for contact with the Portuguese along the coast around the mouth of the Congo River during the period of European expansion, and Afro-Arab slave traders from the east coast of Africa, the peoples of what was to become the Congo lived isolated from outsiders until the 1870s, when agents of King Leopold II (ruled 1865–1909) of Belgium

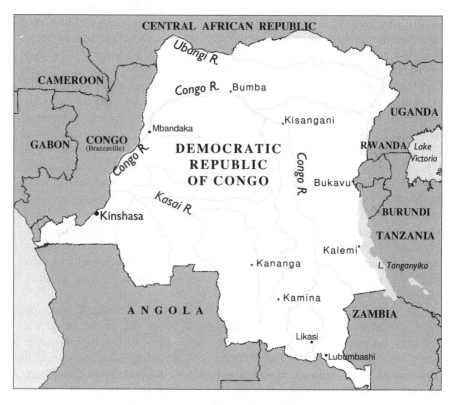

Democratic Republic of Congo

established a rudimentary colony called the Congo Free State, which was recognized by the Berlin Conference as the private domain of King Leopold.[21] In 1908, the Congo Free State was taken over by the Belgian government and renamed the Belgian Congo.

The Belgian Congo was divided into fifteen administrative districts without regard to African political authority, each headed by a commissioner. An army, called the Force Publique, was organized. It was officered by Belgians and its ranks filled with Africans. The Belgian government deliberately created rifts between neighboring African peoples and established administrative hierarchies of African chiefs, who supplied the Belgians with porters, soldiers, and food.

As with other colonized areas, the process of creating a colonial state politicized tribal and regional identities, turning them into social forces around which political loyalties could be organized against others. This set a pattern for the future: to participate in the state, indigenous Africans had few options but to organize themselves around tribal identities. Ethnicity as a political force was both created and politicized by the colonial state.

In the 1890s King Leopold had opened one-third of the Free State's "unknown" territory to private companies, which were given long-term concessions to exploit resources, such as copper, in return for payments to the king. The concessionary companies ruthlessly exploited Africans by forcing them from their villages to work on plantations and in mines, beating them and executing them if they refused, and setting impossibly high work quotas that frequently resulted in death from physical exhaustion. Accounts of the extremely harsh treatment of indigenous Africans raised humanitarian concerns, especially in the United States and Britain, but nothing came of halfhearted attempts to eliminate the forced labor.

After taking formal control in 1908, the Belgian government reduced the power of the concessionary companies and ruled the colony indirectly through African chiefs, whom they appointed and paid. Often the individual appointed as chief over a particular people was not a chief in the eyes of those people. Later, these chieftaincies were grouped together into sectors, and one of the chiefs was appointed to head the sector. These heads were usually individuals who had worked for the Belgians as low-level clerks in the colonial administration or who had served as soldiers in the Force Publique. Thus, an administrative hierarchy was established that was loyal to the Belgians and that simultaneously politicized ethnicity and generated ethnic divisions.

Despite formal Belgian prohibitions against the exploitation of Africans, labor was recruited by force with the assistance of the Belgian colonial administration, which often worked closely with the labor recruiters from the concessionary companies. The colonial authorities in Leopoldville and Belgium turned a blind eye to this practice, justifying it through the racist belief that Africans could be civilized only through regular labor. The colonial authorities also forced Africans to cultivate cash crops, such as cotton, which were difficult to grow successfully in poor African soils but which settlers or foreign markets demanded.

After World War II, the significant number of European-educated Africans in the Congo, known as *évolués* (French, meaning "evolved ones"), began to demand jobs in the colonial civil service commensurate with their level of education as well as equal pay for equal work. They began to organize professional, educational, mutual-aid, and ethnic societies and clubs. By the 1950s they began to demand independence. The first demands came in 1956 from a group of prominent Ngala évolués from Leopoldville. Nationalist political parties began to take shape, based on the already existing mutual-aid and ethnic associations. Only one of these parties, the National Congolese Movement (NCM), led by Patrice Lumumba (1925–1961), a prominent évolué from Leopoldville, claimed to be a colony-wide party.

In June 1959, the Belgian government announced that it was going to "prepare" the colony for independence, suggesting that Africans were not capable of governing themselves. This racist language would provide the Belgians and others with justifications for continued intervention to regulate Congolese sovereignty. Three nationalist leaders, each with a different imagining of the future structure of the independent state, emerged: Lumumba and the NCM were in favor of the establishment of a unitary state for the independent Congo; Joseph Kasavubu (1910?–1969) and his party, the Alliance of the Bakongo, and Moise Tshombe (1919–1969) and his party, the Confederation of Katanga Associations, which was strongly supported by Belgians with a financial interest in the copper-rich Katanga province, were in favor of autonomy for their regions within a federal state. Elections were held in May 1960 for a national parliament and provincial assemblies. Lumumba's NCM won a plurality but not a majority of seats in the Chamber of Deputies, the parliament's lower house. Lumumba became prime minister and formed a coalition government. In June, Kasavubu was elected president.

The tranquility of the first months of independence was broken on July 5, 1960, when the Force Publique mutinied against its Belgian officers. Belgium flew in paratroopers to restore order and evacuate Europeans. Lumumba replaced Belgian officers with Africans and appointed his uncle, Victor Lundula, to be commander in chief and Joseph Désiré Mobutu to be chief of staff. The army's name was changed to the National Congolese Army.

We need to note here the important role of the military in the independent Congo, one of the legacies of colonialism that defines and limits the possibilities of politics in the Congo and elsewhere in postcolonial states.

The military was the element of the state apparatus that the colonial power often most highly developed. Soldiers were well trained, equipped with modern weapons, organized, and disciplined. The independent Congolese state initially maintained Belgian officers, depended upon supplies and training from Belgium, and cultivated a pro-Belgian officer corps. This officer corps enjoyed access to European ideas and was socialized to consider itself as members of the Congolese state with a distinctive responsibility to maintain order and stability.

It is not surprising, then, that civilian leaders would turn to the military for key allies and would give officers important political roles in their governments. This was especially the case given the combination of continued dependence on foreign arms supplies and the willingness of foreign states to back one party against another. Political success came to mean choosing between military patrons. Moreover, the combination of the politicization of tribal identities and the repression of alternative sources of political energy (unions, the working class, or democratic civic organizations) that might challenge forced labor, foreign investment, or the practices of major property owners (especially copper mining by the foreign-owned copper companies) meant that mass support for military and nationalist leaders came to be based in often divisive, exclusionist visions of the state and politics.

The crisis of the early 1960s and General Mobuto Sésé-Sekou's rise to power illustrate this legacy. Tshombe, who had established a one-party government in the province of Katanga, declared it independent of the Congo on July 11, 1960. The Belgian government landed paratroopers in the Congo in support of Tshombe. Lumumba and Kasavubu, who feared that the Belgians were seeking to reoccupy the Congo, turned to the United Nations for assistance. On July 14 the UN Security Council persuaded the Belgian troops to withdraw and dispatched several thousand peacekeeping troops to the Congo.

When the UN troops refused to help him end the Katanga secession, Lumumba turned to the Soviet Union for military assistance. Kasavubu, seeking continued support from the West, dismissed Lumumba and his government and appointed General Mobutu as commander in chief of the army. Lumumba refused to accept his dismissal and accused Kasavubu of high treason. Parliament refused to act. On December 31, 1960, General Mobutu assumed power and demanded the departure of Soviet diplomatic and military personnel. Because Mobutu was unable at this time to establish a unified government, the centralized state all but dissolved. In the chaos that followed, Lumumba was arrested and murdered. In February 1961, the Security Council resolved to give the UN forces the power to bring the Congo together under a single government.

Under UN auspices, a parliament was convened and a broad coalition government, headed by Cyrille Adoula (1921–1978), was formed. Tshombe refused to cooperate, and mercenary troops in the employ of foreign copper companies in Katanga clashed with UN troops. When UN forces gained the military advantage, Tshombe requested aid from the United States. The United States brokered a deal that eventually ended the Katangese succession, brought about the departure of the mercenaries, and sent Tshombe into exile. Tshombe did, however, maintain an army of Katangese police in neighboring Angola while he was in exile.

In mid-1963 the national parliament became deadlocked over the draft of a new constitution. Kasavubu declared a state of emergency for six months, which sparked rebellions in Kuilu and Kivu in early 1964. When, in the following months, rebellions broke out in other northeastern provinces, Tshombe was asked by Kasavubu to return to the Congo and form a transitional government. Utilizing soldiers who had returned with him from exile, Tshombe recaptured rebel strongholds. These successes and his victory in the parliamentary elections of March 1965 made Tshombe a strong contender for the presidency. Therefore, on October 13, 1965, Kasavubu dismissed Tshombe as prime minister. But, because Tshombe's party held the majority of seats, the new prime minister could not form a government. An impasse resulted. The deadlock was ended when, on November 24, 1965, General Mobutu once again took control of the state and forbade all political activity.

Over time, power was increasingly concentrated into Mobutu's hands. Mobutu, who was able to stabilize the situation with U.S. support, became a ruthless, corrupt, patrimonial ruler. On October 27, 1971, Mobutu changed the name of the Congo to Zaire. Other place names were Africanized, and Mobutu changed his own name to Mobutu Sésé-Sekou Kulu Ngbendu wa Zabango. Over a three-month period, foreign-owned plantations and businesses were expropriated and given to Zairens (mostly party loyalists), army officers, and civil servants. In 1974, Mobutu Sésé-Sekou instituted a new constitution that gave the president control over all organs of the state. Mobutu was reelected president in December 1977 and again in July 1984.

Mobutu Sésé-Sekou ruled Zaire until 1997, when his regime was overthrown in a rebellion led by Laurent Kabila, which began in the eastern provinces, primarily among Tutsis, and spread to other ethnic groups. Mobutu survived in power for thirty years because certain European states and the United States needed him. With the end of the Cold War, however, the United States no longer needed Mobutu to support Jonas Sivimbi, the U.S.-backed anticommunist client in neighboring Angola who refused to accept its democratically elected government because of its socialist programs and support by Cuba and the Soviet Union. Consequently, the United States lost interest in Angola and Savimbi. Moreover, Mobutu's regional alliances unraveled. The white regime in South Africa was replaced and, more significantly, the genocidal Hutu regime in Rwanda, which Mobutu supported, was overthrown by a Tutsi and moderate Hutu force. The rebellion in Rwanda created a refugee crisis, sending nearly 2 million Hutu refugees across the border into Zaire, where they were exploited by Mobutu and the remainder of the Hutu government. Mobutu temporarily garnered renewed recognition and support from the United States, and from European states that needed his support, to supply the refugees with humanitarian aid and avoid widespread starvation and disease. He supported the remainder of the radical Hutu military, which used the refugee camps to regroup for an eventual reinvasion of Rwanda, to attack the Tutsi population in Zaire, and to repress political opposition. He also controlled the war economy in eastern Zaire, making a fortune for himself and his cohorts by selling arms and controlling oil supplies in the region. The new Rwandan government invaded eastern Zaire and attacked the remainder of the Hutu army. In doing so, they joined forces with Kabila in order to overthrow Mobutu. Other regional forces backed Kabila, and, somewhat surprisingly, Kabila's forces spread through the country easily. During the final takeover of the state, Kabila refused mediation from the United States or Europe; instead, the final negotiations were made possible by African leaders, most notably Nelson Mandela of South Africa.

Summary

The often turbulent ethnic politics, patrimonialism, and militarization of many postcolonial states are neither the result of neocolonialism nor the failure to modernize, that is, to live up to "modern" standards. Some non-European states, Japan most notably, but there are others, such as China and South Korea, have become powerful states in the current world order. All non-European states, whether directly colonized or externally induced by pressure coming from powerful European states, faced distinctive limits to their sovereignty. These limits were imposed by the historical legacy of colonialism and by continued efforts by powerful European states to regulate their sovereignty so that it conforms to the norms and interests of the states-system and world economy. As we will see in Part 4, such regulating and disciplining of sovereignty has intensified with the globalization of the world capitalist economy.

Notes

1. Sankaran Krishna, "Inscribing the Nation: Nehru and the Politics of Identity in India," in Stephen J. Rosow et al. (eds.), *The Global Economy as Political Space* (Boulder, CO: Lynne Rienner Publishers, 1994): 189–202.

2. Examples of this literature include Leonard Binder et al., *Crises of Political Development* (Princeton, NJ: Princeton University Press, 1971); C. E. Black, *The Dynamics of Modernization* (New York: Harper & Row, 1966); Dankwart Rustow, *A World of Nations: Problems of Political Modernization* (Washington, DC: The Brookings Institution, 1967); A.F.K. Organiski, *The Stages of Political Development* (New York: Knopf, 1965); Walt N. Rostow, *The Stages of Economic Growth* (Cambridge: Cambridge University Press, 1960).

3. Bertrand Badie and Pierre Birnbaum, *The Sociology of the State*, trans. Arthur Goldhammer (Chicago: University of Chicago Press, 1983), especially chapter 2.

4. Such as in Samuel P. Huntington, *Political Order in Changing Societies* (New Haven, CT: Yale University Press, 1968).

5. On the idea of reflexive development that draws on the writings of sociologist Anthony Giddens, see Tony Spybey, *Globalization and World Society* (Cambridge: Polity Press, 1996).

6. See Göran Therborn, "The Right to Vote and the Four World Routes to/Through Modernity," in Rolf Thorstendahl (ed.), *State Theory and State History* (London: Sage Publications, 1992): 62–87.

7. Basil Davidson, *The Black Man's Burden: Africa and the Curse of the Nation-State* (New York: Random House, 1992).

8. David Strang calls external inducement "defensive Westernization." See his piece, "Contested Sovereignty: The Social Construction of Colonial Imperialism," in Thomas J. Biersteker and Cynthia Weber (eds.), *State Sovereignty as Social Construct* (Cambridge: Cambridge University Press 1996): 40–43.

9. See Sanjay Seth, "Nationalism in/and Modernity," in Joseph A. Camilleri et al. (eds.), *The State in Transition: Reimagining Political Space* (Boulder, CO: Lynne Rienner Publishers, 1995): 41–58.

10. Our view of regulated sovereignty is different from Robert Jackson's "quasi-sovereignty" in that emphasis is on regulation and control, whereas his is on creation, entitlement, and "shoring up" of states that do not measure up to the Westphalian-established criteria and norms of sovereignty. See his *Quasi-States: Sovereignty, International Relations, and the Third World* (Cambridge: Cambridge University Press, 1990).

11. For a recent argument that U.S. foreign aid to promote human rights operates as a form of surveillance and discipline of the sovereignty of "developing" states, see Roxanne Lynn Doty, *Imperial Encounters* (Minneapolis: University of Minnesota Press, 1996), chapter 6.

12. The classic argument to this effect was Huntington, *Political Order in Changing Societies*.

13. Robert H. Jackson and Carl G. Rosberg, *Personal Rule in Black Africa: Prince, Autocrat, Prophet, Tyrant* (Berkeley: University of California Press, 1982).

14. René Lemarchand, "Political Clientelism and Ethnicity in Tropical Africa: Competing Solidarities in Nation-Building," *American Political Science Review* 66 (1972): 68–90.

15. Davidson, *The Black Man's Burden*.

16. These details on Japanese statemaking and the following are from Nobutaka Ike, "Japan," in Harold C. Hinton et al. (eds.), *Major Governments of Asia* (Ithaca, NY: Cornell University Press, 1958): 135–154.

17. Eleanor D. Westney, *Imitation and Innovation: The Transfer of Western Organization Patterns in Meiji Japan* (Cambridge, MA: Harvard University Press, 1987); Marius B. Jansen, *The Making of Modern Japan* (Cambridge, MA: Harvard University Press, 2000).

18. Sheldon Garon, *Making Japanese Minds: The State in Everyday Life* (Princeton, NJ: Princeton University Press, 1997).

19. The historical details of the case of Iraq are from Phebe Marr, *The Modern History of Iraq* (Boulder, CO: Westview Press, 1985), 29–122, 153–244.

20. Ibid., 228.

21. The historical details of the case of Zaire are from Irving Kaplan, ed., *Zaïre: A Country Study,* 3d ed. (Washington, DC: U.S. Government Printing Office, 1977).

PART 4

CHALLENGES TO THE STATE

In the final part of the book we address the current challenges and issues facing the state as a form of politico-military rule. What is the future of the sovereign territorial state? To what degree and through what techniques and in what form will states continue to institute sovereignty? Are managerial states being transformed into a new form of the state? Does the spread of a global capitalist economy with its network of disciplinary and managerial institutions suggest a new form of global order is emerging? What does "globalization" mean for the territorial state? Part 4, then, brings the argument of the book together by answering the question raised in the introduction: Are we witnessing the fifth great transformation to a new epoch of global history, one in which the modern territorial state will disappear and a post-territorial form of politico-military rule will become universalized?

11

The Present State of States:
Sovereignty Challenged

We have shown that the modern territorial state is a unique historical creation of relatively recent vintage. It is not eternal, and no form of it is universal. Moreover, it now exists within a world order in which managerial states dominate; indeed, most people live in states whose lives are regulated and disciplined by powerful managerial states, and through these states the norms of the states-system, as well as the organizations of the global capitalist economy.

Military, economic, and social forces are calling into question the state's territoriality, as well as the modern state's insistence on a politics of control from the center. The ability to represent the state as territorially sovereign is diminished by changes in warfare, the globalization of capitalism, the proliferation of international managerial institutions, and the tremendous mobility of people around the globe. Present developments not only seem to be challenging the current form of the state, but are also questioning the possibilities of territorialized, sovereign politico-military power.

This is not to argue that the nation-state is disappearing, but that state sovereignty is facing serious challenges. Territorial states have always had to confront forces that overflow the representation of a sharp boundary between sovereignty inside—that is, the realm in which states claimed to be "in control" and in which the subject population was pacified—and sovereignty outside, that is, the state's independence in a system of juridically sovereign states in a world of perpetual violence and war. These forces are, at a minimum, intensifying in the global order. In this chapter we examine four forces that recently have challenged nation-state sovereignty: (1) changes in warfare; (2) the globalization of capitalism; (3) the fracturing of national identity; and (4) the emergence of "hypermedia" networks.

Post-Territorial Warfare

Since the Peace of Westphalia in 1648, global order has been constructed around the imaginary of "hard-shelled" impenetrable territorial states capable of defending their subject populations and territories from attack and conquest by other states. As one student of the state put it, "the large-area state came to occupy the place that the castle or fortified town had previously held as a unit of impenetrability."[1] Substituting the impenetrable borders of the territorial state for those of castle or fortified town has had a major impact on the practice of war, however.

Before Westphalia, European war was, for the most part, about property and dynastic claims. For example, the Norman Conquest (1066) was carried out by William, Duke of Normandy, who claimed the English throne upon the death of Edward the Confessor; the Hundred Years' War (1337–1453) was fought over lands owned by the English Crown south of the Loire River (Aquitaine), which had been invaded by the French king, and the English king's claim to the French throne; the Wars of the Roses (1455–1485) were struggles between the ducal houses of Lancaster and York over which was the legitimate claimant to the English throne. The rise of the territorial state rendered such dynastic war anachronistic. After Westphalia, the object of warfare became territorial gain. Wars such as the Seven Years' War (1755–1763) between Britain and France and the War of Jenkin's Ear (1739–1748), for example, between Spain and Britain, were about wresting control of small pieces of territory from each other, principally in their colonial empires outside of Europe.[2]

Following the French Revolution and the rise of nationalism, warfare was transformed from being about territorial gain to being about penetrating the hard-shelled state and totally defeating and destroying it as a rival. In other words, the rise of the nation-state ushered in the era of total war. The Napoleonic Wars (1804–1815), World War I (1914–1919), World War II (1939–1945), and the Cold War (1950–1991) were about conquering and occupying the territory of rival states, vanquishing their armies, destroying their infrastructure, and establishing forms of government, economy, and social life acceptable to the conquering state.

Although the rise of nationalism after the French Revolution created the social and psychological conditions that made total war possible,[3] the ability of states to actually override the territorial boundaries of rival states has been aided by the advance of military technology and the general industrialization of warfare. The industrialization of warfare has made war making more dependent upon science and technology, which require formal and informal connections between the military and weapons industries. In 1957, U.S. president Dwight Eisenhower (1890–1969) warned about the influence of what he called the "military-industrial complex." In effect, the industrialization of warfare has made total war even more total.[4] Machine weapons are capable of killing thousands or even millions of people and utterly destroying the infrastructure on which social and economic life in industrial states depends. They require the mobilization of the entire industrial and social capabilities of the states. In the words of one historian, the "old distinction maintained in civilized warfare between the civilian and the combatant population disappeared (with World War I). Everyone who grew food or sewed a garment, everyone who felled a tree or repaired a house, every railway station and every warehouse was held to be fair game for destruction."[5]

Paradoxically, industrial warfare also created new attitudes and social organizations to promote peace and to limit the destructiveness of war. Beginning in the 1890s, international conferences were convened to codify and expand the laws of war. These international laws of war regulated both when it was just and legal for states to go to war, called *jus ad bellum* or "justice of war," and how wars should be conducted, called *jus in bello* or "justice in war." Perhaps most important were attempts to limit or prohibit the use of "cruel and unusual" weapons and prohibitions against targeting civilians. Industrial warfare also generated an international social movement for peace, including the creation of nongovernmental, international organizations the aim of which was to promote peace.[6]

Industrialization also changed the rationale for war, creating a "peace interest." States became more inclined to seek peace and avoid war not out of ethical considerations or concerns for humanity, which animated the international peace movements, but because some sectors of the industrial economy considered peace as necessary to promote industrialization and economic growth. Of course, many other industrialists, especially those directly involved in producing and supplying weapons, recognized how war could be a driving force for an industrial economy and therefore promoted more aggressive foreign policies. The most important sectors of the industrial state that supported peace policies were those whose profit derived in some significant way from trade, especially finance capitalists, who put up the money for industrial enterprises engaged in trade.[7]

Industrial warfare, by allowing mass killing at extremely long range (distances beyond the senses or comprehension of the individual soldier), also fundamentally altered social attitudes toward the meaning of war and, more generally, toward violence and killing. World War I, for example, generated in Britain a remarkable body of writing, especially letters and poetry, by soldiers who attempted to come to grips with the implications of industrial war for human life.[8] Contemplate the following two excerpts from very different writers and times, the first a reflection on the implications of World War I, the second a reflection by a contemporary Native American writer on the implications of modern war.

> We were in a garden at Mons. Young Buckley came in with his patrol from across the river. The first German I saw climbed up over the garden wall. We waited till he got one leg over and then potted him. He had so

much equipment on and looked awfully surprised and fell down into the garden. Then three more came over further down the wall. We shot them. They all came just like that. . . . .[9]

"You were with the others," he said, "the ones who went to the white people's war?" Tayo nodded. . . .

He didn't know how to explain what had happened. He did not know how to tell him that he had not killed any enemy or that he did not think that he had. But that he had done things far worse, and the effects were everywhere in the cloudless sky, on the dry brown hills, shrinking skin and hide taut over sharp bone . . .

But the old man shook his head slowly and made a low humming sound in his throat. In the old way of warfare, you couldn't kill another human being in battle without knowing it, without seeing the result, because even a wounded deer that got up and ran again left great clots of lung blood or spilled guts on the ground. That way the hunter knew it would die. Human beings were no different. But the old man would not have believed white warfare—killing across great distances without knowing who or how many had died. It was all too alien to comprehend, the mortars and big guns; and even if he could have taken the old man to see the target areas, even if he could have led him through the fallen jungle trees and muddy craters of torn earth to show him the dead, the old man would not have believed anything so monstrous. Ku'oosh would have looked at the dismembered corpses and the atomic heat-flash outlines, where human bodies had evaporated, and the old man would have said something close and terrible had killed these people. Not even old-time witches killed like that.[10]

Representations of industrialized, machine warfare in which soldiers are transformed into machines that kill without human feeling, in which the enemy has become nothing more than an object to be routinely, coldly, and efficiently annihilated, have become staples of modern culture. The efficiency and rationality of this form of destruction, rather than being seen as a virtue, are represented as irrational and inhuman, either too efficient or otherworldly and supernatural. Such representations captured and helped to form powerful critiques of not only particular wars but of warfare in general.

Although they were developed to defend territory, modern industrial weapons render the heartland of the state increasingly vulnerable. The most significant developments appear, interestingly, at opposite ends of the spectrum of weapons: large-scale nuclear weapons on one end, and small-scale, even miniaturized weapons on the other, such as portable, easily concealable bombs that can be broken down into their component parts and easily smuggled across borders.

Air warfare and nuclear warfare have affected the territorial impenetrability of nation-states most radically, however. With the development of tactical air warfare during World War I, the perfection of strategic bombing with conventional and nuclear bombs in World War II, and the development of intercontinental ballistic missiles (ICBMs) during the Cold War, the hard shell of the nation-state was decisively blasted away. The development of long-range strategic bombers during World War II made it possible for air forces to fly over the outer defenses of enemy states and directly attack their "soft" hinterlands. Cities, factories, roads, bridges, and civilians came under direct attack. Often the purpose of strategic bombing was not to destroy military targets but to terrorize civilians so that they would refuse to fight or support the war.

The scale of nuclear destruction, however, challenges the very idea that nuclear weapons are "weapons" like other weapons that can "win" wars and achieve political goals. The blast from a nuclear weapon can leave deep craters in the earth of more than a mile in diameter within which everything is instantly vaporized. They generate tremendous heat, which causes "firestorms" that instantly incinerate buildings, trees, roads, and people within a wide radius of ground zero. Such weapons also produce radioactivity that slowly kills thousands more and adversely affects the health of future generations. The scope of their destructive force makes most, if not all, nuclear weapons unusable on the battlefield, although attempts have been made to design tactical nuclear weapons that would confine the effects of blast, heat, and radioactivity. The inability of technology to achieve what many strategic planners consider acceptable limits, along with the concern of military commanders that, in the "heat" and uncertainty of battle, escalation is inevitable, has led many military and civilian strategists to conclude that nuclear weapons are unusable as rational weapons of war. That is, their use serves no strategic purpose in protecting armies and territory or in winning battles.

Nuclear weapons thus challenge state sovereignty not only because of the scale and scope of their destructive power but also because of the ways they are delivered to enemy territory. The first form of delivery was, of course, the strategic bomber (B-17s and B-29s) that dropped the first atomic weapons as gravity bombs on the Japanese cities of Hiroshima and Nagasaki in World War II. Aircraft have remained an important delivery vehicle for weapons, although current technology allows them to avoid flying directly over their targets. Instead they release missiles, called "cruise missiles," which use computerized maps to guide themselves to their targets within enemy territory. In order to ensure a retaliatory nuclear capability that could survive any first strike by an enemy nuclear attack, U.S. strategic planners have developed two additional delivery vehicles for nuclear weapons: land-based and submarine-launched ICBMs. Using computerized guidance systems, ICBMs, launched from hardened land-based silos or from submarines, fly outside the earth's immediate atmosphere across several continents to their targets in enemy territory. Both Russia and the United States continue to maintain all three delivery systems, and other nuclear powers, such as Britain, France, China, Pakistan, and India maintain one or two. All three delivery technologies allow the weapons to jump over, as it were, the territorial borders of an enemy state. Moreover, advanced guidance systems, and "stealth" technology, which makes bombers less detectable by enemy radar, and the sheer speed of ICBMs, which can fly halfway around the globe in less than thirty minutes, have made these weapons impossible to detect with sufficient certainty to ensure a reliable defense against them.

Therefore, air warfare and nuclear weapons have made the territorial sovereignty of even the most powerful nation-states increasingly anachronistic. Even one or two medium-sized nuclear weapons could devastate large swaths of a state's territory. Such weapons make it impossible for states that possess them to go to war against each other without the risk of mutual suicide. In the words of one scholar: "Nuclear weapons . . . [have] finally put an end to the nation-state's ability to guarantee the security of its citizens . . . There is simply no defense against nuclear weapons."[11]

Nuclear weapons have been subject to the rationality of industrialization as much as to strategic considerations.[12] Improvements in them have been subject to the dynamic drive for greater productivity of the large corporations that produce them. In a sense, they are as much the result of the modern penchant for instrumental, means-end rationality as is the zip-lock sandwich bag or double-entry bookkeeping.[13] Improvements are also the result of the modern attitudes toward scientific progress that feed the advanced capitalist economy: if an object (tool, machine, procedure, human behavior) can be improved (i.e., made more powerful and efficient), it should be, according to what is technically possible. The social and political consequences of such technical improvements are seen as exogenous; therefore, technological improvements take on a life of their own. Moreover, the development of miniaturized electronics used to upgrade ICBMs, such as advanced guidance systems that allow multiple, independently targetable warheads to be placed on a single missile, have "improved" conventional weapons as well as making them more powerful, mobile, and concealable.

With the development of miniaturized electronics and the advent of new, more portable means of violence, the global order has become generally militarized. This new technology is not separable from the global context of militarization during the Cold War, which has created both the means and the economic impulses to "microtize" weapons further, and to spread them to private and nonstate groups.[14]

Attempts to humanize war in the 1990s have actually reinforced the war-as-machine paradigm. The first Gulf War was arguably the first computer war. The use of advanced communications and computer technologies, along with more intensive use of realistic gaming to prepare soldiers for the war, have further distanced soldiers, both spatially and cognitively, from killing. The media coverage of the Gulf War and the recent invasion of Iraq, while sanitizing the war coverage to eliminate disturbing images, in the same breadth glorified the abilities of the high-tech weaponry to limit destruction, which helped make the war appear virtuous. This new "military-industrial-media-entertainment complex,"[15] as one scholar refers to it, has been justified by its ability to limit casualties and collateral damage, in essence to limit and control warfare down to its most minute details. But has it? Or does this new form of high-tech warfare make war into a tool of control? Arguably, by making war appear more "surgical," war is becoming a technique of controlling recalcitrant and resistant forces in the world order; that is, war is becoming a way of policing the global order—a development about which many professional soldiers have significant misgivings—especially as war comes to be justified more and more as a collective response of the international community to dangerous "rogue states" or unstable situations.

During the Cold War, nuclear weapons existed in an uneasy peace that was based on the production of nuclear weapons, which everyone agreed could never be used rationally. State territory came to be defended not by national armies and navies but by the fear of mutual destruction. The deaths of hundreds of millions of civilians and the complete destruction of the enemy state's capacity to function as a viable industrial society was sufficient to keep the peace, at least among the European nuclear powers.

Outside of Europe, however, war was frequent, and in almost all cases, warring factions and states were supplied with advanced weapons by the nuclear powers, although neither transferred nuclear weapons to their client states. Most often, this made the client states dependent on the military-industrial complex of their patron, most often the United States or the Soviet Union. Several other European states, such as Britain, France, and the former Czechoslovakia, became major arms suppliers as well, because client states lacked the industrial and scientific base to produce and maintain modern weapons. Also, wars outside of Europe in which the superpowers directly participated—the U.S. war in Vietnam (1964–1975) and the Soviet war in Afghanistan (1979–1985) being the most important—spread enormous quantities of surplus weapons throughout the world, such as automatic rifles, tanks and antitank missiles, artillery pieces, antipersonnel mines, and plastic explosives. Finally, arms production became an important industry in many advanced economies as well as in some newly industrializing non-European states such as Brazil, China, Argentina, and Israel. These non-European states have generated, along with the "leftover" weapons from the proxy wars of the superpowers, a network of arms markets throughout the world in which weapons of all types can be purchased by private persons, movements, or states that cannot produce them themselves.[16]

Such military developments have created a severe challenge to the ability of the well-established European state to defend its territory and maintain the imaginary of impenetrable borders. At the same time, many non-European states are losing their monopoly over the means of physical coercion, one of the basic characteristics of the modern territorial state. In many parts of the world the regular armed forces of the state are in decay or have disintegrated. In such areas there has been a big increase in violence perpetuated by non-state actors and warfare is increasingly becoming privatized. In weak states where the regular armed forces have lost their coherence, non-state actors are assembling their own armed forces to protect their interests and territory. For example, in

> India, tea farmers in the Assam region have assembled an eight-thousand-member private army to protect their interest against two major separatist insurgent groups responsible for a wave of kidnappings and extortion; in Pakistan, large areas beyond the commercial center, Karachi, are controlled by drug barons; in Cambodia, army generals have apportioned important swaths of territory among themselves, which they administer as local warlords; in Guatemala, wealthy landowners have hired entire paramilitary units to safeguard their position of privilege; in the Philippines, the Moro Islamic Liberation Front has hired foreign mercenaries to attack government soldiers.[17]

Thus, with the well-established European state unable to defend its territory against weapons of mass destruction and the weak non-European state unable to maintain its monopoly over the means of physical coercion, we may be entering an age of post-territorial warfare in which war will increasingly take the form it had before the rise of the state and the Westphalian states-system, a "new medievalism."[18] War will increasingly be "low intensity" and involve activities such as assassination, looting, robbery, extortion, pillage, and hostage taking. More and more, armed force will be wielded by nonstate actors who will organize their own armies or will hire mercenary companies, such as Executive Outcomes, Saladin Security, and Sandline International, to put troops in the field, build and maintain military bases, train security forces, and conduct air surveillance, and wars will be fought for individual glory, booty, or profit.[19]

Globalizing Capitalism

The state is also challenged by the globalization of civil society. Globalization has expanded not only the scope of economic activity, but also the ways in which the increasing connections between people across state borders have induced changes in people's perceptions of social space and its boundaries. Social relations that nation-states assume to take place inside their borders—family connections, professional associations, economic activities, friendships—are increasingly constitutive of networks of social interaction across national borders. Civil society at the beginning of the twenty-first century, in important respects, moves rather freely across and through the territorial boundaries of states. This has rendered national civil societies less easy to manage by states and made the imagining of state sovereignty less central to people's identities and more difficult for states to sustain.[20]

Much of the challenge of global civil society stems from the globalization of the capitalist economy. "Globalization" refers to "the complex of economic, technological, ecological, and cultural structures that are emerging on a global scale which ignore or deny the relevance of any state's territory."[21] Globalization challenges the effectiveness of the territorial state as a guarantor of the economic well-being and the national identity of its subject population. States can still intervene in their national economies, often with considerable impact. However, in many important economic areas, states either have chosen not to constrain globalization, by supporting free trade and refusing to restrict capital flows and labor markets, or have felt too restricted by global financial markets or the international division of labor to make any active attempts at managing the economy.

The industrial capitalist system has always been a global system, dependent on networks through which commodities and money circulate. Historically, capitalism has relied on the nation-state and at the same time challenged its sovereignty by undermining the ability of the state to enclose civil society within territorial boundaries. The industrial capitalist system increased the importance of trade in local economies and made long-distance trade economical.[22] It also created a new system of global inequality based on the uneven deployment of industrial technologies. Regions that supplied the raw materials of industrial production, both within states and in relations between states, gained less of the profit from industrial production than did those regions or states that supplied the manufactured goods or provided the financing for manufacturing and trade.

Steam-powered trains and ships, which became large and fast during the nineteenth century, compressed time and space. Steam power resulted in more goods being traded over greater distances more quickly than ever before. This had the effect of spreading the industrial system to all parts of the world, often destroying indigenous economies because imported manufactured goods could be sold more cheaply than locally produced goods.

As we discussed in previous chapters, the British created and dominated the emerging global industrial capitalist system through much of the eighteenth and nineteenth centuries. By the 1870s, Germany and the United States rivaled Britain in industrial power. In the last half of the nineteenth century the Japanese would also embark on the rapid industrialization of their economy. Industrialization became a global phenomenon establishing the terms of hegemony in the European world economy. A core of states with industrial economies came to dominate the world economy by spreading advanced technologies over which they maintained control, promoting norms of free trade, and recolonizing other states through the control of their raw materials and markets.

After World War II, the United States created a globally managed free-trade system, as part of the Fordist social economy, in which goods and investment flowed freely across national borders. The main beneficiary of the system was the large transnational corporation (TNC). These corporations maintained headquarters in their home states but invested directly in other states, where they built factories and bought and otherwise established foreign subsidiaries in order to penetrate foreign markets. They began to organize themselves transnationally in the sense that their "bottom lines" were calculated to include the multinational markets in which they operated. This system has led during the past forty years to a tremendous concentration of wealth that is organized internationally and is highly mobile across borders. According to one estimate, the largest three hundred TNCs, many of which boast sales greater than the gross national product of most nation-states, control nearly a quarter of the world's productive assets.[23]

During the 1980s and 1990s those large corporations that dominate the world economy maintained multinational operations and networks of subsidiaries, many of which are becoming global. These "global corporations are the first secular institutions run by men (and a handful of women) who think and plan on a global scale."[24] They develop products—of which Coca-Cola and the Sony Walkman are two significant examples—that, with minor modifications, can be sold in any country in the world, and they plan their production and distribution to fit a global market. For example, McDonald's adjusts its menus to fit local sensitivities and religious practices. In Israel Big Macs are served without cheese; in India, mutton-based Maharaja Macs and Vegetable McNuggets are served; in Turkey cold yogurt drinks are available; in Italy espresso coffee and cold pasta can be purchased; in Japan teriyaki burgers are available; in Norway grilled salmon sandwiches; in Germany frankfurters and beer; and in Uruguay, egg hamburgers.[25] Moreover, fast food restaurants discipline consumers. Diners are taught to get in line, get their own drinks, napkins, flatware, find their own tables. In effect, diners do much of the labor of eating out in return for low prices.

Such globalization has been made possible by improvements in transportation (bigger trucks, jet-powered air freighters, containerized cargo, superhighways) and spectacular advances in computing and telecommunications technology (digital systems, satellites, fiber optics). These improvements and advances have (1) reduced transaction and communication costs, making goods and services globally tradable that were not before, such as perishable, seasonal items (e.g., flowers, grapes, oranges), fashions, back-office accounts, and design work; (2) made it possible for corporations to coordinate their production, planning, and financial operations effectively and efficiently on a global scale; (3) made information, such as films, compact discs, tapes, software, television news, and programs, tradable; and (4) allowed capital to become highly mobile, which has created a global market for currencies and securities.[26] These developments have made representing the state as securer and manager of an economy inside its territorial boundaries more difficult to sustain. Also, it is more difficult to paint the international and global aspects of economic life as fully outside the territorial state when, for example, subtle changes in interest rates in one state can severely affect jobs in others and when multinational corporations rapidly and frequently shift jobs to low-wage states, producing unemployment and lower wages in other states.

Globalization has, paradoxically, disciplined all states to become more or less managerial; at the same time, management of the economy by the state is increasingly problematic, and has become so in a number of ways. First, the amount of profit-seeking, financial capital flowing electronically around the world far exceeds the amount that any state can marshal from its reserves in order to control the value of its currency. Second, a substantial amount of trade is now intra-industry, rather than international, owing to the specialization of TNCs; therefore, the state can no longer easily distinguish national exports from foreign imports for trade-policy purposes. This means that states have lost much of their ability to protect their domestic markets with tariffs. Third, many TNCs have dissociated themselves from their states of origin and seek to locate their operations where wages and taxes are lower and regulations fewer. For example, the Boeing Corporation, a major aircraft manufacturer located in Seattle, Washington, declared several years ago that it no longer considers itself a U.S. company, but a global one. In 1996, Coca-Cola Corporation, located in Atlanta, Georgia, eliminated the distinction between its domestic and international operations. This means that states have much less control over what happens economically within their territories. States now compete with one another to provide an attractive business environment, such as good infrastructure, deregulated markets, a trained and docile work force, and financial stability, in order to attract and retain more capital and investment from TNCs.[27]

Thus, the global market has increasingly taken on the role of a regulator of sovereignty, creating institutions and generating norms and discourses that make it appear necessary and inevitable that states both adopt free-market economic policies and proffer interpretations of the national interests that conform to the norms of global competitiveness. This is especially true of the poorest states, whose economies are heavily influenced by international regulatory agencies such as the International Monetary Fund (IMF) and the International Bank for Reconstruction and Development, also known as the World Bank, through the conditions they impose on states seeking to obtain new loans from international sources or to renegotiate old ones. In effect, the IMF and the World Bank set monetary and fiscal policy for indebted states.[28]

Despite claims that economic globalization is beneficial for all, the distribution of winners and losers in the global economy does not neatly respect territorial borders. It has created intractable mass unemployment in some states and high levels of unemployment in most states. In others it has led to resource depletion, pollution, and ecological damage. As two analysts of the global economy put it:

> The most disturbing aspect of this system is that the formidable power and mobility of global corporations are undermining the effectiveness of national governments to carry out essential policies on behalf of their people. Leaders of nation-states are losing much of the control over their own territory they once had. More and more, they must conform to the demands of the outside world because the outsiders are already inside the gates. Business enterprises that routinely operate across borders are linking far-flung pieces of territory into a new world economy that bypasses all sorts of established political arrangements and conventions. Tax laws intended for another age, traditional ways to control capital flows and interest rates, full-employment policies, and old approaches to resource development and environmental protection are becoming obsolete, unenforceable, or irrelevant.[29]

The growth of the Internet and other digital networks will make it increasingly difficult for nation-states to tax global commerce effectively. These new technologies are undermining the efficiency of the state as a taxing entity, which may shift authority away from the state and reduce its capacity to raise the financial resources necessary to make war.[30]

Deeper challenges to the state, moreover, stem from the limited possibilities for generating identities bound to territorial sovereignty in the context of a globalized capitalist society. Two factors are most significant: (1) the density of nonterritorial-based global networks of social relations, and (2) the speed and frequency of movements of people, images, and ideas across borders. To these we now turn.

The Fracturing of Identity

Paradoxically, the economic integration of globalization has coincided with the fracturing of national identity, what might be called "deglobalization." Nation and state have rarely coincided in the history of nation-states. State boundaries have rarely conformed to a particular linguistic, religious, and/or cultural community. Therefore, the persistence of representations of the state as a homogeneous national community has had tremendous costs for those marginalized by the national community. Such representations have brought to bear on these peoples' powers of self-discipline (e.g., to make oneself assimilate to the dominant national ideal) as well as overt force and covert surveillance, because those outside the dominant nationality are, in principle, suspect and seen as potential threats. Even those who fit the dominant national representation are forced at times to demonstrate their "true national identity"—their Americanness, Frenchness, Indianness, and so on.

Almost all nation-states contain significant minority ethnic groups, many of which are claiming the internationally recognized "right of self-determination of peoples" found in Article I, Section I, of the charter of the United Nations.[31] Many ethnic groups, such as Basques and Catalans in Spain, Corsicans and Bretons in France, Kurds in Turkey and Iraq, Chechens in Russia, Tibetans in China, Tamils in Sri Lanka, Mayans in Mexico, Québécois in Canada, Kashmiris in India, Ibos in Nigeria, Eritrians in Ethiopia, and Native Americans in the United States, to mention only a few, have demanded autonomy within the state or outright independence from it. Many ethnic groups have come to imagine themselves as a nation and to seek statehood for the following reasons: (1) a sense that the identity of the group is being eroded by strong assimilationist policies of the majority ethnic group that controls the state; (2) a belief that economic prosperity can be maintained and/or achieved only by breaking away from the existing state; and (3) the belief that nationalist aspirations cannot be completely achieved without full, independent statehood.[32] Ethnic nationalisms are exacerbated by the increased regional inequalities within territorial states produced by globalization.

Such fissiparous forces have begun to transform the present states-system by producing new states from existing ones. The collapse of the Soviet Union yielded twelve new independent states, and the collapse of Yugoslavia produced five more. According to one observer, the number of new ethnically based states could go as high as one hundred and fifty.[33] Another observer indicates that the number of potential ethnically pure states could be as high eight thousand![34] No matter the number, there is little doubt that we have entered an age of violent nation-state reconstitution.

The boundaries imposed by the European states during the age of imperialism are being redrawn by the local ethnic groups who were disregarded in the process of creating the present global system of states.

These new states have also begun to transform the global Westphalian states-system, which rests on European principles, regarding the separation of the spiritual and the secular. Increasingly, the imagined nationhood of these new states appeals to religion both as an important source of challenge to European hegemony and as an important form of social solidarity and common will.

The paradigmatic identity as a sovereign identity has also fractured along gender lines. The state as representation of a sovereign nation continues to marginalize women as a subordinate group. Traditional representations of territorial sovereignty have privileged the ideas of military engagement and soldiering as the most important social roles in the state. These roles were tied to the protection of the domestic life of the members of the state and drew symbolically on gendered discourses of public and private. Women and children constituted the private sphere, which male soldiers protected. Modern concepts of responsibility within sovereign, territorial states have clearly drawn on such ontological assumptions of a split between public and private and the representation of women and children as the ones to be protected.

In states in which women have traditionally played important roles in local communities, especially in the agricultural sector, the creation of territorial state sovereignty and nationhood has resulted in a diminution of their position and left them prey to multiple forms of oppression. This is especially the case in the context of globalization, where many states promote export industries and mass industrialization by transforming the local environment in the name of economic development. In such cases, the idea of the sovereign state becomes identified with economic and social trends that destroy the traditional forms of women's (and indigenous men's) authority. Native American women in South and Central America, for example, have organized to protect the environment by promoting representations of identity in which people are presented not as sovereign agents standing outside the environment in order to use it for state development but rather as integral parts of the environment.[35]

An internationalist consciousness among many women's organizations and feminist groups has taken hold; either it challenges the sovereign nation-state or it seeks to reimagine sovereignty in ways more inclusive of not only gender difference, but all sorts of differences that affect the position of women, such as local versus national development, and environmental protection versus economic development. By seeking to reintegrate strong conceptions of liberalism and tolerance into representations of a national community, some women's groups have sought to reimagine sovereignty to be more inclusive of the particular differences of persons. Others have sought new forms of empowerment that often leave the nation-state, and representations of sovereignty, behind, forging alliances with transnational organizations and social movements across national borders.[36]

Because membership in a nation-state can no longer reasonably assure employment, security from poverty and destitution, or a meaningful family and social life, membership in a political community becomes a fleeting and constantly moving horizon for many people rather than a secure, permanent, and lifelong identity. The imagining of politics as located in some central representation of unified, territorially based power (i.e., the state) is difficult to conjure in the minds of ever more nomadic people. Many of the world's poor—and not so poor working class—are left to move in and out of states and to seek new political identities that might secure them a livelihood. In today's global system, one is neither assured of being born into a nation-state nor likely to be able to create one out of some collective will as was assumed by the idea of popular sovereignty. For many in the current global order, one takes whatever nation-state one can find, often at great cost to one's sense of cultural identity.

Economic elites in the global economy are also losing a sense of national political identity. Loyalty to the company—increasingly transnational and global—has supplanted allegiance to a nation-state for managers of major corporations. The pursuit of wealth as a human good and valuable human achievement for the capitalist elite is no longer bound up with the health and well-being of the nation-state into which they were born. This has always been true for many from non-European states, who would leave their home states to be educated and to seek opportunities in advanced capitalist states. But even many of these would eventually return to their home state; this is less the case in the current global economy.[37]

Refugees (political and economic, if they can really be meaningfully distinguished in the current world of drastic inequality), guest workers (who together with their descendants perform a significant amount of the less skilled work in many managerial states), migrants, and dispossessed peoples, among others, are also ripe for appeals of alternative political identities to those of the nation-state.[38] The nation-state promises prosperity and security within secure boundaries, which it can no longer deliver or is not any longer willing to deliver, to the poor as well as much of the working population. Therefore, although many still seek the security, prosperity, and popular sovereignty of nation-states, at the same time they seek out other identities—often ethnic, which requires ethnic "cleansing," or religious, which requires the elimination of the "infidel" or "heretic." As one analyst describes the current predicament: "Where there is no nation, there is no community; where there are no territorial boundaries, there is a search for origins. If you do not define yourself by the place where you live, tell me where you come from."[39]

What does this "strange multiplicity,"[40] as one scholar calls it, mean for the nation-state? One effect is to put pressure on centralized states, especially those in which cultural minorities have been successful in their claims for official recognition. Many minorities use culture to gain concessions from the state, limiting its ability to manage increasingly diverse populations through centralized bureaucratic means.

Another effect is on citizenship. Being a citizen of a nation-state has meant living within the territorial borders of the state, and accepting the legitimacy of the state in return for certain rights and privileges. As we have seen, managerial states have manipulated these elements of citizenship in order to manage politics within them. However, as citizenship becomes more flexible, as in the European Union wherein rights formally reserved only to citizens are available to many noncitizens who reside within the EU, or states such as Israel, Mexico, Portugal, and others that grant rights, including some forms of voting rights, to diasporic communities, manipulating citizenship to manage politics by limiting the range of political contestability becomes more and more difficult.[41] Significantly, rights of citizenship are increasingly being shifted from the juridical system of the nation-state to an emerging global juridical system of human rights. In a another realm, transnational entities such as the World Trade Organization routinely intervene even in advanced states to protect the property rights of corporations. Indigenous groups in Latin America have sued U.S. corporations in U.S. courts over their failure to clean up the pollution they have caused. While citizenship in a nation-state still matters, it is increasingly articulated with alternative, global juridical systems.

Finally, what are we to make of the globalization of culture? While it is doubtful that a singular global culture is emerging, globalization connects culture to politics and the state in new ways. The global circulation of culture seems to be creating hybrid identities for more and more people, identities that draw simultaneously on varied cultural traditions in ways that form novel juxtapositions and syntheses in individuals and groups. Recognizing this, some states have tried to manage cultural multiplicity, attempting to directly manage cultural identity when it threatens the unity of the state. In France, for example, the state seeks to stop Muslim women from wearing head-scarves in public schools and other locations of state authority in order to enforce its vision of France as a secular state. Significantly, the women who wish to wear head-scarves claim to be asserting their human rights as citizens with a distinctive cultural identity, even though this identity is based on the cultural found in other states.[42]

Identity in the current world order is becoming increasingly ambiguous, a situation with the potential for a multiplicity of possible futures, some including and some ignoring the nation-state.

Hypermedia, Community, and Sovereignty

In the previous section, we illustrated how identity in the current world order is becoming increasingly ambiguous, a situation with the potential for a multiplicity of possible futures, complete with social and political forces both "below" and "above" the nation-state. The fragmentation of identity, while not reducible to it, is connected to the more general cultural change often described as "postmodernism."

We must be careful not to take postmodernism to be a clear, discrete movement or category. It is best understood as a loose descriptor of trends and effects in the production and distribution of culture. Postmodernism usually refers to a decentering of the subject, and, in general, a decline in the salience of centralizing and totalizing state authority in favor of more layered, complex relations of authorities within the self, or community. The fragmentation of identity described in the previous section certainly fits this descriptor of cultural change. But multiculturalism and devolving nationalisms do not exhaust the postmodern, nor do they signal all of the effects cultural change is likely to portend for the state and states-system.

Challenges to the state form of rule seem to be coming from changing representations of community. We have already noted how the nation and the state have rarely, if ever, neatly coincided. Nevertheless, the modern state has presumed an intimate, internal connection between community and the state. This internal connection seems challenged by current forms of cultural change. As people are capable of reimaging community, the framework and understandings that establish the collective life that is meaningful for human existence, they can reimagine their political life.

Community is connected to forms of communication. As we discussed earlier, the development of discursive literacy and the invention of printing enabled the development of the imagined community (i.e., the nation) of the territorial state. The territorial form of political authority, while not determined by modes of communication, requires such communication.[43] Postmodernism, while certainly a more general rejection of the centralizing and totalizing methods of modernism, is connected to changes in modes of communication, most significantly the development of "hypermedia." Hypermedia refers to a communication environment that

> reflects a complex melding and converging of distinct technologies into a single integrated *web* of digital-electronic-telecommunications . . . culmi-

nating in the digital convergence that began in the late 1960s . . . the hypermedia environment is not just television, the computer, the fax machine, the cellular telephone, the satellite reconnaissance system, or the hand-held video camera—it is all of the above and more linked *together* into a single seamless web of digital-electronic-telecommunications.[44]

Hypermedia has had significant effects in several areas that challenge the state.

One effect of hypermedia is the refinement and expansion of the technologies of surveillance. No doubt, such technologies have enhanced state capabilities and power, as was shown in our discussion of post-territorial warfare. Hypermedia has also enhanced the state's ability to monitor its population. Stationary surveillance cameras are everywhere, and states have taken advantage of the more mobile capabilities of surveillance to watch citizens. States have also amassed databases and created computer software that link databases into a web of information that violates the liberal ideal of individual privacy. However, hypermedia uses technology that the state cannot monopolize, and it cannot monopolize the effects of that technology or the productive power of those effects. While hypermedia has increased state surveillance, it also enables the monitoring of the social and physical world by private corporations, private security firms, and scientific organizations using satellites and transnational organizations of various sorts.

The important point here is that while hypermedia surely increases state capabilities to monitor and thus manage its population, the state no longer has a monopoly on these technologies, just as some states seem to have lost their monopoly of legitimate military force to nonstate groups. Surveillance is dispersed both below and above the state in international organizations, scientific communities concerned with environmental risks, and in what is increasingly referred to as "global civil society." Space-based satellites were initially created by the U.S. and Soviet militaries during the Cold War. Since the end of the Cold War, the number of states with access to such satellites has proliferated. This access has enabled the Israeli military to target specific persons riding in cars along West Bank roads, and the International Atomic Energy Commission to track power plant emissions, and the Zapatistas to create transnational political coalitions to put pressure on the Mexican government, for example.

Significantly, this global monitoring of states (as well as actors within states) is feeding a reimagining of the global community. To some, the idea of the global village is becoming a "real" virtual community, real in the sense that political and managerial organizations are emerging predicated on a global rather than national community. Human rights become more real when transnational organizations are able to draw in individuals regardless of location. They become institutionalized as valuable human goals and constitutive of human community in general, even if they have no territorially secure container for them. To others, sovereignty appears to be devolving to private groups, such as large transnational corporations.

Hypermedia, then, is productive of networks of data and techniques of surveillance and information flows that shift important aspects of sovereignty to transnational organizations, many of which are increasingly involved in monitoring states, such as transnational economic organizations, human-rights and environmental nongovernmental organizations, private corporations, and "terrorist" groups. Territorial states are nodes within systems of information. As one scholar puts it: "In many respects, a 'space of flows' is coming to dominate and transcend a space of places as the defining characteristic of postmodern world order."[45]

Hypermedia makes it increasingly difficult for the state to control information flows within and across its borders. The "hard shell" of the state is increasingly porous to information. This is in part because of the way in which computer networks work, breaking information down and sending it through many different portals, and partly due to the volume of information and the speed with which it travels. In important ways, computer-based information networks are "democratizing" in the sense of allowing individual input and free creation of information. Whether the form of democracy they enable is statist or not, however, is not at all clear. Rather, it has created new kinds of struggles over the control of information, and over what constitutes useful or real information.

We are not suggesting that "virtual" communities are taking the place of real communities. The argument that the postmodern order is witnessing a transference of sovereignty to globally organized powers, and the state is becoming a functional part of a system of power organized globally through hypermedia, is provocative.[46] Is the state being redeployed, in its managerial or hyper-managerial form, within a system that simultaneously produces subjects through "advertising" (now not merely the hawking of particular products but the propaganda that reinforces the system itself), organizes their lives as productive members of the system, and legitimates itself by appeal to a universal standard of right and justice encoded into global news media and popular culture and policed by military interventions? It is difficult to answer this question at this point. But we are suggesting that hypermedia is creating the means by which people can, and in some modest ways already are, reimagining community in ways more responsive to flows than to space. That the reimagining of community might be a function of new technologies and powers of control, exercised globally, should not be ruled out. The reimagining of community is not likely to replace states with some virtual nonterritorial forms of politico-military rule, but it is already proliferating communal attachments that threaten the sovereignty of territorially based states.

Summary

The ability to represent the state as territorial sovereign has been diminished by the economic and technological forces of globalization. The twentieth century has witnessed a dramatic overriding of territorial boundaries by military technologies and global capitalism. Peoples within states as well as those migrating across state boundaries are being forced to renegotiate their identities. The expansion of global corporations and organizations has extended, and privatized, managerial and bureaucratic control.

In this context, popular sovereignty has diminished. The organs of the state have become less subject to popular input and accountability. Having lost a relatively secure relation to territory, the state has ceased to be able to secure itself as the representation of a distinct people. The globalist and neoliberal ideologies that inform the international organizations and modes of cooperation states enter into in order to manage global capitalism have freed the bureaucratic and managerial powers of the state from their anchors in ideas of "the people" or the "body politic." Hence, state power has grown and politics has become increasingly trivial. In the final chapter we turn to this paradoxical condition.

Notes

1. John H. Herz, *The Nation-State and the Crisis of World Politics* (New York: David McKay, 1976), 104.

2. John J. Weltman, *World Politics and the Evolution of War* (Baltimore, MD: Johns Hopkins University Press, 1995), 26.

3. Ibid., 36–37.

4. On the rise of total war, see Brian Bond, *War and Society in Europe, 1870–1970* (New York: St. Martin's Press, 1983); Ian F. W. Beckett, "Total War," in Clive Emsley, Arthur Marwick, and Wendy Simpson (eds.), *War, Peace and Social Change in Twentieth-Century Europe* (Philadelphia: Open University Press, 1989).

5. H. G. Wells, *A Short History of the World* (London: Casell, 1922), 392.

6. For a history of the attempts to codify the laws of war, and the international organizations that arose to promote peace, see Geoffrey Best, *Humanity in Warfare* (New York: Columbia University Press, 1980).

7. For an account of the peace interest as promoted by finance capitalists up to World War I, see Karl Polanyi, *The Great Transformation: The Political and Economic Origins of Our Time* (Boston: Beacon Press, 1957), chapter 1. For an account of the complex relations between industrial capitalists, finance capitalists, and international power in the twentieth century, see Kees Van der Pjil, *The Making of an Atlantic Ruling Class* (London: Verso Press, 1984).

8. These have been studied and presented vividly by Paul Fussell, *The Great War in Modern Memory* (London and New York: Oxford University Press, 1975).

9. Ernest Hemingway, *In Our Time* (New York: Scribner's, 1925), 29.

10. Leslie Marmon Silko, *Ceremony* (New York: Penguin Books, 1977), 36–37.

11. David Beetham, "The Future of the Nation-State," in Gregor McLennan, David Held, and Stuart Hall (eds.), *The Idea of the Modern State* (Philadelphia: Open University Press, 1984): 215. See also Daniel Deudne, "Nuclear Weapons and the Waning of the *Real*-State," *Daedalus* 124 (spring 1995): 209–231.

12. On the connections between industrial capitalism, technology, and nuclear weapons, see Seymour Melman, *Pentagon Capitalism* (New York: McGraw Hill, 1970).

13. This is most evident in the logic President Truman used to justify the dropping of atomic bombs on Hiroshima and Nagasaki, Japan, at the end of World War II, whatever else one thinks of the morality of the decision. Truman's justification calculated the number of U.S. soldiers who would likely be killed in a full-scale invasion of the Japanese homeland and compared these with the number of Japanese deaths the bombs would cause. He decided, using a calculus that denied the relevance of the distinction between civilians and soldiers and that had racist overtones, that dropping the bombs was more efficient in terms of U.S. lives saved than an invasion; an invasion would also have had significant economic costs, especially to the Americans, and might have had diplomatic costs, too, by giving the Russians the opportunity to enter the Pacific War, which would have allowed them to influence the postwar settlement there.

14. On the idea of a world military order, see Mary Kaldor, *The World Military Order* (New York: Hill & Wang, 1981).

15. James Der Derian, *Virtuous War: Mapping the Military-Industrial-Media-Entertainment Network* (Boulder, CO: Westview Press, 2001).

16. See Anthony Sampson, *The Arms Bazaar: From Lebanon to Lockheed* (New York: Viking Press, 1977); Michael T. Klare, *American Arms Supermarket* (Austin: University of Texas Press, 1984).

17. Ulric Shannon, "Private Armies and the Decline of the State," in Kenton Worcester et al. (eds.), *Violence and Politics: Globalization's Paradox* (New York and London: Routledge, 2002): 33. See also I. William Zartman, ed., *Collapsed States: The Disintegration and Restoration of Legitimate Authority* (Boulder, CO: Lynne Rienner Publishers, 1995).

18. Hedley Bull, *The Anarchical Society: A Study of Order in World Politics* (New York: Columbia University Press, 1977), 264.

19. P. W. Singer, *Corporate Warriors: The Rise of the Privatized Military Industry* (Ithaca, NY: Cornell University Press, 2003). See also Mary Kaldor, *New and Old Wars: Organized Violence in a Global Era* (Stanford, CA: Stanford University Press, 1999); Peter Andreas and Richard Price, "From Warfighting to Crime Fighting: Transforming the American National Security State," *International Studies Review* 3 (fall 2001): 31–52; and Martin Van Creveld, *The Transformation of War* (New York: The Free Press, 1991), chapter 7.

20. Richard Falk, *Law in an Emerging Global Village: A Post-Westphalian Perspective* (Ardsley, NY: Transnational Publishers, 1998).

21. Gianfranco Poggi, *The State: Its Nature, Development and Prospects* (Stanford, CA: Stanford University Press, 1990), 117.

22. Peter Saunders, *Capitalism* (Minneapolis: University of Minnesota Press, 1995), 24.

23. Richard J. Barnet and John Cavanagh, *Global Dreams: Imperial Corporations and the New World Order* (New York: Simon & Schuster, 1994), 15.

24. Ibid.

25. James L. Watson, ed., *Golden Arches East: McDonald's in East Asia* (Stanford, CA: Stanford University Press, 1997), 23–24.

26. Vincent Cable, "The Diminished Nation-State: A Study in Loss of Economic Power," *Daedalus* 124 (spring 1995): 25–26.

27. Ibid., 26–29; Vivien A. Schmidt, "The New World Order, Incorporated: The Rise of Business and the Decline of the Nation-State," *Daedalus* 124 (spring 1995): 79; and Susan Strange, *The Retreat of the State: The Diffusion of Power in the World Economy* (Cambridge: Cambridge University Press, 1996), chapter 4.

28. Beetham, "The Future of the Nation-State," 213.

29. Barnet and Cavanaugh, *Global Dreams,* 19.

30. Roland Paris, "The Globalization of Taxation? Electronic Commerce and the Transformation of the State," *International Studies Quarterly* 47 (2003): 153–182.

31. Robert K. Schaeffer, *Severed States: Dilemmas of Democracy in a Divided World* (New York: Rowman & Littlefield), chapter 1.

32. Raju G. C. Thomas, "Nations, States, and Secession: Lessons from the Former Yugoslavia," *Mediterranean Quarterly* 5 (fall 1994): 47. See also Charles Tilly, "National Self-Determination as a Problem for All of Us," *Daedalus* 122 (1993): 29–35.

33. Daniel Patrick Moynihan, *Pandemonium: Ethnicity in International Politics* (Oxford: Oxford University Press, 1993), 168.

34. James Mayall, *Nationalism and International Society* (Cambridge: Cambridge University Press, 1990).

35. A good summary of the growing literature on women and development is Jan Pettman, *Worlding Women* (New York: Routledge, 1996).

36. On the gendered nature of the institutions, practices, and discourses of global governance, see Mary K. Meyer and Elizabeth Prügl, eds., *Gender Politics in Global Governance* (New York: Rowman & Littlefield, 1999).

37. Christopher Lasch, *The Revolt of the Elites and the Betrayal of Democracy* (New York and London: W. W. Norton, 1995).

38. Myron Weiner, *The Global Migration Crisis: Challenges to States and to Human Rights* (New York: HarperCollins, 1995). See also Christian Joppke, ed., *Challenges to the Nation-State: Immigration in Western Europe and the United States* (Oxford: Oxford University Press, 1998).

39. Jean-Marie Guéhenno, *The End of the Nation-State*, trans. Victoria Elliott (Minneapolis: University of Minnesota Press, 1995), 37.

40. James Tully, *Strange Multiplicity: Constitutionalism in an Age of Diversity* (Cambridge: Cambridge University Press, 1995).

41. On the new forms of citizenship, see Aihwa Ong, *Flexible Citizenship: The Cultural Logics of Transnationality* (Durham, NC: Duke University Press, 1999).

42. See the discussions of Seyla Benhabib, *The Claims of Culture: Equality and Diversity in the Global Era* (Princeton, NJ: Princeton University Press, 2000); Bhikuh Parekh, *Rethinking Multiculturalism: Cultural Diversity and Political Theory* (Cambridge, MA: Harvard University Press, 2000).

43. This argument is made powerfully by Ronald J. Deibert, *Parchment, Printing, and Hypermedia: Communication in World Order Transformation* (New York: Columbia University Press, 1997). In what follows, we draw on Deibert's argument.

44. Ibid., 114.

45. Ibid., 175.

46. Michael Hardt and Antonio Negri, *Empire* (Cambridge, MA: Harvard University Press, 2000). See also Paul Virilio, *The Information Bomb*, trans. Chris Turner (London: Verso, 2000).

12

Conclusion:
A New Global Order?

The state is created and sovereignty instituted under specific conditions at specific times and places. We have traced the evolution of the state as it precipitated out after the collapse of the Roman Empire, as it emerged as a territorial state in early modern Europe, and as it forcefully divided the world into a system of sovereign states linked through global networks of political, economic, and cultural organization as they eventually became nation-states. In the previous chapter, we examined several challenges to the territorial state. We conclude the book by returning to the question raised in the introduction: Is the world experiencing another great transformation to a new global order in which the sovereign territorial nation-state will no longer be the dominant form of politico-military rule and will be replaced by something else?

The End of Modernity?

One of the central attributes of what is known as modernity is the historically created configuration of political space in the form of the sovereign territorial state. Modernity and the territorial state are synonymous. Remember that politics before the rise of the state was based on alternative ways of spatially organizing rule. Among the Germanic tribal peoples who filled in the geographical space of the collapsed Western Roman Empire, for example, the spatial dimension of rule was demarcated by nonterritorial ties of kinship. This was also the case in many places outside of Europe. In Africa, the Americas, the Middle East, and Asia a variety of complex political organizations existed, from traditional empires to tribes. Remember also that in the feudal "states" that grew out of the Germanic kingdoms, rule was fragmented, personalized, and parcelized among a multiplicity of overlapping and competing jurisdictions. There were no clearly demarcated and mutually recognized boundaries between feudal "states," only indistinct frontiers.

As we saw, during the Middle Ages, the territorially indistinct feudal "state" began to be transformed into the territorially exclusive, centralized medieval state. The fragmented, decentralized, personalistic rule of the feudal state was remade into direct, territorially defined, centralized rule over an exclusive geographical space. Political space came to be defined as it appeared from the perspective of an indivisible sovereign, and the rule of that space came to be about maintaining public order and territorial security. After the Peace of Westphalia, reciprocal territorial sovereignty became a fundamental principle of global order. Eventually, no space on the planet, except Antarctica and the open oceans, was left free from the control of a sovereign state, and even the oceans were regulated by international organizations created by sovereign states. The geopolitics of the modern age is grounded in relations among territorially exclusive states and was powerfully reinforced by nationalism after the French Revolution. The story of modernity's triumph, viewed from the perspective of the territorial state, is the story of the victory of reason, science, individualism, law, and rationality, as well as the story of the victory of the Western way of warfare and the conquest of the planet by the European form of politico-military rule.

Modernity is, of course, a complex, multifarious order, and the state does not exhaust it. Moreover, the state participates in and has helped to foster aspects of modernity—developments in science and technology that have brought significant benefits. But the same developments have also had enormous negative effects, such as widespread psychological stress and environmental degradation, for example.

Considerable debate has emerged in current social theory about whether modernity (i.e., the state) has come to an end and is being replaced by something called "postmodernity."[1] Two overlapping questions have been asked in this regard: first, *is* modernity being replaced by a postmodern condition, and second, *should* modernity be replaced? In the case of the state, the question of its demise is not easily answered. State power has widened and increased in significant ways in the context of globalization, even as some of the state's traditional functions as a defender of territory and population have appeared to weaken, as we discussed in the previous chapter. The state remains powerful, and territorial identities, although no longer having quite the monopoly on political identity they once did, are still strong. Nevertheless, arguments about the decline of state power and sovereignty seem plausible. Underlying this paradox is the decline of territoriality as the spatiotemporal frame for politics. Having lost a relatively secure relation to territory, the state has ceased to be able readily to secure itself as a representation of a distinct people. In this concluding chapter we address three results that flow from this state of affairs: (1) the apparent turn throughout the current world order to a "new" type of neoliberal state; (2) political disaffection from the managerial state; and (3) the emergence of a variety of deterritorialized political and social movements.

Neoliberalism: A New Form of the State?

As was mentioned in the introduction, during the 1990s the neoliberal agenda has become widely accepted by major political parties in core European states and has spread to the world order itself.[2] In so-called newly industrializing states such as Singapore, South Korea, and Chile, similar programs of neoliberal economics and often harsh and repressive neoconservative social agendas have been promoted as the way to develop the state economically. The economic success of the former and the appeal to "traditional cultures" and cultural autonomy of the latter have justified restrictions on and often harsh repression of worker and democracy movements. Neoliberal economic programs have been promoted more generally as a way for poorer states to get out from under their enormous debts to Western banks and the International Monetary Fund. Neoliberalism as the hegemonic ideology in international managerial organizations gained credibility after the collapse of the Soviet Union, as did the acceptance of "shock therapy" to turn post-Soviet Russia and other Eastern European states quickly into advanced capitalist ones.[3]

We do not here evaluate the validity or accuracy of the neoliberal assessment of the crisis of the 1970s.[4] We do, however, question whether the advent of neoliberalism marks a fundamental transformation of the state into a new form, as some have argued.[5] We suggest that, in fact, neoliberalism retools the managerial state in response to the accelerating globalization of capitalism since the 1970s.

In our view, rather than fundamentally transforming the managerial state, as the proponents of deregulation and privatization argue, the neoliberal agenda, in fact, actually strengthens key aspects of the managerial state's power to exercise politico-military rule. Most significant is the diffusion and deterritorialization of power. Neoliberalism "externalizes" managerial functions of the state to international organizations and "privatizes" public power to an even greater degree than did postwar Keynesian economic policies.[6] The language of a strictly separate private and public realm is, in fact, reinvigorated by the neoliberal state, for its legitimacy rests on representing the economy as private (meaning outside of government regulation), and the family as private so that it can be deployed as the space in which individual responsibility, patriotism, and traditional "family" values can be nurtured. Let us take each of these points, the delegation of power to international organizations and the world market and the diffusion of state power through privatization, in turn.

It is important to remember that international organizations have been adjunct to the managerial state from its beginnings in the late nineteenth century. During much of the twentieth century, sovereignty was represented by means of the sharp division between inside and outside. For example, economies were represented as national economies with national firms as basic units that operated largely within the confines of the sovereign territorial state.[7] The attempt to represent the state as economically sovereign within its territory, of course, has always included "international" aspects— international organizations, trade, foreign investment, currency exchange-rate mechanisms, and so forth—but these were presented as being *outside* the state. Market theories of the economy supplemented this presentation by situating global aspects of the economy in a cosmopolitan future. As Adam Smith and others argued, the market was the result of a universal human nature, and when all peoples were brought into the system, realizing their basic nature, so to speak, they would create a single, harmonious world order based on the universal principles of the market. The strategies used by states for containing the global and international dimensions of capitalism—representing them as being outside the primary national economy, and legitimizing them as representing a harmonious future—are no longer very successful, however. The markers of the outside increasingly appear inside, and what used to be inside increasingly appears outside. Therefore, neoliberalism has flourished as an ideology because it enables the modern managerial state to deal with globalization, which problematizes territoriality.

From the middle to late nineteenth century, the power of the state (its systems of rational management and its ability to monitor social problems and deploy expert knowledge) began to merge into a system of international unions and organizations designed to manage the expansion of the capitalist industrial system beyond the confines of the territorial state. The number of such organizations already existing by the turn of the nineteenth century is surprising, given the image of the nineteenth century as an age of absolute sovereignty. One scholar of international organizations cites thirty-three such organizations operating in 1914. These covered specific areas such as infrastructure (e.g., the Universal Postal Union [1874] and the Universal Radiotelegraph Union [1906]); industrial standards (e.g., International Bureau of Weights and Measures [1875]); social conflicts (e.g., International Labour Office [1901]); science (e.g., International Council for the Study of the Sea [1901]); and public health (e.g., International Association of Public Baths and Cleanliness).[8]

There came into existence, then, a set of international organizations that, while not part of any particular state, externalized discrete functions of the state in the global order in which nation-states existed. The distinction between international and domestic was an effect of managerialism, or of the limits of managerialism: managerialism constituted politics as an attribute of functional organization and management, and those functions that could not be organized by the individual states, because of politics, technological limits of surveillance, and so forth, were spatially located outside, in a new space of international organization. This space was "territorial" because it was dominated by states that controlled its personnel, set its ideology, and policed its norms of operation; it was at the same time deterritorialized because its organization depended on generating networks of forces and relations that could not be confined within any particular national space.

Neoliberalism presents the modern condition as a deterritorialized world—as a natural system of absolute free trade in which state boundaries do not act as barriers to the flow of goods and services around the globe.[9] If states want to ensure their prosperity, they must be "competitive" in the global capitalist economy. Perceiving the new technological revolution, transnational corporations, and international financial markets as inevitable givens of the modern world system—rather than historical creations of politico-military power and the result of decisions by certain states—states must cede some of their sovereignty to international institutions and organizations (e.g., the European Union, the G-8) that will regulate and manage the new global competitive capitalism efficiently. (The United Nations could be one such institution, but only if it is reorganized to be more efficient and managerial.) Sovereignty is hence reimagined according to a regime of economic and technological necessity. Lost in this reimagining is the idea of popular sovereignty, the sense that the state represents a people to which it is accountable.

The ideology of neoliberalism, in which liberalism is reduced to market economics,[10] argues that states are simply passive vehicles in a globalizing world economy whose momentum they are powerless to stop or control. Downward pressures on wages worldwide and the mobility of firms, which has created unemployment and depressed local economies, are the result of "inevitable," "natural" market forces, so the argument goes. The best states can do is get out of the way.

What this picture does not show, of course, are the ways that states have created and supplement the global capitalist economy. This is impossible for neoliberals to see because their ideology focuses rhetorically on preserving the imagined distinction between state and civil society and state and economy, which their own policies in practice deny. As we saw in Chapter 7, this ideological move was common to the managerial state that neoliberals argue they have supplanted. In many non-European states, such as Indonesia, South Korea, the Philippines, Mexico, and China, wages are kept low by state repression of labor organizations and by restrictions of democratic political activity. In richer European states, market and capital investments are actively promoted over productive capital investments by depressing wages through tight monetary policy as well as by state intervention in labor disputes to break unions or to limit their ability to strike or organize unorganized workers. European states and the United States continue to invest heavily in military industries, reinstituting military Keynesianism, although now with greater emphasis on military exports, which creates a false choice between either increasing state budget deficits or reducing spending on education, health care, and welfare programs.

The emerging model of global managerial politics organized through international organizations does not eliminate the power of bureaucracies, as those neoliberals who fulminate against "big government" would like, but rather privatizes bureaucratic power. It does this internationally, by externalizing power to a network of international organizations; this *insulates power from any form of popular sovereignty* and generates the space for economic liberalism to emerge and appear as legitimate. People, regardless of nationality or political identity, are subject to the discipline imposed by the World Trade Organization, International Monetary Fund, World Bank, transnational corporations, and global financial markets, but they have only very restricted recourse through the political (i.e., electoral) process to hold these entities accountable. In the words of one scholar, "In the current global order Anglo-American ideological presumptions have been transcribed into formal rules of the game, to which individual states must commit themselves or risk becoming economic pariahs."[11]

The privatization of the social-service responsibilities of the managerial state—health care, social security, and welfare most prominently—promotes the neoconservative social agenda, which attempts to reinscribe national sovereignty by means of promoting traditional values. Witness, for example, recent programs in the United States for retooling welfare programs that replace grants-in-aid with "workfare." Although workfare programs in the United States vary somewhat by state, they involve grants or subsidies to private employers who then hire low-skilled workers, most often at below minimum wage, from the welfare rolls. Benefits are limited to a maximum of five years during a person's lifetime and are given under the condition that recipients work. Work is seen as "its own reward." In other words, the jobs are not stable jobs that will give recipients a living wage but are training grounds of the soul; that is, their aim is to make recipients into moral, self-disciplined, and acquisitive subjects who will make their way independently in the new competitive economies. Recipients are subjected to a regime of work (rather than to direct regulation by state agencies and officials) that aims to make them into "productive" members of society. The state is still involved and responsible for the overall regulation of these programs, and without subsidies to employers and administrative rules and laws that permit the payment of wages below the minimum wage, these programs would not work. Although the practices and institutions that do the work of reforming welfare recipients are no longer state agencies, state employees still strictly surveille welfare recipients by monitoring their presence at work.

Witness also the trend toward the "privatization" of the military industry. In the United States and in Great Britain especially, the state has "outsourced" military functions such as building and running military bases to private contractors such as Brown and Root, a subsidiary of the Halliburton Corporation; putting mercenary troops in the field to private military-personnel procurement firms such as Military Professional Resources Inc.; providing bodyguards and security for heads of state to private security firms such as Executive Outcomes (until 1999), Saladin Security, and Sandline International; and providing surveillance to air mapping companies such as Airscam and Dyncorp.[12] We do not accept that such privatization represents a further surrender by the state of its monopoly of the means of coercion. Rather, we see such activity as the furtherance of a political agenda that seeks to wage war in such a way as to insulate it from public scrutiny.

The Politics of Disaffection

One result of the neoliberal ascendancy in the managerial state is a politics of disaffection. The neoliberal view of the relation of territoriality to the "new reality" of global competition, which we have seen renders traditional liberal politics more or less obsolete, has led to widespread disaffection. For many people, it no longer appears feasible and effective to use the electoral system to further and protect their interests because the state appears more responsive to the forces of global capitalism, by presenting itself to the people as having no choice but to make sacrifices to the global reality.

Some have sought to save an element of political liberalism at the edges of neoliberalism by promoting "communitarianism," which argues that individual interests are always framed by shared values. Communitarianism argues that the traditional managerial state has mistakenly overemphasized individualism at the expense of the community.[13] The technocratic and consumer orientation of citizens is seen as a product of a decline in moral values, which are understood as the cement of communities, and states are taken as communities writ large. Revive traditional values, especially traditional family values, whatever these might be, and citizenship will again flourish as it is assumed that it did in some idealized past. Liberal political values for communitarians are depoliticized; that is, they have become shared values that are to be taught by parents to children in a national setting, and promoted primarily through "volunteerism" rather than through political organization and struggle.

Whether communitarianism can successfully revive citizenship in the managerial state remains to be seen. What is clear is that an alternative response, equally depoliticizing, has taken hold. What little political liberalism the managerial state retains has been the primary victim of the deterritorialized politics of the late twentieth century. As we have seen, managerial states limited political liberalism and democracy through the consumerization of the citizen, that is, the transformation of the citizen into a consumer whose normal stance toward the political world is as passive observer, not active participant. Neoliberalism has extended and deepened this transformation by shifting the domain of the political from the electoral system to the privatized bureaucratic systems of the global economy. This shift does not eliminate bureaucratic and managerial power, however. It only insulates that power from any system of political accountability to the people who are its subjects.

In the managerial state that dominates the late-twentieth-century states-system, and in the global system of deterritorialized transnational organizations, politics has become increasingly trivial. That is, there has been a reduction of the significance of the electoral process as a means of deciding public policy and holding the state's decisionmakers accountable.[14]

We saw in Chapter 7 that the evolution of the European state toward greater degrees of rationality has produced the managerial state, which, through its administrative apparatus, dominates and regulates an ever-widening number of aspects of social life. In such states, the bureaucratic sphere has increasingly become the site where real political struggles take place and the political sphere less so. At the same time, the political sphere has increasingly become an arena in which political struggles are represented as consumables for a passive, spectator citizenry. The various ministries, departments, bureaus, and regulatory agencies of the managerial state's administrative apparatus have become "self-regarding and self-referential." They are staffed by a self-confident body of bureaucrats who have tenure, pensions, and autonomy of professional judgment in deciding matters of public significance. For the knowledge to make policy, they are dependent on the private lobbyists with the financial and organizational ability to control the information presented as relevant to policy debates.[15] Thus, the linkage between the political sphere and actual policymaking has been greatly weakened, if not broken. Shifts in the electoral support of opposing parties and changes in officeholders only marginally modify the regulatory activities of the managerial state.

As the site of real political struggles has shifted to the administrative arena—much of which is now situated transnationally, not within particular territories, as discussed in Chapter 11—political parties have lost much of their original reason for being. Political parties have become weak and less capable of presenting to the voters coherent policy alternatives. The traditional dichotomy between "left" and "right," which in the past reflected different ideological views about distributive justice and the role of the state, is disappearing. Old parties of the left and right are being swept away or have adopted policy positions that are scarcely distinguishable. Because political parties are no longer seen as relevant to actual political struggles, the electorate is increasingly turning away from them and staying away from the polls on election day. Party loyalty and identification have declined dramatically in most managerial states. Voters are more and more supporting one party over another not because of its policy stance but, rather, because through it they can obtain some personal benefit—a government job, a position on the board of a public entity, a more favorable disposition of an application for a subsidy, tax breaks, or a positive decision about regulation by a high-ranking government official. Access to such a privatized government—but one not necessarily smaller or less regulatory—is reserved to primarily wealthy organizations and individuals who can buy the information and skills necessary to organize it into self-serving representations.

Mostly, citizens in managerial states are bored and disaffected from a political process in which the state continues to organize their political identity but in which real decisions are taken in the bureaucracies of the state and through the transnational managerial networks of global capitalism. Turnout in elections has declined markedly in all managerial states, and the number of voters who identify strongly with a political party has fallen. People are turning away from politics to entertainment, and to representations of political struggles as forms of entertainment, such as the conventions of the Democratic and Republican Parties in the United States, in order to relieve the boredom that results from the triviality of politics in the managerial state.

Such disaffection, however, feeds the very forces of privatization and the decline of public accountability against which it reacts.

Deterritorialized Politics

The politics of disaffection is countered by various political movements both within and across neoliberal managerial states. In some areas, defined not only as states but subcommunities within states, nationalism continues to have wide appeal,[16] currently most notable among Chechens, Palestinians, Israelis, Tamils, Kurds, and among some fundamentalist Christians in the United States. Significantly, each of these nationalistic movements contains undercurrents or supplements of internationalism within them. Fundamentalist Christians, for example, also seek to create a universal Christian theocracy by spreading their religious beliefs to Latin America, Africa, and Asia. But these are not the only responses to trivialized politics, or even the primary ones. Disaffection and revivals of nationalism are increasingly contested by forms of cosmopolitanism and deterritorialized politics.

It is not surprising in the current context of globalization that renewed interest in cosmopolitanism has emerged. Cosmopolitanism (from the ancient Greek *kosmopolites,* "citizen of the cosmos," or world) arose among European liberal intellectuals of the eighteenth century who traveled widely and developed relationships with intellectuals in other states.[17] They considered their rationalist and scientific orientation as a general creed of life, defining their allegiances to universal principles and humanistic solidarities against the parochial allegiances, especially of nationality and religion, which they held responsible for ignorance, prejudice, violence, and war. They considered human beings, or at least men, to be individuals first, with a universal psychological and moral makeup that created a basis of solidarity, and even community, prior to the division of the human world into territorial states. Therefore, cosmopolitan intellectuals considered themselves citizens of the world first and citizens of particular states second.

Liberal cosmopolitanism was not necessarily antithetical to the principle of state sovereignty. In fact, it developed as an argument against more exclusionist versions of state sovereignty. It did not attempt to reconstruct the political world without sovereignty. It was not interested in engaging in political activity and organization in order to create directly a global or universal society. For example, in what has become the most famous statement of a cosmopolitan politics, Immanuel Kant's essay *Perpetual Peace* (1795), Kant proposed a system in which all states would adopt republican constitutions based on the rule of law. Peace would then follow as these states worked out cooperative, juridical, and diplomatic relations among themselves. He did not propose a world government that would supersede the authority of particular nation-states, although he did enumerate universal principles that he believed engender world peace. Other proponents of cosmopolitanism, such as Charles Louis Montesquieu (1689–1755) in *L'Esprit des Lois* (1748), promoted various models of federalism among states. For the early cosmopolitans, universal principles were realized in states, and the state took on an ethical character.

There has been in the current world a revival of liberal cosmopolitanism of various forms. There are a range of "new federalists" and an interesting variety of proposals for "cosmopolitan democracy" in which principles of liberal representative democracy are transferred from the context of European nation-states to transnational and global institutions.[18] In addition, there has been a revival of neo-Kantian "democratic peace" arguments, that is, arguments that democratic states are less likely to make war on other democratic states, which means that the universalization of principles of liberal representative democracy will produce a peaceful world order.[19]

Also, there has been the revival of a liberal cosmopolitanism among business elites, technocrats in international organizations, legal professionals, and advocates of global capitalism. As we described in Chapter 11, these elites regularly travel and function in a global context, creating personal and professional friendships and solidarity networks that transcend territorial state borders. They consider themselves members of a global community composed of others of their class or profession regardless of their state of origin or residence. Imbued with a vision of an unrestricted global capitalism, these cosmopolitans act politically to secure government policies favorable to their own global economic projects. Indeed, many such cosmopolitans provide crucial support, both financial and ideological, for neoliberalism.

None of these revivals of liberal cosmopolitanism fundamentally challenge the principles of state sovereignty, however. Even if an undercurrent of antistatism runs through the economic cosmopolitanism of the global capitalist business class, its understanding of politics does not challenge the political organization of the world around territorial nation-states, even as its ideology presents the state as more or less irrelevant to global capitalism.

It is important to remember that in spite of the tremendous increase in the movement of people across borders, millions of ordinary people continue to be members of their state of origin, which continues to determine their identities. Moreover, when they do travel, most ordinary people do so as tourists, not for political or economic reasons. If, as we have argued in this book, the state is an ensemble of practices, institutions, and structures that includes the construction of identity, then the state will certainly continue to persist even as rival ways of organizing political space take hold.

However, more-global forms of politics have emerged among those people whose presence in the community of the globalized world is of a different sort from that of the cosmopolitan business class. Political organizations, such as Amnesty International, Doctors Without Borders, and Greenpeace, as well as more general social movements, such as those concerned with the environment, women, and human rights, have emerged. These groups self-consciously adopt antistatist and global identities. Recent United Nations–sponsored conferences on the environment and women gave official status to a multitude of nongovernmental organizations composed of individuals rather than representatives of states and governments. For the most part, these organizations and movements are democratic in a deterritorialized sense; that is, the norms, institutions, and practices of the kind of global society they promote are seen to emerge out of the political activity of ordinary individuals in the course of struggles against particular acts of injustice, inequality, violence, and ecological deterioration.[20]

The most striking recent development has been the rise of politico-religious organizations that seek to desecularize politics, that is, to turn back the "Westphalian synthesis" that brought about the secular state and the current secular global order. Scholars have identified three trends in this regard. First, religious organizations, such as Hindu nationalist parties in India, Muslim parties in Turkey, Orthodox Christians in Russia, fundamentalist Christians in the United States, and Orthodox Jewish nationalists in Israel, have grown in power and are more and more shaping public debate and exercising increasing influence over laws regulating marriage, education, and foreign policy. Second, religious groups and organizations have exercised transnational influence. For example, the Catholic Church fostered democracy in Poland and the Philippines and Jews in the United States have provided strong support for Israel. Third, more and more, religion has influenced the constitutional basis of the state with religious law being incorporated into "the law of the land." This trend has been most dramatic in the Muslim world where *sharia* (Muslim religious law) has become public law in Iran, Sudan, Saudi Arabia, Pakistan, Malaysia, and twelve of Nigeria's thirty-six states.[21]

A deterritorialized or post-Westphalian politics that might emerge out of the agglomeration of such organizations and activities—such a politics eschews blueprints of what a future world might look like—raises important questions: Does the alleviation of suffering and injustice, and the promotion of human rights and equality, including the defining of what these can mean in a multiculturally saturated environment, have to be tied to the secular territorial state? Is politics without sovereignty possible? Since Westphalia the answer has been that progressive, democratic possibilities can only be entertained under the watchful eye of the sovereign territorial state: that a prosperous, valuable human life is only possible if people first and foremost form communities based on allegiances to a secular nation-state. This way of organizing politico-military rule has not yet been rejected by most, but is being challenged by many.

Notes

1. There is now an enormous literature in a number of fields about the modernity/postmodernity debate. In politics, several useful introductions are Stephen White, *Political Theory and Postmodernism* (New York: Cambridge University Press, 1991); Nick Rengger, *Political Theory and Postmodernism* (Oxford: Basil Blackwell, 1995); William E. Connolly, *Political Theory and Modernity* (Oxford: Basil Blackwell, 1994) and *Identity/Difference* (Ithaca, NY:

Cornell University Press, 1991); Richard J. Bernstein, *The New Constellation* (Cambridge, MA: MIT Press, 1992); Steven Best and Douglas Kellner, *Postmodern Theory* (New York: The Guilford Press, 1991).

2. A journalistic account of the rise and "triumph" of neoliberalism is Daniel Yergin and Joseph Stanislaw, *The Commanding Heights: The Battle Between Government and the Marketplace That Is Remaking the Modern World* (New York: Simon & Schuster, 1998).

3. On neoliberalism as shock therapy for the post-Soviet states, see Peter Gowan, "Analysing Shock Therapy," *New Left Review* 213 (1995): 3–60.

4. A critical assessment of Thatcherism and Reaganism is by Joel Krieger, *Reagan, Thatcher and the Politics of Decline* (New York: Oxford University Press, 1986).

5. Herman Schwartz, "Small States in Big Trouble: State Reorganization in Australia, Denmark, New Zealand, and Sweden in the 1980s," *World Politics* 46 (1994): 527–555.

6. Chris Hann, "Subverting Strong States: The Dialectics of Social Engineering in Hungary and Turkey," *Daedalus* 124 (spring 1995): 133–153; and Geoff Eley, "War and the Twentieth-Century State," *Daedalus* 124 (spring 1995): 155–174.

7. David Beetham, "The Future of the Nation-State," in Gregory McLennan, David Held, and Stuart Hall (eds.), *The Idea of the Modern State* (Philadelphia: Open University Press, 1984): 210.

8. Craig N. Murphy, *International Organization and Industrial Change: Global Governance Since 1850* (New York: Oxford University Press, 1994), 47–48. For an interpretation of the European Union in these terms, see Alan S. Milward, *The European Rescue of the Nation-State* (Berkeley and Los Angeles: University of California Press, 1992).

9. This vision has captured business elites and the media, who speak of "globalization" in terms of the creation of an inevitable global economy in which global competitiveness dictates economic conditions and is beyond challenge. On this vision, see Kenichi Ohmae, *The Borderless World* (London and New York: HarperCollins, 1990). For a critical account, see William Greider, *One World, Ready or Not: The Manic Logic of Global Capitalism* (New York: Simon & Schuster, 1997).

10. Stephen J. Rosow, "Echoes of Commercial Society: Liberal Political Theory in Mainstream IPE," in Kurt Burch and Bob Denemark (eds.), *Constituting IPE* (Boulder, CO: Lynne Rienner Publishers, 1997).

11. Peter B. Evans, "The Eclipse of the State? Reflections on Stateness in the Era of Globalization," *World Politics* 50 (October 1997): 71.

12. P. W. Singer, *Corporate Warriors: The Rise of the Privatized Military Industry* (Ithaca, NY: Cornell University Press, 2003).

13. The most influential popularizers of "communitarianism" in the United States have been William A. Galston, *Liberal Purposes: Goods, Virtues, and Diversity in the Liberal State* (Cambridge and New York: Cambridge University Press, 1991), and Amitai Etzioni, *The Spirit of Community: Rights, Responsibilities, and the Communitarian Agenda* (New York: Crown, 1993). Etzioni's philosophy of community was influential in the Clinton administration. In political theory, the communitarians tend to be more thoughtful, although in our view insufficiently aware of the nationalistic and exclusionistic politics that flow, intentionally and unintentionally, from their theories. For a more sophisticated and politically progressive communitarianism, see Michael Walzer, *Spheres of Justice* (New York:

Basic Books, 1983), and Michael Sandel, *Liberalism and the Limits of Justice* (Cambridge: Cambridge University Press, 1982).

14. The discussion of the "trivialization" of politics is from Gianfranco Poggi, *The Development of the Modern State: A Sociological Introduction* (Stanford, CA: Stanford University Press, 1978), 131–144. See also Philip G. Cerny, *The Changing Architecture of Politics* (Newbury Park, CA: Sage Publications, 1990), 105.

15. On the implications of the role of professional lobbyists and the control of information, see Jean-Marie Guéhenno, *The End of the Nation-State,* trans. Victoria Elliott (Minneapolis and London: University of Minnesota Press, 1995), chapter 2.

16. Sheila L. Croucher, "Perpetual Imagining: Nationhood in a Global Era," *International Studies Review* 5 (2003): 1–24. See also Mathew Horsman and Andrew Marshall, *After the Nation-State: Citizens, Tribalism and the New World Disorder* (London: HarperCollins, 1984).

17. See Thomas J. Schlereth, *The Cosmopolitan Ideal in Enlightenment Thought* (Notre Dame, IN: University of Notre Dame Press, 1977).

18. See the contributions to Daniele Archibugi and David Held, eds., *Cosmopolitan Democracy: Agenda for a New World Order* (Cambridge: Polity Press, 1995).

19. See especially Michael Doyle, "Kant, Liberal Legacies and Foreign Affairs," *Philosophy and Public Affairs* 12 (1982): 3.

20. An eloquent argument for the deterritorialized, democratic character of these movements and organizations, written as a composite report of one such organization of scholars, activists, government officials, and academics (the Committee for a Just World Peace), is R. B. J. Walker, *One World, Many Worlds: Struggles for a Just World Peace* (Boulder, CO: Lynne Rienner Publishers, 1988).

21. Daniel Philpott, "The Challenge of September 11 to Secularism in International Relations," *World Politics* 55 (October 2002): 83. See also Mark Juergensmeyer, *The New Cold War? Religious Nationalism Confronts the Secular State* (Berkeley and Los Angeles: University of California Press, 1993); Gilles Kepel, *The Revenge of God: The Resurgence of Islam, Christianity, and Judaism in the Modern World* (University Park: Pennsylvania State University Press, 1994); Susanne Rudolf and James Piscatori, *Transnational Religion and Fading States* (Boulder, CO: Westview Press, 1997).

Bibliography

Abu-Lughod, Janet L. *Before European Hegemony: The World System* A.D. *1250–1350*. Oxford: Oxford University Press, 1989.

Ajami, Fouad. "The Summoning," *Foreign Affairs* (September–October 1993): 2–9.

Alter, Peter. *Nationalism*. 2d ed. London: Edward Arnold, 1990.

Anderson, Benedict. *Imagined Communities: Reflections on the Origin and Spread of Nationalism*. London: Verso Press, 1983.

Anderson, Perry. *Lineages of the Absolutist State*. London: New Left Books, 1974.

———. *Passages from Antiquity to Feudalism*. London: New Left Books, 1974.

Andrew, Vincent. *Theories of the State*. Oxford: Basil Blackwell, 1987.

Andreas, Peter, and Richard Price, "From Warfighting to Crime Fighting: Transforming the American National Security State," *International Studies Review* 3 (fall 2001): 31–52.

Archibugi, Daniele, and David Held, eds. *Cosmopolitan Democracy: Agenda for a New World Order*. Cambridge: Polity Press, 1995.

Arendt, Hannah. *Eichmann in Jerusalem: Report on the Banality of Evil*. New York: Penguin Books, 1963.

Armstrong, John. *Nations Before Nationalism*. Chapel Hill: University of North Carolina Press, 1982.

Ashley, Richard K. "The Poverty of Neo-Realism," *International Organization* 38:2 (spring 1984): 225–286.

Attalí, Jacques. *Millennium: Winners and Losers in the Coming World Order*. Trans. Leila Conners and Nathan Gardels. New York: Random House, 1991.

Aurelio, Bernardi. "The Economic Problems of the Roman Empire," in Carlo M. Cipolla (ed.), *The Economic Decline of Empires*. London: Methuen & Co., 1970: 16–83.

Badian, E. *Roman Imperialism in the Late Republic*. 2d ed. Ithaca, NY: Cornell University Press, 1968.

Badie, Bertrand, and Pierre Birnbaum. *The Sociology of the State*. Trans. Arthur Goldhamer. Chicago: University of Chicago Press, 1983.

Barbour, Violet. *Capitalism in Amsterdam in the 17th Century*. Ann Arbor: University of Michigan Press, 1963.

Barker, Ernest. *The Development of Public Services in Western Europe, 1660–1930*. Hamden, CT: Archon Books, 1966.

Barnett, Michael. "Sovereignty, Nationalism, and Regional Order in the Arab States System," in Thomas J. Biersteker and Cynthia Weber (eds.), *State Sovereignty as Social Construct*. Cambridge: Cambridge University Press, 1996: 148–189.

Barnet, Richard J., and John Cavanagh. *Global Dreams: Imperial Corporations and the New World Order*. New York: Simon & Schuster, 1994.

Barrow, Clyde W. *Critical Theories of the State.* Madison: University of Wisconsin Press, 1993.

Bartlett, Robert. *The Making of Europe: Conquest, Colonization and Culture Change 950–1350.* Princeton, NJ: Princeton University Press, 1993.

Bates, Robert. "Lessons from History, or the Perfidy of English Exceptionalism and the Significance of Historical France," *World Politics* 40 (July 1988): 499–516.

Bean, Richard. "War and the Birth of the Nation State," *Journal of Economic History* 33 (March 1973): 203–221.

Beard, Charles A. *An Economic Interpretation of the Constitution of the United States.* New York: Macmillan, 1913.

Bendix, Reinhard. *Kings or People: Power and the Mandate to Rule.* Berkeley and Los Angeles: University of California Press, 1978.

Benhabib, Seyla. *The Claims of Culture: Equality and Diversity in the Global Era.* Princeton, NJ: Princeton University Press, 2002.

Benjamin, R., and S. Elkin, eds. *The Democratic State.* Lawrence: University of Kansas Press, 1985.

Bercovitch, Sacvan. *The American Jeremiad.* Madison: University of Wisconsin Press, 1978.

Berman, Harold. *Law and Revolution: The Formation of the Western Legal Tradition.* Cambridge, MA: Harvard University Press, 1983.

Bernstein, Richard J. *The New Constellation.* Cambridge, MA: MIT Press, 1992.

Best, Geoffrey. *Humanity in Warfare.* New York: Columbia University Press, 1980.

Best, Steven, and Douglas Kellner. *Postmodern Theory.* New York: Guilford Press, 1991.

Binder, Leonard, et al. *Crises of Political Development.* Princeton, NJ: Princeton University Press, 1971.

Black, C. E. *The Dynamics of Modernization.* New York: Harper & Row, 1966.

Bloch, Howard. *Medieval Misogyny and the Invention of Western Romantic Love.* Chicago and London: University of Chicago Press, 1991.

Bloch, Marc. *Feudal Society.* 2 vols. Trans. L. A. Manyon. Chicago: University of Chicago Press, 1961.

Block, Ernst. *Natural Law and Human Dignity.* Trans. Dennis J. Schmidt. Cambridge, MA: MIT Press, 1986.

Blockmans, Wim. "Voracious States and Obstructing Cities: An Aspect of State Formation in Preindustrial Europe," *Theory and Society* 18 (1989): 733–756.

Bobbio, Norberto. *Liberalism and Democracy.* London: Verso Press, 1990.

Bobbitt, Philip. *The Shield of Achilles: War, Peace, and the Course of History.* New York: Knopf, 2002.

Bodin, Jean. *Six Books of a Commonwealth.* Trans. R. Knolles and ed. K. D. McRae. Cambridge, MA: Harvard University Press, 1962.

Bond, Brian. *War and Society in Europe, 1870–1970.* New York: St. Martin's Press, 1983.

Bonney, Richard. *The European Dynastic States, 1494–1660.* New York: Oxford University Press, 1991.

Bottomore, T. B., ed. and trans. *Karl Marx: Early Writings.* New York: McGraw Hill, 1964.

Botwinick, Aryeh. *Epic Political Theorists and the Conceptualization of the State.* Washington, DC: University Press of America, 1982.

Boxer, C. R. *The Dutch Seaborne Empire, 1600–1800.* London: Penguin, 1965.

———. *Four Centuries of Portuguese Expansion, 1415–1825: A Succinct Survey.* Berkeley and Los Angeles: University of California Press, 1972.

Bozeman, Adda B. *Politics and Culture in International History*. Princeton, NJ: Princeton University Press, 1960.

Bramstead, E. K., and K. J. Melhuish, eds. *Western Liberalism*. London: Longman Group, 1978.

Bratton, Michael. "Beyond the State: Civil Society and Associational Life in Africa." *World Politics* 41 (April 1989): 407–430.

Braudel, Fernand. *The Wheels of Commerce: Civilization and Capitalism, 15th–18th Century*, vol. 2. New York: Harper & Row, 1979.

Braverman, Harry. *Labor and Monopoly Capitalism: The Degradation of Work in the Twentieth Century*. New York: Monthly Review Press, 1974.

Breuilly, John. *Nationalism and the State*. New York: St. Martin's Press, 1982.

Bull, Hedley. *The Anarchical Society: A Study of Order in World Politics*. New York: Columbia Univrsity Press, 1977.

Bull, Hedley, and Adam Watson, eds. *The Expansion of International Society*. Oxford: Clarendon Press, 1984.

Bull, Marcus. "Origins," in *The Oxford Illustrated History of the Crusades*. Oxford: Oxford University Press, 1997: 13–33.

Burch, Kurt, and Bob Denemark, eds. *Constituting International Political Economy*. Boulder, CO: Lynne Rienner Publishers, 1997.

Burchell, Graham, Colin Gordin, and Peter Miller, eds. *The Foucault Effect: Studies in Governmentality*. Chicago: University of Chicago Press, 1991.

Burchell, Scott, et al. *Theories of International Relations*. New York: St. Martin's Press, 1996.

Bush, George, and Brent Scowcroft. *A World Transformed*. New York: Knopf, 1998.

Buzan, Barry, and Richard Little. *International Systems in World History: Remaking the Study of International Relations*. Oxford: Oxford University Press, 2000.

Cable, Vincent. "The Diminished Nation-State: A Study in Loss of Economic Power," *Daedalus* 124 (spring 1995): 23–53.

Calhoun, Craig. *Habermas and the Public Sphere*. Cambridge, MA: MIT Press, 1992.

Callaghy, Thomas M. "The State as Lame Leviathan: The Patrimonial Administrative State in Africa," in Zaki Ergas (ed.), *The African State in Transition*. New York: St. Martins, 1987.

Camilleri, Joseph A., et al. *The State in Transition: Reimagining Political Space*. Boulder, CO: Lynne Rienner Publishers, 1995.

Caporaso, James, ed. *The Elusive State*. Newbury Park, CA: Sage Publications, 1989.

Carnoy, Martin. *The State and Political Theory*. Princeton, NJ: Princeton University Press, 1984.

Castoriadis, Cornelius. *The Imaginary Institution of Society*. Oxford: Polity Press, 1987.

Cerney, Philip G. *The Changing Architecture of Politics: Structure, Agency, and the Future of the State*. London/Newbury Park/New Delhi: Sage, 1990.

Chatterjee, Partha. *Nationalist Thought and the Colonial World: A Derivative Discourse*. Minneapolis: University of Minnesota Press, 1986.

Chodak, Szymon. *The New State: Etatization of Western Societies*. Boulder, CO: Lynne Rienner Publishers, 1989.

Claessen, Henry J. M., and Peter Skalnik, eds. *The Early State*. The Hague: Mouton, 1978.

Clark, Ian. "Another 'Double Movement': The Great Transformation After the Cold

War?" in Michael Cox, Tim Dunne, and Ken Booth (eds.), *Empires, Systems and States: Great Transformations in International Politics*. Cambridge: Cambridge University Press, 2001.

Clark, Robert T., Jr. *Herder: His Life and Thought*. Berkeley: University of California Press, 1969.

Clastres, Pierre. *Society Against the State*. Trans. Robert Hurley. New York: Zone Books, 1989.

Clausewitz, Carl von. *On War*. Ed. and trans. Michael Howard and Peter Paret. Princeton, NJ: Princeton University Press, 1992.

Cohen, Benjamin J. *The Question of Imperialism*. New York: Basic Books, 1973.

Coniff, Michael L., and Thomas J. Davis. *Africans and the Americas: A History of the Black Diaspora*. New York: St. Martin's Press, 1994.

Connelly, Matthew, and Paul Kennedy. "Must It Be the Rest Against the West?" *Atlantic Monthly* (December 1994): 61–88.

Connolly, William E. *Identity/Difference*. Ithaca, NY: Cornell University Press, 1991.

———. *Political Theory and Modernity*. Oxford: Basil Blackwell, 1994.

Contamine, Phillippe. *War in the Middle Ages*. Oxford: Basil Blackwell, 1980.

Coole, Diana. *Women in Political Theory: From Ancient Misogyny to Contemporary Feminism*. 2d ed. Boulder, CO: Lynne Rienner Publishers, 1993.

Croucher, Sheila L. "Perpetual Imagining: Nationhood in a Global Era," *International Studies Review* 5 (2003): 1–24.

Crosby, Alfred W. *The Measure of Reality: Quantification and Western Society, 1250–1600*. Cambridge: Cambridge University Press, 1997.

Currie, Elliot. *Crime and Punishment in America*. New York: Holt/Metropolitan, 1988.

Dahl, Robert A., ed. *Political Oppositions in Western Democracies*. New Haven, CT: Yale University Press, 1966.

Davidson, Basil. *The Black Man's Burden: Africa and the Curse of the Nation-State*. New York: Random House, 1992.

Davies, Norman. *Europe: A History*. Oxford and New York: Oxford University Press, 1996.

Deibert, Ronald J. *Parchment, Printing, and Hypermedia: Communication in World Order Transformation*. New York: Columbia University Press, 1997.

D'Entrèves, Alexander Passerin. *The Notion of the State: An Introduction to Political Theory*. Oxford: Clarendon Press, 1967.

Der Derian, James. *On Diplomacy*. London: Basil Blackwell, 1987.

———. *Virtuous War: Mapping the Military-Industrial-Media-Entertainment Network*. Boulder, CO: Westview Press, 2001.

Diamond, Jared. *Guns, Germs, and Steel: The Fates of Human Societies*. New York and London: W. W. Norton, 1997.

Dorfman, Ariel. *The Empire's Old Clothes: What the Lone Ranger, Babar, and Other Innocent Heroes Do to Our Minds*. New York: Pantheon Books, 1983.

Doty, Roxanne Lynn. *Imperial Encounters*. Minneapolis: University of Minnesota Press, 1996.

Dowdall, H. C. "The Word 'State,'" *Law Quarterly Review* 39 (January 1923): 98–125.

Downing, Brian M. *The Military Revolution and Political Change: Origins of Democracy and Autocracy in Early Modern Europe*. Princeton, NJ: Princeton University Press, 1992.

Doyle, Michael. "Kant, Liberal Legacies and Foreign Affairs," *Philosophy and Public Affairs* 12 (1982): 205–235.

Doyle, Michael W. *Empires.* Ithaca, NY: Cornell University Press, 1986.

Duffy, James. *A Question of Slavery: Labour Policies in Portuguese Africa and the British Protest, 1850–1920.* Cambridge, MA: Harvard University Press, 1967.

Durant, Will. *Caesar and Christ: A History of Roman Civilization and of Christianity from Their Beginnings to A.D. 325.* New York: Simon & Schuster, 1944.

Dyson, Kenneth H. F. *The State Tradition in Western Europe: A Study of an Idea and Institution.* New York: Oxford University Press, 1980.

Eley, Geoff. "War and the Twentieth-Century State," *Daedalus* (spring 1995): 155–174.

Eley, Geoff, and Ronald Grigor Suny, eds. *Becoming National: A Reader.* New York: Oxford University Press, 1996.

Ellis, John. *The Social History of the Machine Gun.* Baltimore: Johns Hopkins University Press, 1975.

Elshtain, Jean Bethke. *Public Man, Private Woman: Women in Social and Political Thought.* Princeton, NJ: Princeton University Press, 1981.

———. *Women and War.* Chicago and London: University of Chicago Press, 1987.

Emsley, Clive, Arthur Marwick, and Wendy Simpson, eds. *War, Peace and Social Change in Twentieth-Century Europe.* Philadelphia: Open University Press, 1989.

Engels, Frederick. *The Origin of the Family, Private Property and the State.* New York: International, 1942.

Ertman, Thomas. *Birth of the Leviathan: Building States and Regimes in Medieval and Early Modern Europe.* Cambridge: Cambridge University Press, 1997.

Etzioni, Amatai. *The Spirit of Community: Rights, Responsibilities, and the Communitarian Agenda.* New York: Crown, 1993.

Evans, Peter B. *Dependent Development: The Alliance of Multinational, State and Local Capital in Brazil.* Princeton, NJ: Princeton University Press, 1978.

———. "The Eclipse of the State? Reflections on Stateness in the Era of Globalization," *World Politics* 50 (October 1997): 62–87.

———. *Imbedded Autonomy: States and Industrial Transformation.* Princeton, NJ: Princeton University Press, 1995.

Evans, Peter B., Dietrich Rueschemeyer, and Theda Skocpol, eds. *Bringing the State Back In.* New York: Cambridge University Press, 1985.

Ewen, Stuart. *Captains of Consciousness: Advertising and the Social Roots of Consumer Culture.* New York: McGraw-Hill, 1976.

Falk, Richard. *On Humane Governance: Toward a New Global Politics.* University Park: Pennsylvania State University Press, 1995.

———. *Law in an Emerging Global Village: A Post-Westphalian Perspective.* Ardsley, NY: Transnational Publisher, 1998.

Falk, Richard, and Robert J. Lifton. *Indefensible Weapons.* New York: Basic Books, 1982.

Febvre, Lucien, and Henri-Jean Martin. *The Coming of the Book: The Impact of Printing, 1450–1800.* London: New Left Books, 1976.

Ferguson, Kathy. *The Feminist Case Against Bureaucracy.* Philadelphia: Temple University Press, 1984.

Ferguson, Yale H., and Richard W. Mansbach. *The State, Conceptual Chaos, and the Future of International Relations Theory.* Boulder, CO: Lynne Rienner Publishers, 1989.

Finley, M. I. "Manpower and the Fall of Rome," in the Carlo M. Cipolla (ed.), *The Economic Decline of Empires*. London: Methuen & Co., 1970: 84–91.

Fletcher, Richard. *The Barbarian Conversion: From Paganism to Christianity*. New York: Henry Holt, 1998.

Flora, Peter, and Arnold J. Heidenheimer, eds. *The Development of the Welfare State in Europe and America*. New Brunswick, NJ: Transaction Books, 1981.

Foucault, Michel. *Discipline and Punishment*. Trans. Alan Sheridan. New York: Pantheon, 1977.

Fowler, Michael Ross, and Julie Marie Bunck. *Law, Power, and the Sovereign State: The Evolution and Application of the Concept of Sovereignty*. University Park: Pennsylvania State University Press, 1995.

Fraser, Nancy. *Unruly Practices: Power, Discourse and Gender in Contemporary Social Theory*. Minneapolis: University of Minnesota Press, 1989.

Friedrich, Carl J., and Charles Blitzer. *The Age of Power*. Ithaca, NY: Cornell University Press, 1957.

Friedrich, Carl J., and Zbigniew Brzezinski. *Totalitarian Dictatorship and Autocracy*. Cambridge, MA: Harvard University Press, 1965.

Fukuyama, Francis. *The End of History and the Last Man*. New York: Free Press, 1992.

———. "The End of History?" *The National Interest* (summer 1989): 3–18.

Fussell, Paul. *The Great War in Modern Memory*. London and New York: Oxford University Press, 1975.

Galston, William A. *Liberal Purposes: Goods, Virtues, and Diversity in the Liberal State*. Cambridge and New York: Cambridge University Press, 1991.

Garon, Sheldon. *Making Japanese Minds: The State in Everyday Life*. Princeton, NJ: Princeton University Press, 1997.

Geary, Patrick J. *The Myth of Nations: The Medieval Origins of Europe*. Princeton, NJ: Princeton University Press, 2002.

Geis, Joseph, and Frances Geis. *Life in a Medieval Castle*. New York: Harper & Row, 1979.

Gellner, Ernest. *Nations and Nationalism*. Ithaca, NY: Cornell University Press, 1983.

Gerth, Hans H., and C. Wright Mills, eds. *From Max Weber*. New York: Oxford University Press, 1958.

Gibson, Charles. *Spain in America*. New York: Harper Torchbooks, 1966.

Giddens, Anthony. *A Contemporary Critique of Historical Materialism*. London: Macmillan, 1981.

———. *The Nation-State and Violence*. Berkeley and Los Angeles: University of California Press, 1985.

Gilbert, Felix, ed. *The Historical Essays of Otto Hintze*. New York: Oxford University Press, 1975.

Gilpin, Robert. *War and Change in World Politics*. Cambridge: Cambridge University Press, 1981.

Given, James. *State and Society in Medieval Europe*. Ithaca, NY: Cornell University Press, 1990.

Goldstone, Jack A. *Revolutions and Rebellion in the Early Modern World*. Berkeley: University of California Press, 1991.

Gowan, Peter. "Analysing Shock Therapy," *New Left Review* 213 (1995): 3–60.

Greenfeld, Liah. *Nationalism: Five Roads to Modernity*. Cambridge, MA: Harvard University Press, 1992.

———. "Transcending the Nation's Worth," *Daedalus* 122 (summer 1993): 47–62.

Greider, William. *One World, Ready or Not: The Manic Logic of Global Capitalism.* New York: Simon & Schuster, 1997.

Grew, Raymond. "The Nineteenth-Century State," in Charles Bright and Susan Harding (eds.), *Statemaking and Social Movements: Essays in History and Theory.* Ann Arbor: University of Michigan Press, 1984.

Guéhenno, Jean-Marie. *The End of the Nation-State.* Trans. Victoria Elliott. Minneapolis: University of Minnesota Press, 1995.

Guenée, Bernard. *States and Rulers.* Oxford: Basil Blackwell, 1985.

Haas, Ernst. *The Uniting of Europe: Political, Social, and Economic Forces, 1950–1957.* Stanford, CA: Stanford University Press, 1958.

Habermas, Jürgen. *Legitimation Crisis.* Trans. Thomas McCarthy. Boston: Beacon Press, 1973.

———. *The Structural Transformation of the Public Sphere.* Trans. T. Berger and F. Lawrence. Cambridge, MA: MIT Press, 1989.

Hall, John A., ed. *States in History.* Oxford: Basil Blackwell, 1986.

———. "Nationalisms: Classified and Explained," *Daedalus* 122 (summer 1993): 1–28.

Hall, John A., and G. John Ikenberry. *The State.* Minneapolis: University of Minnesota Press, 1989.

Hall, Rodney Bruce. *National Collective Identity: Social Constructs and International Systems.* New York: Columbia University Press, 1999.

Hann, Chris. "Subverting Strong States: The Dialectics of Social Engineering in Hungary and Turkey," *Daedalus* 122 (spring 1995): 133–153.

Hanson, Victor Davis. *Carnage and Culture: Landmark Battles in the Rise of Western Power.* New York: Doubleday, 2001.

Hardt, Michael, and Antonio Negri. *Empire.* Cambridge, MA: Harvard University Press, 2000.

Hay, Denys. *Europe: The Emergence of an Idea.* Edinburgh: Edinburgh University Press, 1957.

Hayes, Carleton R. *The Historical Evolution of Modern Nationalism.* New York: Richard R. Smith, 1931.

Heidenheimer, Arnold J., and Donald P. Kommers. *The Governments of Germany.* 4th ed. New York: Thomas Crowell, 1975.

Held, David. *Models of Democracy.* Stanford, CA: Stanford University Press, 1987.

———. *Political Theory and the Modern State.* Stanford, CA: Stanford University Press, 1989.

Held, David, and Stuart Hall, eds. *The Idea of the Modern State.* Philadelphia: Open University Press, 1984.

Held, David, et al., eds. *States and Societies.* New York: New York University Press, 1983.

Helman, Gerald B., and Steven R. Ratner. "Saving Failed States," *Foreign Policy* 89 (winter 1992–1993): 3–20.

Helms, Christine Moss. *Iraq: Eastern Flank of the Arab World.* Washington, DC: Brookings Institution, 1984.

Hemingway, Ernest. *In Our Time.* New York: Scribner's, 1925.

Herf, Jeffrey. *Reactionary Modernism: Technology, Culture and Politics in Weimar and the Third Reich.* Cambridge: Cambridge University Press, 1984.

Herz, John H. *The Nation-State and the Crisis of World Politics.* New York: David McKay, 1976.

Hinsley, J. H. *Sovereignty.* 2d ed. Cambridge: Cambridge University Press, 1986.

Hinton, Harold C., et al. *Major Governments of Asia*. Ithaca, NY: Cornell University Press, 1958.

Hirschman, Albert O. *The Passions and the Interests: Political Arguments for Capitalism Before Its Triumph*. Princeton, NJ: Princeton University Press, 1977.

Hobbes, Thomas. *Leviathan*. Ed. Richard Tuck. Cambridge: Cambridge University Press, 1991.

Hobsbawm, Eric. *Nations and Nationalism Since 1780*. 2d ed. New York: Cambridge University Press, 1991.

————. *The Age of Extremes: A History of the World, 1914–1991*. New York: Pantheon Books, 1994.

Hobson, John M. *The State and International Relations*. Cambridge: Cambridge University Press, 2000.

Hodder-Williams, Richard. *An Introduction to the Politics of Tropical Africa*. London: George Allen & Unwin, 1984.

Hoffmann, Stanley. "Reflections on the Nation-State in Western Europe Today," *Journal of Common Market Studies* 30 (September–December 1982): 21–37.

Hopkins, Andrea. *Knights*. New York/London/Paris: Artabras, 1990.

Horsman, Mathew, and Andrew Marshall. *After the Nation-State: Citizens, Tribalism and the New World Disorder*. London: HarperCollins, 1994.

Howard, Michael. "War and the Nation-State," *Daedalus* 108 (fall 1979): 101–110.

Huntington, Samuel P. *Political Order in Changing Societies*. New Haven, CT: Yale University Press, 1968.

————. "The Clash of Civilizations?" *Foreign Affairs* 72 (summer 1993): 22–49.

Jackson, Robert H. *Quasi-States: Sovereignty, International Relations, and the Third World*. Cambridge: Cambridge University Press, 1990.

Jackson, Robert H., and Carl G. Rosberg. *Personal Rule in Black Africa: Prince, Autocrat, Prophet, Tyrant*. Berkeley: University of California Press, 1982.

Jackson, Robert H., and Alan James. *States in a Changing World: A Contemporary Analysis*. Oxford: Clarendon Press, 1993.

Jacoby, Henry. *The Bureaucratization of the World*. Berkeley and Los Angeles: University of California Press, 1973.

Jansen, Marius B. *The Making of Modern Japan*. Cambridge, MA: Harvard University Press, 2000.

Jessop, Bob. *The Capitalist State*. New York and London: New York University Press, 1982.

Johnson, Chalmers. *MITI and the Japanese Miracle*. Stanford, CA: Stanford University Press, 1982.

Johnson, James Turner. *Just War Tradition and the Restraint of War: A Moral and Historical Inquiry*. Princeton, NJ: Princeton University Press, 1981.

Johnston, R. J. *Geography and the State*. London: Macmillan, 1982.

Jones, David Martin. "Democratization, Civil Society, and Illiberal Middle Class Culture in Pacific Asia," *Comparative Politics* 30 (January 1998): 147–169.

Joppke, Christian, ed. *Challenges to the Nation-State: Immigration in Western Europe and the United States*. Oxford: Oxford University Press, 1998.

Judge, David. *The Parliamentary State*. London/Newbury Park/New Delhi: Sage, 1993.

Juergensmeyer, Mark. *The New Cold War? Religious Nationalism Confronts the Secular State*. Berkeley and Los Angeles: University of California Press, 1993.

Kaldor, Mary. *The World Military Order*. New York: Hill & Wang, 1981.

Kantorowicz, Ernst H. *The King's Two Bodies: A Study in Medieval Political Theory*. Princeton, NJ: Princeton University Press, 1957.

Kaplan, Irving. *Zäire: A Country Study.* Washington, DC: U.S. Government Printing Office, 1977.

Katz, Solomon. *The Decline of Rome and the Rise of Medieval Europe.* Ithaca, NY: Cornell University Press, 1955.

Katzenstein, Peter, ed. *Between Power and Plenty: Foreign Economic Policies of Advanced Industrial States.* Madison: University of Wisconsin Press, 1978.

Kennedy, Paul. *The Rise and Fall of Great Powers: Economic Change and Military Conflict from 1500 to 2000.* New York: Random House, 1987.

Kepel, Gilles. *The Revenge of God: The Resurgence of Islam, Christianity, and Judaism in the Modern World.* University Park: Pennsylvania State University Press, 1994.

Kiernan, V. G. "State and Nation in Western Europe," *Past and Present* 31 (July 1965): 20–38.

King, Roger. *The State and Modern Society.* Chatham, NJ: Chatham House Publishers, 1986.

Klare, Michael T. *American Arms Supermarket.* Austin: University of Texas Press, 1984.

Koch, Hamesjoachim Wilhelm. *Medieval Warfare.* Englewood Cliffs, NJ: Prentice-Hall, 1978.

Kohn, Hans. *The Idea of Nationalism: A Study of Its Origins and Background.* New York: Macmillan, 1944.

Koselleck, Reinhart. *Critique and Crisis: Enlightenment and the Pathogenesis of Modern Society.* Cambridge, MA: MIT Press, 1988.

Koslowski, Rey. "Human Migration and the Conceptualization of Pre-Modern World Politics," *International Studies Quarterly* 46 (2002): 375–399.

Koven, Seth, and Sonya Michel, eds. *Mothers of a New World: Maternalistic Politics and the Origins of Welfare States.* London: Routledge, 1993.

Krader, Lawrence. *Formation of the State.* Englewood Cliffs, NJ: Prentice-Hall, 1968.

Krasner, Stephen. "Approaches to the State: Alternative Conceptions and Historical Dynamics," *Comparative Politics* 16 (January 1984): 223–246.

Kratochwil, Friedrich. "Of Systems, Boundaries, and Territoriality: An Inquiry into the Formation of the State System," *World Politics* 39 (October 1986): 27–52.

Krieger, Joel. *Reagan, Thatcher and the Politics of Decline.* New York: Oxford University Press, 1986.

Lasch, Christopher. *The Revolt of the Elites and the Betrayal of Democracy.* New York: W. W. Norton, 1995.

Lefebre, Henri. *The Production of Space.* Trans. Donald Nicolson-Smith. Oxford: Basil Blackwell, 1991.

Lemarchand, René. "Political Clientelism and Ethnicity in Tropical Africa: Competing Solidarities in Nation-Building," *American Political Science Review* 66 (1972): 68–90.

Levi, Margaret. *Of Rule and Revenue.* Berkeley: University of California Press, 1988.

Lind, Michael. "The Catalytic State," *The National Interest* (spring 1992): 3–12.

Lindberg, L., et al., eds. *Stress and Contradiction in Modern Capitalism.* Lexington, MA: D. H. Heath, 1975.

Lipset, Seymour Martin. *American Exceptionalism: A Double-Edged Sword.* New York: W. W. Norton, 1996.

Lipshutz, Ronnie, and Ken Conca, eds. *The State and Social Power in Global Environmental Politics.* New York: Columbia University Press, 1993.

Livonen, Jyrki, ed. *The Future of the Nation State in Europe.* Brookfield, VT: Edward Elgar, 1993.

Locke, John. *A Letter Concerning Toleration.* Introduction by Patrick Romanell. Indianapolis: Bobbs-Merrill, 1975.

———. *Second Treatise of Government.* Ed. Peter Laslett. Cambridge: Cambridge University Press, 1960.

Lowenstein, Karl. *The Governance of Rome.* The Hague: Martinus Nijhoff, 1973.

Lowi, Theodore J., and Benjamin Ginsberg. *American Government: Freedom and Power.* 3d ed. New York and London: W. W. Norton, 1994.

Lubasz, Heinz, ed. *The Development of the Modern State.* New York: Macmillan, 1964.

Lucas, Angela M. *Women in the Middle Ages.* New York: St. Martin's Press, 1983.

MacArthur, John R. *Second Front: Censorship and Propaganda in the Gulf War.* New York: Hill & Wang, 1992.

Machiavelli, Niccolò. *The Prince and the Discourses.* Ed. Max Lerner. New York: Random House, 1950.

MacIver, Robert. *The Modern State.* London: Oxford University Press, 1926.

MacLeod, W. C. *The Origins of the State.* Indianapolis: Bobbs-Merrill, 1924.

Macpherson, C. B. *The Political Theory of Possessive Individualism.* London: Oxford University Press, 1962.

———. *The Life and Times of Liberal Democracy.* Oxford: Oxford University Press, 1977.

Majone, Giandomenico. "The Rise of the Regulatory State in Europe," in Wolfgang C. Müller and Vincent Wright (eds.), *The State in Western Europe: Retreat or Redefinition?* Newbury Park, CA: Frank Cass, 1994.

Mann, Michael. "State and Society, 1130–1815: An Analysis of English State Finances," in M. Zeitlin (ed.), *Political Power and Social Theory,* vol I. Greenwich, CT: JAI Press, 1980.

———. "The Emergence of Modern European Nationalism," in John A. Hall and I. C. Jarvie (eds.), *Transition to Modernity: Essays on Power, Wealth and Beliefs.* Cambridge: Cambridge University Press, 1992.

———. "Nation-States in Europe and Other Continents: Diversifying, Not Dying," *Daedalus* 122 (summer 1993): 115–140.

Marr, Phebe. *The Modern History of Iraq.* Boulder, CO: Westview Press, 1985.

Mattingly, Garrett. *Renaissance Diplomacy.* Boston: Houghton Mifflin, 1955.

Mayall, James. *Nationalism and International Society.* Cambridge: Cambridge University Press, 1990.

Mayer, Arno J. *The Persistence of the Old Regime: Europe to the Great War.* New York: Pantheon Books, 1981.

McKendrick, Neil, John Brewer, and J. H. Plumb. *The Birth of a Consumer Society: The Commercialization of Eighteenth-Century England.* Bloomington: Indiana University Press, 1982.

McKenzie, Evan. *Privatopia: Homeowner Associations and the Rise of Residential Private Government.* New Haven, CT: Yale University Press, 1994.

McLennan, Gregor, David Held, and Stuart Hall, eds. *The Idea of the Modern State.* Philadelphia: Open University Press, 1984.

McNeill, William H. *The Rise of the West: A History of the Human Condition.* Chicago: University of Chicago Press, 1963.

———. *The Pursuit of Power: Technology, Armed Force and Society Since A.D. 1000.* Chicago: University of Chicago Press, 1982.

Mehta, Uday S. "Liberal Strategies of Exclusion," in Frederick Cooper and Ann

Laura Stoler (eds.), *Tensions of Empire: Colonial Cultures in a Bourgeois World*. Berkeley: University of California Press, 1997.

Meineke, Frederich. *Machiavellism: The Doctrine of Raison d'Etat and Its Place in Modern History*. Trans. Douglas Scott. New Haven, CT: Yale University Press, 1962.

Melman, Seymour. *Pentagon Capitalism*. New York: McGraw-Hill, 1970.

Meyer, Mary K., and Elizabeth Prügl, eds. *Gender Politics in Global Governance*. New York: Rowman & Littlefield, 1999.

Migdal, Joel S., Atul Kohli, and Vivienne Shue, eds. *State Power and Social Forces*. Cambridge: Cambridge University Press, 1994.

Milward, Alan S. *The European Rescue of the Nation-State*. Berkeley and Los Angeles: University of California Press, 1992.

Mitchell, Timothy. "The Limits of the State: Beyond Statist Approaches," *American Political Science Review* 85:1 (1991): 77–96.

Modelski, George. "The Long Cycle of Global Politics and the Nation-State," *Comparative Studies in Society and History* 20 (April 1978): 214–235.

Moore, Barrington, Jr. *Social Origins of Dictatorship and Democracy: Lord and Peasant in the Making of the Modern World*. Boston: Beacon Press, 1966.

Morris, Christopher W. *An Essay on the Modern State*. Cambridge: Cambridge University Press, 1998.

Moynihan, Daniel Patrick. *Pandemonium: Ethnicity in International Politics*. Oxford: Oxford University Press, 1993.

Müller, Wolfgang C., and Vincent Wright, eds. *The State in Western Europe: Retreat or Redefinition*. Newbury Park, CA: Frank Cass, 1994.

Murphy, Alexander B. "The Sovereign State System as Political-Territorial Ideal: Historical and Contemporary Considerations," in Thomas J. Biersteker and Cynthia Weber (eds.), *State Sovereignty as Social Construct*. Cambridge: Cambridge University Press, 1996.

Murphy, Craig N. *International Organization and Industrial Change: Global Governance Since 1850*. Oxford: Oxford University Press, 1994.

Myers, Henry. *Medieval Kingship*. Chicago: Nelson-Hall, 1982.

Nandy, Ashis. *The Intimate Enemy: Loss and Recovery of Self Under Colonialism*. New Delhi: Oxford University Press, 1983.

Nef, John U. *Industry and Government in France and England, 1450–1640*. Ithaca, NY: Cornell University Press, 1964.

Nettle, J. P. "The State as a Conceptual Variable," *World Politics* 20 (July 1968): 559–592.

Neuberger, Benyamin. "The Western Nation-State in Africa: Perceptions of Nation-Building," *Asian and African Studies* 11 (1976): 241–261.

Nicholas, David. *The Growth of the Medieval City*. New York: Longman, 1997.

Nordlinger, Eric A. *On the Autonomy of the Democratic State*. Cambridge, MA: Harvard University Press, 1981.

North, Douglass C. "A Framework for Analyzing the State in Economic History," *Explorations in Economic History* 16 (1979): 249–259.

North, Douglass, and Robert Thomas. *The Rise of the Western World*. Cambridge: Cambridge University Press, 1973.

O'Connor, James. *The Fiscal Crisis of the State*. New York: St. Martin's Press, 1973.

Ohmae, Kenichi. *The Borderless World: Power and Strategy in the Interlinked Economy*. New York: HarperCollins, 1990.

Okin, Susan. *Justice, Gender, and the Family*. New York: Basic Books, 1989.

Olson, Mancur. *The Rise and Decline of Nations.* New Haven, CT: Yale University Press, 1983.

Ong Aihwa. *Flexible Citzenship: The Cultural Logics of Transnationality.* Durham, NC: Duke University Press, 1999.

Onuf, Nicholas. *City of Sovereigns: Republican Themes in International Thought.* Cambridge: Cambridge University Press, 1997.

Opello, Walter C., Jr. "Early Competitors of the State: The Military-Religious Orders," paper presented at the 44th annual meeting of the International Studies Association, Portland, Oregon, February 25–March 1, 2003.

Oppenheimer, Franz. *The States.* Indianapolis: Bobbs-Merrill, 1914.

Organski, A. F. K. *The Stages of Political Development.* New York: Knopf, 1965.

Osiander, Andreas. *The Status System of Europe, 1640–1990: Peacemaking and the Conditions of International Society.* Oxford: Clarendon Press, 1994.

Painter, Sidney. *The Rise of Feudal Monarchies.* Ithaca, NY: Cornell University Press, 1951.

Parekh, Bhikuh. *Rethinking Multiculturalism: Cultural Diversity and Political Theory.* Cambridge, MA: Harvard University Press, 2000.

Paris, Roland. "The Globalization of Taxation? Electronic Commerce and the Transformation of the State," *International Studies Quarterly* 47 (2003): 153–182.

Parker, Andrew, et al., eds. *Nationalism and Secularity.* New York: Routledge, 1992.

Parker, Geoffrey. *The Military Revolution.* Cambridge: Cambridge University Press, 1989.

Parry, J. H. *The Establishment of the European Hegemony: 1415–1715.* 3d ed. rev. New York: Harper Torchbooks, 1959.

———. *The Age of Reconnaissance: Discovery, Exploration and Settlement, 1450 to 1650.* Berkeley: University of California Press, 1963.

Pateman, Carole. *The Disorder of Women.* Stanford, CA: Stanford University Press, 1989.

Pettman, Jan. *Worlding Women.* New York: Routledge, 1996.

Phillips, J. R. S. *The Medieval Expansion of Europe.* Oxford and New York: Oxford University Press, 1988.

Philpott, Daniel. *Revolutions in Sovereignty: How Ideas Shaped Modern International Relations.* Princeton, NJ: Princeton University Press, 2001.

———. "The Challenge of September 11 to Secularism in International Relations," *World Politics* 55 (October 2002): 66–95.

Pierson, Christopher. *Beyond the Welfare State?* University Park: Pennsylvania State University Press, 1991.

Piscatori, James. *Islam in a World of Nation-States.* New York: Cambridge University Press, 1986.

Pjil, Kees Van der. *The Making of an Atlantic Ruling Class.* London: Verso Press, 1984.

Pocock, John. *The Machiavellian Moment.* Princeton, NJ: Princeton University Press, 1975.

Poggi, Gianfranco. *The Development of the Modern State: A Sociological Introduction.* Stanford, CA: Stanford University Press, 1978.

———. *The State: Its Nature, Development and Prospects.* Stanford, CA: Stanford University Press, 1990.

Polanyi, Karl. *The Great Transformation: The Political and Economic Origins of Our Time.* Boston: Beacon Press, 1957.

Porter, Bruce D. *War and the Rise of the State: The Military Foundations of Modern Politics*. New York: Free Press, 1994.

Porter, Michael. *The Competitive Advantage of Nations*. New York: Free Press, 1990.

Poulantzas, Nicos. *Political Power and Social Class*. London: New Left Books, 1973.

Rasler, Karen A., and William R. Thompson. "War Making and State Making: Governmental Expenditures, Tax Revenues, and Global War," *American Political Science Review* 79 (June 1985): 491–507.

———. *War and State Making*. Boston: Unwin Hyman, 1989.

Rasmussen, Jorgen S., and Joel C. Moses. *Major European Governments*. 9th ed. Belmont, CA: Wadsworth, 1995.

Reich, Robert. *The Work of Nations*. New York: Alfred Knopf, 1991.

Reiss, Hans, ed. *Kant's Political Writings*. Cambridge: Cambridge University Press, 1970.

Rengger, Nick. *Political Theory and Postmodernism*. Oxford: Basil Blackwell, 1995.

Reynolds, Susan. *Kingdoms and Communities in Western Europe, 900–1300*. Oxford: Clarendon Press, 1984.

Rice, Eugene. *The Foundations of Early Modern Europe, 1460–1559*. New York: W. W. Norton, 1970.

Rogers, Clifford J., ed. *The Military Revolution Debate: Readings on the Military Transformation of Early Modern Europe*. Boulder, CO: Westview Press, 1995.

Rose, Richard. "On the Priorities of Government: A Developmental Analysis of Public Policies," *European Journal of Political Research* 4 (1976): 247–289.

Rosecrance, Richard. *The Rise of the Trading State: Commerce and Conquest in the Modern World*. New York: Basic Books, 1986.

———. "Long Cycle Theory and International Relations," *International Organization* 41 (spring 1987): 283–302.

Rosow, Stephen J., Naeem Inayatullah, and Mark Rupert. *The Global Economy as Political Space*. Boulder, CO: Lynne Rienner Publishers, 1994.

Rostow, Walt N. *The Stages of Economic Growth*. Cambridge: Cambridge University Press, 1960.

Rothchild, Donald, and Naomi Chazan, eds. *The Precarious Balance: State and Society in Africa*. Boulder, CO: Westview Press, 1988.

Rothman, Stanley. *European Society and Politics*. Indianapolis: Bobbs-Merrill, 1970.

Rowen, Herbert. *The King's State: Proprietary Dynasticism in Early Modern Europe*. New Brunswick, NJ: Rutgers University Press, 1980.

Rudolf, Susanne, and James Piscatori. *Transnational Religion and Fading States*. Boulder, CO: Westview Press, 1997.

Ruggie, John Gerard. "Continuity and Transformation in the World Polity: Toward a Neorealist Synthesis," *World Politics* 35 (January 1983).

———. "Continuity and Transformation in the World Polity: Toward a Neorealist Synthesis," in Robert O. Keohan (ed.), *Neorealism and Its Critics*. New York: Columbia University Press, 1986.

———. "Territoriality and Beyond: Problematizing Modernity in International Relations," *International Organization* 47 (winter 1993): 139–174.

———. *Constructing the World Polity: Essays on International Institutionalization*. London and New York: Routledge, 1998.

Rupert, Mark. *Producing Hegemony: The Politics of Mass Production and American Global Power.* Cambridge: Cambridge University Press, 1995.

Russell, Jeffrey Burton. *Medieval Civilization.* New York: Wiley, 1968.

Rustow, Dankwart. *A World of Nations: Problems of Political Modernization.* Washington, DC: Brookings Institution, 1967.

Sampson, Anthony. *The Arms Bazaar: From Lebanon to Lockheed.* New York: Viking Press, 1977.

Sandel, Michael. *Liberalism and the Limits of Justice.* Cambridge: Cambridge University Press, 1982.

Sassen, Saskia. *Losing Control? Sovereignty in an Age of Globalization.* New York: Columbia University Press, 1996.

Sassoon, Donald. *Contemporary Italy.* New York: Longman, 1986.

Saunders, Peter. *Capitalism.* Minneapolis: University of Minnesota Press, 1995.

Schaeffer, Robert K. *Severed States: Dilemmas of Democracy in a Divided World.* New York: Rowman & Littlefield, 1999.

Schell, Jonathan. *The Fate of the Earth.* New York: Alfred Knopf, 1982.

Schlereth, Thomas J. *The Cosmopolitan Ideal in Enlightenment Thought.* Notre Dame, IN: University of Notre Dame Press, 1977.

Schmidt, Vivien A. "The New World Order, Incorporated: The Rise of Business and the Decline of the Nation-State," *Daedalus* 124 (spring 1995): 75–106.

Schocket, Gordon. *Patriarchicalism in Political Thought.* New York: Basic Books, 1975.

Schwartz, Herman. "Small States in Big Trouble: State Reorganization in Australia, Denmark, New Zealand, and Sweden in the 1980s," *World Politics* (1994): 527–555.

Scott, James. *Weapons of the Weak: Everyday Forms of Peasant Resistance.* New Haven, CT: Yale University Press, 1985.

———. *Seeing Like a State: How Certain Schemes to Improve the Human Condition Have Failed.* New Haven, CT: Yale University Press, 1998.

Seligman, Adam B. *The Idea of Civil Society.* New York: Free Press, 1992.

Service, Elmer R. *Origins of the State and Civilization.* New York: W. W. Norton, 1975.

Seton-Watson, Hugh. *Nations and States.* Boulder, CO: Westview Press, 1977.

Shahar, Shulamith. *The Fourth Estate: A History of Women in the Middle Ages.* London and New York: Methuen, 1983.

Shannon, Ulric. "Private Armies and the Decline of the State," in Kenton Worcester et. al. (eds.), *Violence and Politics: Globalization's Paradox.* New York and London: Routledge, 2002.

Shennan, J. N. *The Origins of the Modern European State, 1450–1725.* London: Hutchison University Library, 1974.

Sigmund Paul E., ed. and trans. *St. Thomas Aquinas on Politics and Ethics.* New York: Norton, 1988.

Silberman, Bernard S. *Cages of Reason: The Rise of the Rational State in France, Japan, the United States, and Great Britain.* Chicago: University of Chicago Press, 1993.

Silko, Leslie Marmon. *Ceremomy.* New York: Penguin, 1977.

Singer, P. W. *Corporate Warriors: The Rise of the Privatized Military Industry.* Ithaca, NY: Cornell University Press, 2003.

Skinner, Quentin. *The Foundations of Modern Political Thought,* vol. 1., *The Renaissance.* Cambridge: Cambridge University Press, 1978.

Skocpol, Theda. *States and Social Revolutions.* Cambridge: Cambridge University Press, 1979.

Skowronek, Stephen. *Building a New American State: The Expansion of National Administrative Capacities, 1877–1920*. Cambridge and New York: Cambridge University Press, 1982.

Smith, Adam. *An Inquiry into the Nature and Causes of the Wealth of Nations*, vol. 1. Ed. Edwin Cannan. Chicago: University of Chicago Press, 1976.

Smith, Anthony D. *Theories of Nationalism*. New York: Harper & Row, 1971.

———. *National Identity*. Reno: University of Nevada Press, 1991.

Smith, G. E., and W. J. Perry. *The Origin and History of Politics*. New York: Wiley, 1931.

Solo, Robert A. *The Positive State*. Cincinnati: South-Western, 1982.

———. "The Formation and Transformation of States," in W. Ladd Hollist and F. Lamond Tullis (eds.), *International Political Economy*. Boulder, CO: Westview Press, 1985.

Solzhenitzen, Alexander. *The Gulag Archipelago 1918–1956*. New York: Harper & Row, 1975.

Southern, R. W. *The Making of the Middle Ages*. New Haven and London: Yale University Press, 1953.

Sparrow, Barthlomew H. *From the Outside In: World War II and the American State*. Princeton, NJ: Princeton University Press, 1996.

Spiegel, Steven L. *World Politics in a New Era*. Fort Worth, TX: Harcourt Brace, 1995.

Spruyt, Hendrick. *The Sovereign State and Its Competitors*. Princeton, NJ: Princeton University Press, 1994.

Spybey, Tony. *Globalization and World Society*. Cambridge: Cambridge University Press, 1996.

Stankiewicz, W. J., ed. *In Defense of Sovereignty*. New York: Oxford University Press, 1969.

Starr, Chester G., Jr. *The Emergence of Rome as Ruler of the Western World*. Ithaca, NY: Cornell University Press, 1953.

Stepan, Alfred. *State and Society: Peru in Comparative Perspective*. Princeton, NJ: Princeton University Press, 1978.

Strang, David. "Contested Sovereignty: The Social Construction of Colonial Imperialism," in Thomas J. Biersteker and Cynthia Weber (eds.), *State Sovereignty as Social Construct*. Cambridge: Cambridge University Press, 1996: 22–49.

Strange, Susan. *The Retreat of the State: The Diffusion of Power in the World Economy*. Cambridge: Cambridge University Press, 1996.

Strayer, Joseph R. *Feudalism*. Princeton, NJ: Van Nostrand, 1965.

———. *On the Medieval Origins of the Modern State*. Princeton, NJ: Princeton University Press, 1970.

Sullivan, Richard E. *Heirs of the Roman Empire*. Ithaca, NY: Cornell University Press, 1960.

Swedburg, Richard, ed. *Joseph A. Schumpeter: The Economics and Sociology of Capitalism*. Princeton, NJ: Princeton University Press, 1991.

Tamir, Yael. *Liberal Nationalism*. Princeton, NJ: Princeton University Press, 1993.

Taylor, Charles. *Sources of the Self*. Cambridge, MA: Harvard University Press, 1989.

Thomas, Raju G. C. "Nations, States, and Secessions: Lessons from the Former Yugoslavia," *Mediterranean Quarterly* 5 (fall 1994): 40–65.

Thompson, Janice E. *Mercenaries, Pirates, and Sovereigns: State-Building and Extraterritorial Violence in Early Modern Europe*. Princeton, NJ: Princeton University Press, 1994.

Thorstendahl, Rolf, ed. *State Theory and State History*. London: Sage, 1992.

Tigar, Michael E., and Madeleine R. Levy. *Law and the Rise of Capitalism*. New York and London: Monthly Review Press, 1977.

Tilly, Charles, ed. *The Formation of National States in Western Europe*. Princeton, NJ: Princeton University Press, 1975.

———. *Coercion, Capital, and European States, A.D. 990–1990*. Cambridge, MA: Basil Blackwell, 1990.

———. "Prisoners of the State," *International Social Science Journal* 133 (August 1992): 329–342.

———. "National Self-Determination as a Problem for All of Us," *Daedalus* 122 (1993): 29–35.

Tilly, Charles, and Wim P. Blockmans, eds. *Cities and the Rise of States in Europe, A.D. 1000 to 1800*. Boulder, CO: Westview Press, 1994.

Titmuss, Richard M. *Essays on the Welfare State*. 2d ed. Boston: Beacon Press, 1963.

Todorov, Tzvetan. *The Conquest of America: The Question of the Other*. Trans. Richard Howard. New York: Harper & Row, 1984.

Trachtenberg, Alan. *The Incorporation of America: Culture and Society in the Gilded Age*. New York: Hill & Wang, 1982.

Tucker, Robert C., ed. *The Marx-Engels Reader*. 2d ed. New York and London: W. W. Norton, 1978.

Tully, James. *Strange Multiplicity. Constitutionalism in an Age of Diversity*. Cambridge: Cambridge University Press, 1995.

Van Creveld, Martin. *The Transformation of War*. New York: Free Press, 1991.

Virilio, Paul. *The Information Bomb*. Trans. Chris Turner. London: Verso Press, 2000.

Walker, R. B. J. *One World, Many Worlds: Struggles for a Just World Peace*. Boulder, CO: Lynne Rienner Publishers, 1988.

———. *Inside/Outside: International Relations as Political Theory*. Cambridge: Cambridge University Press, 1993.

Walker, Robert, and Saul Mendlovitz, eds. *Contending Sovereignties: Rethinking Political Community*. Boulder, CO: Lynne Rienner Publishers, 1990.

Wallerstein, Immanuel. *The Modern World System: Capitalist Agriculture and the Origins of the European World Economy in the Sixteenth Century*. New York: Academic Press, 1974.

Waltz, Kenneth. *Man, the State and War*. New York: Columbia University Press, 1954.

Walzer, Michael. *Spheres of Justice*. New York: Basic Books, 1983.

Watson, James L., ed. *Golden Arches East: McDonald's in East Asia*. Stanford, CA: Stanford University Press, 1997.

Weber, Cynthia. *Simulating Sovereignty: Intervention, the State and Symbolic Exchange*. Cambridge: Cambridge University Press, 1995.

Weber, Eugen. *Peasants into Frenchmen: The Modernization of Rural France, 1870–1914*. Stanford, CA: Stanford University Press, 1976.

Weber, Max. *The Protestant Ethic and the Spirit of Capitalism*. Trans. Talcott Parsons. New York: Scribner's, 1958.

Webster, Graham. *The Roman Imperial Army*. 3d ed. Totawa, NJ: Barnes and Noble Books, 1985.

Weiner, Myron. *The Global Migration Crisis: Challenges to States and to Human Rights*. New York: HarperCollins, 1995.

Wells, H. G. *A Short History of the World*. London: Casell, 1922.

Weltman, John J. *World Politics and the Evolution of War.* Baltimore: Johns Hopkins University Press, 1995.

Westney, Eleanor D. *Imitation and Innovation: The Transfer of Western Organization Patterns to Meiji Japan.* Cambridge, MA: Harvard University Press, 1987.

Wheeler, Wendy. *A New Modernity.* London: Lawrence & Wishart, 1999.

White, Lynn. *Medieval Technology and Social Change.* Oxford: Oxford University Press, 1962.

White, Stephen. *Political Theory and Postmodernism.* New York: Cambridge University Press, 1991.

———. *Edmund Burke.* Beverly Hills, CA: Sage Publications, 1994.

Wight, Martin. *Systems of States.* Leicester, UK: Leicester University Press, 1977.

Wolf, Eric. *Europe and the People Without History.* Berkeley: University of California Press, 1982.

Wolff, Hans Julius. *Roman Law: A Historical Introduction.* Norman: University of Oklahoma Press, 1951.

Wolff, Kurt H., ed. *From Karl Manheim.* Oxford: Oxford University Press, 1971.

Wolin, Sheldon. *Politics and Vision: Continuity and Innovation in Western Political Thought.* Boston: Little, Brown, 1960.

———. *The Presence of the Past: Essays on the State and Constitution.* Baltimore: Johns Hopkins University Press, 1989.

Wriston, Walter B. *The Twilight of Sovereignty.* New York: Charles Scribner's Sons, 1992.

Yergin, Daniel, and Joseph Stanislaw. *The Commanding Heights: The Battle Between Government and the Marketplace That Is Remaking the Modern World.* New York: Simon & Schuster, 1998.

Young, Crawford. *The African Colonial State in Comparative Perspective.* New Haven, CT: Yale University Press, 1994.

Young, Crawford, and Thomas Turner. *The Rise and Decline of the Zairian State.* Madison: University of Wisconsin Press, 1985.

Young, Iris Marion. *Justice and the Politics of Difference.* Princeton, NJ: Princeton University Press, 1990.

Zeitlin, Maurice, ed. *Political Power and Social Theory: A Research Annual,* vol. 1. Greenwich, CT: JAI Press, 1980.

Zolberg, Aristide. "Strategic Interactions and the Formation of Modern States: France and England," *International Social Science Journal* 32 (1980): 687–716.

Index

aborigines (Australia), 219
absolutism, 60, 87–88; and liberalism, 103; monarchical and parliamentary, 88–95; in England and France, 88–95; in Germany 132–133
abstract individual, 105, 125
Abyssinia, *see* Ethiopia
Act of Settlement (1689), 92, 110
Adams, Samuel (1772–1803), 112
Addison, Joseph (1672–1719), 102
Adoula, Cyrille (1921–1978), 238
Adriatic Sea, 28
Afghanistan War (1979–1985), 251
Africa, 67, 167; colonial rule in, 185–187; colonization of, 177, 179, 181–182; independence movements in 208–212
Afro-Arab slave traders, 233
Agincourt, Battle of (1415), 57, 94
Aguinaldo, Emílio (1869–1964), 207
Aid to Families with Dependent Children (AFDC) (1950), 155
Ainu, 225
Airscam, 273
Alaric, Gothic chieftain, 19,33
Alaska, 183
Albania, nationalist movement in, 203
Albuquerque, Afonso de (1453–1515), 173
alcalde, 184
Alcoçaves, Treaty of (1479), 173
Alemmani, 31, 33
Alexander II (r. 1855–1881), czar of Russia, 127–128
Alexander III (r. 1881–1894), czar of Russia, 128
Alexei I (r. 1645–1676), czar of Russia, 127

Algeria, 212–213
alienation, 146; in Hegel, 125; in Marx, 124; in Weber, 137
Ali Jinnah, Muhammad (1876–1948), 206
Aljubaraota, Battle of (1385), 57
Alliance of the Bakango (ABAKO), 236
All-Union Congress of Peoples' Deputies, USSR, 131
Al-Qaeda, 213
American Revolution (1776), 100
Amnesty International, 277
Amuru, Túpac, 199
anarchism, 123
Andropov, Yuri (1914–1984), security general, CPSU, 131
Angles, 31
Anglican Church, *see* Church of England
Anglicanism, 110
Anglo-American ideological assumptions, 272
Anglo-Burmese Wars (1824–1826), 185
Anglo-Iraq Treaty (1929), 229
Anglo-Sikh Wars (1848–1852), 185
Angola, 211, 238
Anjou, 93
Antarctica, 2, 268
anti-semitism, in Nazi Germany, 135–136, 212
Aquinas, St. Thomas (1225–1274), 67–69
Aquitaine, 92, 246
Arab nationalism, 212, in Iraq, 231–232
Arab-Persian conflict, 233
Arendt, Hannah, 136
Argentina, 251
Arif, Abd al-Salam, 231

299

About the Book

This engaging introduction to contemporary politics examines the historical construction of the modern territorial state. Opello and Rosow fuse accounts of governing practices, technological change, political economy, language, and culture into a narrative of the formation of specific state forms. This revised edition reinforces their central argument that the current neoliberal state does not represent a fundamentally new form, but is an attempt to reconstitute the managerial state in the context of globalization.

Incorporating the most recent scholarship, other significant changes in the new edition include more emphasis on the interconnections of state and state-system, discussions of emerging forms of international violence and war, and attention to the increasingly multicultural character of states.

Studies of state formation in Congo, Britain, France, Germany, Iraq, Japan, Nigeria, Russia, and the United States enrich the discussion, which ranges from ancient Rome to the present.

Walter C. Opello, Jr. and **Stephen J. Rosow** are professors of political science at the State University of New York, Oswego.